THE RING
OF
REPRESENTATION

Published by
State University of New York Press, Albany

© 1992 State University of New York

Printed in the United States of America

For information, address State University of New York Press,
State University Plaza, Albany, N.Y., 12246

Production by Marilyn P. Semerad
Marketing by Theresa A. Swierzowski

Library of Congress Cataloging-in-Publication Data

Ross, Stephen David.
    The ring of representation / Stephen David Ross.
        p.   cm. — (SUNY series in contemporary continental
philosophy)
    Includes bibliographical references and index.
    ISBN 0-7914-1109-5. — ISBN 0-7914-1110-9 (pbk.)
    1. Representation (Philosophy) I. Title. II. Series.
B105.R4R67   1992   91-26923
110—dc20   CIP

10 9 8 7 6 5 4 3 2 1

CONTENTS

Anacrusis
vii

ONE
Sonance
1

TWO
Judgment
19

THREE
Representation
49

FOUR
Power
69

FIVE
Desire
91

SIX
Truth
111

SEVEN
History
127

EIGHT
Embodiment
143

NINE
Praxis
161

TEN
Humanity
185

ELEVEN
Nature
203

Notes
215

Index
243

ANACRUSIS

To philosophize after the end of metaphysics, from within its utmost critique. To refrain from metaphysics, then resound to its refrain. To hear nature's sonance within the ring of its representations.[1]

Philosophy has always insisted upon this: thinking its other. Its other: that which limits it, and from which it derives its essence, its definition, its production.

—Derrida[2]

The univocity of being, its singleness of expression, is paradoxically the principal condition which permits difference to escape the domination of identity, which frees it from the law of the Same. . . .

—Foucault[3]

ONE

Sonance

How may we undertake to represent representation? What task unfolds from that endeavor? Do we presuppose an end, a measure, to which any representation may be subjected, or does the representation of representation exceed any scale? Can we speak in a neutral voice that does not represent its own representativity, or does representation's voice drown out any neutrality? Shall we employ a familiar voice that resonates harmoniously in our ear, or a voice that echoes the discordances between any representation and its representativity? And familiar to whom? Who are the "we" so represented? Will "you" listen to an unfamiliar voice that seeks to sound the excesses of its representativity? Will "you" find yourself subjected once more to an alien representation?

Within nature's strife, Heraclitus tells, the harmony of the *logos* resounds.

> It is necessary to understand that war is universal and justice is strife, and that all things take place in accordance with strife and necessity.

> They do not comprehend how, though it is at variance with itself, it agrees with itself. It is a harmony of opposed tensions, as in the bow and the lyre.[1]

We may hear the *logos* as an affinity that overcomes discord or as univocal in its discordances. We may wonder how the single sound of the lyre, its univocity, can keep us from the domination of identity,[2] how the sonance of the One, in nature or in representation, may echo transgression. We hope to listen to nature's sonance, the ring of representation. Does it matter that representation echoes as it shines? Can nature's music echo what remains invisible within its colored rainbows?

What would happen if we were to represent representation's representativity in a sonorescent voice, listening to the ring of representation, echoing the sonance of nature along with its radiance? Would representativity become more aware of itself in its reverberations? Would we make ourselves more familiar with its unfamiliarity?

Shall we with Irigaray envision the luminance of nature's representation within the critique of metaphysics as totalizing and specular?

> What is at stake is not only the hegemony of Western cultures, but also their identities as unified cultures. . . . The West is painfully made to realize the existence of a Third World in the First World, and vice versa. The Master is bound to recognize that His Culture is not as homogeneous, as monolithic as He believed it to be. He discovers, with much reluctance, He is just an other among others.[13]

The Master discovers that He has always been an other among others, heterogeneously, has always imperiled Himself even within His greatest Authority. This discovery doubles, exceeds itself: we are always in danger, in life, in discourse, in representation, and the greatest difficulty is placing ourselves, our authority, at risk. Representation risks everything and nothing, risks subjugation and oppression within a blindness dangerously opaque to every danger. Representation risks even the critique in which it has refused to be at risk, for even though we did not represent it so, it was always in danger. But we have always so represented it. Representation, nature's sonance, places itself inescapably at risk, displaces itself, where one recurrent danger is obliviousness toward any danger.

We find ourselves questioning the ways in which representation has echoed within the recordings of Western thought, has repeatedly sounded discordant tones of images and writing, as if danger resounds incessantly within every familiar representation even as it has been denied. Philosophy has repeatedly sounded its suspicions of representation, from Plato's critique of writing and pictorial representation to Heidegger's critique of metaphysics as the representation of being. "Metaphysics thinks beings as being in the manner of representational thinking which gives reasons."[14] Yet philosophy has repeatedly claimed the truth of its own representations of the limits of representation, claimed authority over itself. In the percussions of this antiphony echo endless questions of representation, of itself and of we, where we find ourselves at risk in representation, and where representation risks itself in us.

Such discordance appears in Plato, who follows his famous critique of writing in *Phaedrus* with the idea of a discourse "written in the soul of the learner, . . . that can defend itself, and knows to whom it should speak and to whom say nothing (*Phaedrus*, 276a),"[15] and his critique of mimetic poetry in *Republic* by questioning whether poetry may "not justly return from this exile after she has pleaded her defense, whether in lyric or other measure" (*Republic*, 607d). Plato's writing is mimetic, and his critique of representation cannot escape the discordances of representation. Why should we imagine that it could? In Kant, the sublime exceeds representation while echoing within it:

> *the sublime is that, the mere ability to think which shows a faculty of the mind surpassing every standard of sense.*[16]

> an object . . . *the representation of which determines the mind to think the unattainability of nature regarded as a presentation of ideas.*[17]

A representation utterly beyond representation makes no sound while the echo of its representation belongs to representation. Here representation returns to place itself at risk as the representation of representation: multiple representation.

In Plato and Kant, the critique and excesses of representation ring in representation. Within the critique of representation there sounds a countermovement that surpasses the limits of representation and its critique, still within representation. The form of that movement echoes the return of representation to itself, the representation of representation as history and time, as danger. The history of history questions itself as both history and representation. The history of representation risks itself as transgression. "The limit and transgression depend on each other for whatever density of being they possess: a limit could not exist if it were absolutely uncrossable and, reciprocally, transgression would be pointless if it merely crossed a limit composed of illusions and shadows."[18] But it rings in representation and marks its excesses by the music of its play.

In Plato and Kant, the self-canceling play of self-representation takes the form of art. In writings after Nietzsche and Heidegger, metaphysics and science, if not history and art, appear deaf to their own representativity, refusing their own discordance in the name of privilege. If we think of refusing even this refusal, still distrustful of privilege, especially of its restoration in the highest and most extreme, the privilege of a Great Refusal, we may return to question representation's diaphonies. We may then sound the possibility of retrieving metaphysics, even science, within its critique through a representation of nature that does not deafen itself to its own representativity, a voice suspicious of every priority, including its own. This refusal of the refusal of metaphysics echoes the percussions of our refrain, reverberating with repercussions of reality and representation. In the ring of representation, unending questions peal forth.

Privilege refuses to countenance its own dividedness, refuses to place its representativity at risk. How might we refuse both privilege and our own refusal? How might we place our own refusal at risk? We refuse privilege by dismembering its authority. To imagine refusing even this refusal, we question the discordance of every representation, including our own, and the mutilation of whatever falls authoritatively into representation. The refusal of representational authority unfolds as question after question of deferral,[19] divided within itself as deference and delay. Deferral echoes acquiescence and postponement, refuses the identity of representation with measure and completion. Yet to question even its own privilege, of an undivided representation of the dividedness of representation, deferral solicits its own deferral, echoes its inexhaustibility. "As long as words of difference serve to legitimate a discourse instead of delaying its authority to infinity, they are, to borrow an image from Audre Lorde, 'noteworthy only as decorations.'"[20] The refusal of epistemic priority echoes a critique of Western representation while the critique of this critique defers its own deferral to question representation's representation, still a critique of Western privilege. In these circular multiplicities of representation and deferral, *technē*, *praxis* and *poiēsis*, materializes as nature's *ergon*, work, whereas truth echoes its untruth. The representation of nature, always *technē*, circles back to echo as nature's *ergon*; the resonances of truth reverberate with excesses of discord and diaphony. In the percussions of these circularities resound the repercussions of representation.

Representation lives in many worlds and in close proximity to countless others. They, in return, reside in representation's vicinity even where they reverberate outside it—a proximity too close to measure. Nature and reality, power, desire, and history, resound in representation. Representation, here, dwells near the limits of nature and history, as they dwell near it, calling forth incessant questions of authority and power. For representation echoes *technē*, inhabits spheres of form and measure. Multiple representation falls between freedom and rule, nature and artifice, sonority and measure, and between the pairs. It returns to question *technē* again and again, as excess and deferral, resounds as *poiēsis*.

This proximity, between nature and representation, composes a region in which we may hope to retrieve philosophy from its close as we retrieve representation from its prohibition. We seek to question Western modernity's critique of itself, but not by repudiating that critique as if it had no truth. We seek instead to avoid a concordant portrayal of the truth of critique, especially a critique of truth. We consider the possibility of a local sonorescence situated among the dissonances between poetry and philosophy, where representation interrogates its truth and where authority repudiates itself.[21] The juncture at which philosophy exceeds and falls into representation echoes politics and truth—the reappearance of the philosopher-king as a figure of transgression. Within that juncture, philosophy represents itself as local, finite, as it rings in representation and as it represents its own representativity. We question the locality of representation through the intonation of its representations: where poetry presents its challenge to philosophy, where philosophy seeks to represent its own representativity, and where we repeatedly echo to ourselves the challenge of our we.

How may we think after modernity, after Nietzsche and Heidegger, Wittgenstein and Dewey, taking hold of their Westernness and maleness? How may we utter what follows our Western tradition after its close and in its refrain? These questions resound of nature and truth. The "of" appears as representation, where we appear as representing and represented, tolling unending questions of this doubling of representation. Questioning it asks us to rethink our time and history, to represent a juncture in our history as a junction within representation and truth. Questioning the limits of representation asks us to sound the limits of our history at the edges of our bodies and our worlds.

When Heidegger speaks of metaphysics, he speaks of representation: "What characterizes metaphysical thinking which grounds the ground for beings is the fact that metaphysical thinking, starting from what is present, represents it in its presence and thus exhibits it as grounded by its ground."[22] He speaks of metaphysics and also representation. Does this mark of representation echo representation? Do we, when we speak of speaking, in our critique of metaphysical representation, always say the same again? May the also of representation in relation to metaphysics be heard again as metaphysics, or does the voice of the end of metaphysics resound as no longer metaphysical, perhaps metamusical? May the representation of representation no longer sound as representational? May it echo excess?

The representation of which Heidegger speaks echoes cacophonically, as that which repeats the obscurity of metaphysics and as an opening within that obscurity. Multiple representation opens a space within representation. This opening within representation reveals the diaphonic circularity of its representations in nature's sonance. "It may be about this multiplicity that philosophy, being situated, inscribed, and included within it, has never been able to reason."[23] Philosophy has never been able to represent its multiplicities. Is this another escape from risk in the "onlyness" of philosophy's relation to its limits?

Philosophy finds itself surrounded by endless "onlys": "only representation," "philosophy only," "only Western," "rational only." The "onlys" represent limits within representation and history whose endless repetitions gesture beyond the limits of representation. The limits of representation sound the limits of what echoes as "only" representation, while representation surpasses every "only." The limits of history echo repetitions of what resounds as "only" history where history includes every every. Each limit presents itself as a univocal, nature's sonance, the single voice of being, history, and representation, even of identity, each disrupting itself, questioning any identity, including its own.

If the univocity of nature permits difference to escape the limits of identity, perhaps the multiplicities of representations may permit nature to escape the limits of its univocity.[24] The escape from identity and representation peals a percussion that requires repercussion, again and again, to escape from itself, again. This escape in time, in repetition, unfolds as *praxis*: another self-canceling identity of history and representation. Each such pervasive form appears as another univocal; history and representation; *technē*, *praxis*, and *poiēsis*; power, desire, and nature; truth and embodiment—with the others, and still others. Each echoes itself. Each echoes the others in circles of circles and questions of questions, dislocating the domination of identity and the dominion of its universality. Nature rings out as fragmentary, discordant, multiple; harmony and diaphony, consonance and dissonance. Our nature, multiple and fragmentary, appears to escape the dominion of its identity "only" in the embrace of its materiality, weighed down by oppressions of race and class, sexuality and gender, by rule of law.

We may wonder if, where thought questions its limits, representation may question its relations to itself, its self-understanding, and its relations to others, its self-forgetfulness. We may wonder if, where self-forgetfulness and self-understanding include themselves, where understanding may be forgotten and forgetting deepens into a form of understanding, modernity might become excessive—*our's* or *some other's* modernity—and reflexivity might exceed itself. This excessive excess, exceeding itself, echoes the self-forgetfulness that questions self-understanding. It redisplays representation and nature as questions, the one repeatedly of the of, the other of itself.

In the predominant Western tradition, challenged throughout, to question reason's nature is to question science's truth. Is science the name of that form of representation in which truth and reason know themselves most fully; or are scientific reason and truth unable to represent their own limits truthfully? "By contrast, science is not an original happening of truth, but always the cultivation of a domain of truth already opened."[25] Our Western modernity materializes as a site where science faces the challenges of its own, if silent, multiple reflexivities, where its multiple representativity places it in incessant danger. Even where reason appears dialectical and reflective, knowing itself and its limits, it does not—some say cannot—know the limits of its knowledge of its limits. This insight defines the "problem of reflection."[26] In Western modernity, philosophy dwells among the others that define the scientificity of science and among the sames that define the rationality of reason. It resides among the sites where modern science becomes science, by defining its limits. Yet it also dwells among the sites where science receives its greatest challenge, by questioning the limits that define its authority. The modern proximity of science and philosophy defines a region in which philosophy dissolves. Other such limiting regions are the proximity of truth and desire and of power and representation. We ask if they are regions from which may emerge questions of the truth of science and philosophy and their relatedness, questions of their and.

If science defines our modernity, then if we are to understand modernity, science calls for questioning from whatever vantage point can be taken toward it, including those we do not, and some of which we will never, know how to take. The plausibility of this conclusion is offset by the realization that the plurality of vantage points whereby science may be interrogated defines a plurality of sites for the definition of science and philosophy: art, religion, and practice no less than the reciprocity of philosophy and science, as well as *our* or *any other* modernity, Western or non-Western. The multiple limits whose representation defines philosophy, along with their limits, tear open the fabric of reason and its truthfulness, disharmonize nature's cacophonies. We find excess in excess, surplus in surplus. Excess and surplus have no (or every) name. The limits of the limits that define reason, reality, and history resound in reason, reality, and history plurally, recurrently, and discordantly. The limits of representation have no determinate representation, however oblique, without disowning the representation of their limits.

Foucault defines power in terms of four principles.[27] The last concerns us here: "Where there is power, there is resistance, and yet, or rather consequently, this resistance is never in a position of exteriority in relation to power." Such a sweeping conception may be considered metaphysical. "Power is everywhere, not because it embraces everything, but because it comes from everywhere"[28]: immanent, productive, nonbinary, and nonsubjective. How can the "everywhere" not be metaphysical? Foucault's response is that power is pervasive without being total, since it does not include everything. This transgressive notion of an everywhere without totality unfolds questions of the possibility of a local metaphysics without metaphysicality. Could a philosophy be pervasive but not total if it cannot represent everything and cannot be represented by anything more sovereign? Nature here would be power and resistance. Reality would be everything, including its own unreality. Being would include its own nonbeing, dislocating itself. Can these univocal countermovements dismantle metaphysical authority within the ring of its musicality?

In Foucault, power includes its own alterities. Its limits lie within and without, and may be thought from within the pervasiveness of power. Or rather, resistance is neither power nor its differences, but transgression. Resistance is more of the same, to be thought within, and disruptive, shattering any established hegemony. Within every representational formation that defines power and truth, there unfolds resistance, understood as power and truth but also their difference. "There is a plurality of resistances, each of them a special case."[29]

Power presses upon us within the relations of reason to itself whose truth includes its own defilement. Reason materializes inseparable from unreason, truth from untruth, power from resistance, and production from violence. We ask how each might stand forth as the others while their nature lies between. Questioning the truth of power suggests that truth is made by power, faced and defaced by it. Questioning ideology disrupts the sanctity of a *logos* through which truth might be transparent to itself to name a between in which truth finds itself before its opposite, defined and defiled by it. The self-understandings of truth and reason cancel themselves as the will to truth.[30] Power materializes as the institutional, nonsubjective, self-deceptive will that constitutes and imperils subject and truth. It belongs together, inseparably, with desire. The self-deceptions of power that limit its truth themselves resound as limited by desire. In this interrogative space inhabited by the limits of illusion echoes the will to truth achieving its goal.

Our time lies between any modernity and its futures, haunted by whether our modernity will be the same again and how it might be different. In this conflict echo questions of the localities of history. History emerges as a pervasive site at which we may question the multiple movements of practice, deferral's deferral. In the localities of history unfold the limits of our humanity. In the localities of the of echo representations of our relationship to nature and the limits of every representation of our nature. Otherness to oneself—locality's locality—marks our nature's *technē*.

defers itself as resistance; resistance relates to power by deferral. Deferral calls forth a double movement of transgression, echoes unending questions and more questions. Everything and totality sound their transgressiveness, with locality, inexhaustibility, and the absolute, echoing the limits of their limits.

We are exploring a sonorescent representation of locality, of *place*, where locality's locality echoes the limits and work of place. We join two thoughts in Aristotle's *Physics*:

> things which exist are *somewhere* . . .[35]

> *nature is a source or cause of being moved and of being at rest . . .* in virtue of itself. . .[36]

Nature moves of itself, from somewhere to elsewhere, where somewhere and elsewhere echo order together with disorder. What belongs somewhere echoes locally in place, but within itself, within its locality, belongs inexhaustibly elsewhere, works in many places. The movement echoes desire; the relevance of elsewhere echoes power; the reflexivity echoes representation; representation performs its work. Locality echoes multiply in virtue of its locality, a locality of representativity and ergonality.

Power, desire, and representation compose a triangle chiming locality and inexhaustibility, locality's excess, echoing locality's inexhaustibility and inexhaustibility's locality as their ergonality, excesses exceeding and dislocating themselves. Power, desire, and representation resound in our sonorescence as locality, inexhaustibility, and ergonality, echoing relevance and excess. Locality here repeats and displaces place, its order and disorder, places place at risk elsewhere. Locality's locality, its excesses and inexhaustibility, places metaphysics and science at risk through their ergonality. Whatever their truth, it echoes in virtue of their ergonality, the local and inexhaustible work they do. We seek to represent power, desire, and representation locally and excessively where the excesses reverberate together as their ergonality, and where ergonality resists metaphysical authority. We confront the question of how our local representations may exceed themselves, may place themselves at risk, how the work of representation may risk incessant danger.

Locality's locality echoes in place where each location works, is relevant, elsewhere, in other places, each location exceeding itself. The displacement of language echoes at the heart of our sonorescence. We sound our univocal names clattering all at once, chattering their multiple locality among themselves, echoing their ergonality. These univocal sonorescences of locality and inexhaustibility represent their ergonality, dismantling any privilege, even their own.

> A *locus*, located and locating, in spheres of relevance: a *locale* of its *ingredients*; an ingredient of other locales.

An ingredient, one among many other ingredients in a locale: as one, a *unison* with many *resonances*, the other ingredients relevant to it in that locale. A unison including many other unisons: a *superaltern unison* located in a *superaltern locale*.

An ingredient with a superaltern unison in a superaltern locale *belongs* there, otherwise it *departs*. Every ingredient belongs to and departs from any of its locations in *harmony* and *disharmony*.[37]

An ingredient together with other alternatives ingredient in a locale: such an ingredient works there in *polyphony*, otherwise in *stillness*, lacking possibilities. Every ingredient echoes stilly and polyphonically in any of its locations.[38]

A locus comprises a locale of relevance for its ingredients and works in many other locales as ingredients among their other ingredients. As locale-ingredients together, a locus does its work, does different and conflicting work, wherever located. The univocals reverberating in our sonorescence, with their proliferating prepositions (in, of, for, by, et cetera, always et cetera), represent inexhaustibly different ergonalities of location, multiple workings in place, frame different representations of order and disorder, locality and excess: a locale of ingredients, an ingredient in a locale, many locales; a unison composing an ingredient's unitariness in a location, other relevant ingredients its multiple resonances in that location; a superaltern unison including many subaltern unisons, each unison working somewhere as superaltern, elsewhere as subaltern; each ingredient with a superaltern unison belonging in that location, otherwise departing, harmonious and disharmonious; ingredients working together as polyphonic alternatives in a location, otherwise still in their location; always other locations. Order and disorder belong together as multiple location, locality and inexhaustibility, concord and discord. Locality and inexhaustibility belong together in virtue of their ergonality, each echoing the other displaced by work in other locations. Locality echoes ergonality, the different work that loci and ingredients do in different locations, where no single or overarching location, no totality, defines a locus's work. Its work comprises its inexhaustible multiplicities, excesses of locality and their locality, multiple representations of order and disorder and their representativity.

A locus—the proximity of locale and ingredient—belongs to many local spheres of relations and comprises a local sphere of relations for others. The locality, pervasive and everywhere, repudiates totality: no overarching location delimits a locus, no supreme superaltern unison. The inexhaustibility, pervasive and everywhere, calls for displacement, echoes further locations with their excesses. The ergonality, pervasive and everywhere, repudiates univocity, sounds the limits of every limit, including the limits of its own univocities. For any unison, in any location, multiple resonances resound exceeding any relation. For any superaltern unison, a locus belongs to many other locations exceeding any identity. Among the other ingredients in a locale, an ingredient echoes stillness and polyphony, each exceeding the other in that locale, together expressing excesses in relation to other locales. Locality echoes relevance as power, each exceeding, resisting, itself; inexhaustibility echoes excess, each exceeding itself; ergonality works as representation, exceeding itself as representation. The multiple localities of power appear as excesses in which representation exceeds its representativity.

How shall we hear the reverberations of this univocal discourse? We may hear the proximity of Aristotle's categories, locale and ingredient as substance and accident, unison and resonance as one and many, harmony and disharmony as identity and difference, stillness and polyphony as actuality and possibility, rest and motion. How shall we hear the differences? The sound, the music, of nature's sonance echoes an ergonality that does not repeat *techne*, does not resonate as instrumentality or form, norm or rule. Rather, each univocal departs from wherever it belongs, departs from norm or rule while it belongs together with them. Each of the sonorescent univocals expresses location and the limits of that location. Locality's locality resounds through each pair of sonorities as inexhaustibility, deferral's deferral, echoes nature's *ergon*.

Each of the sonorities echoes excess, and each of the pairs echoes further excesses. The togetherness of locale and ingredient within each locus echoes its proximity to other locales, belonging together with them, but every belonging departs. This disharmony echoes ergonality, refuses the totality of nature under any representation, material or spatial, even local. A locus works somewhere, many wheres. In its many locations, it belongs and it departs, and no totality of all locations composes it, no totality of work exhausts it. Harmony and disharmony express the inexhaustible proximities of loci among themselves and to us. Stillness and polyphony express the inexhaustible determinations and excesses of possibility, the want of necessity in necessity. Unison and resonances doubly echo the excesses of identity and propriety throughout inexhaustible locations. Each pair of sonorities sounds a certain proximity of determination and excess. Each exceeds the others and itself.

Excess echoes here in two pervasive ways. One is the ergonality of every sonority, of every locus, representing the inexhaustible locations to which it belongs. The second, refusing totality, echoes the intransitivity of location. Locality and relevance demand intransitivity, repudiate infinite chains of relevance composing totality. Transitivity constitutes a total measure, each locus relevant to another, that locus relevant to a third, and so forth, the first thereby relevant to every other. Locality and ergonality entail no supreme harmony, no great chord, of relevance, transitivity, or power. Intransitivity represents excess.

The reciprocity, multiplicity, and intransitivity of relevance echo the principle that power is everywhere, dislocated by resistances. If power materializes as

local, everywhere, it cannot materialize as everything, always echoes the discords of reciprocity. Relevance materializes everywhere—equivalent with locality—displaced by other relevances. The everywhere belongs with intransitivity,
surrounded by unending possibilities. Its univocity represents resistance to authority including the authority of every resistance.

If we associate relevance with power, then power appears to echo generically, defining representation and desire.[39] Yet how can power materialize as the
defining idea of locality without excluding resistances in relations of power to
desire and truth, without excluding the pervasiveness of representation and desire? How can the truth of relevance be heard except as a local truth, limited
and dislocated by representation and desire? The question unfolds whether the
truth of the multiple reflexivities of locality and inexhaustibility is defined by
Western culture, embodied in the irrelevance of philosophy's history to a
future pervaded by unending stories it tells to its futures of the nature of relevance. The alternative unfolds that the univocity of being rings out unending univocities, unending deferrals, echoing here as locality, inexhaustibility, and ergonality; as power, desire, and representation; as locale-ingredient, unison-
resonance, harmony-disharmony, stillness-polyphony; and more. Locality,
inexhaustibility, and ergonality represent respectively power as relevance, desire
as excess, and representation as nature's work, as the sonorous pairs represent
their own locality, inexhaustibility, and ergonality, each echoing deferral and
excess.

The traditional metaphysical voice speaks of reality without speaking of its
own reality. The transcendental turn, in turning back onto itself, repudiates that
voice as unreflexive. The multiple reflexivity that emerges turns representation
back onto itself, questioning the limits of that repudiation. Among the forms in
which this multiple limitation may be questioned resound the midworlds of representation, power, and desire, the sites of history, practice, and humanity. Our
sonorescence includes, within its reflexivities, pervasive representations of these
other movements. Our sonorescences dismantle the dominion of identity through
the inexhaustibility of their univocity.

Will those who accept the traditional metaphysical project hear the sonorescences of locality and inexhaustibility as too strange? Will those who repudiate
metaphysics hear our sonorescent univocals as too authoritative? Will the re-
trieval of the metaphysical project within its critique be heard as too dangerous or
too familiar? In every case, the danger and familiarity place themselves at risk.
The Master's voice finds its authority broken, its rule heterogeneous, under any
authority. The risk under which we place ourselves dismantles His (and Our)
authority from within and without, echoing the disharmonies of repetition and the
repetitions of the others. We sound a metamusical sonorescence that would repudiate every authority, even that of Being, without reinstating another privilege,
even the privilege of the Other.

Locality, in its sonorescent representations, including the univocals but also the representations that displace them and represent their dislocations, echoes unending questions of the reflexivities of representation, desire, and power, of the multiple reflexivities of inexhaustibility. The truth of nature sounds its reflexivities both because truth and nature echo reflexivity and because the territory between them is occupied by our reality. Our reality echoes its locality, and no firm opposition between reality and unreality resounds within it. The multiple reflexivities of reality include the reflexive unrealities within it, where each reflexivity dislocates the others, representing within each departure its departures from itself. In this way, reality remains reality as much as it changes, and changes as much as it remains the same. Similarly, multiply reflexive representation remains representation even as it echoes misrepresentation. Each sounds its locality and inexhaustibility. Each disperses and includes its others.

Speaking of truth and knowledge rings of representation. Yet despite our multiple representations of the percussions and repercussions that echo between reality and truth, this figure represents representation and its deferrals locally, in a certain way. We may seek another paradigm of reflexivity and truth by means of which to question representation historically. Judgment tolls as the traditional Western representation of the midworlds in which truth and nature resound. It rings between reality and representation. Local judgment occupies a site of deferral at which, pervasively, locality and inexhaustibility meet the ring of their representations.

TWO

Judgment

n Kant's Third *Critique*, judgment occupies the terrain between two domains
of law, understanding and practical reason, that together exhaust the territories of necessity. Kant's description of the conflict resounds with aporia:
"Understanding and reason exercise, therefore, two distinct legislations on
one and the same territory of experience, without prejudice to each other."[1] These
two domains must interact, but cannot. Moreover, judgment composes another
aporia.

> Now even if an immeasurable gulf is fixed between the sensible realm of the con-
> cept of nature and the supersensible realm of the concept of freedom, so that no
> transition is possible from the first to the second, . . . There must, therefore, be a
> ground of the unity of the supersensible, which lies at the basis of nature, . . .[2]

> in the family of the supreme cognitive faculties there is a middle term between the
> understanding and the reason. This is the judgment, . . .[3]

Judgment appears as the middle term where there can be no middle, echoes in
between, leading to the sublime, that which exceeds every representation.[4] Representation occupies a doubled territory, at once within itself, related to sense,
and exceeding itself in a thought that surpasses every representation. The idea of a
thought that must surpass itself to remain within itself echoes inexhaustibility. It
passes into the idea of a judgment for which representation and its excesses resound together.

Does the distinction between judgment and the sublime tempt us to represent judgment as a third that falls *within* representation, mediately, neglecting the
intractable gulf between the poles that judgment mediates and the movement in
judgment from representation to its excesses? Within the scope of this question
images of excess and in between appear inseparable. The location of excess
stands in between, in nature's sonance. We may consider some thoughts of excess
in judgment.

First, we speak of the sublime as we speak of being, nature, and the world,
also of the supersensible and its greatness. Shall we hear this recurrence as an
inevitable movement within judgment toward unity and infinity or as a self-can-

To speak of the sublime without great and small, without measure's infinite, it appears that we must turn from the mathematically sublime to Nature's dynamically sublime. Yet Kant repeatedly denies that the sublime pertains to Nature.

> Now we may see from this that, in general, we express ourselves incorrectly if we call any *object of nature* sublime, although we can quite correctly call many objects of nature beautiful.[17]

> It is a magnitude which is like itself alone. It follows hence that the sublime is not to be sought in the things of nature, but only in our ideas; . . .[18]

He also repeatedly speaks of the sublime in nature. "We may describe the sublime thus: it is an object (of nature) *the representation of which determines the mind to think the unattainability of nature regarded as a presentation of ideas.*"[19] He seems inescapably drawn to the natural sublime for excess, though we wonder if music's sonance might be sublime, representation's excess. Kant's critique of metaphysics is at once affirmed and belied by the natural sublime, which represents nature as unattainable yet presents that unattainability to us in aesthetical ideas. There echoes in Kant the idea of a metaphysics of excess where neither involves measure or limit but escapes the rules of representation. Judgment, here, echoes excess.

The dynamically sublime sounds nature's might without dominion, without a measure of greatness. It presents us with an unpresentable, an excess in and over representation, without rules or regulation. Judgment echoes as the representation of representation,[20] a figure within the critique of metaphysics and its critique, excess exceeding itself. Nature and representation have echoed excess and plenitude throughout the Western metaphysical tradition: Spinoza's absolutely infinite Substance, Leibniz's windowless but representational monads, Whitehead's Creativity, also, on Heidegger's reading, Aristotle's *physis*. The sublime becomes, on this reading, a local movement whereby philosophy exceeds itself along with everything local—two excessive terms. Here nature echoes both the totality of all representations and a cacophony that exceeds any totality. It resounds as judgment, exceeds itself in the figure of the sublime, rings as deferral.

Images of mediation where mediation is impossible, of the reflexivity of a midworld that dislocates itself in its self-representation, characterize our sonorescence. Judgment, not the understanding or reason, materializes as the site at which thought thinks itself as excess. Understanding and reason—science—represent modernity's knowledge, but appear as neither reflexive nor dissonant enough without judgment to compose multiple reflexivity. Rather, reason and understanding, freedom and science, echo judgment in its midworldliness. A wonderful passage in Foucault speaks to this point: "The description of the archive . . . establishes that we are difference, that our reason is the difference of discourses, our history the difference of times, our selves the difference of masks.

That difference, far from being the forgotten and recovered origin, is this dispersion that we are and make."[21] Difference sounds in the between: the poles echo discourse, history, and subjectivity. Reason, history, and self emerge as differences dispersed among the dispersions of representation. Reason, truth, and judgment meet in the middle region of representation among repeated questions of its limits.

What might it mean to think of locality inhabiting the midworlds of power and desire and of judgment inhabiting the midworlds of representation? Locality, inexhaustibility, and judgment resound together in our sonorescence, not in the fullness of being but judgment's excesses, repeating judgment. A local philosophy seeks to draw into itself the deferrals of judgment and truth. To deny it this possibility withholds from philosophy the capacity to criticize itself presupposed in calling it into question.

We are supposing that judgment, along with power, truth, and desire, inhabits every human midworld, thereby also every natural midworld through its representations, where representation includes every site at which nature is inhabited by representation. The repeated everys here speak not undividedly of totality but of deferral within the multiple reflexivities of judgment. Representation and judgment echo each other as the same, though each dislocates itself and the other. Each sounds the same as the other and its excess. That we can think of, even inhabit, nature "only" through representation asserts the local excesses inherent in its limitation. That every thought or practice—everything human—materializes as judgment asserts the deferrals of judgment within its midworldliness. Our task unfolds as one of locating and dispersing the middles that judgment inhabits without intimating their overcoming, accepting its deferrals while sustaining their representations, allowing it to ring out as itself without insisting that it sound either within the same or without.

Judgment, as representation, echoes nature's *techne* in its univocal voice as desire and power echo inexhaustibility and locality. Power, desire, and ergonality represent one side of judgment, which echoes their excesses and betweens in its own excessive voice. Judgment mediates where mediation is impossible, echoes in the midworlds of unisons and resonances, harmony and disharmony, stillness and polyphony. Each univocal pair echoes order and disorder, identity and excess; the pairs together echo further excesses; representation represents further excesses as judgment's judgment, nature's *ergon*, *techne*: *praxis* and *poiesis*. Nature's work of representation echoes judgment where judgment judges and exceeds itself.

We do not follow Kant to the infinite, over or into the abyss, but remain where representation and judgment limit themselves and their limitations. Excess exceeds itself. Abysmalness abysms the abyss. Judgment judges itself, defining reason. We may think of reason inhabiting the same midworlds of representation and truth, theory and practice, as judgment. We may think the same of science.

Contrasts between science and thought, truth and unconcealment, knowledge and fiction, the confines of reason and the freedoms of unreason, disperse into the midworlds of judgment where representation and truth disharmonize themselves.

In this diaphony, the capacity of judgment to exceed itself echoes its capacity to produce and destroy. The bringing forth of judgment, here, echoes its reason, inseparable from its violence. Images of destruction constantly reappear in relation to the representation of judgment as production. They are contrasted with an equally important emphasis on judgment as the same.

Arendt interprets Kant's view of judgment as "being able to 'think in the place of everybody else' and which he therefore called an 'enlarged mentality.' . . . The power of judgment rests on a potential agreement with others."[22] She follows one side of Kant in emphasizing agreement and shared experience. Judgment postulates common sense. Taste presents the model rather than genius. We can understand the rejection of genius as repudiation of the inflated transcendental subject. Yet we hesitate to accept the model of taste as defining the public as community, even in Arendt herself:

> the reality of the public realm relies on the simultaneous presence of innumerable perspectives and aspects in which the common world presents itself and for which no common measurement or denominator can ever be devised. . . . Being seen and being heard by others derive their significance from the fact that everybody sees and hears from a different position.[23]

In her strongest formulation, she rejects agreement: "The end of the common world has come when it is seen only under one aspect and is permitted to present itself in only one perspective."[24] She is speaking of a mass public, but the conflicting values turn on the normality that defines normativity. The common world sounds perspectivally divided. Its singularity and commonality mark it as transgressive. We ask, what may be shared in such a common world without a common measure? Why are differences in norms not as relevant as agreement? Why, in the name of truth, do the differences that divide not delimit conditions of knowledge as much as the connections that join?

No one in our time is more concerned with ideology and repression yet more adamant about the presence of consensual norms than Habermas:

> the paradigm of the knowledge of objects has to be replaced by the paradigm of mutual understanding between subjects capable of speech and action.[25]

> With Hegel and Marx, it would have been a matter of not swallowing the intuition concerning the ethical totality back into the horizon of the self-reference of the knowing and acting subject, but explicating it in accord with the model of unconstrained consensus formation in a communication community standing under cooperative constraints.[26]

He accepts the primacy of the transcendental subject but disallows the multiply reflexive deferrals of representation as too threatening to normativity. He repudiates in the name of liberation any radical critique of the oppressiveness of commonality and the repressiveness of normality while affirming a critique of the oppressions of late capitalist society. He accepts the dominant Western tradition in which understanding is consensus and reason is shared, rejects the possibility of a reason or truth for which sharing is unlikely or oppressive in some cases and unintelligible in others, disallows a locally normative public defined by difference.

Such a public is by no means foreign to Arendt where she rejects the intelligibility of a single perspective characterizing the public realm. Yet she too follows that side of Kant in which taste predominates over genius in relation to judgment, emphasizing common sense rather than departure, accepts the maxim that normality takes precedence over abnormality.[27] Her interpretation of taste is indistinguishable from Habermas's: "what Kant demanded in the *Critique of Judgment* of judgments of taste, is 'general communicability.' 'For it is a natural vocation of mankind to communicate and speak one's mind, especially in all matters concerning man as such.' "[28] She appears to ignore the possibility that judgments of taste might unfold locally, culturally and historically situated, imposing agonistic conflicts around standards of representation invaded by desire and power. She rejects the possibility that norms of artistic and political representation might stand in unending disarray, effectively denies that communicability depends on difference as well as agreement, that a public truth inhabits a space of misunderstanding and untruth. The result neglects the oppressions of every public normativity, defined by exclusion. The alternative within our sonorescence echoes local universality, inexhaustibility rather than infinity, normativity as deferral rather than consensus, nature's work as the ring of representation and the crash of judgment.

If judgment belongs to the middle regions of representation and truth, the possibility resounds that truth and representation possess exteriorities that shatter them, others that lie without yet within. Does this mean that truth cannot be truly thought except as sundered into untruth? Does it mean that the modern paradigm of truth, propositional or scientific, is included or excluded—or both? May we think of science as presenting untruth as its excess even while negating it? If so, then Heidegger's rejection of science along with metaphysics calls for questioning.

> When and insofar as science passes beyond correctness and goes on to a truth, which means that it arrives at the essential disclosure of what is as such, it is philosophy.[29]
>
> What characterizes metaphysical thinking which grounds the ground for beings is the fact that metaphysical thinking, starting from what is present, represents it in its presence and thus exhibits it as grounded by its ground.[30]

Representation and science, together with every form of knowledge and truth, may be heard within the middle regions in which order establishes itself together with disorder and normality cohabits with abnormality. Madness and reason echo each other.[31]

Presence and ground unfold as midworldly figures, incompatible with the idea of essential disclosure. We hope to retrieve science, along with metaphysics, from the appearance of full presence, restoring it to midworldliness. We listen to the dissonant proximity of truth with judgment within and to a multiplicity of modalities of judgment without. Reason here, like representation, judgment, power, and desire, both includes its other and questions itself as its own excess.

After Kant, we may think of judgment in the proximity of displacement, echoing the reciprocation of harmony and disharmony within representation. Similarly, locality echoes the reciprocation of belonging together and departing within nature. The question unfolds of how we are to hear the dislocation of judgment and locality when they echo everywhere, how we may think of them as exceeding and deferring themselves. We have answered that everywhere rings out as a transgressive figure. The world resounds as one and many worlds, each exceeding the others, where excess exceeds itself. One locale divides into many locales; many locales belong together as one. The harmony and disharmony that define judgment and representation echo their own harmony and disharmony. This doubling defines the multiple reflexivities of judgment.

To think of judgment as representation entails that *theōria*, *praxis*, and *poiēsis* both belong to and depart from representation, that they both exceed and repeat *technē*.[32] We live in experience "only" an indeterminate part of which can be understood in terms of *theōria*.[33] Reflective knowledge is surrounded and exceeded by *praxis* as *praxis* is guided though never determined by reflection and *poiēsis* is inseparable from and exceeds them both. This reciprocity of excesses echoes midworldliness. *Poiēsis* and *praxis* fall outside representation, surpluses, while also falling within. Science, art, and politics together inhabit the midworlds of judgment and truth.

In these reverberations, we find that, although we may represent every modality of judgment as representation, *praxis* reverberates within it among its departures, exceeding it while belonging within. If judgment rings as middleness itself, between, then judgment includes *praxis*, for *praxis* falls between past and present, present and future. Judgment requires *praxis* and *poiēsis*—every modality—as the others that define its disruptive limits.

Habermas speaks of the development of autonomous value spheres as characterizing cultural modernity: "In the modern world, 'value spheres' have been differentiated out from each of these moments [the cognitive-instrumental, moral-practical, and expressive moments of the intramundane linguistic functions of representation, interpersonal relation, and subjective expression . . .]"[34] Among his most strenuous criticisms of poststructuralism is that it denies the autonomy of different knowledge systems. He does not pursue the strongest argument available to him, that without autonomy, a knowledge system would be impervious.

Without other knowledge systems defining its limits, how could a knowledge system avoid closing on itself, unable to know itself? The closure would occur in an extreme of reflexivity without multiple reflexivity. Yet Habermas's own notion of autonomy echoes undeferred deferral.

A multiplicity of autonomous spheres of judgment echoes the midworldliness of judgment, demanding exteriority as well as interiority. In our sonorescence, judgment mediates in its differentiations, divides in its unities, discords in its concords, departs in its belongings, exceeds itself. It can do so "only" dispersed into multiplicities of deferral, modalities of judgment. In its dispersion, judgment repudiates any origin, any starting point of the hegemony of reason, any rational necessity. Yet reason itself echoes as a midworldly figure, joined with an unreason that both belongs with it and departs. Reason and unreason, with sanity and madness, truth and untruth, represent their own authority and dismantle its credibility.

Within our Western experience, there unfold many modalities of judgment. Each unfolds both as a particular kind or sphere of judgment and as judgment itself, a deferred univocity in multiplicity. Similarly, there echoes a truth appropriate to each modality of judgment, including art and *praxis*. This truth echoes its displacement by truths of departure as well as belongings within. Judgment, representation, and truth express reciprocal discordances and dislocations. The modalities of judgment sound its deferrals as our sonorescent univocals echo nature's ergonalities. The modalities of judgment resound among the cacophonies of relevance, echoing the multiple ergonalities of locality and inexhaustibility, multiply sounding the sonorities of locale-ingredient, unison-resonances, harmony-disharmony, and stillness-polyphony. Nature's work echoes through our sonorescences and resounds through judgment's modalities, in both cases cacophonically.

The classic triad of judgmental modalities goes back to Aristotle's distinction among saying, doing, and making, preserved in Kant among understanding, reason, and judgment as well as in Hegel's dialectic. Is it reasonable to ask why the faculties are divided into three, why every third is not divided inexhaustibly by the invasion of others, and how the mediating third of sublation can itself be sublated? If every pair requires a third for mediation, then does each of the pairs engendered by the third require another third? Does this regress of middles echo inexhaustibility?

Mediation echoes consonance and dissonance. Dispersion echoes exteriority. We find ourselves within a multiplicity of judgmental modalities, first, as excesses in judgment, but second, as a canon in relation to whose repeated measure an inexhaustible plurality of disciplinary modalities rings out. The canonicity of modalities of judgment sounds the repetitions of its disciplinariness. The presence of a set of disciplines, each with its autonomous sphere of rational legitimacy, sounds the will to truth while "incapable of recognising the will to truth

> At the foundation of all the empirical positivities, and of everything that can indicate
> itself as a concrete limitation of man's existence, we discover a finitude—which is
> in a sense the same: it is marked by the spatiality of the body, the yawning of desire,
> and the time of language; and yet it is radically other; in this sense, the limitation is
> expressed not as a determination imposed upon man from outside (because he has a
> nature or a history), but as a fundamental finitude which rests on nothing but its own
> existence as fact, and opens upon the positivity of all concrete limitation.[39]

The humanity of judgment materializes as specific and contingent, empirical and historical. It does not presuppose a subject or an agent, any particular forms of representation or judgment—presuppose them, that is, anhistorically. The multiplicities of reflexivity and limitation suggest that there resounds no unqualified essence to human being, for in the representation of that essence there echo the limits of that representation, and no unqualified necessity to its representation. Humanity appears inexhaustible along with representation. Humanity resounds as inexhaustible because finite, local, empirical, and contingent.

Without the presence of human beings, "subjects," can there be judgment, representation, power, desire, or truth? The relevance of human beings to judgment presupposes the relevance of judgment to human beings, the constitution of humanity by the judgmental locales, the perspectives, to which human beings belong, including history, embodiment, and practice as well as representation, desire, and power. Humanity, judgment, and perspectivity reciprocally constitute and exceed each other.

The constitution of human being by the deferred modalities of human judgment rings in a circularity within whose margins sound the displacements and promulgations of the truths of lived historical experience, including dispersion of the subject and constitution of different subjects. Here "the subject," each individual human being, exceeds and dislocates itself. There can resound no judgment without a judge, though that judge may sometimes stand forth as an agent, sometimes a group, sometimes known by name, sometimes anonymous, sometimes natural, sometimes artificial. The public worlds that judgments inhabit to be effective "only" sometimes materialize defined by individual human subjects, even where such subjects appear. The timelessness and universality of reason and truth unfold dispersed by the historicality of human agents. The grounding of judgment and truth in individual human experience echoes as dispersed by the public nature of historical experience.

We ask, then, whether the relevance of human beings to judgment may be understood, not as a recurrent condition, but as a multiple deferral in which the limits of the limits of human being resound. Is it possible that no differences obtain between natural locales and human perspectives except for the presence of human beings, who make every difference and none at all? Is it possible that nothing ultimate is at stake between humanity and animality save the arbitrary privilege of the former, where language and art make every difference and none at all? May there resound no differences between one person's public perspectives and another's, except that different human beings make every difference and none at all? In this interplay of same and other in judgment rings the inexhaustibility of humanity and its others.

In our sonorescence, we hear the ring of judgment as a pervasive midworld figure of representation situated at the local sites of differentiation where human life is carried on, including complex forms of reason and everyday practical experiences, a function of the locales it comprises and the ingredients that compose it, representation of itself and its truths and dislocated within itself. How it presents itself as so dislocated, however, cannot be thought transcendentally, through a subject, or transcendently, through its objects, but as multiply situated in lived historical experience, public and private. Let us, then, imagine two ways of marking this inexhaustibility in representation, the arbitrariness of the dividedness of judgment: through the diverse modalities of judgment inherited within our philosophic tradition and through the multiplicity of disciplines that compose modernity. And let us also acknowledge that any preference between them, even for the pair together, is arbitrary. The locality of knowledge echoes the locality of judgment, represented in inexhaustibly manifold ways.

We may imagine that each of the three functions described by Aristotle and repeated by Kant materializes as a modality of judgment. Questions emerge of how these modalities may show themselves as distinct where they are not autonomous, and how judgment may resound generically as there appears nothing with which it may be contrasted. Here the reciprocity of the modalities of judgment with judgment itself appears fundamental. As representation, judgment echoes many others, dislocated by and open within to alterity.

How pervasive is judgment? In what ways does it belong to nature? Does it include whatever human beings produce, possibly other representational beings, that modifies or reinforces human, or other, locales? Human beings stand in natural surroundings as material presences, weights and masses. Do perspectives require the relevance of human beings as judges, involve representation? Shall we say that a perspective resounds as a locale in which beings function representationally as judges while judgment transforms or reinforces perspectives through representation? To the extent that representation and judgment are reciprocal, nature's work, judgment includes whatever nature yields that modifies or reinforces its perspectivity.

This circularity in representation, judgment, and perspective serves to identify and displace them. The conjunction of their identity and difference defines representation and judgment in proximity to their limits and the limits of those limits: reciprocity and excess. The midworldliness of judgment echoes in its perspectivity as the midworldliness of perspective sounds in judgment. The spaces between different judgments and modalities of judgment, like the spaces between perspectives, echo repetition and nothing, the nonbeing of the repetition of repetition.

The circularities and excesses of judgment and perspective define the limits in whose limits can be found the multiple reflexivities of representation and truth. The circularity of repetition and difference opens the inexhaustibility of judgments and perspectives in two ways: in the multiplicity of forms of knowledge and in the inexhaustibility of judgments and perspectives, realized together with the limits of their representations.

We are asking whether whatever a human being brings about transpires as a judgment, given that human beings function as natural beings as well as judges in perspectives. We are asking whether wherever a human being is found a perspective appears as well. Yet how can we avoid saying that in whatever a human being produces, and wherever such a product appears, judgments and perspectives may transpire, where this possibility echoes excess? The natural world of locality and inexhaustibility is situated at the limits of each judgment and perspective, on both sides of its limits. Reciprocally, do judgment and perspective echo at the limits of every locus, again on both sides of its limits? Judgment and perspective both are and are not equivalent with humanity, as power, desire, and representation both are and are not equivalent with human locality. In the complex excesses of these sites of humanity we may find the deferred historicality of human perspectives and the deferred truthfulness of human judgments.

In our sonorescence, not every locale in which human beings are located materializes as a perspective, "only" one in which human beings function as judges, whereas judgment may transpire in any human locale. This broken circularity echoes transgression. Not everything brought about by a person materializes as judgment, but one that reinforces or modifies a perspective, whereas anything brought about may do so. This broken circularity of judgment echoes its deferred truth. The multiplicity of modalities of judgment entails a multiplicity of modalities of truth. Truth appears as a site at which representation defines and fragments itself.

We find ourselves located within many modalities of judgment and truth, and many modalities of reason. Each appears unintelligible from the standpoint of any other; each appears inseparable from the others. We may take these pluralizations of judgment and representation to define the midworlds of deferral in which every judgment makes its home, at once within a single modality that defines it yet also within other modalities that redefine it. The canonical Western modalities of judgment may be heard as propositional, practical, and fabricative; philosophy and religion suggest another, syndetic judgment, pertaining to the whole. Non-Western and subjugated writings suggest still others, emerging and yet to emerge. The corresponding Western modalities of reason resound as science, politics, art, and philosophy, with religion and mythology sources of endless questions. Among these sites of judgment and representation stand the midworlds that define order, truth, and intelligibility. These sites appear midworldly, fragmented and discontinuous. The thought that science and philosophy are undivided—can represent themselves as undivided—places them outside reason and truth.

The identification of truth with science echoes a Western theme going back at least to Aristotle, though it competes with faith through medieval thought. Our concern here is not whether some form of science is more rational or truthful—a form perhaps yet to evolve, the culmination of Western history into a later modernity—but with science's authority and privilege. In the Western tradition, truth represents and emerges from privilege. Reason and truth appear founded on the tombstones of unreason and untruth. Science sounds the emblem of the limits of a reason that cannot tolerate its other.

Identifying science as the form of reason predominantly concerned with propositional truth makes two representations at once: accepting the authority of propositional truth in its own domains, dividing that authority over other spheres of truth; and calling into question the legitimacy of propositional truth in its historical supremacy. In the extreme, this challenge to rational authority passes into repudiation of any authority to question whether truth can be heard without repudiating its other, whether it presupposes exclusion.

The locality of truth requires its others. We question how science's others may be sounded, as bad science, failed science, nonscience, madness; as science's limits, its fallibility and deferral, including the limits of those limits, echoing again and again; as inexhaustible resonances surrounding every unison, as inexhaustible disharmonies within every harmony, as unexpected polyphonies among the stillnesses, as the unending surprises in judgment and further judgment. We question whether untruth belongs within science or without, question its authority and privilege, whether science possesses hegemony over its others, within and without, whether reason possesses supremacy over unreason.[40] One answer rings in a multiplicity of modalities of truth, each irreducible to the others, unintelligible as such a modality from the standpoint of the others, inseparable from every other. To science, ethical values, political decisions, artistic masterpieces, and religious faith all appear unintelligible as truthful products, appear irrational. Yet reciprocally, the truths of science appear unintelligible from the standpoints of politics, religion, and art. The irreducibility of multiple modalities of truth to any single modality reflects the displacements that characterize the selectivity of the will that composes them. Yet no judgment can resound within but one modality. Does not every propositional assertion exercise power and embody desire? Does not every scientific claim materialize as a fabricative judgment? Does not every scientific practice embody values, exercise power, and contribute to a sense of the whole? Does not every science define a limit of reason, where reason is dislocated by its others—here other sciences and their limits?

We have supposed that science's repetition of the same unfolds with unisons, harmonies, and stillnesses more than with resonances, disharmonies, and polyphonies, with necessities more than with possibilities. This supposition fails in both directions: resonances echo in every unison, disharmony in every harmony, polyphonies in every stillness, possibilities everywhere; science can be concerned no more with one than the other. Each works differently, heterogeneously; each works together with the others. The dream of undisordered order belongs to science "only" in a Western dream of reason's privilege, the madness of reason without madness. Within the sphere of propositional judgment, ergonality's representations echo the unintelligible limits of intelligibility.

Propositional judgments canonically present themselves within the repercussions of truth and falsity. Yet they live in historical experience by being judged themselves. Judgments live in time through future judgments. We may call this judgment upon judgment *semasis*, judgment's work; and every judgment summons further judgments in its work or will be forgotten. Semasis and truth appear inseparable, and truth resounds through semasis as deferral. Representation, once begun, initiates further representations and rerepresentations; signs, in Peirce, initiate unending interpretants;[41] judgments may—and may not—give rise to subsequent judgments indefinitely. Semasis echoes judgment's multiple deferrals.[42] Even directed toward the past, as memory, judgment materializes in future judgments and that future's future, always outside itself. It is in virtue of this outside that truth is possible. But truth is not the "only" outcome of semasis.

Judgment's judgment, semasis, echoes among our sonorescences as their ergonality, repeating the play of locality and inexhaustibility. The determination of judgment resounds in the unisons and stillnesses among whose reverberations semasis belongs. The indeterminations and excesses of judgment echo in the resonances and polyphonies that pervade the temporality of semasis, belonging to its own history as deferral and disharmony. Judgment echoes in semasis, where its truth is judged, consonantly and dissonantly. The unending repetitions of semasis in time resound cacophonically and concordantly.

Where judgment is judged, we may hear criticism. Where the criticism is criticized, we may hear inquiry. Inquiry echoes as unterminating, multiply reflexive propositional interrogation, criticism, and more criticism. It presents itself as the "only" form of propositional reason, inexhaustibly dispersed, and may in our time be identified with science—one that sounds its limits through other modalities of judgment and truth. Where science closes upon itself by claiming that its methods alone determine the course of its development, where it subordinates propositional reason to itself, to that extent it repudiates its own rationality.

The deferrals through which propositional judgment represents its others echo through diverse modalities of judgment and truth that recurrently include and exclude each other. The deferrals in which inquiry interrogates its others peal forth through other forms of reason than science: forms that possess public standing and authority through the inclusions and exclusions that define them, and forms that question public authority on the basis of personal experiences. The ongoing other to propositional judgment echoes both as judgment itself and divided into multiple modalities interrogated through semasis. The ongoing other to inquiry materializes as *query*, reason itself, the unremitting, polyphonic interrogation of perspectival possibilities of judgment. Query resounds as both inquiry's genus and its univocal other. In response to modernity's claim that the norms of reason must be established within reason itself, our sonorescence responds that the norms of reason are established within query, but query rests on the possibilities within it of overthrowing any norm, including its own. Query echoes self-fulfillment through interrogative excess, exceeding itself.

Propositional judgment presupposes authority while in its empirical forms rejects every authority. This circularity defines an aporia characteristic of modern science: to accept no authority as free from challenge while proclaiming the supreme authority of the discipline through which every authority is challenged. This aporia leads to the presumption that propositional truth will triumph over all competitors, that science eliminates every alternative in the establishment of its truth. Such a truth, seeking to abolish its exteriority, denies itself in denying its other. May there sound forth an understanding of scientific truth that can affirm the authority of its others?

Science echoes as fragmented and dislocated, excessive within and without. Without, it reverberates divided by other modalities of reason and truth; within, divided into many sciences, natural and human sciences, by new theories, methods, and instruments that challenge the intelligibility of older theories; in relation to nature, fragmented by inexhaustible resonances and polyphonies. Propositional reason displays itself as divided by other forms of reason. Propositional query—science—resounds as one of many modalities of query. Nature rings among inexhaustible univocals. Reason and its truths reveal themselves as inexhaustibly divided.

Reason echoes query, intermodal and multimodal. Propositional query—again intermodal and multimodal—echoes science, characterized by the diaphonic ingredients that constitute its epistemic authority. May we say that such authority derives from repetition, repeatedly masked by appeals of certainty and necessity? Does the authority of modern science lie in repetition even where the singularity of events is unrepeatable and the abstractness of form makes repetition unintelligible? Does the standard of modern science appear as repetition even where science demands for its rationality the unending transformation of established truths? Does repetition as a standard deafen itself to the ringing of its disharmonies, resonances, and polyphonies?

Reason as repetition is traditionally referred to Plato, whose representation of the *eidos* defines the repeatability that makes contingent events intelligible. Here intelligibility appears as repetition—though Plato seldom repeats himself—a theme repeated 2,000 years later in the mathematization of modern science and in the regularization that defines the intelligibility of empirical experience. The truth of propositional reason sounds a repetitive truth in at least two ways: in the laws whose repetitions define the intelligibility of events, and in the repetitions in experience that define the ground of empirical science.

This principle of intelligibility as repetition continues throughout modernity into Hegel's dialectic, where among the historical contingencies whose sublation defines the activities of Spirit, Spirit manifests itself in the self-identity of its repetitions, however different. Repetition also continues to define norms of intelligibility in the atomisms whose representational repetitions constitute scientific intelligibility under law. How else, except as based on a principle of repetition, explain the continued return to law in nature outside human practices and in lived historical experience, where the singularity of events and persons forcibly manifests itself in the narratives told about them?

Repetition appears in our tradition as measure. Modern science grounds its authority in the metricization of truth. We wonder how questions of measure can avoid falling within science and without, within the natural and social sciences, politics and art, the procedures of science, logic and epistemology, and the experiences and understanding of human social life in which they are embedded. The thought that the truth of science may be represented "only" within science presents a closure that makes such a truth deaf to the power and desire that compose it. The thought that the truth of science, or any truth, expresses what can be measured denies the dislocations of what exceeds measure and of measure itself. To deny that the limits of science and reason lie in unscience and unreason repudiates the limits that define them. The locality of scientific reason echoes in the inexhaustibility of repetition, expressed in the displacements of our sonorescent univocals: resonances, disharmonies, and polyphonies. The inexhaustibility of scientific reason resounds in the inexhaustibility of other modalities of judgment and forms of query that provide science with means whereby it may be criticized.

The reflexivity of science is limited, a mark of its locality, as every modality of query is local. These limits compose the exclusions of reason. Science cannot represent its nature without overlooking the deferrals that compose its limits. It must either be judged under closure, under a principle of repetition, or judged from the perspectives of other modalities of judgment and truth. Art and philosophy do not compete with science as much as they define it. Science divides within into many sciences and without into many modalities of reason. Reason reveals itself as intrinsically divided.

The mark of modern science resounds as repetition, under evidence or law. For science to be the "only" form of truth makes repetition equivalent with truth although repetition cannot repeat itself without departure. Arendt's understanding of the multiplicity of perspectives that composes a public pertains to science, in which public life appears essential to its truth. In the publicity of its repetitions appears the dividedness of multiple perspectives for which repetition is departure. In the public life of science lie the polyphonies that mark the stillnesses of its truths.

Propositional judgment has traditionally sought a doubly repetitive truth: in the repeatability of its claims and in the repetitions of its laws. It passes into query where repetition remains at the center while fragmented by relentless criticism.

Scientific query rests on a ground of repetition although the finite and contingent events of the natural world are never repeated and query requires continual invention. There remains a fundamental tension in scientific query between the repetitive grounds of scientific truth and the unrepeated processes composing scientific activities, between the stillnesses of law and the polyphonies of history.

The presiding aporia of modern science presents it as defying all epistemic authority, thereby establishing itself as a supreme authority. Truth cannot be based on authority alone, of any kind, but is based on reason and empirical observation. Yet the nature of such reason and observation lies in repetition, and repetition grounds a new authority. The aporia resounds that a repeated science might have epistemic authority although science's authority bases itself on variation and invention.

The aporia has two resolutions: one that science's principle of repetition defines it, entailing that other modalities of reason delimit and rupture science; the other that external disruptions carry the disruptiveness of judgment from without to within, so that science cannot truly conform to a supreme principle of repetition. The truth of science echoes a repeatable truth that cannot be repeated, a stable truth that cannot conform, a deferred truth of deferral. Recognition of the instability of propositional judgment in relation to other modalities of judgment infiltrates the interior of scientific truth to disperse it into a cacophony of local truths. The locality of science echoes within its repeatability.

How may we think of the locality of science, given the tradition in which it is equated with repetition? Does science echo its locality in its historical situations and social relevance? Does it echo in a distinctively Western voice in the name of its universality? Does modern science echo its relevance, despite its movements toward universality, "only" to particular perspectives, "only" to perspectives defined by its and our modernity? Science's perspectivity echoes that it cannot sound its limits from within, "only" from without, through philosophy, art, religion, and practice; through non-Western voices challenging Western mastery; through unknown modalities of query. In return, science's perspectivity may resound in its heterogeneous polyphonies, the cacophonies of nature's work.

In our modernity, philosophy appears as science's other, both of them divided by the modalities of query. Yet art and practice also echo as science's others. Do we not find a plurality of others, a multiplicity of modalities of query? Moreover, these others resound divided by the others within science, dislocated into many sciences and other forms of propositional reason and by its own multi-modalities and intermodalities. The truth of science peals forth in proximity to repetition, producing the departures manifested by philosophy, politics, religion, and art. The truth of practice reaches forth in the space of failure, producing the achievements of science, religion, philosophy, and art.

May we suppose that failure belongs to practice in the irresistibility of time and history, the relevance of a past whose meaning forever remains indeterminate and a future that threatens every past with dissolution? May we suppose that time belongs to practical judgment as it does not belong to any other modality, while every judgment materializes as practical, influenced by its past and requiring its future, and while every judgment appears semasic, preceded by past judgments and succeeded by future judgments? The temporality of judgment multiply pertains to every modality but especially to practice: that mode of judgment for which the future looms as determination and excess.

Let us say that time belongs generically to judgment as semasis and deferral, the unending succession of judgments composing the continuities and dislocations of history. Let us also say that time belongs to judgment through multimodality, the relevance of every judgment to every modality, supplementing and displacing it. The latter condition entails that every judgment presses upon us as a practical judgment, if also assertive, fabricative, and syndetic. This practicality of judgment expresses its materiality in three successive forms: in relation to the future, where succession unfolds as prospective; in relation to other judgments, past, present, and future, where succession unfolds as semasic; and in relation to the heterogeneous univocals representing the sonorescences of time and nature. Practical judgment circles back through other modalities of judgment to its past; and politics, despite its irresistible movement toward the future, finds itself inescapably relevant to its past. The materiality of judgment manifests its practicality, for any judgment may be invaded by others unknown to it and us. The materiality of judgment dances before us as its deferral.

The ways in which time belongs to practical judgments compose the perils and subjugations of materiality. Like every judgment, practical judgments inhabit the succession of historical events and their disruptions within the reciprocities of historical time. Yet in addition, practical judgments belong to time as means and causes, unisons and resonances, harmonies and disharmonies, stillnesses and polyphonies—all echoing the displacements of time. Assertive and fabricative judgments in science and art belong to history and semasis, for without a future they would have no meaning, require a future in which they may again be judged. Practical judgments require their future twice, for their practicality and for their truth. They stand as causes with future consequences as well as semasic judgments. They materialize as judgments with consequences, opening possibilities of failure.

In our sonorescence, every judgment materializes as practical, including propositional and fabricative judgments. Every judgment unfolds as material, influences the future, displacing the present and dislocating the past. Every judgment, however practical, unfolds as propositional, fabricative, and syndetic. Within these circularities of modalities of judgment and truth, we hear intermodality and multimodality. Propositional truth is pervaded by materiality; practice is invaded by science and art. Intermodality and multimodality express the multiply reflexive interrelations of judgments without which no form of reason could interrogate itself. In this entanglement of judgmental modalities resounds truth,

divided by its others within—truth and untruth, representation and misrepresentation—and by its others without, other modalities of judgment and their truths.
Truth rings as its own deferral.

The irresistibility of time in practice defines the irresistibility in practice of
desire and power, of inexhaustibility and locality. Desire and power inhabit multiple times in which each future sounds fulfillment of a past through which it is
determined and dislocation of a past whose materialities displace it. This reciprocity tolls the historicality through which desire and power exceed any temporal determinations. The irresistible temporality of practical judgment is invaded
by the inescapable temporalities of power and desire.

The defining ingredient of practice may be heard as failure: a possibility in
every future, an inescapable reality in some perspectives. Its threat underlies what
Foucault and Derrida call the perils of discourse and representation, but its understanding goes back to Nietzsche's will to truth. It struggles as the excesses in
practice that repeat the excesses of time and judgment. We undertake practical
judgment facing an indeterminate future; any limit may be transgressed in the
determination of any future; every norm echoes its locality, no longer normative
in certain perspectives however normal it may be in others. Propositional and
fabricative judgments never as such materialize as failures, though they may be
untrue. They nevertheless echo failure as practical judgments.

Failure presents itself within the semasic condition that a practical judgment
is succeeded by others. No matter our efforts in controlling nature, we fail in
unanticipated ways. No matter our successes in controlling nature, control has
consequences that escape control. No matter our successes in resisting control,
our practice influences the future. Failure in mastery transpires not as hegemony
but reflexivity: it cannot master itself. Failure in practice follows from the fact
that it cannot avoid its own materiality. These failures appear as the unwork that
disperses and defers the work that practical judgments do.

A recurrent strain in the Western tradition maintains that to seek to control
nature while unable to control oneself is a defect. Self-knowledge and self-control
represent epitomes of mastery. Yet they represent not the limits of the self in
relation to nature, or conversely, but failure to master oneself. Self-control appears not as self-mastery but acknowledgment of one's otherness to oneself, failure as self-deferral.

Failure, power, and desire stand forth as pervasive conditions of practical
judgment, therefore of the forms of representation—politics and ethics—that define practical query. Each appears divided within; each divides the others. Failure
unfolds in virtue of the circular deferrals of temporality, the locality of a future
that constitutes the past while constituted by it, and of unending futures. Power
and desire stretch out as excesses in practice and representation, manifested as
failure. Desire reaches out as excesses in will to abrogate the truth of any judgment in relation to its future. Power weighs upon us as excesses in materiality

whereby any judgment may influence a future that will nullify it. These excesses sound the opacity of judgment without which failure would be unrepresentable. Excess in practical judgment appears as failure.

Failure echoes as the locality of practice, divisible into charity and sacrifice.[43] Charity echoes inexhaustibility. Sacrifice echoes locality. Both resound as failure in the ergonality of practical judgment. Together they compose valor, the practical truth of any locus, its inexhaustible deferrals and excesses over any representation, the inescapable limitations of practical judgment. Valor materializes as the inexhaustible excess of any locus in relation to practical judgment: excess and practical judgment's excesses. Valor represents the possibility of a touchstone for practical judgment even within its dislocations, a touchstone but not a norm or measure, each of which must sacrifice to its efficacies the inexhaustibility of local sonorescences. Valor's touchstone echoes the excesses of locality within the work of practical query.

Practical query takes two traditional forms: politics and ethics. Where the latter is associated with morality, with practice under law, its regulation imposes order over sacrifice and charity. Here politics appears to express practical reason more than ethics, a practice of inescapable risk and deferral. Yet ethics also may be based on valor, in this way indistinguishable from politics except for its public representations. Here we may again heed Arendt.

> Power preserves the public realm and the space of appearance, and as such is also the lifeblood of the human artifice, which, unless it is the scene of action and speech, of the web of human affairs and relationships and the stories engendered by them, lacks its ultimate *raison d'être*.
>
> Without action to bring into the play of the world the new beginning of which each man is capable by virtue of being born, "there is no new thing under the sun"; without speech to materialize and memorialize, however tentatively, the "new things" that appear and shine forth, "there is no remembrance"; without the enduring presence of a human artifact, there cannot "be any remembrance of things that are to come with those that shall come after." And without power, the space of appearance brought forth through action and speech in public will fade away as rapidly as the living deed and the living word.[44]

Representation endures in the public realm of action whereas power is its own representation. We add two provisos: that power and representation make a difference to history, bring forth risks and threats, and that the public representational space of power stands divided by multiple perspectives and diverse representations.

Practice stands as a site at which power, desire, and representation meet, each dislocating the others while inseparable from them, each divided within. Power contains its others in resistances, each a repetition of power, each a threat to destroy it. Desire contains its others in an infinite play that exceeds any strategy to contain it. Representation contains its others in the deferred spaces of repetition it opens to excess. In these middle regions emerge the historicality of politics and the instrumentality of embodiment. Our bodies dance within the entanglements of power, representation, and desire where, subject to the oppressions of power, they exceed any form of representation; where overwhelmed by the whirlwinds of desire, they exceed any gratification; where sites of the inscriptions of power and desire, they exceed any representation of its nature.

For Heidegger, art inhabits the rift between world and earth, a midworld in whose space truth establishes itself in the work. "Truth establishes itself in the work. Truth is present only as the conflict between lighting and concealing in the opposition of world and earth."[45] He suggests the unique midworldliness of art, to make a work, while denying that art is alone at the middle region of truth. "One essential way in which truth establishes itself in the beings it has opened up is truth setting itself into work. Another way in which truth occurs is the act that founds a political state."[46] "Only" science is excluded from the middle region, the clearing in which truth is established.

In the embrace of nature and representation, art rings as fabricative query, *poiētic* reason. Query unfolds as unending semasis, fabrication unfolds as *poiēsis*, and *poiēsis* unfolds as *technē*. The region occupied by judgment sounds between, defined less by its poles than by proximity to its others. We may wonder why fabricative judgment might sound more midworldly, science less reflexive and reciprocal, less open to its disharmonies, than practice or philosophy. Yet we may find something deeply important in Heidegger's view of science, at least the physical and mathematical sciences. Science may not explicitly include its own midworldliness within its purview, may not present itself as reflexively reflexive. Modern science sounds fragmented into many sciences, some of which— the social, historical, and human sciences—interrogate the cultural and historical conditions of the others, which in their purity deny the *ergon* of their own locality.

Such a denial cannot be sustained, yet neither can the belief that overt midworldliness is more truthful than covert expression. Both echo beliefs without deferral. Science peals its midworldliness despite its own denials and reveals itself as disruptive in virtue of them. It cannot present itself as the sole form of reason and truth, but neither can philosophy and art represent themselves as the sole forms of true thought.

Art displays itself as fabricative query, a pervasive form of reason. In modernity reason belongs with science, and science is pervaded by exclusion, especially the exclusion of *praxis* and *poiēsis* from reason. Reason here is propositional: mathematical and experimental. Art is relegated to imagination, to the sphere of representation. Yet if representation includes its others, can we exclude imagination and art? If representation reflects itself as repetition, does it do so by dislocating repetition and representation? Without art, can science's truth be rational? Reciprocally, does art need science for its truth? May each need the other, unending others, to define the regions in which the truth and untruth of judgment are defined in their departures?

Fabrication materializes as bringing forth, *poiēsis*. Every judgment, in every mode, shapes itself as fabricated, brought forth, as every judgment moves toward the future, conjoined with others that constitute its ground. Every judgment belongs to every mode, intermodally and multimodally.

Multiply reflexive representation belongs to propositional judgment insofar as truth appears in question, to practical judgment insofar as time appears in question, to fabricative judgment insofar as becoming appears in question, and to syndetic judgment insofar as belonging together appears in question. Truth resounds as propositional, practical, fabricative, syndetic—and more. Fabricative judgment and query inhabit the midworlds of truth in ways unknown to science, philosophy, religion, and practice, yet inseparable from them. Science's truth echoes repetition, displaced by departure. Practice's truth brings forth control, displaced by failure. Art's truth works as the unending interplay of materiality and sounding forth.[47]

Art shows itself as representation, inhabited by imagination, both midworldly figures. Imagination dwells at a site where judgment finds its others, within and without, equivalent with representation. Representation sounds divided within and without by misrepresentation, in two directions: toward a being that echoes as representation's other, present "only" through the otherness of representation, and toward the multiple reflexivities of judgment, where judgment finds its others within, canceling and augmenting itself. Here, in art, we may repudiate the exclusions that form the limits of truth in modern science and practice by other limits, without authority. Propositional reason resolves the midworldliness of its truth into exclusion of its others, claiming ultimate authority. Practical reason resolves the omnipresence of failure into failure's other, claiming authority over others within the limits of sacrifice. In our Western tradition, science and politics, religion and philosophy, resound as rational "only" where they possess authority over their others. Art possesses no such authority, though the Western tradition at times has claimed authority for it following the models of propositional and practical reason. Fabricative query claims no authority over its others, but maintains itself between. It echoes in the spaces opened within the polyphonies of judgment, the misrepresentations of representation.

Multiple reflexivity is modeled after art, though it belongs to all query. Art works in a middle region of its fulfillment, needing neither authority nor exclusion of others from itself. In this calming image of habitation erupt the most violent disturbances. More than practice, but without the immanence of failure, art confronts the violence and saving grace of bringing work forth. Art shows itself free from failure as art, free to pursue otherness while surrounded by violence and conflict. These confront art with the threat of failure; art and practice together, agonistically, occupy a middle region of life and death.

In the interplay of same and other as art lies the midworldliness of representation and imagination, where imagination resounds as both within and other to representation, representation as its misrepresentation. Where midworldliness sounds inescapable and perilous, it must, as practice, be resolved into one of its poles. Where inescapability takes precedence, art turns peril into giddiness and threatens the most dangerous of human sacrifices with denials of the threats of otherness.[48] The other becomes a principle of the same, however perverse, and the unending play of same and other becomes its own repetition. This echoes the aestheticization of practice in art, the dominion of the same as other within the unending play of harmony and disharmony. Adorno calls it "fetishization"[49]: a fascination with the other that collapses into the same. The peril of art, expressed in aestheticization, threatens to obscure the terrible otherness of the other behind a veil of fascination.

Where peril takes precedence, art turns into practice and risks losing its truth as art. The other threatens failure and dissolves into undying repetitions. Practice without art knows "only" failure. Art without practice knows nothing of failure. Together, they occupy midworlds of transgression.

The representation of representation and limitation of limitation forbid collapsing different modalities of reason into one. Although multiple reflexivity and representation define art in our local modernity, and although science and politics echo multiple reflexivity, they cannot all sound the same without destroying the others that define them. Art presents a model for a form of reason in our modernity that cannot become authoritarian without violating its own otherness. Music presents a model for a form of art that cannot become privileged within the same.

In propositional judgment, truth is based on a compulsion of the same residing in evidence and proof. In practical judgment, truth is based on the threat of temporality, the movement from past to future, a principle of repetition disrupted by time. In fabricative judgment, truth is based on materiality and deferral, each representation displaced by others without and within. In syndetic judgment, truth looks toward union and division, movements of the same divided by its others. Same and other occupy the center of fabricative judgment and art; a work emerges in the play of same and other that echoes the emergence of thing and work.

Art is inseparable from its history although it looms as monumental. Art is represented as atemporal although it emerges as historical. This midworldliness shows its prominence less in art than in the forms that would represent it, above all in the discipline of art history and in the forms of reason disrupted by it. The history of art is not art history: the latter is defined by a canon, based fundamentally on a principle of the same, a discipline that dwells in the spaces of its canonicity. The history of art echoes whatever stories we can tell, inexhaustibly and disruptively. For this reason, art history's rationality is constantly invaded by others that would disrupt it, although to do so would be to displace the entire space of art. In this way, art history occupies a unique midworldly space different from the spaces of history and art, music and dance.

As query, philosophy inhabits every between through the generic forms of its representations, pervaded by the excesses of query. Judgment rings as the between in representation, divided by a multiplicity of modalities of judgment. If this is so, then perhaps we may expect that at least one modality—possibly emergent in the midworldly spaces of the others—would have the work of representing the multiplicity of modalities generically and univocally. Perhaps, given one modality with that function, we should expect to find others. The generic representation of the space of otherness in judgment presents itself as syndetic judgment. Its predominant modern Western form of reason echoes as philosophy, syndetic query. Its most famous modern Western form resounds as metaphysics. The truth of metaphysics echoes aporia, reason based on its own deferral. Western metaphysics always appears beside religion, asking whether religion's truth shares in the displacements of metaphysics.

Metaphysics has always been thought profoundly culpable in refusing to condone the different modalities that define the plurivocities of query. At the heart of this denial lie the midworldliness of judgment and representation, the dividedness of truth and reason, and rejection of the exclusions that compose the authority of science. The latter rejection, repudiation of the disciplinariness of truth even in science, can be found in the most scientific of metaphysics, the aporias that compose the emptiness of the authority of philosophy. For in the West, philosophy has never possessed authority, but has always represented another sovereignty, God or science.

The absence of authoritative truth in philosophy has not been due to its refusal to claim such authority, and Nietzsche condemns philosophy for defining its truth and reason as the presiding forms. What Nietzsche may overlook—he recognizes it in relation to the will to power in Socrates and Christ—is that the opponent he reviles is weak. Socrates and Christ represent the absolute authority of the personification of a certain truth and reason. In their persons they possessed power and authority, constituted by their will to truth. Yet the truth they achieved has little power, for it influences the future less as philosophy than as practice. The aporia of philosophic reason is that it is caught inescapably between its own impotence and the powers that gather round it.

Philosophy struggles as practice like every mode of judgment, occupying the spaces defined by its materiality. Every mode of judgment materializes as practical and every mode echoes as propositional and fabricative. In addition, every mode reflects itself as syndetic: occupying the univocal spaces defined by the dividedness of judgment. Syndetic judgment unfolds as judgment of the dividedness in judgment. The late modern critique of metaphysics is that its judgments are overriding principles of the same within an experience disrupted by many others. The critique's rejection of the dominion of the same as the hallmark of truth echoes our sonorescent truth. Its limited understanding of the locality of metaphysics sounds our modernity's untruth. Its limited reflection of the pervasive hold religion presses on human life echoes another of our sonority's untruths.

The critique of metaphysics and religion as dogmatic rests on the authority of science and fails to acknowledge the dislocations of religion and philosophy in relation to scientific truth. It is a critique without thought of the dividedness of propositional reason. At the other extreme, the critique of metaphysics as a thought in full presence rejects with it the rational authority of science and demands a thought of the discordances that disrupt every truth. Both critiques, opposed as they are in spirit, speak to the inexhaustible displacements that reason requires to compose truth: the untruths of truth, the misrepresentations of representation; the aporias of aporia. They speak as well to the unholiness of the holiness of our being and the holiness of the unholiness of our lives. They toll of valor and the excesses that compose it.

Syndetic judgment resounds as that mode of judgment for which the unending dance of same and other appear unendingly as the aporia of the same, stillness in polyphony. Philosophy, but especially metaphysics, reverberates as the inexhaustible representation of harmony and disharmony within representation and judgment, where the other belongs to judgment as promise and as threat. The truth of metaphysics unfolds as aporia. The critique of metaphysics as undivided representation posits the truth of philosophy to be both propositional and totalizing. Rather, a local philosophy echoes unendingly deferred semasis and query of the multiple limits of multiple representation from standpoints within and without. The truth of philosophy appears neither propositional nor scientific, though one of the disruptive thoughts that has recurred throughout the history of philosophy echoes of a science whose representations would be the "only" truth. The generality of philosophy both fails to provide undivided representations and divides the dividedness in reason and truth into aporia. Aporia sounds the music of truth. It echoes transgression.

Aporia finds itself where representation reaches its limits and displaces itself. It echoes at the site where the univocities of syndetic query confront the limits of its representations, either in what exceeds representation or in the circularities of limitation and representation. Aporia stands at the site where philosophy acknowledges the limits of its multiple representations. The generality of philosophical query transmutes otherness into aporia. The appearance of otherness as aporia within syndetic query sounds the locality that defines philosophy and religion within our modernity.

Whitehead speaks of the relation between philosophy and religion in terms divided into emotion and reason, temporality and eternity.

> Religion should connection the rational generality of philosophy with the emotions and purposes springing out of existence in a particular society, in a particular epoch, and conditioned by particular antecedents. Religion is the translation of general

ideas into particular thoughts, particular emotions, and particular purposes; it is directed to the end of stretching individual interest beyond its self-defeating particularity. . . . Religion is an ultimate craving to infuse into the insistent particularity of emotion that non-temporal generality which primarily belongs to conceptual thought alone.[50]

If he unwisely accepts the bipolarities of emotion and reason, generality and particularity, temporality and eternity, he is deeply concerned with the relations of disharmony and polyphony that inhabit syndetic judgment. Metaphysics echoes the syndetic representation of nature, its *ergon* and *technē*, realized as aporia, the unending call of semasis. Religion peals the local echo of multiple representation, where *ergon* and *technē* echo valor in the passing harmonies that put failure away. We cannot escape failure in any judgment, a consequence of its materiality. But we can live with charity and sacrifice in the ring of valor, occupying syndetic query together with practical judgment. Religion sounds this way of being human whose truth appears as valor but whose untruth does not ring of failure.

Diverse modalities of judgment lead through semasis to judgments between the modes. Syndetic query rings as a predominant form of representation of what falls between, producing the pervasive aporia that results from philosophy's generality: the insistent others that fall within its repetitions. Yet the thought of generality and otherness is not restricted to philosophy, and the regions between the modes of judgment are occupied by other forms of judgment and query or, where empty, pose questions of their absence. This plurality in modality reverberates as a heterogeneity in which otherness divides even repetition in judgment as the same in itself. When judgment turns back on itself through semasis, intermodality and multimodality echo their predominance. They sound especially predominant in the heterogeneity within new forms of query: psychoanalysis, ethnology, structuralism, poststructuralism, psychohistory, and new discursive forms, new forms of religion. The emergence of such multimodal forms fulfills the imperatives of a divided reason.

It may seem strange to think of such a fulfillment. For how can there be fulfillment of a divided norm where the same is both divided and dislocated by an other? How can there be fulfillment without a norm, or where norms are emergent, including every norm of norms? How can deferral be fulfillment? In what can fulfillment echo but stillness? Yet is not such polyphonic fulfillment essential to an ethics of charity and a politics of sacrifice? Without such a normless norm of fulfillment, intermodality and multimodality could not emerge. The presence of limits—certain definite, if proximate, forms of query—sounds essential to the broaching of limits, the disruption of what falls between. It is the reason why resistance always follows power and why representation returns representation to itself.

Intermodality and multimodality echo not as unitary forms of judgment that triumph over the separateness of differentiation, or as bridges that divide and connect established domains of judgment, but as judgmental midworlds inhabiting the spaces among many entrenched forms of truth as representations of deferral. Intermodality and multimodality sound the betweens of judgment's betweens, unisons among its resonances; stillnesses among its polyphonies. Semasis and its inventions unfold the forms of deferral judgment wears to judge itself in relation to its future. Semasis, in multimodality and intermodality, resounds as representation of the judgment of judgment, the midworldliness of midworldliness. Even judgment, pervasive throughout representation, must disrupt its sames to realize its others.

Judgment occupies betweens in which representation turns back on itself reflexively. The midworld spaces of judgment divide into diverse modalities, each irreducible, each unintelligible as a mode of judgment from the standpoint of the others, each polyphonic in its stillnesses. The autonomy of each of the modes is essential to the heterogeneity of the midworld spaces of judgment and representation—an autonomy that defines excess, each in relation to the others. Yet even here excess echoes excesses, represented by the differences among modalities of reason and truth. Intermodality and multimodality in judgment echo another excess where judgment relates to itself and its limits. Yet the disruptive side of excess forbids judgment of the limits of judgment from within judgment alone. The limits of representation, limitation, judgment, reason, and truth are transgressed within every particular mode of judgment and truth. This may be understood not as a representation of limitation but as the capacity of judgment and reason to sacrifice themselves to establish their truth. In this sense, intermodality and multimodality resound among the untruths that compose truth.

THREE

Representation

By any name—mimesis, judgment, language, or artifice—representation rings in the middle, echoing itself and the others. This midpoint, alongside the traditional representation of representation as repetition, reverberates where representation rasps transgression and truth departs from itself as untruth. Turning back, judgment dislocates itself. In this circularity, representation dismembers itself. Within science, transgression echoes unreason. Within philosophy, it reverberates as aporia. Within practice, it unfolds as sacrifice. Within art, it brings forth art. Art brings itself forth as transgression, except that in this identity we efface the transgressions of science, practice, and philosophy, disown failure and untruth, above all, disavow misrepresentation. In the identities named by representation, we annul the others that allow the same to be the same and the different names by which we know it, abrogate them even as their univocities mute the dominion of their identity.

The names of representation; the identity of mimesis, representation, language, and judgment; the modalities of judgment—all reverberate as judgments of judgment. The judgment of judgment echoes semasis; the repetition of repetition resounds as excess; the nature of nature reverberates as artifice, judgment and representation. Semasis sounds the deferrals that mark representation, that name its different names within itself. In the aura of representation, locality echoes its others, deferral and its simulations.

Judgment repeats representation discordantly as semasis disharmonizes judgment. Nature, here, diaphonically echoes itself. Similarly, locality discordantly echoes power; inexhaustibility diaphonically repeats desire; nature's *ergon* sounds the dissonances of *technē*; representation harshly rings of artifice. Within the repetitions of representation echo the others that dislocate it.

Representation peals locality where locality discordantly echoes itself. We name this discord nature's *ergon*: nature echoing its work, its *technē*, representation as judgment. The form in which truth displaces itself opens into untruth, power into resistance, desire into itself, representation into misrepresentation.[1] Our sonorescence echoes the misrepresentation of representation. The unnaturalness of nature echoes artifice, the work done by loci in inexhaustibly different locales.

The middle regions where rèpresentation echoes transgression may not be heard without representation, but may be listened to beyond representation. What may be heard beyond representation does not depart from representation, from judgment, but belongs to it as deferral and excess, including excesses of excess. The transgression of representation by representation sounds beyond representation through representation, exceeding judgment as semasis.

In his travels, Gulliver visits the island of Lagado, where members of the Academy propose that we stop using words for things, with all their confusions, and carry things themselves about, things both being and representing things. The excesses of words over things passes into the excesses of things over themselves. The story suggests that such excesses arrive with language. Rather, although things do not always mark themselves, they cannot "simply" be themselves. Nature echoes its own excesses. This truth exceeds itself in its untruth. Our antiphony sounds at this point of dislocation where language, representation, and truth, also nature and philosophy, echo their unlimits, exceeded by the others that delimit and disperse them. Reality here rings its inseparability from unreality, truth from untruth, representation from misrepresentation. This inseparability reverberates as deferral's deferral.

The middle regions where representation echoes its belonging together with transgression unfold not of truth alone, even with untruth, but belong together with practice and art. The middle regions dwell between truth and untruth, rulers and ruled, necessity and freedom. Ideas of sovereignty and power, governance and rule, occupy the same midpoints of representation, for no power can be effective without implementation where the latter moves by representation. We speak of unrepresentative government, as if "only" certain forms of governance were representative, as if "only" certain forms of judgment were representation. Where these "onlys" define the terrain of thought, they move away from the limits of their limits. Where these "only's" define the terrain of practice, they situate practice far from transgression, defining it by rule. The capacity of representation to circle back to destroy itself echoes where the same finds itself divided by others that define, defy, and defile it. As every thought resounds as representation, divided by its circularity, every government stands as representative, divided by resistances that compose its power and deferrals that compose its misrepresentations.

Chapter Sixteen, "Of Persons, Authors, and Things Personated," in *Leviathan*, marks the end of Part I, "Of Man," and precedes Part II, "Of Commonwealth." It is where Hobbes makes his transition from human beings to politics. In it he depicts sovereignty and power in terms of representation. "A person is he whose words and actions are considered either as his own or as representing the words or actions of another man, or of any other thing, to whom they are attributed, whether truly or by fiction."[2] Fundamental here are artificial persons and representation by fiction. The idea of a person involves action as representation, including misrepresentation as well as truth. Otherness lies coiled within the ideas of both representation and being a person, and the latter is inseparable from representation. "When they are considered as his own, then is he called a *natural person*; and when they are considered as representing the words and actions of another, then is he a *feigned* or *artificial person*."[3] Representation here rings its togetherness with fiction and truth, artifice and nature. The circularity of representation opens a space of misrepresentation and untruth, of pretense, fraud, and deceit; the idea of a person occupies that space, rests on misrepresentation and deception. The idea of action at the center of Hobbes's theory of practice echoes the stage: representation as performance, deception, illusion. Within the idea of a person resounds the notion of representation as misrepresentation: of performance behind a mask, in disguise. One personates oneself or another where personation is impersonation.

> The word *person* is Latin, . . . which signifies the *face*, as *persona* in Latin signifies the *disguise* or *outward appearance* of a man, counterfeited on the stage, and sometimes more particularly that part of which disguises the face, as a mask or vizard; . . . So that a *person* is the same that an *actor* is, both on the stage and in common conversation; and to *personate* is to *act* or *represent* himself or another; . . .[4]

The idea of a person resounds as portrayal behind a mask because personation echoes representation and representation echoes misrepresentation. The idea of action here belongs together with its counterfeit. Representation rings up a dramatic performance where every role suggests deceit. The truth of performance unfolds as the truth of deception. Truth in practice echoes its counterfeit.

This antiphon of representation sets the stage on which Hobbes defines his view of sovereignty. The sovereign acts as the representative of the people with or without consulting them or concerned with their desires, exercising their authority. The question of power in collective human life presses forth as one of representative authority, of how and when a person can act as representative for a person or thing, where one's actions stand for another's. This absent presence echoes at the heart of representation and public life. Behind the idea of politics resound the discordances of the representations and powers that constitute a public. The movement from the state of nature to a commonwealth in Hobbes is from natural powers without representation to powers defined by representation.

Fundamental to Hobbes's account echoes the proximity of representation and fiction. Representational truth resounds as representational untruth. In his view of words, this recognition implies that fiction presents a constant threat that must be ruthlessly weeded out. "Compound imagination" is "but a fiction of the mind."[5] More important are four "special uses of speech" with "four correspondent abuses": "First, when men register their thoughts wrong by the inconstancy of the signification of their words, . . . and so deceive themselves. Secondly, when they use words metaphorically . . . and thereby deceive others."[6] The idea of representation here, in relation to imagination and speech, is pervaded by deception. Untruth must be purged. Fiction inhabits representation. The fiction of an artificial person underlies the dispersion of authority, the possibility of power, and the idea of a person. Power echoes representation's misrepresentations.

Within this upsurge of misrepresentation belonging to authority and truth, we may hear a certain refrain. Truth shines in the radiance of untruth; representation rings in the sonance of misrepresentation. Yet where we hear the ring of representation, the sonance of nature as its artifice, do the antiphonies within truth and representation resound oppositionally as untruth and misrepresentation? Does the fiction in representation belong to its sonance as truly as to its radiance? Or shall we hear it as judgment's deferrals?

The "mis-" of representation, like the "un-" of truth, traditionally shines in the light of adversarial judgment. In the ring of representation, we may hear instead the sonance of a misrepresentation and untruth that, like dissonance, belongs to music's harmony even while dividing it, to its unisons and to its resonances. The refrain of our sonorescent music peals as its antiphonies, belonging with them and departing from them. We hear our refrain as forbearance rather than abstention.

In Hobbes's extraordinary analysis authority appears unintelligible without representation's misrepresentations. We can discern a similar view in Machiavelli, though falling short of Hobbes's: "When it happens that some one does something extraordinary, either good or evil, in civil life, he must find such means of rewarding or punishing him which will be much talked about. And above all a prince must endeavour in every action to obtain fame for being great and excellent."[7] Essential to civil life is being talked about, obtaining fame. Representations of greatness and excellence appear as important as achievements. Public life stands as one of representation, and representation appears together with power.

An analogous view appears in Arendt:

> The term "public" signifies two closely interrelated but not altogether identical phenomena:
>
> It means, first, that everything that appears in public can be seen and heard by everybody and has the widest possible publicity. For us, appearance—something that is being seen and heard by others as well as by ourselves—constitutes reality.[8]
>
> Second, the term "public" signifies the world itself, in so far as it is common to all of us and distinguished from our privately owned place in it. This world, however, is not identical with the earth or with nature, as the limited space for the movement of men and the general condition of organic life. It is related, rather, to the human artifact, the fabrication of human hands, as well as to affairs which go on among those who inhabit the man-made world together. To live together in the

world means essentially that a world of things is between those who have it in common, as a table is located between those who sit around it; the world, like every
in-between, relates and separates men at the same time.[9]

The public world shows itself constituted by appearance, by representation as a
public, by the making of artifacts. Being seen and being heard, in a public space
constituted by fabrication, transpire as representation. This representational public is an "in-between," at once separating and relating. Arendt's understanding of
this play of same and other is unsurpassed.

Under the conditions of a common world, reality is not guaranteed primarily by the
"common nature" of all men who constitute it, but rather by the fact that, differences of position and the resulting variety of perspectives notwithstanding, everybody is always concerned with the same object. . . . The end of the common world
has come when it is seen only under one aspect and is permitted to present itself in
only one perspective.[10]

The "same object" appears within a representational public defined by differences. The presence of one perspective destroys it, a common public, fabricated
as an artifact, shared as difference. Arendt's is a powerful sense of what commonality can mean in public in virtue of representation, definitive of sovereignty. Yet
she does not emphasize as forcefully as Hobbes the fictiveness of representation,
the misrepresentative side of public life. Hobbes's view that authority is a ficti-
tious creature surpasses Machiavelli's and Arendt's.

None, however, seems to hear the possibility that representation's antiphony may be represented by music and dance. May we think of authority's dispersion more as the evanescent temporality of a musical performance than in terms of
enduring works? The dividedness of personal authority pertains to representation
itself, not "just" to words and deeds. Representation inhabits the space where
authority is constituted and divides that space in ways that resist any undivided
presence. Once words are words, once songs are recorded, the authority that surrounds them becomes institutional, historical, dispersed.

Representation always rings reciprocally as public and private. Even so,
Arendt defines the public world exclusively in relation to representation and appearance, leaving the private realm to fall outside representation:

To live an entirely private life means above all to be deprived of things essential to a
truly human life: to be deprived of the reality that comes from being seen and heard
by others, to be deprived of an "objective" relationship with them that comes from
being related to and separated from them through the intermediary of a common
world of things, to be deprived of the possibility of achieving something more permanent than life itself.[11]

The private realm falls away from representation although the shelter it requires
from the harsh glare of commonality requires another representation. Arendt

maintains a Kantian distinction between objectivity and subjectivity that passes into her view of publicness and privateness, a distinction overthrown when representation circles back upon itself. In the public nature of words and acts, authority ceases to belong exclusively to subjects, dwells everywhere and nowhere. A public space presents itself as representational in the doubled reverberations of meaning and authority. In a public world with an unknown future, no one can own one's words as no one can own one's sounds or deeds. Representation marks this negativity positively as deferral.

In Hobbes, the doublings of representation point toward both the fictiveness and artificiality that define it and the bonding on which power depends. The achievement of a commonwealth requires the creation of a public space that would be impossible without representation. "A commonwealth is said to be instituted, when a multitude of men do agree, and covenant, every one with every one, that to whatsoever man, or assembly of men, shall be given by the major part, the right to present the person of them all, that is, to say to be their representative."[12] To be a person is to exercise representational activity. A commonwealth is a representational object. The sovereign appears as the representative of each and all and can serve that function "only" by fiction and artifice. More important, the determination of a lasting public depends on the deferrals of representation. "A multitude of men, are made *one* person, when they are by one man, or one person, represented; . . . For it is the *unity* of the representer, not the *unity* of represented, that maketh the person *one*. And it is the representer that beareth the person, and but one person; and *unity*, cannot otherwise be understood in multitude."[13] Unity appears as a fiction, artificially constructed by representation, or sounds forth "only" in virtue of representation. The unison of a public depends on the divided reciprocities of representation and misrepresentation. One consequence is that the capacity of the sovereign to represent the multitude is inseparable from the capacity to tyrannize them. The sovereign's authority, in virtue of his representativeness, has limits, and those limits have limits, dividing the authority, truth, and efficacy of his misrepresentations. The monstrosity of the future, embodied in the state of nature, is not alleviated by the institution of sovereignty, but carries into and pervades the entanglements of its representations and misrepresentations. The aporias of representation, its displacements and reciprocities, provide the soil on which its authority rests.

Hanna Fenichel Pitkin represents the "paradox of representation" by two quotations:

> Either the representative must vote as his constituents would vote if consulted, or he must vote in the opposite sense. In the latter case, he is not a representative at all, but merely an oligarch; for it is surely ridiculous to say that a man represents Bethnal Green if he is in the habit of saying "Aye" when the people of Bethnal Green would say "No."[14]

The essence of Representation is that the power of the people should be parted with, and given over, for a limited period to the deputy chosen by the people, and that he should perform that part in the government which but for his transfer, would have been performed by the people themselves. It is not Representation if the constituents so far retain a control as to act for themselves. They may communicate with their delegate . . . but he is to act—not they; he is to act for them—not they for themselves.[15]

We may wonder at the idea that votes can "only" be for or against. Does it suggest denial of difference's betweens? What of the idea of acting for a person who has no standing? If issues must be voted on without a between, or a representative government gives up power to another with no remainder, does representation ring without excess or deferral? Is political representation without displacement representation at all?

Pitkin portrays the conjunction of autonomy and repetition paradoxically:[16] "the concept of representation just does seem to be paradoxical in meaning, is intended to express a dichotomous idea."[17] We hear the conjunction as aporia rather than paradox, a difference between a thought that thinks itself as excess and one that knows its limit to regulate it.

The aporia of representation sounds a representation of its midworldliness. In Pitkin's case, it echoes between repetition and autonomy. To represent is to be "autonomously repetitive," "freely mediative," following while breaking rules. Representation materializes as practical judgment, acting for or in the place of another—even all others—by acting as the representative decides, while acting always stands for another. These aporias have no resolution, not because there is no rule, but because representation, like judgment, falls between. Like translation, they echo transgression.[18]

Pitkin's treatment of the doubled nature of political representation resists its symbolic side. Words are one thing, acts another. Yet both forms of representation share the departures whereby representation echoes both itself and others. One of Pitkin's striking assumptions lies in her expectation of what it might mean to represent representation:

But the single, basic meaning of representation will have very different applications depending on what is being made present or considered present, and in what circumstances. . . . What we need is not just an accurate definition, but a way of doing justice to the various more detailed applications of representation in various contexts—how the absent thing is made present, and who considers it so.[19]

We may think of the concept as a rather complicated, convoluted, three-dimensional structure in the middle of a dark enclosure. Political theorists give us, as it were, flash-bulb photographs of the structure taken from different angles. . . . Yet there is something there, in the middle in the dark, which all of them are photographing; and the different photographs can be used to reconstruct it in complete detail.[20]

Yet if representation, like words, makes absence present, does it not make presence absent? Although there is little sense in Pitkin of this reciprocal movement that lies at the heart of representation's representation, there is a powerful sense of the midworldliness of representation, with the proviso that the "something there" can be reconstructed from the photographs without deferral. In the midworlds of representation, every representation of representation repeats and dislocates itself.

The dream of perfect representation has been with us always despite the failure of every repetition. This failure is not "just" a reflection of differences between signifier and signified, word and thing, but is found in things themselves, in their identity. Identity rasps discordantly of dislocation in its limits and the others that delimit them. Nothing can be itself without excess. Even in a perfect democracy, human beings cannot represent themselves perfectly, pursuing their interests and values, not because they fall short, but because they cannot be perfectly or simply themselves, do not possess undivided identities, interests, and values. In a complex world, interests and values, like representations and presences, appear as misrepresentations: counterfeits and deceits, artifices and simulations.

The dividedness of political representation materializes in words and symbols but more generally in things and powers. One direction we may pursue is that of locality, represented by a thought that includes its others within itself excessively. Another is that of judgment, understood to disperse itself. Representation materializes as the site at which these dissonances sound together.

It follows that representation cannot be normalized within its displacements:

> representing here means acting in the interest of the represented, in a manner responsive to them. The representative must act independently; his action must involve discretion and judgment; he must be the one who acts. The represented must also be (conceived as) capable of independent action and judgment, not merely being taken care of. And, despite the resulting potential for conflict between representative and represented about what is to be done, that conflict must not normally take place. The representative must act in such a way that there is no conflict, or if it occurs an explanation is called for. He must not be found persistently at odds with the wishes of the represented without good reason in terms of their interest, without a good explanation of why their wishes are not in accord with their interest.[21]

Missing here are the deferrals that compose power and desire. Political representation is situated at a point where power and desire meet. Its paradoxes do not mark complex human lives, which, with good will and devotion, we will find a way to order successfully. They mark power exceeding itself transgressively, along with representation and desire.

Representation, verbal or practical, finds itself thrown upon its limits by its reciprocities and reflexivities. It turns back on itself, multiply, and in doing so, dislocates itself. In this disturbance, its perseverance presses forth as transgression. This displaced sense of the limits of limitation may be contrasted with Pitkin's closing words:

> The concept of representation thus is a continuing tension between ideal and achievement. This tension should lead us neither to abandon the ideal, retreating to an operational definition that accepts whatever those usually designated as representatives do; nor to abandon its institutionalization and withdraw from political reality. Rather, it should present a continuing but not hopeless challenge: to construct institutions and train individuals in such a way that they engage in the pursuit of the public interest, the genuine representation of the public; and, at the same time, to remain critical of those institutions and that training, so that they are always open to further interpretation and reform.[22]

She normatively represents modern political practice as rational "only" if it pursues institutions that seek to make power responsive to those who do not possess it and if it maintains continuing criticism of every effort undertaken in the name of representation. Such a view presupposes that liberation belongs within power comfortably, that representation belongs to representation without discordance.[23]

In our sonorescence, representation echoes its own excesses. Yet from the Enlightenment, the theme of accurate representation resounds, first in terms of mirrors and diagrams—visibilities rather than sonorities—today embodied in the idea of a representative sample, where the few reproduce the identity of the whole. This notion of the whole reverberates as a figure of transgression, yet does not sound it. Measure presupposes a totality of all states and arrangements, without limits that exceed themselves.[24]

The metrical theme in representation goes back to Pythagoras, allied with the mathematical side of the Western tradition, associated with Aristotle's view of *technē*. A mathematical emphasis, even glorification, echoes in Descartes and Leibniz, Galileo and Newton, in philosophy and science.[25] Less plausibly resounds its association with measure, for many forms of mathematical order have no metric. Whitehead displays a striking thought of order without measure, yet no philosopher offers a more profound sense of the mathematical nature of things.[26] A metric presupposes equivalent units to be exchanged for each other without undermining their identity whereas Whitehead's metaphysics emphasizes the unrepeatable identity of actual things, each of which is a unique experiencing subject that cannot be replaced by any other.

The idea of exchange equivalence echoes wealth: the transformation of tangible things into currency. Foucault discusses an exchange economy in the sixth chapter of *The Order of Things*, perhaps the most comprehensive analysis of representation yet undertaken. "The two functions of money, as a common measure between commodities and as a substitute in the mechanism of exchange, are based upon its material reality. A measure is stable, recognized as valid by everyone and in all places, if it has as a standard an assignable reality that can be compared to the diversity of things that one wishes to measure."[27] Essential here, the presiding theme of *The Order of Things*, is the pervasiveness of order that money provides to representation: a common measure of all things in an overarching economy.

Foucault characterizes the order of exchange within classical representation as based on three great parallels among language, wealth, and natural order.[28] This system of identities and differences characterizes what he calls "classical" representation, but echoes today within the systems of exchange that characterize contemporary thought. For Saussure, the mark of a linguistic sign resides in its arbitrariness and the value of a sign—"only" difference—resides in its role in a system of substitutions and equivalences.[29] The notion of difference here embodies no sense of displacement. The sign of that lack appears in the systematic play of differences that constitutes *langue*. In a synchronic sense of language abstracted from *langage* and *parole*, *langue* forms a system of equivalences while no exact equivalences echo in a living language. The system of exchange hides its transgressions from itself. For Freud, the pleasure principle defines a double system of identities and differences in which each desire appears irreplaceable, each lack unfulfillable, yet each pleasure is exchangeable, through sublimation, with infinitely many others. The idea of sublimation inhabits this middle region between equivalence and uniqueness, repetition and valor, that characterizes so many Western theories of experience. For if sublimation confronted excessive desires that could not be diverted, it would be inert. It presupposes that desire is its own difference while positing an exchange relation within that difference. In both Saussure and Freud, difference dwells at the center of the theory in a substitutive form that dissolves it into an economy of the same.

At stake is representation's multiple reflexivity through the linguistic sign. Language echoes as if represented by itself, either in its fecundity, so that excess multiplies through its representations, or in its totality, each sign by every other. This latter sense of relation to another posits a system of equivalences, a metric whereby representation defines a universal measure. The value of each sign appears measured against its equivalents as each pleasure appears measured against other pleasures, determined within a system of substitutions. An exchange system posits a totality pervaded by a universal basis of representation. Wealth appears as model for all, represented by money in a system of exchange. "For Classical thought in its formative phase, money is that which permits wealth to be represented. Without such signs, wealth would remain immobile, useless, and as it were silent."[30] An economy in which desire, power, and representation appear represented echoes a system of exchange determined by an underlying metric that defines the mobility of its currency without excess.

Throughout the West, the idea of value has repeatedly been grounded in a system of exchange equivalences. In utilitarianism, value appears both calculable and systematic, the good defined in terms of interests and desires determined on the whole. Such a calculation is based on the premises that values and desires are always comparable, that each may be exchanged for any other; and that all may be calculated together as if none was incompatible with the others. Utilitarianism may appear extreme in its calculations "on the whole," but not in its assumptions of equivalence. These are canonical in classical theory. The totality of values and their liquidity replace the uniqueness and inexhaustibility of valor.

For Foucault, the idea of exchange is an offshoot of classical representation:

> The theory of money and trade responds to the question: how, in the movement of exchange, can prices characterize things—how can money establish a system of signs and designation between kinds of wealth? The theory of value responds to a question that intersects this first one, . . . why are there things that men seek to exchange; why are some of them worth more than others, why do some of them, that have no utility, have a high value, whereas others, that are indispensable, have no value at all? . . . why objects of desire and need have to be represented, how one posits the value of a thing, and why one can affirm that it is worth this or that.[31]

Multiple reflexivity suggests a more sweeping view. Foucault makes the striking point that within such a system of exchange, value depends on sacrifice. "The creation of value is therefore not a means of satisfying a greater number of needs; it is the sacrifice of a certain quantity of goods in order to exchange others. Values thus form the negative of goods."[32] This double idea, that values in a system of exchange presuppose sacrifice and that sacrifice echoes excess, characterizes the representations that make goods into values. Desire emerges as that whose representation defines value and whose excesses bring forth the sacrifices required by a system of exchange.

The notion that defines an exchange metric is equivalence,[33] the idea that imposes sacrifice; for if things were not equivalent or equivalent "only" locally, then the economy in which they were located would have to sacrifice any excess, any good not represented within the economy. The economy represents desire and power, and their exchanges define the excesses whose sacrifice is required if desire and power are to be represented. Representation therefore unfolds as sacrifice. This aporia defines the truth of representation's representation, revealed, for Foucault, by Sade, neglecting the monstrous ways in which he sacrifices women: "Sade attains the end of Classical discourse and thought. He holds sway precisely upon their frontier. After him, violence, life and death, desire, and sexuality will extend, below the level of representation, an immense expanse of shade which we are now attempting to recover, as far as we can, in our discourse, in our freedom, in our thought."[34] Foucault continues with the comment: "But our thought is so brief, our freedom so enslaved, our discourse so repetitive, that we must face the fact that that expanse of shade below is really a bottomless sea."[35] This excess, this endless sea, echoes at the point at which the representation of representation opens into multiple deferral. Foucault appears to reject such a view of representation, relegating representation to its classical period. Yet the excesses in representation may be heard nowhere more compellingly than in *The Order of Things*, where both representation and its excesses ring forth identified with order. That identification, with its differences, echoes the play of representation with its truth, misrepresentation.

The Order of Things recounts the movement from classical to modern representation as the decline of representation. It does so in such a way as to emphasize the relevance of representation after its disappearance. Representation doubles twice: once in its occurrence and decline, then in its perpetuation. The decline of classical representation echoes within the perpetuation of representation. These doublings ring within representation, a truth unheard in *The Order of Things*, though it reverberates in *The Archaeology of Knowledge* and later essays:

> I have sketched a genealogical history of the origins of a theory and a knowledge of anomaly and of the various techniques that relate to it. None of it does more than mark time. Repetitive and disconnected, it advances nowhere. Since indeed it never ceases to say the same thing, it perhaps says nothing. It is tangled up into an indecipherable, disorganised muddle. In a nutshell it is inconclusive.[36]

A representation that knows itself to be representation, that circles back to include itself, also dislocates itself, throws itself into transgression. It goes far from itself, advances nowhere, and is written without a face that might define its purpose. A morality and countermorality here demand the same within the displacements whereby representation defines its others. Here to say nothing is not to have nothing to say but whispers the misrepresentations that enable representation to represent itself.

Foucault tells us that *The Order of Things* is about order, conscious and unconscious, explicit and implicit, in knowledge and in things, where inseparable from representation. "The fundamental codes of a culture—those governing its language, its schemas of perception, its exchanges, its techniques, its values, the hierarchy of its practices—establish for every man, from the very first, the empirical orders with which he will be dealing and within which he will be at home."[37] These codes and what they govern—language, perception, and exchange—define empirical order, which is constituted by the historical a priori.[38] Elsewhere, Foucault associates it with the "archive,"[39] the general system of the formation of order. We have echoed his extraordinary remarks concerning the archive:

> The analysis of the archive, then, involves a privileged region: at once close to us, and different from our present existence, it is the border of time that surrounds our presence, which overhangs it, and which indicates it in its otherness; it is that which outside ourselves, delimits us. . . . In this sense, it is valid for our diagnosis. . . . In this sense, the diagnosis . . . establishes that we are difference, that our reason is the difference of discourses, our history the difference of times, our selves the difference of masks. That difference, far from being the forgotten and recovered origin, is the dispersion that we are and make.[40]

This difference and dispersion, that which delimits "us," rings out in multiple representation where discourse, time, and self fall into representation. The site of privilege, in the archive, resounds not as the origin, but where representation echoes its transgressions.

As its subtitle, *An Archaeology of the Human Sciences*, indicates, *The Order of Things* is concerned with how the human sciences perpetuate representation after the decline of classical representation, though Foucault also speaks of the strangeness of language, its excesses.[41] His focus falls on the space between the birth of the modern sciences and classical representation,[42] on the difference between modernity in science and modernity in representation. In this gap between two modernities reverberates what Foucault calls the birth and death of "Man,"[43] a creature of representation who feints at the limit but represents himself nontransgressively.

> man for the human sciences is not that living being with a very particular form (a somewhat special physiology and an almost unique autonomy); he is that living being who, from within the life to which he entirely belongs and by which he is traversed in his whole being, constitutes representations by means of which he lives, and on the basis of which he possesses that strange capacity of being able to represent to himself precisely that life. (OT, p. 352)[44]

The unthought composes the frame of both the book and representation, present in the excesses of language but echoing in different guises. The human sciences seize the unthought in the name of the unconscious,[45] while in Borges's Chinese encyclopedia a taxonomy appears about whose unthinkable monstrosity Foucault asks,[46] "But what is it impossible to think, and what kind of impossibility are we faced with here?" (OT, p. xv). The answer lies in the excesses of language. "Where else could they be juxtaposed except in the non-place of language?" (OT, p. xvii). A nonplace of disorder, where order echoes representation. The disorder of the Chinese taxonomy sounds an order that exceeds our capacity for representation. "There would appear to be, then, at the other extremity of the earth we inhabit, a culture entirely devoted to the ordering of space, but one that does not distribute the multiplicity of existing things into any of the categories that make it possible for us to name, speak, and think" (OT, p. xix). Representation, order, and classification join to define intelligibility, and within each echoes the other that disharmonizes it: misrepresentation, discord, and misclassification.

The theme of the unthought, that which exceeds representation, returns obliquely where "Man" echoes as a figure that closes the circle of empirical knowledge and its origin: "The question is no longer: How can experience of nature give rise to necessary judgments? But rather: How can man think what he does not think, inhabit as though by a mute occupation something that eludes him, animate with a kind of frozen movement that figure of himself that takes the form of a stubborn exteriority?" (OT, p. 323).[47] In modernity, the unthought reverberates in the empirico-transcendental circle that defines humanity as both knower and known, may be heard in the space that defines their differences within the circle of their identity. "Man" closes that circle in denying the excesses of thought and representation that lie in language.

The circle here sounds the aporias of representation, appearing in the *The Order of Things* as multiple representation, the space in which representation represents itself as misrepresentation.[48] This space of representation, understood transgressively, echoes where sign and symbol, word and thing, reverberate as same yet other, where the great domination of the same echoes representation. Representation's prepositions, *of*, *through*, *in*, and *by*, haunt every representation. In this space where representation folds back on itself a middle region unfolds between ordered and known truth.

> Thus, between the already "encoded" eye and reflexive knowledge there is a middle region which liberates order itself: . . . This middle region, then, in so far as it makes manifest the modes of being of order, can be posited as the most fundamental of all: anterior to words, perceptions, and gestures, . . . Thus, in every culture, between the use of what one might call the ordering codes and reflections upon order itself, there is the pure experience of order and of its modes of being. (OT, p. xxi)

The middle region dwells in the betweens at which limit and transgression may be heard. It "liberates order *itself*," is most fundamental, is where we find the possibility of a "pure experience of order and of its modes of being." These primacies and purifications are aporias within representation and order, where disorder appears indistinguishable from order and where representation misrepresents itself. In the invisibilities that surround representation dwell the "only" representation we may find of pure representation as dislocation.

> [In *Las Meninas*] representation undertakes to represent itself here in all its elements, with its images, the eyes to which it is offered, the faces it makes visible, the gestures that call it into being. But there, in the midst of this dispersion which it is simultaneously grouping together and spreading out before us, indicated compellingly from every side, is an essential void: the necessary disappearance of that which is its foundation—of the person it resembles and the person in whose eyes it is only a resemblance. This very subject—which is the same—has been elided. And representation, freed finally from the relation that was impeding it, can offer itself as representation in its pure form. (OT, p. 16)

This pure representation rings as representation itself, freed from its classical bonds to subject and object, free to sacrifice itself. Representation can represent itself "only" by representing what exceeds it. The "pure" form of representation may be heard in Foucault, not as the origin of representation, but as the ring of transgression, where representation represents itself by dislocating itself. Representation in the web of the human sciences claims to represent itself without excess. Within this grid echoes the absent self whose sovereignty emerges in the solidity of its representations.

Classical representation is contrasted in *The Order of Things* with what preceded it, the prose of the world, and what followed, modernity. The latter is defined by what exceeds representation. "Our" modernity emerges when what exceeds representation is known to belong to it, however aporetically. What preceded classical representation appears more striking: the play of the world entirely within the same, based on resemblance. Even here, Foucault cannot avoid speaking of representation: "It was resemblance that largely guided exegesis and the interpretation of texts; it was resemblance that organized the play of symbols, made possible knowledge of things visible and invisible, and controlled the art of representing them" (OT, p. 17).

The prose of the world rests on similarity and resemblance, in four forms whereby anything may be joined with anything else within the same: convenience, emulation, analogy, and sympathy.[49] Anything anywhere can answer anything anywhere else. Anything can resemble anything else. In this unending play of likenesses and resemblances, differences are transformed into unending domination of the same, the reason why sympathy requires antipathy. What is so important to classical representation and modern science, being in the true surrounded by the false, has no place in so mighty a sense of the same. "The same remains the same, riveted onto itself" (OT, p. 25).

Even so, the same cannot know, cannot *be*, itself without representation, without displacement. The plethora of knowledge in the same cannot be knowledge if it is not defined by the whisper of the other that is either not known (exceeding knowledge) or untrue. Resemblances can be known "only" through the signatures that echo as themselves. "There are no resemblances without signatures. The world of similarity can only be a world of signs" (OT, p. 26).[50] Similarities and resemblances, every relation under the same, can be known "only" insofar as each makes itself a sign. Each term of a resemblance visibly marks it in a relation of resemblance and displacement.[51] The presence of signatures, of visibility, opens a rift in the seamlessness of the same. Here representation enters a nonspace where truth has its home. Language (and representation) belong to the natural world and mark its excesses. "Language stands halfway between the visible forms of nature and the secret conveniences of esoteric discourse. It is a fragmented nature, divided against itself and deprived of its original transparency by admixture; it is a secret that carries within itself, though near the surface, the decipherable signs of what it is trying to say" (OT pp. 35–36).

Even here, within the plethoric interplay of similitudes and signatures, the rasp of excess sounds a limit that cries for regulation.[52] In the unending play of the same, knowledge appears a thing of sand, entirely in vain, in virtue of its repetitions. The same cannot be truth; its other both exceeds truth and makes it possible. The regulation of excess, emphasized in classical representation, emerges as a requisite for science and its knowledge. Language echoes the excesses that science fails to bring under regulation.

The story of *The Order of Things*, the narrative that defines its history, recounts an epic drama whose hero is language, captured in one *epistēmē*, seduced in another, but always exceeding its captors' grasp. Immersed in resemblances and similitudes, inseparable from the order of the world, nevertheless, in the space opened by its otherness, language exceeds itself and the world, an excess whose restlessness leads to classical representation.[53] Language belongs to and calls forth the world when the very things that resemble each other in their play of the same show the marks of their similitudes. Language belongs to the world, but departs from, exceeds, it and itself. The parallel excess emerges that the world exceeds both itself and language, that things in their affinities mark their disaffinities.

The three notions that define classical representation are natural order, wealth, and language. Each, in classical representation, appears without excess, defining for us our understanding of truth and value as measure.[54] The most prominent structure, representative of the others, is that of wealth. Money circulates as the universal measure, the structure of wealth repeating the structures of language and nature.[55] This triangle of structures, each mirroring and dividing the others, shapes a representation of classical representation. The demise of this view of representation transpired when the table of identities opened up into the excesses of representation. Foucault ascribes this efflorescence to Sade. But his project is to define modernity as the transformation from representation without excess to the excesses of representation in the circular movements within the triad of life, labor, and language, each of which comes to represent its excesses within and over itself.[56] In this transformation, modernity emerges, with two predominant themes: the unthought, and "Man" as empirico-transcendental doublet.

Two important qualifications remain. One Foucault speaks of openly: the excesses that emerge within representation, that present themselves as the unthought, definitive of modernity, do not escape the clutches of representation, for in the reciprocity and circularity of modernity, representation turns back onto itself in the form of the human sciences to seize its origins. The human sciences define an "anthropological sleep" in which the excesses of language sound the name of "Man."[57] The historical role of the human sciences here is to step aside from the main track of modernity, in which excess emerges as the unthought, to seek to complete the task of classical representation, to close representation onto itself, containing both its origin and its limits. The human sciences seek to find in human being its empirical and transcendental conditions.

> And so we find philosophy falling asleep once more in the hollow of this Fold; this time not the sleep of Dogmatism, but that of Anthropology. . . . The anthropological configuration of modern philosophy consists in doubling over dogmatism, in

dividing it into two different levels each lending support to and limiting the other: the pre-critical analysis of what man is in his essence becomes the analytic of everything that can, in general, be presented to man's experience. (OT, p. 341)

The second qualification constitutes the focus of our discussion. Representation, even while turning back onto itself to regulate its excesses within the same, echoes excess within itself. Representation divides itself transgressively while remaining within the dominion of the same. The explicit narrative of *The Order of Things* tells of language's escape from representation; the implicit narrative calls forth representation's escape from classical representation. The greater epic tells the escape of alterity from the dominion of the same, "only" to know—to represent—to itself that it was "always" within and without. This recognition marks the ring of representation's representation, both metaphysics and anthropology, as transgression.[58] Foucault poses the question of the limits of representation from the standpoint of "another metaphysics," which he hears as falling outside representation. "Criticism . . . opens up at the same time the possibility of another metaphysics; one whose purpose will be to question, apart from representation, all that is the source and origin of representation; it makes possible those philosophies of Life, of the Will, and of the Word, that the nineteenth century is to deploy in the wake of criticism" (OT, p. 243).

Questions of the limits of representation and of its source and origin coincide. They lead to metaphysics: how questions of the limits of representation may be posed "apart from representation" and whether such questions may be posed at the limits of metaphysical representation or without, whether posing them is transgression. The question of the origin of representation may be heard as Greek; the question of its limits may be heard as transcendental. That either question might be posed from within representation closes representation upon itself. That either might be posed from without traces the closure of that standpoint onto itself. The traditional metaphysical movement is the representation of this closure. The question, for both metaphysics and its representation, echoes whether posing questions of their limits and origins posits closure. The circularity of representation imposes a realization that if such questions do not fall within, then both representation and metaphysics fall outside the limit that they have struggled so hard to regulate. The alternative is that the limits of representation fall within representation transgressively, within and without, where the percussions of representation echo multiple repercussions, metaphysics echoes locality, and locality echoes excess.

Representation belongs to both politics and discourse. In their three-fold belonging together echoes representation's displacement. Such a togetherness has been sharply criticized. Noting that in German the distinction is marked by two different words, *vertreten* and *darstellen*, Gayatri Spivak claims that to confuse speaking for and about is to reinstate the male European subject.[59] In Deleuze, for example,

> Two senses of representation are being run together: representation as "speaking for," as in politics, and representation as "re-presentation," as in art or philosophy.[60]

> In the guise of a post-Marxist description of the scene of power, we thus encounter a much older debate: between representation or rhetoric as tropology and as persuasion. *Darstellen* belongs to the first constellation, *vertreten*—with stronger connotations of substitution—to the second. Again, they are related, but running them together, especially in order to say that beyond both is where oppressed subjects speak, act, and know *for themselves*, leads to an essentialist, utopian politics.[61]

She also associates the sites of purity in Foucault—"pure" madness, "pure" representation, order "itself"—with the pure presence of an oppressed subject. Political practice is overwhelmed by multiple representation, by too much talk of talk. Where the subaltern is Third World and female, there is no point from which she can speak for herself. To think there is names an undivided Other that, by a reverse movement, reinstates the European Subject. Rather, Spivak suggests, we may take the site of oppression to call forth unrelenting critique where the European's task reverberates as neither to speak *for* the other nor to *let* the other speak but to speak for "himself" from within the dividedness of his representations. The masculine pronouns are explicit.

Two of her arguments are especially relevant.[62] In her discussion of the two senses of representation, Spivak addresses *The Eighteenth Brumaire of Louis Bonaparte*, concluding that: "Marx is obliged to construct models of a divided and dislocated subject whose parts are not continuous or coherent with each other."[63] She does not consider the possibility that the same movement away from continuity and coherence applies to distinctions within as well as totality. Sharply distinguishing the two meanings of representation posits another coherent narrative. Every narrative may be heard as incoherent (including this one).

Power's dispersion materializes as its heterogeneity. It includes its other, resistances, within itself. Desire, similarly, reaches forth as its other, always departing from itself, the reason why it can be manipulated and controlled, and why it can never be completely manipulated and controlled. Representation, too, echoes as its own other—its misrepresentation—the reason why there unfolds no science of sciences or narrative of narratives, no representation of representation, that tells its undivided truth. The truth of knowledge's truth echoes in its divided untruths as its disharmonies. Western truth appears "only" Western; the European subject sounds "only" one subject among others. To "let the subaltern speak," where "she" does not already speak, indeed is arrogance, no less than speaking for her or claiming she has nothing to say. The arrogance, however, belongs to the representation as well as to the colonization. It is the arrogance of a representation of representation that does not acknowledge its own incoherence. The site where the subaltern may speak resounds as one where culture meets representation. Culture emerges as another univocal that echoes its own displacement, between power and representation.

Among the themes of poststructuralism that Spivak admires is the heterogeneity of any narrative about narration, representation, or truth, but also about power and desire. This heterogeneity has two important features: that representation, power, desire, history, and truth belong together, composing truth; and that the multiplicity of truths about these constellations accommodates no overarching truth, resonate disharmoniously and polyphonically. The truth of truth reverberates as its untruth, where power, desire, and representation with their sonorescent univocals, but also history and embodiment, echo the untruths of truth. The distinction between theory and practice, resounding between *darstellen* and *vertreten*, becomes irrelevant.

How do we express the incoherencies of representations of truth, power, desire, and representation itself? If the ways in which we represent representation express both incoherence and specificity, one danger is totalization, whether of representation or subjectivity itself, anonymously, or of any distinction that appears in anonymous garb. The alternative unfolds of speaking in a particular historical and cultural voice. Yet every voice speaks multiply, whereas to specify a voice denies its multiplicity. It follows that among the voices we may—but must not say "must"—employ to speak of the heterogeneity of representations and truths echoes a multiply reflexive voice in which the totality of representations turns back on itself, where the representation of representation sounds so multifariously and incoherently that it echoes misrepresentation, where the truth of truth sounds untruth and the power in power presses upon us as resistance. History and culture emerge as each other's deferrals, and our time's historical juncture irrupts in the challenge of other cultures. Our sonorescence is ours but not "only" ours, and where others appear, they are not "only" other, but within our history.

To acknowledge difference—sexual, gender, racial, ethnic, cultural, class, and so forth—is to inhabit at least two representational and practical spaces: to represent each difference uniquely and to represent differences as difference, where the latter disrupts every epistemic authority, including its own.

> The Master is bound to recognize that His Culture is not as homogeneous, as monolithic as He believed it to be. He discovers, with much reluctance, He is just an other among others.
>
> As long as words of difference serve to legitimate a discourse instead of delaying its authority to infinity, they are, to borrow an image from Audre Lorde, "noteworthy only as *decorations*."[64]

Our concern is with the "infinity" of this deferral, which cannot be given any particular form. Epistemic authority slips away into heterogeneity. Knowledge never belongs to everyone and never belongs "only" to someone. It belongs to someone and belongs to others, private and public, is situated at a time and place while it slips away into other times and places.

That a white, male, middle-class philosopher may speak "only" from within a divided representation of his representational locale does not belie their limits or transgressions. A local philosophy of the multiple reflexivities of representation within oppression and privilege may represent itself as divided even while reinstating privilege, itself divided. This divided representation seeks to dislocate the privilege of one perspective over another without escaping privilege, hopes to disrupt representation through its misrepresentations without escaping representation. To see the "of" in representation "only" as a conjunction of speaking for and speaking about in which oppressed people are oppressed once more represents it as a synthesis blind to its misrepresentations. Hobbes suggests that the play between power and representation can shatter the relationship in classical representation between signifier and signified as the duplicity of the latter can shatter the naming of privilege within the authority of political representation. The single word "representation" marks not a unitary presence, but a discordant unison. Here misrepresentation belongs to representation as untruth belongs to truth, and conversely. The multiple displacements within reflexive representation dislocate its privilege and itself. It cannot then be the "only" voice in which representation's privilege is protested.

FOUR

Power

n our refrain, power beats in the chords of relevance and relevance echoes dispersion, reciprocity, and intransitivity, expressions of its multiple deferrals. In our sonorescence, relevance echoes locality, divided and pervasive. Power includes its others and is dislocated by them, by the resistances that both repeat power and alter it. In this aporia, throughout power, representation, and desire, resound the transgressions that our sonorescence requires to express power locally—to tell its truth without obscuring the masks that eclipse it. In this reciprocity of power with its others echo its discordances, unmastery with mastery, resistance with power. To be, Plato suggests, is to exercise power. Yet whatever exercises power is exercised by it. To be is to inhabit local spheres of relevance where power dislocates itself.

This understanding of power sounds its doubled locality, a view of power close to Foucault's, with an important difference, that its dissonant voice echoes the cacophonies of metaphysics, exuberant while aporetic in its sonorities that power beats everywhere—but not universally; or rather, that universality always dismembers itself from within, excessively. The displacement of universality by transgression manifests the dislocation of philosophy by ontology, equally dislocated, into a univocal voice that echoes its own locality, its will to truth as its untruth. We may challenge metaphysics as a thought that fails to think its own transgressions, that does not circle back to displace itself. We ask in return, what belongs to such a dislocation if not metaphysics? May it be heard as the ring of our sonorescence? Power beats the chords of relevance among nature's stillnesses and polyphonies.

The decentering of the subject within our refrain echoes repudiation of neither human beings nor subjectivity, but of a center of activity that does not voice its own displacements, does not acknowledge the ways in which being an object for and among others tears the subject apart at the same time that it constitutes an inescapable condition of human subjectivity. In this repudiation of its agency, the subject sounds its own dispersion, affirming its powers and subjugations.

The essential contemporary work on power, definitive of its locality, is Foucault's *History of Sexuality, Volume I.* (Nietzsche's *Will to Power* is its forerunner.) It may be no accident, though it may be regrettable, that such a "metaphysics of power" should receive its most compelling formulation in relation to sexuality. It may be no accident because the relation of power to desire materializes intrinsically, reciprocally, and transgressively. It may be regrettable because power materializes everywhere; yet desire echoes everywhere together with power, locality's inexhaustibility. The inseparability of power from desire makes the autonomy and excess of each all the more important and puzzling. In our refrain, power, desire, and representation echo respectively as relevance, inexhaustibility, and judgment. Each sounds its inseparability from the others everywhere along with the excesses that pertain to each, its autonomy relative to the others. This conjunction of entanglement and excess echoes the dispersions that characterize multiple locality, defined by the multiple reflexivities of representation, desire, and power.

Foucault claims that power is to be understood not as the control inherent in the inequalities of human public life, the state apparatus, but as the network of multiple relations within which a public emerges, though restricted neither to the public nor to subjugation. Power is immanent as the field of relevances in which institutions define themselves.

> It seems to me that power must be understood in the first instance as the multiplicity of force relations immanent in the sphere in which they operate and which constitute their own organization; as the process which, through ceaseless struggles and confrontations, transforms, strengthens, or reverses them; as the support which these force relations find in one another, thus forming a chain or system, or on the contrary, the disjunctions and contradictions which isolate them from one another; and lastly, as the strategies in which they take effect, whose general design or institutional crystallization is embodied in the state apparatus, in the formulation of the law, in the various social hegemonies.[1]

He specifically repudiates the bipolarities and repressions of power, themes intrinsic to the identification of desire with sexuality. The repudiation rests on the distinction within Western history between power and "Power." Power (in general, univocally but not universally) is everywhere. "Power" is the specific form power has taken in the premodern West. It appears in the form of Law, which belongs to Power but is not essential to power. Above all, Power is marked by exclusion where power is marked by inclusion, including Power. "The omnipresence of power: not because it has the privilege of consolidating everything under its invincible unity, but because it is produced from one moment to the next, at every point, or rather in every relation from one point to another."[2]

The omnipresence of power whispers metaphysically: everywhere but not everything. Rejected with its "invincible unity" is its totalization: "everything." Two thoughts of universality echo here: First is totality, all and every, inclusive. Metaphysics speaks here in the voice of "Metaphysics" as power speaks in the voice of "Power." Totality and universality echo "Totality" and "Universality."

Second, emphasizing locality, we reject the Totality and Universality of totality and universality. Universality whispers its locality and univocity, its deferrals and excesses, its resonances and polyphonies. For us, universality asks whether a local sonorescence can echo its univocals, power, desire, and representation, history, embodiment, and truth as the murmuring of its transgressions.

What may be heard as omnipresence but not invincible unity, not total totality? What may be heard as a local "everywhere"? These questions define our sonorescence. In relation to power, relevance echoes its transgressiveness. To be is to be relevant, where relevance echoes reciprocity and displacement. To be is to be local, located and locating, thereby relevant, exercising power and being exercised by it. The fundamental transgression of power in our sonorescence resounds in the relation of power to Power, of relevance to oppression, displacements within the rule of Law.[3]

Two aporias define the materialities of power within our modernity. The theme of everywhere in relation to power rings the aporia of universality: everywhere but not everything. In addition, power crystallizes into networks and hegemonies, displays domination even when divided within itself. Power produces strategies and apparatuses from within, produces Power, even though the two are always distinct. Power sets itself apart from "Power" while always producing order. This aporia marks the fundamental division on which Western power rests, the aporia of universal history: to appear both as everything and something material. The conjunction of materiality with universality expresses the aporia that gives power its historicality, realized in our Western tradition as Power. The aporia of power in relation to Power institutes our historical relation to power: the positive side of the negativity of domination.

Why does power take the form of Power? Why does power exercise domination and control when everywhere? Why does power organize into hegemony and oppression, utilize strategies and produce order, materialize as authority? Why does power crystallize into institutions, apparatuses, and laws? Why does it produce domination if everywhere? Why, if power is relevance, is it not innocent as relevance appears to be—innocent as well as guilty? Why does power not dissipate itself into anarchy and chaos? Why is violence inescapable? Should these questions be repudiated? Do they follow from the locality of power?

Power materializes, everywhere and always, in the forms of dissipation and production, disruption and hegemony, innocence and guilt, each multiple deferral. As productive, power produces order, in materiality and truth, thought and things, representation and reality. It produces order, transforming it into Order and Power. As productive, it produces disorder. Power produces determinateness and order, unisons, stillnesses, and harmonies. In this production, it produces multiple displacements, resonances, polyphonies, and disharmonies.

Power stands among the pervasive representations of the reciprocity of order with disorder. Its deferrals lie in the gestures that define its universality. Its excesses lie in its otherness to itself—its resistances but also Power: "Power is everywhere; not because it embraces everything, but because it comes from everywhere. And 'Power,' insofar as it is permanent, repetitious, inert, and self-reproducing, is simply the over-all effect that emerges from all these mobilities, the concatenation that rests on each of them and seeks in turn to arrest their movement."[4] Power comes from everywhere but does not embrace everything. Power echoes everywhere but not permanently. Nevertheless, there transpires a Power that represents itself as permanent and self-reproducing, echoing its Stillness as if without polyphony. The relation between power and Power manifests multiple deferral, for power cannot escape the embrace of Power. This reciprocity defines a local movement. Power produces "Power" as both the materiality through which we experience power, its resistance, and the other that dislocates it, while power displaces Power. The excesses of relevance within locality are marked by the excesses of power's Power.

Power cannot echo a universal condition within an undivided history of "Power," but materializes in a particular historical form before it can possess generic force. The most powerful of Foucault's writings concern the transformation of Power into power, where the latter has already been realized in the rule of a modernity that would deny any rule. His discussions of the rule of power, its productivity, surge within our modernity in relation to sexuality, madness, and criminality, in each case to produce themselves as others: sexuality rather than desire, unreason rather than madness, criminality rather than nonconformity with law. Disciplinary power becomes a fact before it materializes as a universal—a material fact incompatible with universal universality. Power, desire, and representation displace the universality of universality, replacing it with the pervasiveness of a unison of disharmonies that resonates with its own excesses.

What force can the embrace of universality have when power comes from everywhere? What might press upon us everywhere but not universally? How can power come from everywhere while not relevant to everything? Within the ring of our sonorescent univocals we may understand how universality must be limited—how everything must be limited, including limitation—therefore locality and inexhaustibility as well. Relevance echoes everywhere along with irrelevance. Irrelevance sounds the deferral of relevance; resistance sounds the deferral of power.

Loci echo their relevance to each other when they have ingredients in common. If two loci differ, then some of their ingredients differ. It follows that some of their subaltern ingredients materialize irrelevant to each other. What sounds its universality over all locales cannot echo its universality over all their ingredients and subaltern ingredients. Otherwise everything would echo the same, riveted on itself. Irrelevance rings the locality of universality.

Foucault describes power as coming from everywhere but not including everything. The everything speaks of every locus including its ingredients and the

ingredients of those ingredients—a condition that cannot be expressed even locally, the aporia that defines inexhaustibility. The "everywhere" speaks of each
inexhaustible locus in its spheres of relevance, the aporia that defines locality.
Locality and inexhaustibility echo aporetic moments of relevance and excess. In
particular, their aporias define the excesses that make universality intelligible: its
locality. Analogously, power's dividedness defines its intelligibility. "Only" because power is Power (though also other) can power be represented. Similarly,
"only" because power includes the resistances that displace it can power represent
itself as deferral.

The distinction between power and Power defines each. In relation to sexuality, Power echoes mastery even while desire refuses to be controlled:

> These are some of its principal features:
> —*The negative relation*. It never establishes any connection between power and
> sex that is not negative: rejection, exclusion, refusal, blockage, concealment, or
> mask. . . .
> —*The insistence of the rule*. Power is essentially what dictates its law to sex.
> Which means first of all that sex is placed by power in a binary system: licit and
> illicit, permitted and forbidden. . . .
> —*The cycle of prohibition:* thou shalt not go near, thou shalt not touch, thou
> shalt not consume, thou shalt not experience pleasure, thou shalt not speak, thou
> shalt not show thyself; ultimately thou shalt not exist, except in darkness and se-
> crecy. . . .
> —*The logic of censorship:* . . .
> —*The uniformity of the apparatus.*[5]

These five moments of Power belong to power.

First, Power knows itself as negating, obstructing. In relation to sexuality,
Power stands forth as mastery and domination, achieved by repression, based on
silence. "Power" and power inhabit the same spaces of silence and repression: the
one a generic moment in the denial of sex definitive of gender and sexuality, the
other a figure defining a particular sexuality. A local sonorescence, here, represents itself in the spaces it inhabits between power and Power.

"Power" unfolds as juridico-discursive power while power unfolds as its
parent and progeny, excesses emergent within the Law. The rule of law that defines Power passes into deferral and transgression, but the transgression requires
Power to define itself. Power and "Power" silently echo each other. Without this
relation, we could not speak of the everywhere of power or of domination and
subjugation. The productiveness of power demands its inseparability from Power
as well as their distinctness. "Only" thereby can we speak of domination:

> In a sense, only a single drama is ever staged in this "non-place," the endlessly
> repeated play of dominations. . . . This relationship of domination is no more a
> "relationship" than the place where it occurs is a place; and, precisely for this rea-
> son, it is fixed throughout its history, in rituals, in meticulous procedures that im-

pose rights and obligations. . . . Humanity does not progress from combat to combat until it arrives at universal reciprocity, where the rule of law finally replaces
warfare; humanity installs each of its violences in a system of rules and thus proceeds from domination to domination.[6]

The rules impose the violences without which power cannot impose itself, cannot
dominate. Power's productivity engenders "Power," gives rise to negativity,
domination, and subjugation. Domination materializes as the Power within
power, though the latter stands forth as alternative to Power. In this respect relevance is not innocent, for it gives rise to Power.

Second, the Power that masters sex by dictating its rule to it cannot disappear, to be supplanted by a power that produces sex without a rule. Not only may
power exercise domination through a system of rules—its violences—but law,
rule, and language may transpire as means whereby power produces its materialities. This is the message of the "rule" that domination is everywhere. The universality of power does not entail that thought and practice must transpire by means
of binary oppositions, licit and illicit, permitted and forbidden; yet power materializes "only" within binary oppositions that realize its productivity. Mastery here
may be reviled while pursued, the other within whereby power echoes both Power
and resistance. "Only" in this circularity can power echo transgression. Power
echoes power's deferral; power sounds deferral of the Law of Power.

Third, "Power" works by prohibition; power works positively and materi-
ally. Yet the language that manifests the forcefulness of power always speaks of
prohibition and denial—the reason why sexuality appears in relation to prohibitions: not because power prohibits, but because it produces in the shadow of its
excesses, Power. Some of this truth echoes in the "only's" and "nothing more's"
that surround the definition of Power. Power echoes excess in relation to "Power"
defined by mereness and onlyness, its nostalgia. Power echoes the excesses
within, the dominations and violences, that define the orderings of power. Without Power, power could not determine order. The order of sexuality determined
by power, and that exceeds it, also determines the disorder within Power, whose
prohibitions are requisites of the positive workings of power.

Fourth, it follows that silences within the violences of power whisper of
Power within, of its inseparability from its dominations. This truth expresses the
point of the "nonspaces" and "nonexistences" that define the truths of power and
its representations. The relevance of resistance within power echoes the power
within that defines its differences with Power.

Fifth, the circle of local universality closes where the uniformity of the
apparatus echoes the same while always departing from itself. Rule and law define the uniformity in Power; their negativity defines uniformity's excesses, materializing in the representations of power. Power knows itself by the differences
within it that define its relations with itself: its togetherness with Power and resistance.

The relation between Power and power defines the figures whereby power can unfold in transgression. It is summarized on one side by Foucault:

> Underlying both the general theme that power represses sex and the idea that the law constitutes desire, one encounters the same putative mechanics of power. It is defined in a strangely restrictive way, in that, to begin with, this power is poor in resources, sparing of its methods, monotonous in the tactics it utilizes, incapable of invention, and seemingly doomed always to repeat itself. Further, it is a power that only has the force of the negative on its side, a power to say no; in no condition to produce, capable only of posting limits, it is basically anti-energy. This is the paradox of its effectiveness: it is incapable of doing anything, except to render what it dominates incapable of doing anything either, except for what this power allows it to do.[7]

Striking in this description of Power is its incapacity: it does and allows nothing "except" and "only." These appear as either "nothing . . ." or "anything . . ." since the rule of law echoes inexhaustible deferral. Power emerges within "Power" as the other that was "always present," hidden as the form of excess, to be realized, in our modernity, as its own excess, definable "only" as "Power."

Power rustles as the transgressions within "Power" that define its historicality. The poverty of resources that pertains to Power echoes in its subservience to rule and law, the impoverishment of normality. Power sounds excess and transgression within "Power": the positivity and affirmation—Nietzsche's "Yes"—in response to the "No" of "Power"; transgression rather than conformity to limits; productivity rather than taboo; obedience rather than disruption. Yet to the exclusions of Power, we reply that negativity, limitation, taboo, and law irresistibly echo their others, so that within the Power that they define emerges the power that produces otherness within.

"Power" materializes as power's other, displacing it from within—not, however, its "only" other: power materializes everywhere dispersed by multiple resistances. Power unfolds everywhere, but not everything: dispersed, fragmented; not owned or seized, manipulated or utilized. "Power is not something that is acquired, seized, or shared, something that one holds on to or allows to slip away; power is exercised from innumerable points, in the interplay of nonegalitarian and mobile relations.[8] The "everywhere" of power echoes its locality; the "innumerable points" do not define a totality of power, always regulated by the same, but its mobilization into nonegalitarian relations—domination and oppression—divided by the deferrals that constitute them. Here power becomes Power, a transformation essential to its disclosure everywhere. Relations between power and Power echo transgression; power resounds not as Power, seized or owned, but multiply in its mobilizations and strategies, including Power. This may be why power produces subalterns and superalterns. The authority of difference lies coiled within power as what defines it—between rulers and ruled—but also within the reciprocities of power and Power.

Power materializes as relevance, what makes a difference, and always differs by the difference it makes. Power exercises those who mobilize it as much as they exercise it, the reciprocity of local relevance. Power, then, materializes within the weight, the authority, of difference, including differences between rulers and ruled. The efficacies of power give rise to Power under Law as the particular form of hegemony that defines the West. The mobilities of power give rise to authority and domination. These belong to power from within, dividing it, although they may also echo as its others. The immanence of others within it marks the multiple reflexivities of power with desire.

> —Relations of power are not in a position of exteriority with respect to other types of relationships (economic processes, knowledge relationships, sexual relations), but are immanent in the latter; they are the immediate effects of the divisions, inequalities, and disequilibriums which occur in the latter, and conversely, they are the internal conditions of these differentiations;[9]

Otherness murmurs its disharmonies within and without. Similarly, power materializes within and exceeds the relations of human experience, defined by them and influential upon them. Sexuality and truth materialize within power and desire while each imposes its excessiveness on the others, imposing autonomy. Autonomy does not sound freedom from influence and power but excess. The reciprocity of freedom and necessity, autonomy and relevance, echoes immanence and deferral.

That power cannot be seized or held, manipulated or acquired, appears incompatible with a subject whose will constitutes power. Alternatively, power materializes as held and seized, gained and lost, not by subject-centers of activity, but dispersed and fragmented. The question of "where" power may be found then appears absurd, for no agent holds it, no *technē* directs it. From a local standpoint, the everywhere of power always occupies a site—many dispersed and local sites—whose localities define the future. Similarly, power materializes as oppressive without being wielded. The opposition between rulers and ruled belongs to Power and not to power—with the aporia that Power belongs historically and culturally to power and cannot be evaded within it. "Power comes from below; that is, there is no binary and all-encompassing opposition between rulers and ruled at the root of power relations, and serving as a general matrix."[10]

That power comes from below in one sense denies that it comes from above, owned by those who rule, wielded by agents. In another sense, power materializes somewhere even if it comes from everywhere. Relations between rulers and ruled materialize as transgression and excess. In this excess lies the everywhere that disrupts the somewheres that locate power in agents.

Power materializes as relevance and not will. Will emphasizes the agency of an individual subject, as if we who wield it are not influenced by it. It defines an absolute, not local center.

—Power relations are both intentional and nonsubjective. If in fact they are intelligible, this is not because they are the effect of another instance that "explains" them, but rather because they are imbued, through and through, with calculation: there is no power that is exercised without a series of aims and objectives. But this does not mean that it results from the choice or decision of an individual subject; . . .[11]

Power thrusts itself on us dispersed and fragmented throughout a regime, constituted by the authority of no subject. Yet it materializes through intentionality and teleology. We could have said the opposite, that power materializes without intention, grounded in the will of no subjects, but through collective subjectivity, constituting a unity of purpose. The decentering of the subject here echoes the centering of a masked subject, the unities of difference that constitute the strategies of power, domination and oppression. Yet decentering the subject does not abrogate the politics in which it is located, does not even abrogate a subject, "only" certain representations of its powers and desires. The centering of a subject is hostile to any politics, which materializes in relation to a dispersed public.

Power relations form constellations with goals and ends. They materialize as nonsubjective in their dispersion, repudiating the aura of the subject. They impose themselves as oppressive without centering. Power forcefully manifests the impoverishment of any ends in nature or subject. Oppression needs no human purposes for its definition.

Power materializes as transgressive in virtue of the presence of its others within it, dividing and dislocating. "Where there is power, there is resistance, and yet, or rather consequently, this resistance is never in a position of exteriority with respect to power."[12] Power's other lies within it, departing from it: power again. Wherever there is power—everywhere—there is resistance. Wherever there is relevance, in each location, there is multiple relevance in inexhaustibly multiple locations. It follows that power and resistance can take no particular form or location, though they can materialize "only" as located. Resistance murmurs everywhere along with power, but resistance divides power as it cannot divide itself by repetition. "These points of resistance are present everywhere in the power network. Hence there is no single locus of great Refusal, no soul of revolt, source of all rebellions, or pure law of the revolutionary."[13] Power is not "Power." It materializes as plural rather than singular, dispersed and fragmented rather than at a given site, everywhere while nothing and nowhere. Power as resistance includes its own excesses, above all exceeding any particular representation, though it cannot materialize without representation.

Instead there is a plurality of resistances, each of them a special case: resistances that are possible, necessary, improbable; others that are spontaneous, savage, solitary, concerted, rampant, or violent; still others that are quick to compromise, interested, or sacrificial; by definition, they can only exist in the strategic field of power relations.[14]

That resistances divide power, that power unfolds everywhere along with resistances, defines resistance and power as both the same and each other's other. In this interplay of harmony and disharmony, power and resistance become each other while always resisting. Resistance dislocates power while belonging with it; power displaces resistance by stratifying it into another violence. Resistance echoes power's other while remaining power. Power materializes as resistance's other by, in a particular history, becoming "Power."

There unfolds no single locus of power but fragmented and dispersed power, always other to Power while always the same, always other to itself. There transpires no single locus of resistance but fragmented and dispersed resistances, some spontaneous, others compromising. Compromise, sacrifice, opportunism, all materialize as resistances, repeating and dividing power. Resistance and power materialize as each other in the deferral of deferral.

Power and desire, along with history and embodiment, define the voices through which judgment, representation, and truth participate in the reciprocities of harmony and disharmony. In each case, the voice of power in judgment speaks through the departures within it and without: its others, in particular, the voices of resistances. Moreover, resistances rasp everywhere along with the everywhere of power: everywhere and in every way, but not everything; everything but not the totality. Power and resistance sound the ways in which locality presents and exceeds itself.

History's excesses transpire at every point within it, here the ways in which resistance exceeds power and itself. Compromise, sacrifice, and opportunism, in the first instance, echo Power, but in the second interrupt it, echoing departure, "only" thereafter, third, repeating power. As power crystallizes within the play of everywhere surrounded by constellations of order, resistances repeat the play of order disruptively. Disorder materializes in no one place, nor does order, but pervade locales everywhere as conditions of their locality. Power, resistance, desire, and representation echo locality's locality by defining it univocally, pervasively, everywhere, while not everything.

Within Power, the sites of domination and hegemony, liberation and revolution, disperse throughout the play of differences. Liberation crystallizes polyphonically throughout complex, divided, and fragmented interstices of power and diverse and dispersed movements of resistance. Power and resistance belong together except that some constellations of power resist the others. Power and resistance depart from each other except that resistance repeats power wherever it materializes.

No power can materialize without the dislocations of its regimen; no resistance can escape wearing the clothes of Power. Here sacrifice echoes Power even in resistance and liberation, echoes authority, domination, and oppression. These movements within resistance echo the deferrals that define power.

Shall we suppose that power comes first, in its network of relations, with resistance following as shadow or mirror? Or shall we gather instead that within power, first and last, resound the polyphonic disharmonies that compose resistance? If the latter, then power echoes resistance because resistance echoes power. No system of power can close off resistance. Disharmonies inhabit every sphere of power, resistance, desire, or representation. Limits unfold, even in transgression, at the edges of thought and practice. Resistance resists power to the limit, requiring transgression. Resistance materializes as representation of the edges that mark power—its limits—"only" by having edges of its own, marked by the deferrals of power.

The differences between power and Power, aside from the difference that each marks within the other, echo within their joint deferrals. In relation to power, deferral lies within: power appears as our tradition's public representation of deferral. Where Power echoes its dominance, a rule of the same, resistance turns transgression into its other without departing from itself. It turns transgression into domination in the regime of Power: domination and liberation. But liberation also materializes within the hegemony of Power. Resistance does not always materialize as liberation, nor as the origin from which resistance derives; it rather echoes the always-present transgressions without which no liberation could transpire. That resistance always divides power as its other entails that we do not have to find a mysterious origin of liberation within a regime of oppression. Regimentation divides by differences—by alternative powers and resistances—as much as repetitions unify.

The play of repetition and variation emerges as a play of belonging and departing. Its ontology repeats and differs from the ontology of things and thoughts: fragmented, dispersed, wasteful, but sedimented and crystallized into kinds. The universe sings of countless things whose histories can be told, surrounded and pervaded by tales without beginnings and endings. Locality expresses this play of order and disorder as a play of limit, doubly, even triply and more, echoing excess: the broaching of limits into other limits as dispersion and dislocation. Locality represents a sonorescence of power, where every term echoes the deferrals of resistance.

It follows that although resistance materializes everywhere together with power, and power emerges always divided, dispersed, fragmented, and opposed, inseparable from its others, the play of power and resistance, like that of same and other, echoes excess: polyphonies, resonances, and disharmonies. In state regimes and social constellations, the tug of hegemony and domination resounds repeatedly, offset by two recurrent resistances: other hegemonies and oppressions and the fragmentations of domination into disorder. Disorder appears trivialized when represented as the other of order, where power echoes as the same within order, within an agonistic struggle of one domination over another, one domination succeeding another, but also within an antagonistic struggle of domination with dispersion—a dispersion that sounds domination's other although not liberation. Liberation materializes at the point where domination meets dispersion: "humanity installs each of its violences in a system of rules and thus proceeds from domination to domination."[15]

Violence upon violence, domination over domination, impose themselves within power where each, like power and resistance, unfold together and depart. In their reciprocity lie oppression and liberation. The succession of domination upon domination, the promulgation of violence upon violence, express the play of power, altogether different from but inseparable from the Law that has defined its history. "Resistances do not derive from a few heterogeneous principles; but neither are they a lure or a promise that is of necessity betrayed. They are the odd term in relations of power; they are inscribed in the latter as an irreducible opposite."[16] Resistances echo as "odd terms" in power, surpluses and excesses. Within the regime of Power, otherness materializes as oppositional. Within the play of power and resistance, otherness materializes as agonistic, no less contentious or competitive, but echoing difference as difference rather than under Law.

> Are there no great radical ruptures, massive binary divisions, then? Occasionally, yes. But more often one is dealing with mobile and transitory points of resistance, producing cleavages in a society that shift about, fracturing unities and effecting regroupings, furrowing across individuals themselves, cutting them up and remolding them, marking off irreducible regions in them, in their bodies and minds.[17]

It seems natural, in the West, to think of power as Power, as binary under Law, as if power should be Law itself, dividing into domination and subjugation, rulers and ruled. In such a representation, power finds its other entirely without, unable to represent the truth that it belongs together with its other. To think of liberation within such a view of Power always appears paradoxical more than aporetic: liberation without power appears empty while utilizing Power.

On one side, the thought of power falls within utopia and despair. Power must be used without becoming Power but power belongs to Power. On the other side, Power cannot materialize except through alternatives that oppose each other from without, enemies across a chasm, unable from within to represent themselves as their others. Our local sonorescence rings of a Power that recognizes its polyphonies and disharmonies within, of a Power that gives way to the fragmentations of power, as Law gives way to judgment, Truth to representation, and the Repetitions in representation give way to inexhaustible deferral.

Resistance crystallizes as the other in power that defines its same, the reason why power and resistance remain indistinguishable despite their differences. The excess within resistance—an "odd term" in power—falls within Power without being governed by rules: ruling without rules. Power echoes rule and transgression. Resistance materializes as the limit in power: everywhere but nowhere in particular, in every form, but in no form in particular. Power and resistance await an undetermined future whereby they may be distinguished and rethought, each transformed into the other. Yet this is not awaiting history's destiny to tell us Truth, any more than the future will bring about Power or Justice or tell us their Truth. Rather, truth unfolds in the disruptions and transgressions of resistances within power. The play of same and other echoes in power as resistance—the same as power although different; in truth as untruth—also the same although different; in desire as desire—different although always the same. But also, the play of same and other resounds in power as Power and as desire and truth.

Power can be power—and Power—"only" through opposites that tear it apart, "only" to reconstitute it as its others. That is why power is inseparable from Power, why the play of resistance in power cannot fall outside Power or Law.

Aristotle's notion of potency speaks as progenitor of power's identity with relevance, preceded by Plato's criterion of being as power. "'Potency' then means the source, in general, of change or movement in another thing or in the same thing *qua* other, and also (2) the source of a thing's being moved by another thing or by itself *qua* other. For in virtue of that principle, in virtue of which a patient suffers anything, we call it 'capable' of suffering."[18] Potency joins with actuality as a reciprocal pair of categories of local relevance. In our sonorescence, they resound as stillness and polyphony. Polyphony does not, however, represent what moves, even at rest, but one way of making a difference, the multiplicities silent in stillness.

A famous aporia in Aristotle is that although there are many ways of being-something—four modes of causation, four kinds of substance—one, the individual, is first *in all ways*. Actualities are first logically and chronologically although potency in time typically precedes its actualization, states and affects of an individual logically determine it, and individuals are unknowable. Power is potency but actuality precedes potentiality, reality precedes possibility. Power's indeterminateness subordinates it to what is determinate in all ways. This notion of determinateness in all ways echoes Heidegger's full presence and appears in Aristotle here and there, inseparable from other forms of determinateness and indeterminateness: potency, matter, final causation. In our sonorescent refrain, the pairs of univocals compose the play of harmony and disharmony, constituting and dividing each member of the pair. No ontological priority echoes in locality, "only" priority within a particular locale, and no priority within a pair of sonorescences. Each resounds as a local determinant of the other.

Aristotle's, Nietzsche's, and Foucault's theories are not the only major theories of power in the Western tradition. Others are Locke's view of causal powers and Spinoza's *conatus*, one of the few places in the tradition where power joins desire. Whitehead may be the only major writer in the tradition to build on the affinities of Locke's and Spinoza's views of power. What all require that Nietzsche and Foucault provide is explicit realization that power unfolds as both innocent and guilty, inseparably, in the violences and dominations that surround it. Nietzsche's unsurpassable realization is that although power materializes everywhere it does so violently everywhere as well, including the violences of truth and goodness, and the violences it imposes on itself.

On the empirical side of materiality nothing surpasses Locke's view of causal powers. In *Process and Reality*, Whitehead claims that Locke anticipated Whitehead's entire theory. First Locke:

> Thus we say, fire has a power to melt gold; . . . and gold has a power to be melted; . . . Power thus considered is twofold; viz. as able to make, or able to receive, any change: the one may be called "active," and the other "passive," power. . . . I confess power includes in it some kind of relation,—a relation to action or change; as, indeed, which of our ideas, of what kind soever, when attentively considered, does not? . . . Our idea therefore of power, I think, may well have a place amongst other simple ideas, and be considered as one of them, being one of those that make a principal ingredient in our complex ideas of substances, as we shall hereafter have occasion to observe.[19]

Locke speaks of power as a simple idea ingredient in our idea of substance. He might have said that we cannot think of substance—of whatever moves, acts, or changes, or is moved, acted upon, or changed—without thinking of power: the substance's powers and the powers of others. Being here echoes power, where power unfolds as relation and activity.

Whitehead comments: "But Locke, throughout his *Essay*, rightly insists that the chief ingredient in the notion of 'substance' is the notion of 'power.' The philosophy of organism holds that, in order to understand 'power,' we must have a correct notion of how each individual entity contributes to the datum *from which* its successors arise and *to which* they must conform."[20] The comment emphasizes the generality of Locke's view of power: power echoes everywhere, with substance and being. What cannot be heard in Locke's view, though present in Whitehead's, are the antiphonies of power. Locke's causal powers materialize without transgression, living in two worlds at once without aporia: that of being and that of the ideas whereby being is thought. The dividedness and circularity of activity and passivity seem, here, nontransgressive.

In Whitehead, by way of contrast, following the line of thought whereby powers constitute the subjects that employ them and objects that they influence, powers make actual entities what they are although each entity determines itself and the ways in which it is determined by others. It materializes in the form of deferral.

How do determination by others and self-determination, deferral and its deferral, coincide without being equivalent? How do we represent excess in power where power irrupts everywhere, coincident with every actual thing? Actual entities arise amid the powers that constitute their relations to the past and to which they must conform, but they determine their own conditions of conformation. Actualities exceed the powers that constitute them but such powers do constitute them as well as other actual entities. In this way, there resound both power and excess in Whitehead, but not excesses within power, represented by us as desire, the will to power. In particular, an entity constituted by the past exceeds what constitutes it, but not conversely: no theory echoes in Whitehead of how the past exceeds the future, entailing violence and requiring sacrifice. No theory sounds how the past may be determined by the future, although each exceeds the other. A limited historicality may be heard in Whitehead. But there echoes a powerful sense of sacrifice.

> The ultimate evil in the temporal world is deeper than any specific evil. It lies in the fact that the past fades, that time is a "perpetual perishing." Objectification requires elimination. . . . The nature of evil is that the characters of things are mutually obstructive. Thus the depths of life require a process of selection. But the selection is elimination as the first step towards another temporal order seeking to minimize obstructive modes. Selection is at once the measure of evil, and the process of its evasion.[21]

Evil emerges as the unresolvability of difference into the same within the regime of power. Yet Whitehead's own view seems largely characterized by a priority of the same within the unending excesses that constitute relevance. Each entity exceeds the powers that compose it, and among the selections that result from such excesses, obstruction and sacrifice sound their inescapability.

Power cannot materialize in an experiential world without excess. This appears true even in so deterministic world as Spinoza's, where power is pervasive. First, the determinism appears as the result of the power of God, but the power of God *is* God: "The power of God is His essence itself."[22] Second, the being of each individual thing is identical with its powers:

> The effort by which each thing endeavors to persevere in its own being is nothing but the actual essence of the thing itself.[23]

> By virtue and power I understand the same thing, that is to say, virtue, in so far as it is related to man, is the essence itself or nature of the man in so far as it has the power of affecting certain things which can be understood through the laws of nature alone.[24]

The actual essence of the thing is both its power and its effort to persevere—its *conatus*. The latter echoes Spinoza's theory of desire as power: "*Desire* is the essence itself of man in so far as it is conceived as determined to any action by any one of his modifications."[25] Every being endeavors to persevere in its being and this striving is its actual essence. But each actual thing is relational, related causally to other beings. The relation of each thing to other things, in virtue of its essence, is its *conatus*, power and desire. Spinoza's is one of the very few theories in the tradition in which power and desire are pervasive and inseparable.

What may be missing from Spinoza's view is what may be missing from White-head's, a strong sense of how power and desire exceed each other, how their otherness may collapse into the same.

We have heard how the selectiveness of locality entails evil in Whitehead. Another place to hear the violence in desire is in Plato, where desire of the Good is inseparable from knowledge and being. In *Republic*, philosophy is love of wis-dom, and the erotic side of truth pervades the powerful lures of Cave and Sun. In both *Symposium* and *Phaedrus*, the lure of the Good draws the soul toward the beauty of truth. In Plato, being resonates together with power, truth with desire, all four meeting in the Good. Yet the unity of being and truth, power and desire, appears constantly disrupted by the polemics of the dialogues, where agonistic confrontations rule, pervaded by magic spells, potions, and incantations.[26] Truth echoes unified and divided by desire, suggested by the contrast between the im-ages of beauty in *Phaedrus* and the chariot of the soul. There can be no philoso-phy without eros, no love of truth without desire, no movement without the wings of desire, but desire divides being and truth even as they are constituted by it.

Desire and power divide truth and being in Plato, but the notes of mutual violence there are muted, manifested more in the dialogic exchanges than in any other form; for example, in the famous images that define Thrasymachus' charac-ter. The violence and domination inherent in power and desire do not appear again in canonical form until Nietzsche, who did not acknowledge their impor-tance in Plato. In contrast with Nietzsche's view of power as violence and domi-nation, though closely allied with its pervasiveness, there echoes a more Aristo-telian view of power as potency, inseparable from the everywhere that defines power yet opposed to it in the priority of actuality in the regimes that manifest power.

A beautiful expression of this play of same and other, activity and potenti-ality, appears in Gadamer, where power and desire manifest the historicality of human experience in contrast with the timelessness of Platonic Ideas. Here Hegel replaces Plato and Kant, though the images of the potency of the same remain. "Power is obviously the central category of the historical view of the world."[27] Power echoes here a timeliness inseparable from historicality despite the remark-able sense in Spinoza and Aristotle that power belongs to being as such rather than to its historicality. At stake is deferral.

The historical view of the world echoes, in Heidegger's words, as "ek-static," elsewhere and when, dislocation; in Whitehead, as the multiple presence of any actual thing, caught up in a past that makes it, moving toward a future that cannot be without it. Yet Whitehead is silent on something present in Hegel and Nietzsche: the sense that the future needs the past, circumscribes it. This may be heard as the ekstatic sense of temporality. Power materializes both as relevance within a past to what follows and as dependence on what follows it. Power echoes as reciprocity and displacement: whatever power works on works on it; this mutuality echoes excess and dislocation. "The concept of power has a central place within the historical world view because in it interiority and exteriority are held in a peculiar unity in tension."[28]

We may add that this circularity of interiority and exteriority does not belong uniquely to power, but also pertains to desire and truth—creatures of power as well as creators of it. Gadamer emphasizes the potency of power more than its temporality, returning to Aristotle.

> All power exists only in its expression. The expression is not only the manifestation of the power, but its reality. Hegel was right when he developed dialectically the inner correspondence between power and expression. But this dialectic also shows that power is more than its expression. It possesses potentiality also, ie it is not only the cause of an particular effect, but the capacity, wherever it is used, to have that effect.[29]

If we think of power in relation to resistance as both other and itself, then we may think of resistance and power as exceeding themselves.

> It follows from this that power cannot be known or measured in terms of its expression, but only experienced as an in-dwelling. The observation of an effect always shows only the cause, and not the power, if the power is an inner surplus over the cause that belongs to the effect. This surplus, of which we are aware in the cause, can certainly be understood also in terms of the effect, in the resistance it offers, in that the offering of resistance is itself an expression of power. But even then it is an awareness in which power is experienced.[30]

Gadamer's conclusion echoes Nietzsche's and Foucault's: power is everywhere and sole condition of itself. Yet in this repetition of the same, power is always displaced by its others. "Interiority is the mode of experiencing power, because power, of its nature, is related to itself alone."[31]

The notion of potency here marks not another form of presence, possibility within actuality, but an interiority that divides itself from without, stillness and polyphony, harmony and disharmony. Power as potency materializes everywhere always different as the same. Amid the excesses in Gadamer there echoes no mark of violence. Power's capacity to destroy in the name of building is silent within its complex unity.[32] History's sacrifices remain unthought.

The inescapable traits of power, in Nietzsche and Foucault, echo their materiality and positivity. Activity and passivity, actuality and potentiality, do not voice this domination and violence within their materiality, though it appears within the implied priority of actuality and activity. In stillness and polyphony, no priority belongs, yet stillness imposes its own violences upon its polyphonies, that of determination and exclusion. In the use of power, in its exercise, there unfolds no escape from violence. Power requires rules, "only" to pass into Power.

> The nature of these rules allows violence to be inflicted on violence and the resurgence of new forces that are sufficiently strong to dominate those in power. Rules

are empty in themselves, violent and unfinalized; they are impersonal and can be bent to any purpose. The successes of history belong to those who are capable of seizing these rules, to replace those who had used them, to disguise themselves so as to pervert them, invert their meaning, and redirect them against those who had initially imposed them; controlling this complex mechanism, they will make it function so as to overcome the rulers through their own rules.[33]

The opposites of power, violence, and domination may be heard as power, violence, and domination again. Rules belong to power insofar as it cannot be distinguished except in name from Power. Rules and sovereignty represent the dispersions of power against itself.

In relation to sexuality, Foucault says the following:

the question that we must address, then, is . . . In a specific type of discourse on sex, in a specific extortion of truth, appearing historically and in specific places (around the child's body, apropos of women's sex, in connection with practices restricting births, and so on), what were the most immediate, the most local power relations at work? How did they make possible these kinds of discourses, and conversely, how were these discourses used to support power relations?[34]

Power crystallizes into "Power," into specific dominations, manifested in the rules of discourse. Yet power materializes in dispersions as well as constellations, surrounded by representations, violences, and dominations.

This may be understood as much from the side of discourse as of power.

I believe we must resolve ourselves to accept three decisions which our current thinking rather tends to resist, and which belong to the three groups of functions I have just mentioned: to question our will to truth; to restore to discourse its character as an event; to abolish the sovereignty of the signifier.

. . . We must conceive discourse as a violence that we do to things, or, at all events, as a practice we impose upon them; it is in this practice that the events of discourse find the principle of their regularity.[35]

The will to truth reaches forth as the power within discourse and representation—the power behind it, though we must not forget resistance: "Discourses are not once and for all subservient to power or raised up against it, any more than silences are. We must make allowance for the complex and unstable process whereby discourse can be both an instrument and an effect of power, but also a hindrance, a stumbling block, a point of resistance and a starting point for an opposing strategy."[36] A reciprocal movement appears, so far neglected in our discussions, from representation to power. We may question how representation constitutes power, a relationship fundamental to the notion of discourse.

Arendt speaks of the public realm as constituted by power and representation.

Power is what keeps the public realm, the potential space of appearance between acting and speaking men, in existence. . . . Power is always, as we would say, a power potential and not an unchangeable, measurable, and reliable entity like force and strength. While strength is the natural quality of an individual seen in isolation, power springs up between men when they act together and vanishes the moment they disperse.[37]

Her understanding of power is based on a threefold distinction among power, force, and strength: "Under the conditions of human life, the only alternative to power is not strength—which is helpless against power—but force, which indeed one man alone can exert against his fellow men and of which one or a few can possess a monopoly by acquiring the means of violence."[38] Strength is the efficacy of one agent against another and cannot be divided, is "nature's gift to the individual which cannot be shared with others":[39] "(The story of David and Goliath is only metaphorically true; the power of a few can be greater than the power of many, but in a contest between two men not power but strength decides, . . .)."[40] Strength belongs to an individual, manifests that individual's capabilities. Force imposes coercion in a social space, involves violence, implied or actual. Strength and coercion materialize as capacities respectively of individuals and groups, independent of the public realm and representation.

Arendt's emphasis on potency emphasizes dispersion. She lacks Foucault's strong sense of material discontinuity and fragmentation. The potency in power echoes its excess, that it is not situated "simply" at a given location. Locality entails that nothing belongs "only" to one location. More important is the emphasis on discontinuity within the materialities of power. These materialities include representation. That is what Foucault means by discourse.

How can force, strength, or power materialize independent of representation? Arendt's reply is that power—including force and strength and their tributaries—belongs to representation as profoundly as representation belongs to power. Power occupies a public space that can neither materialize nor be thought without representation.

> Power preserves the public realm and the space of appearance, and as such it is also the lifeblood of the human artifice, which, unless it is the scene of action and speech, of the web of human affairs and relationships and the stories engendered by them, lacks its ultimate *raison d'être*. Without being talked about by men and without housing them, the world would not be a human artifice but a heap of unrelated things to which each isolated individual was at liberty to add one more object; without the human artifice to house them, human affairs would be as floating, as futile and vain, as the wanderings of nomad tribes.[41]

Power unfolds everywhere and nowhere; no person or group owns or wields it. The everywhere here echoes dispersion and fragmentation. The nowhere echoes power's refusal to be wielded like an instrument (though instruments themselves refuse ownership). If we cannot think without gesturing toward mastery and control, every such figure represents aporia, displaces itself and represents that displacement. Power materializes not so much everywhere as nowhere in particular, in a public space constituted by representation. Arendt presupposes that public power unfolds through the natural capacities of individuals and groups: strength and force. Foucault replies that individual powers echo how we think of them and pursue them, include representation as well as desire.

One dimension of Arendt's understanding is very important: power materializes in a public, representational space—that of human togetherness—and would not appear apart from the representation of belonging together that composes that space. Individual human beings may occupy a territory together and may pursue collective ends and practices, but they compose a public "only" where the collectivity unfolds as both represented and representational. Social groups may engage in social practices as well as individual undertakings, but among their determining practices resounds the representation of the group as a public to itself.

Arendt speaks of a public realm as a sphere in which human beings act together, in common, and as a realm in which collectivity appears collective. She does not discuss how the two themes of togetherness here conflict. In one case, commonality is presupposed, and the realm of power materializes where human beings share events and meanings and seek to enhance their commonality. In the other case, collectivity is represented as appearance while within the collectivity, difference speaks. Commonality manifests itself as difference:

> the reality of the public realm relies on the simultaneous presence of innumerable perspectives and aspects in which the common world presents itself and for which no common measurement or denominator can ever be devised. . . . Being seen and being heard by others derive their significance from the fact that everybody sees and hears from a different position. This is the meaning of public life, . . .
>
> . . . The end of the common world has come when it is seen only under one aspect and is permitted to present itself in only one perspective.[42]

In Arendt, the public world is that which human beings have in common, where commonality is displaced by differences and where the same is inexhaustibly deferred. We may contrast this view with Whitehead's understanding of the public:

> The theory of prehensions is founded upon the doctrine that there are no concrete facts which are merely public, or merely private. The distinction between publicity and privacy is a distinction of reason, and is not a distinction between mutually exclusive facts. The sole concrete facts, in terms of which actualities can be analysed, are prehensions; and every prehension has its public side and its private side.[43]

Whitehead's claim to reciprocity is stronger than Arendt's and Foucault's: being is inseparably public and private. An actual entity is what it is, in that sense private, and dwells with other entities in a public world. Public and private here do not entail representation but prehension, perspectivity, being-for and being-with. Perspective, judgment, desire, and power unify and divide each other. This complexly entangled interrelation materializes as nature's work.

Foucault concludes "Truth and Power" with the words:

> Truth is a thing of this world; it is produced only by virtue of multiple forms of constraint. And it induces regular effects of power. Each society has its regime of truth, its "general politics" of truth: that is, the types of discourse which it accepts and makes function as true; the mechanisms and instances which enable one to distinguish true and false statements, the means by which each is sanctioned; the techniques and procedures accorded value in the acquisition of truth; the status of those who are charged with saying what counts as true.[44]
>
> The political question, to sum up, is not error, illusion, alienated consciousness or ideology; it is truth itself. Hence the importance of Nietzsche.[45]

We may hear in these words two discourses on truth: one concerning its "regime," the other its truth. On the one hand, we are within a society whose microstrategies force us to speak the discourse of its truth, produced by ordered procedures within a political economy. On the other hand, this truth *is* the truth of truth, true for "us" and true in some form for every society.

These two discourses open a strange and conflicted space, especially if we hear them as fundamentally political. The political question is truth itself. *That* is the importance of Nietzsche: archaeology as the representation of subjugated local truths; genealogy as their insurrection. In Foucault, truth "itself" is found within two conflicting discourses: one concerned with the microtechniques of its production and regulation, the other concerned with its truth, where *that* truth refers again to the microtechniques and regulation of truth but also speaks of the violence, masks, and will to power that constitute it.

That the political question is truth itself represents the belonging together of power and truth in their departures, where the truth of truth echoes power while truth sounds the repetition of and resistance to power. That is the importance of Nietzsche, to recognize that the truth we ring in representation belongs to power while the powers of power echo in the departures of its truths.

The interplay of power, desire, and truth forms a triangle within which our sonorescence echoes itself. It chimes without a center, whose absence is defined through representation but whose representation includes the inescapability of desire and power. Power here unfolds as the fluid, conflicted medium through which loci relate to each other, desire as the impetus within them that defines and exceeds their relations, representation the voice in which each whispers its truth.

In this triangle of multiple reflexivity, each vertex—power, desire, and representation—belongs together with the others, found everywhere with them, and departs from them. In multiple reflexivity, each of these reciprocally divided relations resounds as same and other to the others. Power materializes as what relevance requires—to make a difference—"only" to be dislocated by the differences that it makes, to be displaced by itself and the others.

The others of power inexhaustibly unfold within the limits that compose it. Each other sounds a limit of power that, in its own limits, unveils a space for power to exceed itself in unending repetition. This space of power opens a space of representation and desire: that of public representation, exceeded by itself and by public and private desire. Here power divides within and without, inseparably, into resistances within and Power without.

We may hope to close this circle without sacrificing the displacements within power. When Foucault distinguishes power from Power, he represents the former as the mobilizing and productive medium within which life and practice circulate, appearing to leave aside, banished, the oppressions and dominations that characterize the history of Power. The claim that power escapes the rule of rules and circulates without a center entails that it can be neither controlled nor mastered, but neglects the control and mastery that always seem to fall within its hegemony. "Power" materializes as the violence that falls within power inescapably, "only" to be denied its sovereignty.

"Power" materializes as power's other and its same. In the excesses of the spaces opened up between them in the discovery that power is not Power lie the oppressions and subordinations that compose Power, the dispersions and fragmentations that compose the materialities of relevance, and the differences that undermine the sovereignty of the Law. The difference between Power and power resounds within their identity and difference as the sovereignty of Law and a challenge to every rule. To neglect the dispersions of power within and around Power is to make a fetish of Power, of violence and oppression. To neglect the dominations of Power within power is to make violence and oppression universals, making a fetish of power instead, neglecting the material differences of oppression and domination. Sovereignty appears as the play of the same again and again—the repetitions that constitute Power—and the differences that divide Power into power. Power echoes as one name of the play of same and other that constitutes our modernity, but can name that play "only" within the dominations constituted by the inescapability of Power.

FIVE

Desire

Desire reaches out as power's other—and its same; as truth's other—and its same: echoes their inexhaustibility. The triangle of representation, desire, and power chimes unending questions of repetition and deferral, a figure whose absent center is occupied in turn by each, though it is always time for each and there is never enough time for one to resound without the others. In its repetitions of power and truth, desire joins each, divided within and without. As power displaces itself within and without into resistances and Power, desire and truth, desire repeats the others, finds itself everywhere but never alone, dislocated by itself, by power and representation, always departing from itself. As power divides into Power and resistance, desire divides into Desire—lust, greed, ambition—and itself, into different and imagined desires, bodies, and environments, into unending deferrals.

Truth belongs to representation in virtue of its misrepresentations, for the truth of truth echoes its untruths. Similarly, power and desire resound in the unending disharmonies that compose them, including the bodies that compose their truth. This is one reason why in our modernity, sex and politics career from utopia to revulsion and back again, excesses of desire and power. Desire's infinite absence seems to permit no satisfaction, "only" the turning of the same bodies under different gazes. This narrative of the infinity of desire, mirrored in the unlimits of power, defines our tradition, countered within it at sporadic moments. Yet these moments present ringing examples of how the canon exceeds itself, along with desire and power, without exceeding the limits of the limits that define it.

The figures of the untrammeled desires that characterize our tradition—for truth, sex, God, and wealth; in every bodily part, from any center that circumscribes its origin; obsession, infatuation, and compulsion—all portray themselves as inexhaustibly divided yet disdain the circularities that would disrupt their purity. Sexuality presents an example, where it and sex represent not alternative sites of desire, but a pair whose reciprocities define representational spaces inhabited by each body with its history, culture, and illusions but also other bodies, along with power, truth, and the future—and much more. Each body, here, with its orifices and extrusions, materializes as both object and seat of desire without in the least containing it, while the capacity of a body to enjoy pleasure or pain without infinite repetition is severely circumscribed. The seat of our embodiment dwells inexhaustibly divided by the polyphonies within its stillnesses.

The unlimit of desire in relation to embodiment craves inexhaustible repetition, divided here and there by longings for displacement. The pleasures of the body lie in its capacity for repetition and in repeated representations of its capacity to escape from repetition. The regulation of desire within the body by the prohibitions that define it delimit mirrors of the repetitions that represent desire surrounded by variation and disharmony. It is as if we can inhabit sexuality "only" by repetition after repetition, while the pleasures that define it mark an unceasing dance of departures. For Augustine, God represents escape from the pleasures of the body but especially from the cloying repetitions of its sinfulness. God, supreme emblem of the same, represents desire's escape from one same into another. The same within desire sounds the origin of its power and regulation, displaced at its center and periphery by excesses of pain and pleasure.

This mimetic movement within desire echoes in the tradition as Platonism, though in Plato himself it resounds as departure. Desire, in our tradition, represents both the overpowering inertia of repetition and desire's capacity to dislocate every same. Two great images in Plato characterizing desire have come to define the tradition that represents it, as if every subsequent expression of desire might appear but as a repetition, if "only" of masculine desire. One rings the triangle of desire and truth that represents the power of reason within our tradition—why Nietzsche is so unyielding on Plato. The power of reason joins in Christianity with images of self-abasement, denying the power and will in reason in the name, first, of humility, thereafter of science. The second sings of the soaring flight of desire attracted by the lure of beauty and the good. The first image echoes dividedness without, the second excesses within.

We may hear the yearning in Plato of a desire whose life joins inextricably with departure, caught up, nevertheless, within the same. In its pervasiveness, desire interrogates reason, truth, and power deeply and profoundly, not as their enemy, but as their polyphony. Philosophy resounds as excessive love of wisdom, and Plato repeatedly returns to the obsessive desire that defines that love. It echoes as what always exceeds the bodies, ideas, and history that circumscribe it. It echoes as what always exceeds itself.

Although the triangular image of the charioteer with two horses echoes twice in dialogues that concern themselves with desire and truth, *Republic* and *Phaedrus* treat *Eros* as a far greater force than can be represented by even a wild and powerful horse. The desires to be brought under the control of reason are appetites whose deficiencies lie in their powers and ends, but also in blindness to themselves. When *Eros* stands forth as herself, in all her glory, she overpowers Socrates himself. That above all signifies her divinity.

The images of control that appear in the last paragraph mark desire's powers. Desire overwhelms us, and we desire to control it. Both images express desire's power, and desire reaches toward us together with power—its repetition—in the drives and forces that impel it. What moves us are desires, and insofar as we are moved without, toward any objects, human or inanimate, we are subject to their powers as our desires. By contrast, that we might be moved within—in the name of the tradition, by reason and truth—appears miraculous. Among Hume's greatest insights is this aporia, that we cannot think of being moved except by desire, yet desire bears no relation in our tradition to truth or to ourselves. The self-knowledge for which Socrates gave his life appears inexplicable to the extent that it lacks desire.

Yet it does not lack desire in Plato, a truth with which the tradition has not lived comfortably. He is not the first to emphasize desire and does not seek "merely" to control it, though the tradition has assigned him that role. For Nietzsche and his followers, including Heidegger, the shadow of reason fell upon desire in the persona of Socrates, whose primary act was to oppose the inexhaustibility of power and desire with the force of rational truth. What this tradition ignores is the play of excess throughout the dialogues, particularly in relation to the dialogues themselves, as written and remembered, that is, in relation to truth and desire. Wherever desire appears in the dialogues, it reaches forth in obsessive garb displaying its excessiveness.

Four of the greatest dialogues speak expressly of desire: *Symposium*, *Phaedrus*, *Philebus*, and *Republic*. The latter two overtly address the good, but that is the point: desire and the good either move together as opposites in the continuing conflict where human beings live their lives, or they are movements within an identity of the same, divided by their differences. *Republic* is the major case in point. Two great images of desire appear, that of the charioteer with two steeds and that of philosophy herself, a wisdom grounded in inexhaustible desire. The former image presents the appetites brought under the control of reason with the power and support of higher emotions. Even here, desire wells up excessively within the good life under the control of reason. In relation to philosophy, however, desire moves as at least coequal with reason, no more regulated by it than regulator. "But the one who feels no distaste in sampling every study, and who attacks his task of learning gladly and cannot get enough of it, him we shall justly pronounce the lover of wisdom, the philosopher, shall we not?" (*Republic*, 475c).

Philosophy echoes inescapably as desire—love of wisdom and truth—in that respect fundamental to power. The traditional image, reaching culmination in Hume, of a beleaguered reason under domination of the passions, is forestalled by a truth regulative of desire and exceeded by it. Excess falls on every side of desire, power, and truth. In *Republic*, the truth of power echoes in the desires that determine it, yet "only" desire for wisdom can constrain the unbridled will to power that contaminates every other form of rule. Desire, here, displaces itself, its other, and stretches forth as other to power.

Desire pertains to philosophy as well as to the appetites. Yet an important difference looms between a desire embodied in the image of an unbridled horse, driven toward different objects of desire but not invested in any, and a desire directed toward wisdom and beauty, for which the goal is predominant. Desire, we may say, turns toward an object, fulfills itself "only" in relation to that object, and invests its objects with its own excesses. Appetite invests its excesses in mundane objects. Higher desires mate their inexhaustibility with the inexhaustibility of their fulfillments.

To this we add the excesses of the love of wisdom. Socrates suggests that "only" in relation to truth and power can desire find its limits—limits that both circumscribe and exceed. It follows that power and truth echo as desire's polyphonies, not without but within. They resound, in Plato, as songs of desire, situated where desire turns back to claim and displace itself. In this turning back, the place where desire dislocates itself shines in relation to its excesses; here lies the love of wisdom, where truth appears as another excess. Nothing in Plato, as in his descendants, suggests that desire's excesses may be regulated by philosophy. Rather, the unlimit of desire fulfills itself as truth's excess.

The first image of desire, that of the charioteer, appears mundane in the supporting images that surround it. Some appetites for wealth and fame contaminate the truth and goodness toward which they strive. The latter image portrays a wisdom whose object overcomes, through its excesses, the very forms that delimit it. Desire moves toward the good, impelled by beauty. Or rather, in *Symposium* and *Phaedrus*, desire moves within itself. Reason presents us with the question whether desire can be moved by an other without as well as one within. We may wonder, not whether truth exercises sovereignty over desire, but whether it exceeds desire's grip, exercising power in return.

For in Plato the power echoes in desire and truth whereby each controls the other, "only" to collapse under the weight of its disharmonies. Philosophy sings not of freedom from desire but of a greater desire that overcomes the limits of the lesser. Desire in Plato moves in relation to an object that stands behind the worth of its sacrifices. It also moves, in relation to philosophy and truth, against the limits of every other that might limit it. Every form of truth, in every way, sings as embodiment of truth's desire.

The good, then, may be understood either as an object controlling desire by exercising control over reason, or as that which exceeds any object and any desire, as desire inexhaustibly exceeds itself. The good reaches forth as that object toward which all desires flow, exceeding every object as desire exceeds every impulse. We are led to wonder how within its movement desire might know itself as inexhaustibly divided.

Unlike *Republic*, *Phaedrus*, and *Philebus*, *Symposium* speaks entirely on desire. Or rather, it sings entirely of love, implicitly asking how love and desire are related. Yet Plato elsewhere displays the multiplicity and breadth of desire: for things, for truth, even for itself. Desire for material things is appetite and is qualitatively different from desire for other human beings or truth. Yet the desire for truth exercises power over the appetites. Desire cannot avoid deferring itself.

Symposium is framed by desire at beginning and end in the person of Socrates who, as embodiment of desire, exceeds any representation. He is Apollodorus' and Alcibiades' beloved, exceeding their desires in the distance he maintains from them and in their limited comprehension of his truth. Apollodorus, like Glaucon to whom he has been speaking, was a mere child when the banquet took place and narrates the speeches that he has heard from Aristodemus, who "did not pretend to reproduce the various speeches verbatim, any more than I could repeat them word for word as I had them from him" (*Symposium*, 178). Even within an oral tradition and despite the irony that the dialogue was written by Plato, the relation of the narration to its truth is multiply displaced, as far, perhaps, as the distance of the other protagonists from Socrates. The representation of the truth of desire in *Symposium* is at a multiple remove, as if representation and desire cannot know themselves undivided, as if their truths lie in a region quite unlike the regions of truth that succeed them.

The truth of desire dwells in the displaced truths of its representations, in *Symposium* portrayed by set speeches on love framed by intoxication. The party is not to be a drunken one but the participants are overwhelmed by its temptations; similarly, desire overwhelms us by its temptations even, or in virtue of, its regulation by reason as reason is overwhelmed by its own temptations—the will to truth.

The theme of *Symposium* is the regulation of desire in the form of love. Phaedrus begins with a eulogy that denies that desire requires regulation, because "Love is the oldest and most glorious of the gods, the great giver of all goodness and happiness to men, alike to the living and to the dead" (*Symposium*, 180b). Love is wonderful to all, a tribute oblivious to its terrible nature, the unhappiness it causes and the surplus whereby it exceeds any grasp. It is said to need no regulation. Pausanias replies that there are two kinds of love, heavenly and earthly, the latter shallow and vulgar, the former innocent of any lewdness. Lewdness marks excess and regulation, that movement within sexuality that threatens more than the future of humanity, but its nature, as a consequence demanding regulation. Love, here, is with its parent, desire, situated at the juncture at which humanity defines itself and regulates its excesses—a schism of male and female, licit and illicit.[1]

Pausanias tells of lewdness and propriety, of lovers who should be encouraged and lovers who should be shunned, of morality and decency, all in terms of the regulation of desire. Within these pairs he represents the latter terms as heavenly despite their earthly natures, the former terms as earthly despite their heavenly impulses. He therefore regulates desire twice, once by prohibition, the other in relation to heaven and earth. What desire requires for its regulation are both the most stringent of human rules and the powers of the gods, as desire contains within itself unbridled excess. The regulation consists in defining what is acceptable and what prohibited, licit and illicit, falling under rule.

The regulation of sexual desire is achieved by defining its excess as falling outside acceptability: certain orifices of the body, certain objects, certain kinds of behavior, and not others. Sade defies all of these categories, forcing us to recognize that they fall within desire's normality, however obsessive, not outside. Obsession and fascination belong to desire's normality.

The name of the regulations—even in Sade—that pertain to sexuality is *Woman*. In Freud's words:

> When you meet a human being the first distinction you make is "male or female?" and you are accustomed to making the distinction with unhesitating certainty.[2]
>
> Anatomical science shares your certainty at one point and not much further. The male sexual product, the spermatozoon, and its vehicle are male; the ovum and the organism that harbours it are female. In both sexes organs have been formed which serve exclusively for the sexual functions; they were probably developed from the same [innate] disposition into two different forms.[3]

Irigaray responds: "Silence, then, on the subject of that extreme assurance which keeps you from being mistaken *at first sight* about the sex of the person you run across. The important point, it seems, is for you to be firmly convinced, without possible hesitation, that you cannot be in error, that there is no ambiguity possible."[4] We think we *must* be sure, concerned with the taxonomy into which all human beings must fit without excess, but also with the rigidity of our determinations, marked by presence or absence of a penis. Yet penises are normally concealed and secondary characteristics unreliable. We must defer the certainty of our determinations, "only" to find, hidden in tales for the perverted, that penises are also indeterminate, that sexuality contains within itself the same uncertainties that besiege the worlds of desire.

Freud denies that men and women are unambiguously distinct, grounded in his view that both were originally bisexual. The question becomes not what a man or woman is, but of how each comes into truth. The answer, Irigaray points out, is that "THE LITTLE GIRL IS THEREFORE A LITTLE MAN. . . . The little girl uses, with the *same* intent her *still smaller* clitoris . . . a penis *equivalent*.[5] The fundamental form of sexual desire is masculine, and women are assimilated to the presence and absence of a penis, not merely anatomically, but seat and object of desire. "We can assume that any theory of the subject has always been appropriated by the 'masculine.' When she submits to (such a) theory, woman fails to realize that she is renouncing the specificity of her own relationship to the imaginary. Subjecting herself to objectivization in discourse—by being 'female.'"[6] "Such a" view both defines woman and regulates desire in such a way that Woman sounds the name of the regulation of desire. Desire is named as masculine through its other, thereby regulating it. That the penis appears as the object of desire for both boys and girls promotes it to an excess of symbolic representation.[7] The little girl's object of desire inhabits a fetishistic movement initiated beyond her own determination. Within this imposed regulation, we may hear the question, "But what if the 'object' started to speak?"[8] Desire's excesses irrupt on every side of this question. Where desire joins power, where locality meets inexhaustibility, violence irrupts as both order and disorder, in the exclusions of any location and in the insurrections that echo within that location drawn from other locations.

This digression began with Pausanias' distinction between higher and lower goddesses of desire, mimicking the almost universal movement of thought into a bifurcation between acceptable and prohibited desires, above all, into higher and lower pleasures. Mill's is the most well-known voice here, as in his *Utilitarianism* he must hold that there are higher as well as lower pleasures and that the distinction is immediate even though many human beings do not know it. Without higher pleasures, we are at the mercy of desire, moved in any direction by it. Regulation falls within desire, not without, in power. Higher desires possess no ground outside themselves. Desire reaches out as both its other and its same. "Only" as both can it regulate and exceed itself. Desire regulates itself by investing itself in an object that falls within its control "only" to be exceeded by that investment.

The theme of regulation by division continues after Pausanias through the speeches of Eryximachus and Aristophanes. Love is divided, like the body, into virtue and vice—divided as the body is divided. There are bad and morbid desires as well as sound and healthy ones. Biology and medicine define the truth of desire's alterity. Love presides over these oppositions, "only" to fail to acknowledge her own internal dividedness.

It remains for Aristophanes, after recovering from the deferrals of his hiccups, to define a technically perfect regulation of desire within an understanding of its impossibility. On the one hand, he defines sexuality almost exactly as does Freud: "besides the two sexes, male and female, which we have at present, there was a third which partook of the nature of both" (*Symposium*, 189e). The difference is that where Freud treats woman entirely in terms of what she lacks, the other within man's desire, Aristophanes is perfectly symmetric: "And so, gentlemen, we are all like pieces of the coins that children break in half for keepsakes— making two out of one, like the flatfish—and each of us is forever seeking the half that will tally with himself" (*Symposium*, 181e). We may wonder at the images, however comic, of the determinateness of the object of desire in relation to itself and its other and of the completeness of desire within its dividedness. Excess within desire is captive here, regulated by an other that matches its curves and angles perfectly. Aristophanes offers a technical-perfectible view of love and desire within a substitutive model, an economy of lack based on a truth of equivalence. It is no wonder that the perfect realization of desire's obsession is found in death.

> How would you like to be rolled into one, so that you could always be together, day and night, and never be parted again? . . .

> We may be sure, gentlemen, that no lover on earth would dream of refusing such an offer, for not one of them could imagine a happier fate. (*Symposium*, 192e)

Desire is captive to repetition, if "only" in a mirror, obliterated by its regulation. Surrounded by unending polyphonies, it finds fulfillment in stillness; yearning for stillness, it finds itself constantly disharmonized by excesses.

Aristophanes' is a supreme rendition of object-centered, mimetic desire, not simply its profane embodiment, but the perfectibility inherent within its dividedness, however elusive perfection may be. Following his speech no further discussion of the perfectibility of desire is possible. Desire passes into excess, first in Agathon's extolling of its divinity, then in Socrates' explanation. First Agathon: "And so I say, Phaedrus, that Love, besides being in himself the loveliest and the best, is the author of those very virtues in all around him" (*Symposium*, 197c). Then Socrates, returning to question desire as lack: "Love is always the love of something, and . . . that something is what he lacks" (*Symposium*, 201). Desire is absence, lack, even where divided and excessive. Above all, it seeks an object worthy of its excesses: beauty and the good. Yet as Diotima says, emphasizing excess rather than lack:

> And if, my dear Socrates, . . . man's life is ever worth the living, it is when he has attained this vision of the very soul of beauty. And once you have seen it, you will never be seduced again by the charm of gold, of dress, of comely boys, or lads just opening to manhood; you will care nothing for the beauties that used to take your breath away and kindle such a longing in you, and many others like you, . . . (*Symposium*, 211d)

Shall we say that love is always for a beauty derived from absence? Or must love be achieved to be desire?

> But if it were given to man to gaze on beauty's very self—unsullied, unalloyed, and freed from the mortal taint that haunts the frailer loveliness of flesh and blood— if, I say, it were given to man to see the heavenly beauty face to face, would you call *his*, she asked me, an unenviable life, whose eyes had been opened to the vision, and who had gazed upon it in true contemplation until it had become his own forever. (*Symposium*, 211e)

Desire pursues beauty even more strenuously after achieving it. Desire for the good strengthens upon possessing its object. The important distinction echoes here between desires that vanish when satisfied and those that grow when fulfilled. Fulfillment, here, in relation to desire, divides in two: death and deferral. Hunger and thirst disappear when satisfied. Love enlarges even as lust. Wherever desire and power join as will, they exceed themselves. Obsession, compulsion, and irresistible fascination belong to desire as its fulfillments except where overcome by death. Here desire exceeds even the absence that defines it, since its strength measures its achievement as well as loss. The object of desire exceeds itself without eliminating desire.

The dialogue does not end with Socrates' speech, but with Alcibiades', on Socrates himself. Desire echoes excess throughout. To this point, no one has spoken of the concrete embodiment of the life of desire though it has been represented throughout in the person of Socrates. Alcibiades' drunken speech extols not love but Socrates, the living incarnation of desire. Desire has no intelligible meaning apart from its incarnations.

Alcibiades praises Socrates for what we expect: "Besides, when we listen to anyone else talking, however eloquent he is, we don't really care a damn what he says. But when we listen to you, or to someone else repeating what you've said, even if he puts it ever so badly, and never mind whether the person who's listening is man, woman, or child, we're absolutely staggered and bewitched" (*Symposium*, 215de), and beyond:

> There was one time when the frost was harder than ever, and all the rest of us stayed inside, or if we did go out we wrapped ourselves up to the eyes and tied bits of felt and sheepskins over our shoes, but Socrates went out in the same old coat he'd always worn, and made less fuss about walking on the ice in his bare feet than we did in our shoes. (*Symposium*, 220b)

His remark about repetition pertains to himself and Plato, who bask in reflected light from Socrates' beauty. The stories of the Ideas work upon us and our desires through the model Socrates represents. When all is said and done, desire in Plato does not pass from this world and its shadows to the light of the sun, but fastens upon those embodiments it finds around us, however excessive. For Socrates is no god and perfection is unintelligible around him. More than any other embodiment of our aspirations, he falls short of perfection without tarnishing his inspiration.

Within the Greek inspiration, before Christianity took hold, ideality appeared incompatible with perfection. The final words of *Symposium* express this truth as a double possibility within representation, that one person might be both low and high—"capable of writing both tragedy and comedy" (223d)—without losing an ideal capacity for representation. The highest ideal is neither perfectible nor pure, a striking response to the images in *Republic* of the sun (but not of the desire that moves toward it) and of the myth of metals. Moving from *Symposium* to *Philebus*, we find that: "Our discussion has made it plain to us, now as at the outset, that we must not look for the good in the unmixed life, but in the mixed" (*Philebus*, 61b). With this recognition pertaining to desire wherever acknowledged, that its object can never be pure, we note the closing words:

> Pleasure is not the first of all possessions, nor yet the second; rather, the first has been secured for everlasting tenure somewhere in the region of measure . . .
>
> And the second lies in the region of what is proportioned and beautiful, . . .
>
> And if you . . . put reason and intelligence third, you won't be very wide of the truth.
>
> Nor again, if beside these three you put as fourth what we recognized as belonging to the soul itself, sciences and arts and what we called right opinions, inasmuch as these are more akin than pleasure to the good.
>
> And as fifth, the pleasures which we recognized and discriminated as painless, calling them pure pleasures of the soul itself . . . (*Philebus*, 66bc)

All of these, not alone the good, beauty, or Ideas, embody and fulfill desire. Pleasure is fifth because it is pure as the sun and as pure fails desire. Desire in Plato moves before us mixed, like virtue and writing, and possesses a divided role in dialogues whose existence depends on having been written. Truth and writing, like truth and desire, cannot be separated and, consequently, cannot be thought or imagined pure. Purity is incompatible with virtue, desire, and representation, which always come before us mixed.

The play between representation and desire is represented by Plato himself in *Phaedrus*, mated with magic and illusion,[9] but also with power. *Phaedrus* is writing on the subject of writing, or representation, and desire where desire and representation conceal themselves within their performances. It can be no surprise that *Phaedrus* hides its misrepresentations from itself and its readers as Phaedrus hides Lysias' speech. "Do you expect an amateur like me to repeat by heart, without disgracing its author, the work of the ablest writer of our day, which it took him weeks to compose at his leisure? That is far beyond me, though I'd rather have had the ability that come into a fortune" (*Phaedrus*, 228). Socrates replies that he knows that Phaedrus spent hours memorizing the speech; moreover, he has spied the text hidden under Phaedrus' cloak. More important than the limits of memory Phaedrus speaks of in relation to repetition is his description of himself as an "amateur." The idea of a professional in the art of truth is anathema—Plato's strongest criticism of the Sophists. The dissembling nature of representation appears twice here, both in relation to writing, the most famous passage of the dialogue:

> written words . . . seem to talk to you as though they were intelligent, but if you ask them anything about what they say, from a desire to be instructed, they go on telling

you just the same thing forever. And once a thing is put in writing, the composition, whatever it may be, drifts all over the place, getting into the hands not only of those who understand it, but equally of those who have no business with it; it doesn't know how to address the right people, and not address the wrong. And when it is ill-treated and unfairly abused it always needs its parent to come to its help, being unable to defend or help itself, . . . (*Phaedrus*, 275e)

and in relation to mimesis, to the displacements that occur with memorization and repetition. Living truth can be neither memorized nor repeated. The parent here is truth, whose children—words and truths—always slip away. Knowledge and truth cannot be possessed, a theme Socrates never tires of repeating: "lucidity and completeness and serious importance belong only to those lessons on justice and honor and goodness that are expounded and set forth for the same of instruction, and are veritably written in the soul of the listener, and that such discourses as these ought to be accounted a man's own legitimate children—" (*Phaedrus*, 278). Parents and, especially illegitimate, children are images of desire. But representation cannot escape the disruptive coils of writing, having been "veritably written in the soul." The faults for which Socrates criticizes writing are inescapable rifts of representation, even in the soul, of the *logos* and Ideas, of knowledge and truth, and as much virtues as defects. In its most stable forms, truth echoes representation, writing, with the masks all texts possess in a public world. Truth here mirrors desire, captured in the extraordinary image of writing as *pharmakon*: recipe, medicine, drug, remedy, philter, magic potion, poison, pigment, a deferred figure of deferral.

These two types of repetition relate to each other according to the graphics of supplementarity. Which means that one can no more "separate" them from each other, think of either one apart from the other, "label" them, than one can in *the pharmacy* distinguish the medicine from the poison, the good from the evil, the true from the false, the inside from the outside, the vital from the mortal, the first from the second, etc. Conceived within this original reversibility, the *pharmakon* is the *same* precisely because it has no identity. And the same (is) as supplement. Or in differance. In writing. If he had *meant* to say something, such would have been the speech of Theuth making of writing as a *pharmakon* a singular presence to the King.[10]

Among the "outsides" of the "insides" that define *Phaedrus* are thought in relation to writing and truth, yet still written on the soul, love in relation to appetite, both falling within desire, and the walls of the city where Socrates and Phaedrus have their talk. Talk outside the city—outside power—echoes freedom from the regulation of the *polis*, with the qualification that in human life there can be no such outside—of politics and power, desire, or representation, with their multiple turnings and obsessions. These twists and turns fall within the *pharmakon*, with Socrates as *pharmakeus* and *pharmakos,* where "The *pharmakon* and writing are thus always involved in questions of life and death."[11] The *pharmakon* echoes writing as writing echoes desire and desire, like power, resounds as a *pharmakon*. In these circles sound the inside and outside of life and death.

"Writing is desire" as "desire is power." Both identities are false, since writing and desire are not the same, nor are desire and power. The unison that they are not echoes their disharmonies. The writing that embodies desire is the "only" truth worth having: "Why, life itself would hardly be worth living save for pleasures like this [writing and writing on writing]—" (*Phaedrus*, 258e), and full of life, "any discouse ought to be constructed like a living creature, with its own body, as it were; it must not lack either head or feet; it must have a middle and extremities so composed as to suit each other and the whole work" (*Phaedrus*, 264c), though in our reading divided and uplifted by the wings of desire.

The two great images of the dialogue are of the charioteer with his two horses and the living body. In both cases, desire stretches before us divided by its own image: the doubling of the steeds, the body into its parts and organs. Similarly, writing marks itself divided into parts and chapters, arguments and movements. On the one hand, Socrates strenuously opposes the "evil steed," the "wanton horse," overwhelmed by lower desires, as he opposes the closure of writing, though even that "evil steed casts off his wantonness" (254e). On the other hand, truth resounds as "veritably written on the soul" while desire invades reason as itself.

Truth unfolds as materiality, impressing itself firmly on the soul, where the imprint manifests power. Kafka is our narrator of the ways in which desire disrupts itself through its others. When truth is written on the body, when it shines directly on the soul, then the soul finds its truth "completely"—never mind the images of domination and mutilation. Kafka sounds the underside of what Plato makes a higher truth: that desire and truth dismember themselves, that the orderliness and purity on which Socrates insists is belied by his own different roles, belied wherever truth echoes forth divided.

We wonder whether the reminders in the soul of writing and declamatory prose (*Phaedrus*, 278) may echo not fixed and absolute truths, but a truth profoundly dislocated by its representations. Desire echoes the inward state of relation-to-truth but also relation-to-representation. The object of desire outstrips every attempt to control it, both in its resistances and its truths. Truth and power echo ways in which desire obliterates itself.

The closing prayer of the dialogue may be repeated in different mediums of exchange: "May I count him who is wise, and as for gold, may I possess so much of it as only a temperate man might bear and carry with him" (*Phaedrus*, 279e). Overwhelmed by the deferrals of representation, power, and desire, we may be blessed if we are surrounded by "only" so much as a temperate person can bear. For each exceeds the others even as desire echoes as deferral deferring itself. It resounds polyphonically at the center of truth and power where they exceed themselves and their others—everywhere.

This inexhaustible excess in desire appears in Plato surrounded by reason's truth, so that we must find desire within that truth to grasp Plato's truth. Philosophy moves as desire—the will to truth—far more than as truth or power: it moves as power where power makes it so.

The most far-reaching Western theory of desire is Spinoza's view of *conatus*: "The mind, both in so far as it has clear and distinct ideas and in so far as it has confused ideas, endeavors to persevere in its being for an indefinite time, and is conscious of this effort."[12] This endeavor is the essence of every thing, finite or infinite. Every thing is both object and subject of desire, striving for its own preservation: "The effort by which each thing endeavors to persevere in its own being is nothing but the actual essence of the thing itself" (Spinoza, *Ethics*, III, Prop. VII). To be is to endeavor, to be moved by desire and to exercise power. Power and desire occupy the center of Spinoza's theory of human being:

> This effort, when it is related to the mind alone, is called "will," but when it is related at the same time both to the mind and the body is called "appetite," which is therefore nothing but the very essence of man, from the nature of which necessarily follow those things which promote his preservation, and thus he is determined to do those things. (Spinoza, *Ethics*, III, Prop. IX, Note)

They are conjoined there with representation as a consequence of the most famous of Spinoza's propositions: "The order and connection of ideas is the same as the order and connection of things" (Spinoza, *Ethics*, II, Prop. VII).

Power has a double meaning, one related to God and every essence: "The power of God is His essence itself" (Spinoza, *Ethics*, I, Prop. XXXIV). "Therefore, the power of a thing, or the effort by means of which it does or endeavors to do anything, either by itself or with others—that is to say, the power or effort by which it endeavors to persevere in its being—is nothing but the given or actual essence of the thing itself" (Spinoza, *Ethics*, III, Prop. VII, Demonstration). This power is causal and geometrical. The order of the universe, in ideas and things, is indistinguishably logical and causal, expressed in the geometric structure of the *Ethics*. Geometry here is the order within and without, of the universe and of our ideas, with the merest whisper that a living being wrote the work in which the universe appears in its order and necessity. The power of a finite thing always lies outside itself as well as within.

The second meaning of power, then, concerns the relations of things to one another: "By virtue and power I understand the same thing, that is to say, virtue, in so far as it is related to man, is the essence itself or nature of the man in so far as it has the power of effecting certain things which can be understood through the laws of its nature alone" (Spinoza, *Ethics*, IV, Definition VIII). Finite individual things exist in their essence as caused by an infinite number of other things and also caused by God.

> An individual thing, or a thing which is finite and which has a determinate exist-
> ence, cannot exist nor be determined to action unless it be determined to existence
> and action by another cause which is also finite and has a determinate existence; and
> again, this cause cannot exist nor be determined to action unless by another cause
> which is also finite and determined to existence and action, and so on *ad infinitum*.
> (Spinoza, *Ethics*, I, Prop. XXVIII)

In these double causal relations lie the networks of power that define finite desire.
In relation to human beings, the second meaning of power refers to "the body."
"The mind endeavors as much as possible to imagine those things which increase
or assist the body's power of acting" (Spinoza, *Ethics*, III, Prop. XII). The body
is the site at which power and desire work, together with the ideas of the body.
Desire, here, reflects independently but inseparably through mind and body.
Each is identical with but exceeds the other.

Even within his view of the self-certainty of knowledge and truth, Spinoza
holds that desire and truth belong together. On the one hand, he maintains an
extraordinarily strong sense of the truthfulness of truth: "He who has a true idea
knows at the same time that he has a true idea, nor can he doubt the truth of the
thing" (Spinoza, *Ethics*, II, Prop. XLIII). Truth certifies itself undivided by error.
On the other hand, truth is divided both by desire and will and by the unending
contingencies of finiteness: "The force by which man perseveres in existence is
limited, and infinitely surpassed by the power of external causes" (Spinoza, *Ethics*, IV, Prop. III). Among the resonances of this truth of truth is that it is always
situated, along with desire and power, in relation to the body, even when infinite:
"The object of the idea constituting the human mind is a body, or a certain mode
of extension actually existing, and nothing else" (Spinoza, *Ethics*, II, Prop. XIII),
and "The human mind perceives no external body as actually existing unless
through the ideas of the modifications of the body" (Spinoza, *Ethics*, II, Prop.
XXVI), although "Every idea which in us is absolute, that is to say, adequate and
perfect, is true" (Spinoza, *Ethics*, II, Prop. XXXIV). The body materializes as
the site of truth, power, and desire, where they meet and divide themselves and
each other.

Spinoza's understanding of excesses in desire and power is remarkably explicit. The canonical reading of Spinoza as monist and rationalist suffers from
several textual difficulties. In particular, he twice explicitly distinguishes God
from finite things.

> I think it is plain that by *natura naturans* we are to understand that which is in itself
> and is conceived through itself, or those attributes of substance which express eter-
> nal and infinite essence, that is to say, God in so far as He is considered as a free
> cause. But by *natura naturata* I understand everything which follows from the ne-
> cessity of the nature of God or of any one of God's attributes, that is to say, all the

modes of God's attributes in so far as they are considered as things which are in God, and which without God can neither be nor can be conceived. (Spinoza, *Ethics*, I, Prop. XXIX, Note)

a thing which is the cause both of the essence and of the existence of any effect must differ from that effect both with regard to its essence and with regard to its existence. (Spinoza, *Ethics*, I, Prop. XVII, Note)

God cannot be identified with finite modes, but with their cause. "God is not only the efficient cause of the existence of things, but also of their essence" (Spinoza, *Ethics*, I, Prop. XXV). Even here, however, there is excess, for in addition to God, who is the efficient cause of the existence and essence of all things, finite things follow from each other inexhaustibly.[13] Here finiteness appears as excess.

Wherever Spinoza defines the closure of the universe, either finitely or infinitely, we find excess. God is not only infinite, but absolutely infinite, unlimited in infinite numbers of ways. God exceeds both himself and his and our comprehension. We know "only" of the attributes of thought and extension. The limits of God's knowledge of himself appear in his unity among an infinite number of attributes each of which expresses his infinite essence. God is one but cannot be thought, even by himself, except as divided.

God exceeds himself but resounds as the immanent cause of all things. We cannot take refuge from the excesses of finite things in God's infiniteness, for they exceed him in their infinite causal relations to each other. Moreover, each finite thing exceeds its relations to other things in its essence: desire and power. The *conatus* represents the excess present in every finite thing *as finite*, an effort to persevere that exceeds any causal relation.

Finally, through the identity of ideas and things, these excesses reunite—another excess—as emotion, situated at the juncture of desire and power. "By emotion I understand the modifications of the body by which the power of acting of the body itself is increased, diminished, helped, or hindered, together with the ideas of these modifications" (Spinoza, *Ethics*, III, Def. III). Emotion appears as the togetherness of mind and body in relation to the powers of the body, exceeded twice: by relations to God, whereby eternity belongs to human beings insofar as they are active rather than passive; and by the excesses of ideas over the body even where ideas and things perfectly correspond. These excesses come together in one of Spinoza's most extraordinary propositions: "He who possesses a body fit for many things possesses a mind of which the greater part is eternal" (Spinoza, *Ethics*, V, Prop. XXXIX).

It may seem perverse that enhancement of the powers of the body should increase the powers or eternity of the mind. Yet if we think of these, not as moments demanding mediation, but as excesses, mirroring and mirrored by excesses in desire and power, then as power and desire exceed each other in their togetherness, as God and finite modes exceed each other, eternity and temporality exceed each other in the excessive powers of the body. Spinoza tells us repeatedly of the polyphonies of our embodiment: "the joy by which the drunkard is enslaved is altogether different from the joy which is the portion of the philosopher—" (Spinoza, *Ethics*, III, LVII, Note). Our bodies differ inexhaustibly, from each other and within themselves.

Involved in this play of desire with power and representation is the nature of the body, the site at which these performances take place. As each is divided within and without, promoting mutual excesses, bodies are divided within and without. On the one hand, they belong to a causal order within which they are regulated by natural laws and liberated from human laws by the necessities of their causal relations. On the other hand, whatever causal necessity pertains to them, whatever their biology, bodies are regulated and liberated by the customs and conventions of historical social life. On one hand, the biology of bodies permits them to be socially regulated, a site of power and control. On the other hand, the biology of bodies exceeds their regulation.

Desire, here, both inexhaustibly mirrors power and representation, as they inexhaustibly mirror it, and departs from their regulations. Repetition and deviation, harmony and disharmony, echo the inexhaustible polyphonies of desire within and without. In this sense, the body, desire's recurrent and inescapable site and object, invested with its inexhaustible energies, is delimited by unending repetition "only" to signify, through repetition, the disharmonies that exceed every representation in the reciprocities of power and desire. Here we may understand desire as the inexhaustible site of inexhaustible deferral.

Desire's excesses within material embodiment both confirm and give the lie to the most influential modern theory of desire as the form whereby a conscious subject relates to another subject to reaffirm its own subjectivity. "This opposition of its appearance and its truth finds its real essence, however, only in the truth—in the unity of self-consciousness with itself. This unity must become the state of *Desire* in general."[14] The great part of Hegel's *Phenomenology of Spirit* represents the working through of self-knowledge by a subject in the form of desire, where the other side of desire manifests truth and freedom. Here, in Hegel, desire moves not as other to truth but as its representation in the form of subjectivity.

Among the truths of the dialectic is that the Idea reappears at every level of the system, drawing circles upon circles in the famous image of systematicity:

> Each of the parts of philosophy is a philosophical whole, a circle rounded and complete in itself. In each of these parts, however, the philosophical Idea is found in a particular specificity or medium. The single circle, because it is a real totality, bursts through the limits imposed by its special medium, and gives rise to a wider circle. The whole of philosophy in this way resembles a circle of circles. The Idea

appears in each single circle, but, at the same time, the whole Idea is constituted by the system of these peculiar phases, and each is a necessary member of the organisation.[15]

The images represent the infinite. The bad infinite corresponds to the image of a straight line. The image of the good infinite corresponds to the image of a circle.

The image of the progress to infinity is the *straight line*, at the two limits of which alone the infinite is, and always only is where the line—which is determinate being—is not, and which goes *out beyond* to this negation of its determinate being, that is, to the indeterminate; the image of true infinity, bent back into itself, becomes the *circle*, the line which has reached itself, which is closed and wholly present, without *beginning* and *end*.[16]

Both images, good and bad, express desire. The inexhaustibility of desire is either infinite and intractable or turns back to control itself. Absent from both infinites, good and bad, are excesses whereby desire surpasses itself in the form of power and truth. Such excesses echo here as inexhaustibility, desire circling back to itself as its own deferral.

Where most Western philosophers presuppose that within desire, for good or God, there is a limit to the violences called forth in its relationship to power, Hegel understands desire as fundamentally rooted in destruction.

And self-consciousness is thus only assured of itself through sublating this other, which is presented to self-consciousness as an independent life; self-consciousness is *Desire*. Convinced of the nothingness of this other, it definitely affirms this nothingness to be for itself the truth of this other, negates the independent object, and thereby acquires the certainty of its own self, as *true* certainty, a certainty which it has become aware of in objective form.[17]

Desire irrupts as violence to oneself, as a subject, through another. Power belongs to desire as the violence whereby self-consciousness may attain unity with itself while violence unfolds as the transgressive movement within desire of overcoming itself by reason and love. Desire's circularity manifests its belonging together with destruction. Violence within desire echoes the truth that composes its obsessions.

Hegel's view appears governed by the assumption that the autonomy of self-consciousness is the overriding concern. Desire is overcome, not by itself and its truth and not by power including violence and destruction, by its own displacements, but by the unifying movement within self-consciousness that manifests its impulse toward its own being. Desire is overcome by freedom and truth, and violence gives way to community under law, effectively repudiating the insight that desire, in virtue of the bodies in which it is situated, is inseparable in its highest forms from obsession, mastery, and violence. The site in Hegel to which desire returns again and again is the self-conscious subject, and its return blunts the realization that desire is destruction including destruction of its own destruction.

Desire circles back on itself from and within truth "only" to find that every truth is contaminated by desire, distorted yet made possible by it. When Foucault speaks of the pervasiveness and truth—the "scientificity"—of ideology, we hear him speak of desire as well:

> 1. Ideology is not exclusive of scientificity. . . .
> 2. . . .
> 3. By correcting itself, by rectifying its errors, by clarifying its formulations, discourse does not necessarily undo its relations with ideology. The role of ideology does not diminish as rigour increases and error is dissipated.[18]

Ideology presents itself as power and desire, situated where they meet, their togetherness and departure. Power and desire, ideology and violence, sovereignty and mastery, emerge as locations where truth happens, is instituted and collapses. Representation and truth belong to desire as desire belongs to power and as each belongs to the others and departs from them. These circularities express the authority, the will, of truth and power. Desire, here, falls into power and truth, determining, through its own laws and excesses, the discourses that delimit itself and power. Desire and power excessively define disruptive moments within truth.

Freud opens *Civilization and Its Discontents* with reference not to reason or pleasure, but to power. "The impression forces itself upon one that men measure by false standards, that everyone seeks power, success, riches for himself and admires others who attain them, while undervaluing the truly precious things in life."[19] It appears here in the form of a contrast with higher values, though as Freud immediately points out, the truth is one of variety and multitude. "And yet, in making any general judgement of this kind one is in danger of forgetting the manifold variety of humanity and its mental life."[20] The name of this variety echoes desire, including representation and power. Although this excess in desire has always been known, it has been traditionally resisted in the name of reason. To the French, Sade represents the historical moment at which desire emerged in its awesome, obsessive inexhaustibility, inseparable from representation, truth, and language, sexuality and death, violence and power.

> Sade attains the end of Classical discourse and thought. He holds sway precisely upon their frontier. After him, violence, life and death, desire, and sexuality will extend, below the level of representation, an immense expanse of shade which we are now attempting to recover, as far as we can, in our discourse, in our freedom, in our thought. But our thought is so brief, our freedom so enslaved, our discourse so repetitive, that we must face the fact that that expanse of shade below is really a bottomless sea.[21]

This immense expanse of shade illuminates the excessiveness and obsessiveness within desire, divided by power and representation, all divided and maintained by the objects of desire: those to which it attaches, in which it invests, and to which it gives rise through its investments. We may think, here, of life and death, not "only" as moments within this expanse of desire, but as objects of desire determining the polyphonies of their power and truth.

Yet the images of shade, of a bottomless sea, shine as images of excess without multiple reflexivity. They are moments within modernity whereby the transparency of truth to itself is challenged by what exceeds it, but may not be moments where excess exceeds itself. Desire for us represents the excesses of excess over itself.

SIX

Truth

Truth echoes locality. It resounds within representation and without; within nature and without; within desire and power and without. It echoes without because it resounds within, and what belongs within must exceed its limits to be limited by them. It belongs within because its limits limit in virtue of an other—many others. Belonging and departing belong together and depart. Truth echoes the diaphonies of others that exceed it while it exceeds them and itself.

Truth belongs to representation when embodied: sounded, inscribed, or thought; it departs from representation where "word breaks off," where the music ends, where representation exceeds its materiality. Harmony and disharmony, here, in relation to representation, repeat nature's work, repeat the relations that *techne* bears to truth. The relations between representation and reality express embodiment's transgressions.

The political question is truth itself because the truth of truth is always in question, questioning its authority, constituted by power, and power's truth, constituted by representation. Power works for us by constituting our truth, by forcing us to speak the truth. Truth works for us by constituting the authority of power. Truth and power belong to each other. What we hope to represent here are the disharmonies in this belonging together, the ways in which the untruth of truth constitutes power and resistance to power constitutes truth.

When Aristotle says of *nous* that "the thinking part of the soul must be, while impassible, capable of receiving the form of an object; that is, must be potentially identical in character with its object without being the object,"[1] he speaks of knowledge and the knowing mind, of the repetitions that define them; he also speaks of truth, its togetherness with its object in virtue of their departures.[2] In Spinoza's words, "the order and connection of ideas is the same as the order and connection of things."[3] This unison of ideas and things echoes in the realm of truth,[4] a belonging together that can be heard "only" through its departures. That is why truth cannot be its own standard, why it cannot be true that "He who has a true idea knows at the same time that he has a true idea, and cannot doubt its truth."[5] Truth can be its own standard "only" by exceeding itself, a unison that echoes "only" in its displacements, and these can be heard "only" through the same. The truth of truth echoes inescapable departures from truth. The truth of truth, like the representation of representation, whispers violence, resounds where truth achieves itself by tearing itself apart. The truth of truth echoes its untruth.

The tradition, from Aristotle to Spinoza to the present, composes a canon, alive "only" at its edges, in which truth echoes itself as undivided, as if truth transpired "only" in its regulation: "The world is all that is the case,"[6] "the totality of facts."[7] The totality of facts is nature; truth falls outside into representation. "A picture agrees with reality or fails to agree; it is correct or incorrect, true or false."[8] Truth echoes between reality and representation, within neither, except for that fated word "agree" echoing correctness and incorrectness. In the agreement of picture and fact echoes dominion of the same although they are two "only" in virtue of their differences. When truth sounds agreement it passes into an opposition that demands regulation by repetition.

The "totality of facts" echoes a different movement, in which truth opens to its others in the totality. This movement sounds more powerfully where Hegel defines truth in the totality:

> The truth is the whole. The whole, however, is merely the essential nature reaching its completeness through the process of its own development. Of the Absolute it must be said that it is essentially a result, that only at the end is it what it is in very truth; and just in that consists its nature, which is to be actual, subject, or self-becoming, self-development.[9]

> In common life truth means the agreement of an object with our conception of it. We thus pre-suppose an object to which our conception must conform. In the philosophic sense of the word, on the other hand, truth may be described, in general abstract terms, as the agreement of a thought content with itself.[10]

Given Hegel's repeated emphasis on deferral, the identification of truth with agreement sounds remarkable even within thought's return to itself. Is the belonging of thought to itself also its departure from itself? Does the totality include difference with agreement, difference from itself? Do we hear, in this displacement, the arbitrariness of representation, inner and outer?

The tradition before Hegel defined truth in opposition with falsity, sounding an opposition in which truth belongs to measure in relation to the whole. In Aristotle's words:

> it is obvious that the one-sided theories which some people express about all things cannot be valid—on the one hand the theory that nothing is true . . . on the other hand the theory that everything is true. These views are practically the same as that of Heraclitus; for he who says that "all things are true and all are false" also makes each of these statements separately, so that since they are impossible, the double statement must be impossible too.[11]

Everything cannot be true, including the contradictory of this statement; nor can everything be false. Yet the comparison with Heraclitus is instructive. That all is flux does not preclude a measure, "only" an unchanging measure outside the flux, a measure of equivalence. Within there sounds a more or less, a quick or slow. Moreover, we may listen to the discordant side of Heraclitus where justice is strife and truth is falsity. That everything is true and everything is false does not retell the aporia that everything is both true and false. The latter, closer to Heraclitus, speaks not of truth as a canon, but as a truth whose truth rings antiphonally. If truth expresses a measure, then the truth of truth sounds no measure at all, but truth belonging to and departing from itself as disharmony. The play of truth and falsity in language and thought echoes their deferral.

The Western tradition represents truth as a measure. Yet even Aristotle cannot always treat it as the same. "As there are in the mind thoughts which do not involve truth or falsity, and also those which be either true or false, so it is in speech. For truth and falsity imply combination and separation."[12] Truth and falsity resound as qualities, sometimes present, sometimes not, that represent diversity. Yet of all truths about truth, that it differs from a quality is as true as anything can be—true while false. Truth echoes either as no predicate or as a predicate that predicates nothing, resounding univocally. Further, the nothing that it predicates says what it is not: untruth with truth. Not that anything is both true and false, in an overarching economy of predication, but that truth and falsity are not predicates—are and are not predicates.

Truth unfolds as falsity's opposite "only" within a canon defined by exclusion, by and for men in the presence of the absence of women, by a center circumscribed by its periphery. The canon expresses a brotherhood in truth, a fraternity that excludes women and the temptation of evil along with falsity and death. Here, as always, Spinoza presents an exception, refusing the opposition of falsity with truth, stepping outside the canon, though regrettably not outside its brotherhood.[13] Falsity is inseparable from truth as its lack. "Falsity consists in the privation of knowledge which inadequate ideas, that is, fragmentary and confused ideas, involve."[14] Privation may be heard to define another opposition between falsity and truth, still one of privilege, of completeness over incompleteness, eternity over temporality. Yet the incompleteness of the totality echoes in Spinoza in infinite numbers of infinite attributes, each a representation equivalent with God except for the disharmonies within them. Privation echoes here as inexhaustible deferral.

In Hegel also, privilege in opposition emerges into a unity of difference in the notion, displacing the primacy of truth over falsity. "Just in the interest of their real meaning, precisely because we want to designate the aspect or moment of complete otherness, the terms true and false must no longer be used where their otherness has been cancelled and superseded. . . . falsehood is not, *qua* false, any longer a moment of truth."[15] The whole in which truth unfolds comprises truth and falsity together even as it supersedes them. Truth stands forth as agreement in the same including its disharmonies, dissolving falsehood. Even in Peirce's famous definition, truth resides among ultimates and fatalities, the destiny of agreement joined with reality: "The opinion which is fated to be ultimately agreed to by all who investigate, is what we mean by the truth, and the object represented in this opinion is the real."[16] Reality echoes its locality but dwells with privilege in the sovereignty of the one. Yet if reality sounds its inexhaustibility, disharmonized by simulation, then truth echoes its antiphonies in the aporias of representation and reality.

Heidegger speaks of the "essence of truth": "the one thing that in general distinguishes every 'truth' as truth."[17] We may have difficulty in our sonorescence taking such a transcendental turn in relation to truth. What represents truth as truth echoes neither as one nor in general. What makes truth truth sounds its inexhaustibility. The truth of truth echoes untruth; the truth of the truth of truth echoes deferral. This truth sounds its own locality. Our time unfolds as an age of truth where nature and truth echo artifice and untruth in the form of representation. The truth of truth resounds for us as simulation, where truth appears indistinguishable from untruth but where their difference marks truth; where reality echoes unreality, nature sounds unnatural, and unnaturalness belongs to nature in the form of artifice. The indistinguishability expresses the reciprocities and excesses of reality and unreality and of truth and untruth—simulation. The artifice of simulation echoes reality: working somewhere, multiply and excessively. The truth of truth echoes the inexhaustible work of nature's loci.

The answer Heidegger gives to the question of the essence of truth is freedom: "The essence of truth reveals itself as freedom. The latter is ek-sistent disclosive letting things be."[18] The truth of truth echoes freedom. Or shall we say that truth resounds as freedom as the truth of truth echoes the truth of freedom and the freedom of truth, always untruth? In every case, truth dislocates and is dislocated by others. Wherever we listen to truth we hear untruth; wherever we hear freedom we listen to necessity. Falsity belongs to truth as the untruth of the truth of truth. Necessity belongs to freedom as its deferral. Freedom belongs to necessity to mark the limits of its limits. The truth of freedom echoes necessity; the truth of necessity echoes freedom. Stillness and polyphony sound together.

The freedom of truth is "letting things be." This theme, with its passive voice, resists the mastery of a rational tradition that would impose itself on things in the name of their truth. It is resistant to what Foucault calls being "within the true":

> a proposition must fulfil some onerous and complex conditions before it can be admitted within a discipline; before it can be pronounced . . . "within the true."
>
> It is always possible one could speak the truth in a void; one would only be in the true, however, if one obeyed the rules of some discursive "policy" which would have to be reactivated every time one spoke.[19]

The passive voice, however, the "letting-be" in truth's freedom, exercises a different privilege, possibly one also resisted by Foucault: "In letting things as a whole be, which discloses and at the same time conceals, it happens that concealing appears as what is first of all concealed."[20] The entire world with its truths rings in this "first of all" although truth has no such world. The truth of truth echoes the twin dangers of first and "only," priority and incompleteness. Heidegger escapes the second but exercises privilege repeatedly in the firstness of the first. Yet from the belonging together of concealment and unconcealment we may repudiate the privilege of any first. Truth departs from itself as untruth, unconcealment as concealment.

> That which is can only be, as a being, if it stands within and stands out within what is lighted in this clearing. . . . And yet a being can be *concealed*, too, only within the sphere of what is lighted. Each being we encounter and which encounters us keeps to this curious opposition of presence in that it always withholds itself at the same time in a concealedness. The clearing in which beings stand is in itself at the same time concealment.[21]

Unconcealment brings about concealment, truth brings about untruth. More extremely, truth belongs to untruth, unconcealment belongs to concealment. This truth composes nature's work. To be is to belong somewhere, "many wheres." To be is to work somehow, "many hows." The truth of truth echoes the union of this someplace with its many places.

Two additional themes, untruth and error, disclose mystery.

> In letting things be, which discloses and at the same time conceals, it happens that concealing appears as what is first of all concealed. Insofar as it ek-sists, Dasein conserves the first and broadest undisclosedness, untruth proper. The proper non-essence of truth is the mystery.[22]

> Man's flight from the mystery toward what is readily available, onward from one current thing to the next, passing the mystery by—this is *erring*.

> Man errs. Man does not merely stray into errancy. He is always astray in errancy, because as ek-sistent he in-sists and so already is caught in errancy.[23]

> Errancy is the essential counter-essence to the primordial essence of truth.[24]

The circularities of representation pass into the errancy of truth. The truth of truth belongs together with its countertruth, its truthfulness in the proximity of mistruth. Again, in the extreme, untruth belongs to truth and the truth of truth belongs to untruth, both figures of diaphony, repeating the misrepresentations of representation. Representation represents itself as its misrepresentation. Truth tells its truth as its untruth. We seek to know this truth without naming the totality of truth: to dissipate the onlyness of truth while maintaining its locality. Even where totality includes its own displacement, it remains a local totality, a fragment among the fragments. Mystery resounds in the stillnesses of these polyphonies.

Hegel echoes for us as philosopher of difference as well as of the Absolute, above all, as philosopher of the "only." In him, in the totalities that pertain to truth, we greet its "loneliness," where truth abides in its "ownliness." This ownliness echoes the "only" truth of truth.

> The truth is the whole. The whole, however, is merely the essential nature reaching its completeness through the process of its own development. Of the Absolute it must be said that it is essentially a result, that only at the end is it what it is in every truth; and just in that consists its nature, which is to be actual, subject, or self-becoming, self-development.[25]

How are we to hear this movement to totality? As completion or as its denial? As result or including the development? The Absolute "is essentially a result," but the result, at the end, is self-becoming and self-development. The totality resounds as not "merely" the result, but the whole including the opposing moments that pass into it. "Only at the end" is the Absolute what it is in truth. "Only" at the end is truth. But the truth is not the end without its beginning, enfolds beginning and end together. This togetherness is truth. "Only" it is the whole. Hegel speaks to this directly in relation to the ground.

> We must be careful, when we say that the ground is the unity of identity and difference, not to understand by this unity an abstract identity. Otherwise we only change the name, while we still think the identity (of understanding) already seen to be false. To avoid this misconception we may say that the ground, besides being the unity, is also the difference of identity and difference.[26]

The ground is the identity but also the difference of identity and difference. Similarly, the Absolute is the return to itself of the Notion *in all its difference*. The word "all" here works transgressively, suggesting the totalizing movement that characterizes one side of Hegel offset by his constant repetition that the totality includes its differences in the belonging together of identity and difference.

The resolution of all diversity and negation into the Idea echoes abstraction, lacking the totality. The totality is all: outside and inside, affirmation and negation, identity and difference, truth and untruth. The totality includes more than the unity of identity and difference, but also the difference of identity and difference. It also includes the difference of the identity and difference of identity and difference, and so forth, though that inexhaustible movement of deferral never resounds in Hegel without ambiguity. But why should we expect this ambiguity to resound unambiguously, since it falls within the differences between identity and difference?

This theme, of the inexhaustible differences in the unity of the Absolute, tends to obscurity in Hegel, overwhelmed by the repeated thunder of totality. Yet it can be heard in a variety of moments: in the great shapes of Recollection that repeat the Idea after its abstract realization; in the sacrifices Spirit makes of its

subjectivity into Nature; in the process to which the Idea must return to be concrete; and in the abstractness of the Logic, wherever only modifies itself.

> Consequently, it [the Idea] is the certitude of the virtual identity between itself and
> the objective world.—Reason comes to the world with an absolute faith in its ability
> to make the identity actual, and to raise its certitude to truth; and with the instinct of
> realising explicitly the nullity of that contrast which it sees to be implicitly null.[27]

The nullity discharges where the totality is only a totality. Actuality emerges
where the end contains its beginning, where the totality is not only a totality. The
certitude of the identity between the Idea and the world either displaces unreason
to outside the Idea or includes its opposites and differences. Hegel speaks to this
question explicitly in relation to the relevance of error within truth. "Error or
other-being, when superseded, is still a necessary dynamic element of truth: for
truth can only be where it makes itself its own result."[28] Even the totality may be
only a totality, the Absolute only Absolute.

> Logic shows that the subjective which is to be subjective only, the finite which
> would be finite only, the infinite which would be infinite only, and so on, have no
> truth, but contradict themselves, and pass over into their opposites. Hence this tran-
> sition, and the unity in which the extremes are merged and become factors, each
> with a merely reflected existence, reveals itself as their truth.[29]

Wherever totality and absolutes become complete, they become null. The "onlyness" of the Absolute echoes as its "alsoness."

It follows that the unity and totality of the Absolute echo not the unity and
totality *of* differences, the same within them that they are not, but the unity and
totality *in* a multiplicity of differences that is univocally the same with them while
always different. This disharmony within and by means of the unison of belonging together echoes the univocity of aporia; its primary manifestation is time.

Two sides of the only manifest themselves recurrently in relation to truth.
One emerges as time, the reciprocity of harmony and disharmony as deferral. The
other emerges as science, represented as system. Spirit cannot relate to itself except through time, where time moves as the process identity needs—with science
and truth—to be itself. This historicality of truth speaks to the contradictoriness of
thought, replacing it with aporia. "It [the ordinary mind] does not conceive the
diversity of philosophical systems as the progressive evolution of truth; rather, it
sees only contradiction in that variety."[30] To think of the Absolute as timeless is
to think of its contradictions as falling within or without. Only through time can
they belong to the Absolute within and without. The whole is the process with its
result, though no thought can comprehend them both. "For the real subject-matter
is not exhausted in its purpose, but in working the matter out; nor is the mere
result attained the concrete whole itself, but the result along with the process of
arriving at it."[31] To think the result without its development is empty. To think

the process without its end is blind. Both are corpses, dead remnants of the living development that they mask. Hegel is caught up in the inexhaustible movement of desire, far surpassing that sense of desire restricted to the subject. Desire strives forth as end *in* means and means *in* end, though the two together fall apart into nature and experience.

Truth lies in the end, in the beginning, and in the process—in "all" their differences. Only within can we think of truth and falsity, and the development of their interrelations manifests science and reason. "The systematic development of truth in scientific form can alone be the true shape in which truth exists."[32] Even here, the key words are "systematic" and "scientific." Science may be known *in* and *through* the process, entailing that we think it as both result and never having arrived.

> But science, in the very fact that it comes on the scene, is itself a phenomenon; its "coming on the scene" is not yet *itself* carried out in all the length and breadth of its truth. In this regard, it is a matter of indifference whether we consider that it (science) is the phenomenon because it makes its appearance alongside another kind of knowledge, or call that other untrue knowledge its process of appearing.[33]

"Coming on the scene" can be taken lightly, as the advent of science in a world that lacked it, thereafter exercising sovereignty. Yet Hegel explicitly says that it must be thought *both* alongside other knowledges and within them in its process of appearing. The alongside emerges as a theme that defines our modernity in response to the within of past modernities.

Hegel suggests that truth and falsity are opposed, their unity contradictory, in the moments that precede their full scientific revelation, and they are unified, no longer contradictory, within the unity of subject and object, mind and matter. The question is whether the higher truth replaces its moments so that they no longer stand displaced, no longer possess a dislocated truth opposed by falsity as a standard, or whether this higher truth echoes both the unity and the dislocation, the result and the moments, however aporetically. The question then arises of the onlyness of truth in which it either contradicts falsity or appears as one with it. Yet neither alternative alone appears true; each presents itself as an only as their togetherness presents another only. Truth contradicts falsity and echoes its same. Can we fail to sound this truth without giving up hope of thinking truly?

One way this aporia echoes in Hegel rings in his continuing emphasis on process: "its having its own otherness within itself, and the fact of its being a self-initiated process—these are implied in the very simplicity of thought itself. For this is self-moving inwardness, the pure notion. Thus, then, it is the very nature of understanding to be a process; and being a process it is Rationality."[34] Only as a process can truth unify all its oppositions and differences. If Hegel still speaks as the philosopher in whose voice we think difference, we have barely begun to hear thought as a process, never achieved, always becoming, yet not for that reason compromised, with its fulfillment present within itself though never arrived on the scene. "If we identify the Idea with thought, thought must not be taken in the sense of a method or form, but in the sense of the self-developing totality of its laws and peculiar terms."[35] The totality includes the development in all its circuitousness and cunning, including its disharmonies and hesitations. If science and truth are processes, are not only the result, they are both incipiences and fulfillments. The recurrent onlys mark the differences in the totality along with the totality in the differences, mark them in their restlessness.

Truth here echoes the process turning back upon itself. As process it sounds the rhythms of becoming, a togetherness of movement and representation that cannot avoid aporia though it may hope to avoid, by means of aporia, the contradictions in its movement. Truth as process echoes truth together with falsity. Yet as both it echoes neither. The truth of truth sounds the nonopposition of the opposition of truth and falsity. We avoid representing truth as triumph over falsity. We also avoid representing truth without a need to triumph, as if truth and falsity were no longer opposed. In the timbres of its development, truth sounds the displacements that define its truth.

That falsity defines truth speaks of truth in opposition and as a canon. That truth and falsity, in the Absolute, no longer oppose each other suggests a truth that no longer needs untruth, that ceases to voice its own truth. That the Absolute sounds its unity with its moments echoes the development of truth as both opposition and nonopposition, where truth passes into its other and remains at war with it. We may mark here a distinction between a truth in truth that continues to be won from untruth and a truth of truth that cannot be thought without untruth. The distinction represents truth as representation while also representing the limits of the limits of that representation. The circling back may occur in time as history. It may echo representation and system.

For process is not the only way in which the aporias of truth appear in Hegel. Development is not the only truth of truth. Among its other truths are science and necessity. These join in the development. "The systematic development of truth in scientific form can alone be the true shape in which truth exists. . . . The inner necessity that knowledge should be science lies in its very nature; and the adequate and sufficient explanation for this lies simply and solely in the systematic exposition of philosophy itself."[36] Science echoes the true shape of truth; necessity shows the form it wears through time. The necessity here, like science and truth, lives at the end of time, at the beginning, and at a particular time—effectively every time with its displacements. Necessity joins with totality as the beginning, middle, and end, all together. Science is always coming on the scene, truth is always unfolding as development, necessity always echoing within freedom.

> Developed actuality, as the coincident alternation of inner and outer, the alternation of their opposite motions combined into a single motion, is *Necessity*.[37]

> This truth of necessity, therefore, is *Freedom*: and the truth of substance is the Notion, . . .[38]

Freedom wins over necessity and falls within it, as science triumphs over its others—nonscience, unreason—and delimits them within itself, as man defines himself over woman as his Other and includes her within himself, and as truth falls inside and outside untruth. It is only an approximation to say that truth is the totality given that the totality includes every disharmony, every falsity. Truth is the totality but the totality never sounds without the antiphonies of its disharmonies. Truth echoes in the inexhaustible play of opposition and resolution, where the resolution cannot give up the opposition without losing itself.

Consciousness, here, echoes truth and falsity as it represents necessity and freedom. That truth can be its own standard, in Spinoza, echoes aporia, for it must include itself by departing from itself. This broken reflexivity manifests the circularity that defines the totality of science, truth, and necessity, a circularity that displaces each of its moments, alienating them in its name. No external standard exists for truth;[39] science falls entirely within itself; reason exercises its own rule; not because there is no other standard, but because there is no externality. There is exteriority but not externality, a totality that becomes a supertotality and in doing so, brings falsity within truth, freedom within necessity, and conversely.

The totality of truth falls into the falsity of truth and its truth. The Absolute divides truth and falsity into their oppositions no less than it joins them in their reciprocities. The standard of truth in opposition to falsity, upon which the Western tradition largely rests, though always called into question, defines a norm only in virtue of a whole that redefines its opposition. Truth opposes falsity and requires extraordinary devotion and rigor—except that within such rigor and devotion questions cannot be asked about truth in relation to its own truth, however devotedly and rigorously. The canonicity of truth echoes in constant tension with privilege and opposition. The opposition of truth to falsity must be maintained without privileging any canon.

In a Hegelian circle, Heidegger asks us to think of the "essence" of truth—what we have called its truth—as *freedom*:

> The essence of truth is freedom.[40]

> Freedom is not mere absence of constraint with respect to what we can or cannot do. Nor is it on the other hand mere readiness for what is required and necessary (and so somehow a being). Prior to all this ("negative" and "positive" freedom), freedom is engagement in the disclosure of beings as such.[41]

Freedom and truth open toward beings, toward their disclosure but letting them be. This "letting" emerges where Heidegger seeks to depart from Hegel, not in the freedom of truth and the truth of freedom, not in the disclosure of beings or being of disclosure. Freedom echoes the *letting be* of beings rather than their appropriation and mastery.[42] Hegel's words, in a passage that calls for inversion, are that "[Spirit] . . . discovers this world in the living present to be its own property; and so has taken the first step to descend from the ideal intelligible world, or rather to quicken the abstract element of the intelligible world with concrete selfhood."[43] That the world might be Spirit's property seems at odds with letting things be, the freedom of a Spirit within the totality at odds with finite freedom. Yet as the totality divides into the differences within its unity, and truth divides into untruth, freedom divides into unfreedom, and letting-be divides into the repetitions of time. The property of the world echoes transgression.

Even more striking in Heidegger's description of the essence of truth is its onlyness. Freedom issues not as absence or constraint, but absence and constraint, as truth is untruth, unconcealment is concealment, and letting-be is comportment. "Precisely because letting be always lets being be in a particular comportment which relates to them and thus discloses them, it conceals beings as a whole. Letting-be is intrinsically at the same time a concealing."[44] Letting-be, together with unconcealment, echoes at the same time and in the same way as concealment. Truth echoes untruth, echoes onlyness. "Man *is* essentially this relationship of responding to Being, and he is only this. This 'only' does not mean a limitation, but rather an excess."[45] This onlyness appears as untruth in relation to truth, concealment in relation to unconcealment, as truth belongs to and departs from itself, exceeds itself.[46] Yet Heidegger speaks of concealing "as a whole," bringing back the notion of totality in its internal dividedness. He does not relinquish nostalgia toward the totality of the world.

> The concealment of beings as a whole, untruth proper, is older than every openedness of this or that being. . . . Nothing less than the concealing of what is concealed as a whole, of beings as such, i.e., the mystery; not a particular mystery regarding this or that, but rather the one mystery—that, in general, mystery (the concealing of what is concealed) as such holds sway throughout man's Da-sein.[47]

This theme of the whole, of the only and merely that define the totality, return in the untruth without which truth cannot sound. Themes of privilege echo "throughout" in the "one mystery," even in the proximity of the "older" of concealment, reminding us of Anaximander.[48] Women along with every minority, male or female, for whom difference echoes both curse and promise, must experience privilege and domination in the oneness of the mystery of the world, in the unity of "man's" *Dasein*. Heidegger repudiates neither canonicity nor its privilege, only a certain privilege within it. The canon remains within its recession.

Two themes resound. One echoes the mystery at the heart of *alētheia*, from which escape is "erring." "Man's flight from the mystery toward what is readily available, onward from one current thing to the next, passing the mystery by—

this is *erring*."[49] The mystery is granted privilege, defined by man's authority. The other theme echoes the way of truth as restlessness and movement, disharmony and polyphony. Here *errancy* belongs to truth as the disharmonies within that make truth possible. Truth is freedom because it lies in possibility, not necessity—or rather, rings where truth divides into untruth, stillness into polyphony. Errancy echoes the untruth in truth that enables it to open to representation, freedom's movement within truth's necessity.[50]

Heidegger seems to preserve the privilege that surrounds truth and being, both in the totality and in the sense of straying from the mystery of Being. "The glimpse into the mystery out of errancy is a question—in the sense of that unique question of what being as such is as a whole."[51] The mystery and the way from which errancy departs grant a certain primacy to *alētheia* as one way of truth. The way of untruth asserts primacy over the way of truth in this reciprocity, so that untruth belongs to truth more than truth to untruth. We may seek a more displaced truth of the truth and untruth of truth. The truth of truth echoes the truth of truth, the untruth of untruth, and the truth and untruth of the untruth of truth and the truth of untruth. And so on. We reject the privilege of the first and only. "Truth happens only by establishing itself in the conflict and sphere opened up by truth itself."[52] Such a privilege excludes certain differences defining certain human beings and the forms of their freedom. The freedom of the truth of truth wins at the expense of those who never lived at the center of our Truth.

With rejection of this privilege goes a more powerful rejection of Truth, expressed in our return to science. For Heidegger's privileging of unconcealment passes into a questionable untruth about truth: "science is not an original happening of truth, but always the cultivation of a domain of truth already opened, specifically by apprehending and confirming that which shows itself to be possibly and necessarily correct within that field."[53] As if there were a technical truth that did not concern us, as if we might be too profound, too deep, too heretical, or too primordial to care about correctness, too correct to hear its excesses. The truth of science suffers from loneliness like all finite creatures, echoes the untruths of its truths. The loneliness of truth sounds departure from truth wherever it belongs with untruth. But neither echoes everywhere and everywhen.

The aporia of truth belonging together with untruth echoes wherever truth resounds. "Only because truth and untruth are, *in essence, not* irrelevant to one another but rather belong together is it possible for a true proposition to enter into pointed opposition to the corresponding untrue proposition."[54] This reciprocity peals even within science—perhaps most of all. To say that science does not know this truth may not be important; it cannot help but represent it. But science must sound its untruths with its truths to unfold as science, must echo, however softly, that it slips away in every representation of its authority. No local truth can resound less dissonantly than another, and none can echo further from the mystery. Science's concealment expresses its own ways of unconcealment.

The theme of privilege echoes repulsion. It sounds among the oppositions that define truth and freedom, with the forms of restraint that define the ideality of human thought and being. Science lives among the limits that both contain it and repulse the others that threaten its hegemony. Yet such repulsions echo not only within science, but in every domain of representation: "Within its own limits, every discipline recognises true and false propositions, but it repulses a whole teratology of learning. . . . there are monsters on the prowl, however, whose forms alter with the history of knowledge."[55] The truth that every discipline inhabits has the task of repulsing dragons. Yet the monsters that threaten reason and intelligibility gnarl not of the errors that fall within the bounds of truth, not even at its boundaries, but without, with no outside. To follow scientific method offers no guarantees of truth, only places us in the true. Sovereignty is exercised over truth from within—but not only within. It stands at the limits of representation with the forms of order that circumscribe the walls that keep the dragons of untruth at bay. It stands as truth limiting itself by its untruth without knowing it as its truth.

Untruth echoes here at least twice: *within* the true, defined canonically, and *as* the true, defining the canon. This doubling sounds its locality. No line, no perimeter draws forth at which one may stop and say "here prowl monsters," "watch for the abyss." The monsters roar within and without, wherever privilege and intelligibility join.

Error echoes untruth, yet truth and error belong together. Error always falls within the castle, untruth at its walls. Like K., we cannot tell where the authority of each begins and ends, in an infinite cycle or regression. The name of this deferral sometimes echoes power, sometimes desire or representation. Truth names the disharmonies that resound within every thought or representation, exercising and exercised by power, exceeding itself as desire. Truth names itself within theory as truth, within desire and power as freedom, within history as fact, within embodiment as its materiality, within nature as its work.

These meet at the truth of the will to truth: "True discourse, liberated by the nature of its form from desire, and power, is incapable of recognising the will to truth which pervades it; and the will to truth, having imposed itself upon us for so long, is such that the truth it seeks to reveal cannot fail to mask it."[56] Truth lives under masks, denying its will and desire. The desire for truth reaches forth as desire for Truth where fulfillment echoes the exercise of power over the dragons at the gate. Oblivion to the walls and monsters outside it does not mark a True discourse, but regulates necessity in the freedoms that delimit it. The thought transpires of a truth that knows its own ideology, the will that defines and dislocates it, the masks that obscure its borders. The truth of the truth of power dislocates its authority. The authority of the will to truth displaces its truth. Power and truth belong together in the polyphonies of their disharmonies.

The thought that truth is ideology, unconcealment is concealment, openness is another mask, untruth is freedom, and truth is necessity echoes a multiply reflexive movement toward truth and reality. Otherness echoes in many ways, one as simulation, where reality sounds its unreality in the multiple reflexivity of representation, where truth divides itself. In these repetitions we face the masks that define the alterities of truth, another way to express the onlyness of truth.

The possibility unfolds that the truth present in doubled form in the true echoes the only truth there is, including its heterogeneities and antiphonies. In the true echoes within and without, the truth that falls within regulation and the truth that constitutes its borders. These truths emerge dislocated by their others, by untruths and misrepresentations, by power and desire with their multiple representations and reflexivities, by the deferrals of time and the doublings of sexuality. The truth within echoes as a truth of representation, including falsity and misrepresentation. Within the latter, truth joins simulation: the appearance of a truth that cannot be distinguished from its untruth.

> All things come to an end in their redoubled simulation—a sign that a cycle is completed. When the reality effect, like the useless day-after Messiah, starts uselessly duplicating the course of things, it is a sign that a cycle is ending in an interplay of simulacra where everything is replayed before death, at which point everything falls over far behind the horizon of truth.[57]

The intervention of simulacra into our experience as the only things whose truths we know represents the representativity of truth as death. Life and death echo the doubled moments within which representation passes into misrepresentation, truth into untruth, and their return. Simulation resounds where truth and representation join forces.[58] Along with truth as a standard, reality transpires as the touchstone that marks the privilege of repetition over misrepresentation within representation, where science exercises hegemony. "As long as you consider that there is a real world, then by the same token there is a possible position for theory. . . . In my opinion, theory is simply a challenge to the real."[59] Baudrillard inflates the hyper in the real, calling it simulation; Hegel exaggerates the absoluteness of the Absolute, calling it science. In both cases, in Simulation and the Notion, truth defines reality and collapses under it. Reality echoes at the limits of power as truth echoes at the limits of desire. In the doubling of these limits, truth and untruth echo each other, a simulation of simulation that fails to tell how it exceeds itself.[60]

The sacrifice of truth into falsity echoes simulation. The sacrifice of reality into unreality echoes hyperreality. Neither sounds rejection of truth and reality, but acknowledges the disharmonies that make reality reality and truth truth. In these reciprocities echo both the utmost seriousness of the human project and the laughter that divides it into its truth. "I think there is a destiny of theory. There is a curve we can't escape. You know that my way is to make ideas appear, but as soon as they appear I immediately try to make them disappear. That's what the game has always consisted of. Strictly speaking, nothing remains but a sense of dizziness, with which you can't do anything."[61]

To those outside the walls, the dizziness echoes irresponsibility. The question of truth resounds as one of high seriousness, among oppressed minorities and suppressed majorities, not of laughter at the seriousness of truth. Yet the tragic view of truth, along with power and desire, echoes its own locality and must be represented through its others. Without laughter we cannot begin to know the seriousness of truth. Here laughter repeats life and death: another function of nature's truth, inseparable from simulation.

SEVEN

History

History sings where representation and *praxis* call to each other in time, where representation echoes deferral and *praxis* materializes in embodied life and thought, where *praxis* unfolds as representation and representation echoes *praxis*, where time advances divided by past, present, and future. Along with *praxis* and representation, history includes every opposition resolved into unity and every unity fragmented in the working of time, including the displaced totalities of history's history and dislocations of every every. History echoes as one history and many histories, and even this doubling echoes one and many, unisons and resonances, stillnesses and polyphonies. History harmonizes the totality of totalities and disharmonizes every totality. It peals where *praxis* divides the unity of history and history divides the unity of *praxis*.

Questions of time and truth, along with past and future, echo their belonging together. They resound, in our sonorescence, as its reflection on itself. Named as a time in which history may be thought multiply reflexive, our sonorescence delimits a truth of history that circles back to dislocate itself in time. This timeliness resounds as history's truth, the truth of the truth that history tells repeatedly. Every truth echoes a particular story at a particular time; every story tells its truths and untruths to and for other times. The other times in any time compose history—others within its repetitions. Truth and untruth meet in history at the juncture of representation and *praxis*. The truth of history echoes *praxis*; the truth of *praxis* resounds as history, each deferred by the polyphonies of its untruths. The truth of truth echoes where history and *praxis* resonate together polyphonically, where the stories told of *praxis* diverge within the repetitions that define historical understanding and where desire and power delimit each other.

The stories of history can be told in many ways. Each tells another history, and there can be heard no Total History that delimits the plurality or regulates it except within another history. History's repetitions echo the locality of any story within history even as a totality of which many stories are told. These doublings of locality and totality find their others in this many despite the historical truth that history repudiates dividedness and that the History of which we speak is largely Western.

Hegel echoes history's onlyness, each moment only that moment, awaiting its future for fulfillment. "Of the Absolute it must be said that it is essentially a result, that only at the end is it what it is in every truth; and just in that consists its nature, which is to be actual, subject, or self-becoming, self-development."[1] Hegel echoes history's loneliness, each moment sacrificing itself into its future. "Knowledge is aware not only of itself, but also of the negative of itself, or its limit. Knowing its limit means knowing how to sacrifice itself."[2] And Hegel echoes history's "ownliness": "It thus discovers this world in the living present to be its own property; and so has taken the first step to descend from the ideal intelligible world, or rather to quicken the abstract element of the intelligible world with concrete self-hood."[3]

Shall we hear in Hegel's truth of truth in the Absolute Idea that it be absolutely certain that history is one? "[The Idea] is the certitude of the virtual identity between itself and the objective world.—Reason comes to the world with an absolute faith in its ability to make the identity actual, and to raise its certitude to truth."[4] Or shall we hear this certitude as a moment in which history's self-unity dissolves, broken into pieces, a moment where truth gives up the certitude of certitude as its criterion? Is the totality of history's truth broken apart by its multiple circularities so that it confronts with absolute certitude the untruths of its onlyness? "Logic shows that the subjective which is to be subjective only, the finite which would be finite only, the infinite which would be infinite only, and so on, have no truth, but contradict themselves and pass into their opposites."[5] And so on. The onlys go on forever, as every unity, every resolution, only becomes another only, where the Absolute is only absolute. "As the idea is (*a*) a process, it follows that such an expression for the Absolute as *unity* of thought and being, of finite and infinite, &c. is false; for unity expresses an abstract and merely quiescent identity."[6]

History tells unending telling—story after story after story, representation after representation after representation—representing the onlyness, loneliness, and ownliness of events in time, consequently of itself. This triad echoes locality and inexhaustibility in time, in *praxis*, resonates between stillness and polyphony, harmony and disharmony. Here truth falls into history. Yet while every fulfillment of history realizes only some fulfillment and not others, every such fulfillment yearns for and belongs to others. Every truth echoes only a particular truth and not other truths, but every truth echoes elsewhere. Even the whole echoes as only the whole, beyond itself. The totality emerges as more than any totality, more than itself, history's loneliness. Truth unfolds in history as an only repeatedly belied by history's ownliness while exceeded by its loneliness. History echoes the fragmentation of every certainty and the harmonization of every disharmony, the unity in every plurality and the pluralization of every unity. History's onlyness echoes Hegel's totality with its differences, except that even absolute totality is only Absolute and only Totality. And even this Absolute Totality is only Our Totality, only male and only Western (still longing for Its Others).

The representativity of history echoes representation: the turning back of representation upon itself in the fragmentation of every continuous story and the continuity across every break, the limitation of every story and the limitation of those limitations. Every representation, every break, every harmony, every disharmony, every representation of representation, every reflexivity, every every, belongs to history, where every disharmony harmonizes and every harmony is displaced. History echoes the totality of what has no totality, a polyphony that contains all dissonances within itself as another only, including the dissonances of onlyness. History's aporias echo that every every rings as both only and a totality.

Every history belongs to history as every representation belongs to representation, in both cases, departing. The stories history contains displace it while they constitute its truths. The turning of history into itself through representation and *praxis* reflects their multiply circular reflexivities. Every representation represents itself in its representations of another; every action delimits action. This multiple reflexivity constitutes the deferrals of representation and *praxis*. Similarly, history both never and always tells the story of the world: there rings forth no such story and no such world while the movement of representation against its limits opens the limits of those limits within the totality of history, itself countermanded by history.

The terrible thing about history is not its pastness but the inescapability of its presence. That is why we struggle over history, over whose story will triumph—men's or women's, colored or white, rich or poor, mine or yours—even within the repudiation of struggle. This agonistic presence of the past within every present haunts us as history. Yet remembrance alone does not define the monstrosity of the past within the present, neglecting the monstrosity of the future. This monstrosity emerges from the repetitions of repetition, the multiple stories of many pasts, presents, and futures that join in history displaced by the restlessness of time. This restlessness imposes itself on us as both memory and praxis, past and future. The practicality of history echoes its terror and its promise.

The truth of history sings the truth of truth, inseparable from the truth of nature and the nature of truth. It resounds in many ways, as the many stories that compose history and as the many judgments that compose semasis. The truth of history resounds inseparable from the representation of representation, from *ergon* and *technē*. In a given place, we can tell only a particular story of history and its truth. That story, here, recounts its lownlyness, divided into three: onlyness, loneliness, and ownliness. This triangle chimes our modern history as torn asunder by power, desire, and representation, by others within and without. The lownlyness of history echoes its locality and inexhaustibility, shattered along lines of stress defined by *praxis* and *technē*. The lownlyness of history echoes its practicality, dislocated at points of representation and embodiment by desire and power.

The onlyness of history sounds the locality of *praxis* where history and nature echo neither History nor Nature. This repudiation of the totalities that constitute the metaphysical tradition's ontotheology—but not the truth of its aporias—echoes in Hegel and Heidegger no less than in Derrida and Foucault. The Absoluteness of the Totality, in Hegel, echoes a movement toward its locality: the onlyness of the totality. We hear in this circling movement, however obscurely, both inexhaustibility and aporia. The thought of totality resists totalization. The thought of history resists the Totality of History.

Hegel's System, a circle of circles, each containing the Idea, seems to demand a System of History and a History of the System. Yet his surpassing genius—but not his Genius—is to acknowledge the inseparability of totality and fragmentation: the totality and fragmentation of totality and fragmentation—"the ground, besides being the unity, is also the difference of identity and difference."[7] Hegel's truth flashes multiple reflexivity within the circling play of representation's representation.

In our sonorescence, we do not echo difference only in relation to identity, fragmentation and dispersal only in the shadow of the totality. Nor do we sound Difference only in relation to Being: harmony and disharmony resonate incessantly and reciprocally. They belong together in their departures, and their belonging together belongs together and departs. The onlyness of truth echoes within the inexhaustibility of history as many histories that have no History, many stories that tell no living Practice, as the many stories belong together in their departures from each other. History here represents neither the Totality of History nor an opposition of History and histories but deferral of every such opposition. We write the opposition to repudiate it, thereby reinstating it. Similarly, Being represents not an origin, but the recession of any origin including the recession of every recession, where the "of" pertains to the multiple reflexivities of representation and recession. We may be tempted to add "in its full radicality." *Being is the recession of the origin in its "full" radicality.* Yet the radicality repudiates the totality of its fullness, intimates onlyness. The radicality echoes the irresistibility of the only: history's lownlyness, the lownlyness of truth and goodness, the polyphonies haunting every stillness.

The truth of truth echoes its onlyness: the locality of its locality. The truth of history echoes its onlyness: partiality, incompleteness, the unending disharmonies that compose repetition's repetition. In each case, parts imply a whole, incompleteness suggests completeness, difference yearns for identity, as disharmony dislocates and is dislocated by harmony. History resonates as representation and its representation, also *praxis* and its *praxis*: onlyness recognizing its onlyness and consequent loneliness. History resounds where this play of onlyness stretches toward its limits, toward locality's locality. Here we reach one of Hegel's limits, where Spirit's Absoluteness takes precedence over onlyness. The onlyness of history lies within the movement from representation to truth, nature to *praxis*, truth to justice. The onlyness of truth echoes its injustice—except that no other justice can be heard. Justice resounds as the inexhaustible deferral of injustice, unending sacrifices and retributions.

The onlyness of truth echoes every untruth, where every every suffers onlyness. The onlyness of history echoes the locality of every story, the sacrifices that compose any history. No one expresses the importance of sacrifice in history more profoundly than Hegel:

> Knowledge is aware not only of itself, but also of the negative of itself, or its limit. Knowing its limit means knowing how to sacrifice itself. This sacrifice is the self-abandonment, in which Spirit sets forth, in the form of free fortuitous happening, its process of becoming Spirit, intuitively apprehending outside it its pure self as Time, and likewise its existence as Space. This last form into which Spirit passes, *Nature*, is its living immediate process of development.[8]

The sacrifice is infinite: utter self-abandonment. Within its play no room remains for waste. That is the terrible truth of the couplet that resounds in Hegel's later writings:

> What is reasonable is actual;
> and, What is actual is reasonable.[9]

If onlyness resonates here, it whispers absolutely. No space is heard for lowlyness while the absence of such a space tolls the greatest loneliness of all. Hegel's Spirit possesses lownlyness without waste, without the loneliness of injustice. That is why it comes on the scene always too late. There lies, in its unending procrastinations, infinite sacrifice into waste without knowing anything of the injustices of waste.

The difference between sacrifice and waste echoes the difference that marks lownlyness, where injustice is absolutely unavoidable although absolutely intolerable. Spirit must sacrifice itself freely into Nature to be Spirit. It is therefore not profoundly threatened by the injustice of its sacrifices, however terrible they may be. This theme of sacrifice without catastrophe is inseparable from several others essential to the Absoluteness of the Absolute:

> The thing is nothing in itself; it only has significance in relation, only through the ego and its reference to the ego. . . . The trained and cultivated self-consciousness . . . retains itself, therefore still in the thing, and knows the thing to have no independence, in other words knows that the thing has essentially and solely a relative existence.[10]

> It thus discovers this world in the living present to be its own property; . . .[11]

An unmistakable if countermanded theme here echoes Spirit's sovereignty. It may be heard as absence of waste in the infinity of sacrifice, sacrifice without charity, where charity expresses what belongs to things against the injustices of others, what demands restitution. Charity echoes lownlyness. It threatens every lawful *praxis* inexhaustibly, providing its inexhaustible fulfillment as history.

For this reason, *praxis* relates repeatedly to its past in the form of retribution, where retribution echoes deferral's deferral, refusing every authority including its own, especially History's Authority, under Western Law. "As long as words of difference serve to legitimate a discourse instead of delaying its authority to infinity, they are, to borrow an image from Audre Lorde, 'noteworthy only as *decorations*.' "[12] The form of history's deferral is retribution; the form of History is Restitution. Disharmonies and polyphonies resonate as the waste of history, imposing retribution.

The rhythms of history reverberate as flow and obstruction, tempo and rest. The timbres of history echo the unfolding of human life in the murmuring of the only, where either all makes sense or none does—or something in between, in onlyness. This in between resonates as the story of history, its truth. Its unfolding resounds as the onlyness of history and time: every present only its time and not any other; every present other times, however differently. The truth of truth echoes the history of history, each displaced by the other. History, like representation, reverberates as the Onlyness of the Same—lonely without its others. History, like representation, echoes the truth of truth as the history of history. This circular movement sounds the dislocations of transgression.

The terror of the onlyness of history threatens as an inescapable present, not as past. Yet the form of its presence appears as both the influence of the past upon the present and that it is only past—that is, nothing—without present and future. Every history echoes as only one time's history, nothing without it, yet every history belongs to many futures. Every present awaits unending futures for its truths. The truth of history's truth sounds in its unending presents as each present's truth echoes its unending histories.

For this reason, *praxis* relates to its past in the form of retribution, where retribution echoes deferral's deferral, refusal of even its authority. The loneliness of history dwells at the point where the onlyness of its truth passes into *praxis*, where the future looms over every present as entirely anticipated and monstrous deceit, both representations of its representativity. History echoes its loneliness as only only, in relation to *praxis*, faced with catastrophes exceeding any story that can be told, including the story of catastrophes. Every story that composes history must destroy the concord that defines it as history, some part of its totality. The destruction is the loneliness of history's truth. Only the ownliness of history permits us to experience the loneliness of this only, the monstrosity of locality.

The onlyness of history echoes its locality. The loneliness of history echoes its inexhaustibility, both belonging to time as semasis. We have heard in history and truth the sound of another triad that repeats and displaces our other triads: locality, inexhaustibility, and ergonality; power, desire, and representation; now onlyness, loneliness, and ownliness. The question unfolds how this triad belongs with our others. In our sonorescence, history presents itself as a major site where these triads meet.

Onlyness expresses locality: to belong to only a particular moment of history while every moment belongs to others, yet differently to each, effectively to none; to belong to only a particular locale while always belonging to other locales, but never to All. Onlyness expresses locality in the reverberations of unisons, stillnesses, and harmonies, obliquely echoing the limits of their limits in resonances, polyphonies, and disharmonies. Here history's onlyness posits totality though totality conflicts with onlyness, echoing inexhaustibility. Abandoning the totality manifests the loneliness in history's onlyness as inexhaustibility. No story of history can be told without a repeated only—and, similarly, no truth echoes free from onlyness. No story can be told of history that does not sound a lonely story, craving resolution into a totality that resounds as only a totality and, consequently, that faces the inexhaustibility of its inexhaustibility: the promise and threat of always more, the polyphonies of every story.

This terrible threat echoes unending promise and deferral. Both reverberate within history as the future with its future: inexhaustible promise of the demise of present struggles and terrible threat of the unknown together with disruption of every past. The representativity of history constitutes the onlyness and loneliness of time, each moment crying out for its past and future, each seeking its lost and future times, each torn apart by repetition.

Faced inescapably with the future and loss of the past, with sacrifice and waste, history sings recurrent refrains of onlyness, surrounded by loneliness. This loneliness neither contrasts with an awe-inspiring infinite nor tolls gloomy melancholy at its disappearance, but presents finiteness as finite, local and inexhaustible, discordantly present in each moment. Loneliness echoes inexhaustibility, both unending promise of more, irresistible whisperings of onlyness, and inescapable nostalgia for a past whose onlyness dissolves into inexhaustibly many futures, each transforming every past into its past.

The onlyness, but not the terrible loneliness, of history finds expression in Gadamer, where loneliness passes into universality:

> However much it is the nature of tradition to exist only through being appropriated, it still is part of the nature of man to be able to break with tradition, to criticise and dissolve it, and is not what takes place in the work of remaking the real into an

instrument of human purpose something far more basic in our relationship to being? To this extent, does not the ontological universality of understanding result in a certain one-sidedness?[13]

The historical movement of human life consists in the fact that it is never utterly bound to any one standpoint, and hence can never have a truly closed horizon. The horizon is, rather, something into which we move and that moves with us.[14]

The openness of every horizon to other horizons manifests the onlyness within which it finds itself: always one standpoint among the others; only one horizon open to others. But the movement that composes our historicality and its representations echoes not only openness to others, but sacrifice and loss. Each horizon loses itself as it opens to others, loses its truth. Its loneliness materializes as the sacrificial movement of its togetherness with others. It appears lonely among them in its loss. Catastrophe echoes cacophonically in the polyphonies of time.

The malleability and permeability of tradition make it lonely, for it cannot share itself with others without losing itself, cannot belong to a community and still belong to itself, cannot belong to itself except through a community, cannot fall into time without a past and future, before and after, each a difference within it, each imposing loneliness upon it. The gathering and belonging in Heidegger of truth and being in the Open are only and ownly; they are not so clearly lonely, not so clearly shattered by their appropriation. The rejection of loneliness in Gadamer echoes through universality, in Heidegger through nostalgia: the omnipresent near within what is far. Nostalgia echoes a hope directed toward a past that would overcome the terrible loneliness of loss. The same hope directed toward the future dreams of loss as sacrifice but not waste—not only sacrifice.

The idea of tradition—Gadamer calls it "effective-historical consciousness"—echoes onlyness without loneliness, without cacophony: "Historical consciousness in seeking to understand tradition must not rely on the critical method with which it approaches its sources, as if this preserved it from mixing in its own judgments and prejudices. It must, in fact, take account of its own historicality. To stand within a tradition does not limit the freedom of knowledge but makes it possible."[15] It limits knowledge and makes it possible, or makes it possible by limiting it. But limitation echoes not only polyphonies of freedom but devastating losses. In the loneliness of effective history, the form of its thinking denies the terrible nature of its losses. It replaces loneliness by nostalgia. It finds another way to be oblivious to the catastrophes of waste.

Loneliness echoes where time meets repetition, and repetition transpires as the home of loneliness. Yet loneliness does not belong to difference only within the same but departs, even from itself. Facing itself, repetition dwells in loneliness, the impossibility yet inescapability of repetition amid the displacements of its repetitions. Repetition echoes loneliness. Dislocation echoes onlyness, both in time. Waste and catastrophe belong to history and its temporality.

In Dewey:

> Individuality conceived as a temporal development involves uncertainty, inde-
> terminacy, or contingency. Individuality is the source of whatever is unpredictable
> in the world.[16]

> To say this is not arbitrarily to introduce mere chance into the world. It is to say that
> genuine individuality exists; that individuality is pregnant with new developments;
> that time is real.[17]

> The mystery of time is thus the mystery of the existence of real individuals. It is
> a mystery because it is a mystery that anything which exists is just what it is.[18]

The "uncertainty, indeterminacy, or contingency" of time constitute its onlyness
and loneliness. The individuality of individuality constitutes its ownliness. The
mystery of time echoes its temporality, where onlyness, loneliness, and ownliness sound in unison as lownlyness. Unnamed here is waste, the catastrophic
truth of contingencies in time.

It rings in the discontinuities that plague Foucault's sense of history.

> I have been careful to accept as valid none of the unities that would normally present
> themselves to anyone embarking on such a task. I have decided to ignore no form of
> discontinuity, break, threshold, or limit.[19]

> Discourse must be treated as a discontinuous activity, in different manifestations
> sometimes coming together, but just as easily unaware of, or excluding each
> other.[20]

This discontinuity marks what Foucault calls the "positivities" of discourse,[21]
defining the onlyness and loneliness of history. "Thus conceived, discourse is not
the majestically unfolding manifestation of a thinking, knowing, speaking subject, but, on the contrary, a totality, in which the dispersion of the subject and his
discontinuity with himself may be determined. It is a space of exteriority in which
a network of distinct sites is deployed."[22]

Foucault cannot avoid replacing one set of unities by another: sheer discontinuity, like sheer difference, resides at the limits of intelligibility.

> I set out with a relatively simple problem: the division of discourse into great unities
> that were not those of *oeuvres*, authors, books, or themes.[23]

> But, in fact, was I not all the time in that very space that has long been known as
> "the history of ideas"?[24]

The answer is "of course." For the history of ideas sounds as one of the forms of
history that, amid its yearning for the All, finds itself lonely in its inexhaustibility. The onlyness of the history of ideas echoes totality and nothing. In the spaces
opened up between these regions lies the loneliness of history.

Foucault's answer is that his account is provisional, on the side of onlyness.

> I have sketched a genealogical history of the origins of a theory and a knowledge of anomaly and of the various techniques that relate to it. None of it does more than mark time. Repetitive and disconnected, it advances nowhere. Since indeed it never ceases to say the same thing, it perhaps says nothing. It is tangled up into an indecipherable, disorganised muddle. In a nutshell, it is inconclusive.[25]

This inconclusiveness—this nothing—unfolds as the onlyness of history. "So, the main point to be gleaned from these events of the past fifteen years, their predominant feature, is the *local* character of criticism."[26] And history. Criticism and history, and the criticism of history and the history of criticism, all transpire as local: only local, positing a local totality; the onlyness of their locality, echoing polyphony.

Foucault adds to this onlyness the loneliness of history and truth, characteristic of the retributions of *praxis*: "it also seems to me that over and above, and arising out of this thematic, there is something else to which we are witness, and which we might describe as an *insurrection of subjugated knowledges*."[27] The sacrifices of knowledge and truth in history compose its onlyness; the insurrection calls out its loneliness, either from the Totality of Truth, Knowledge, and History within which no story gets lost, devoid of waste, or from within the inexhaustibility of truth and history that displace every sacrifice with questions of waste and retribution, the onlyness of onlyness, leading to genealogy:

> In a sense, only a single drama is ever staged in this "nonplace," the endlessly repeated play of dominations.
>
> Humanity does not gradually progress from combat to combat until it arrives at universal reciprocity, where the rule of law finally replaces warfare; humanity installs each of its violences in a system of rules and thus proceeds from domination to domination.[28]

This play of domination upon domination manifests the loneliness of history's *praxis*, caught up in the dream, but not the possibility, of resolution and universality, in the "always more" that belongs within the inexhaustibility of violence and domination. Here loneliness resounds as anything but onlyness: violence and domination but also violence against violence and the domination of domination. "The nature of these rules allows violence to be inflicted on violence and the resurgence of new forces that are sufficiently strong to dominate those in power."[29] Loneliness echoes the yearning within the locality of history, not for a Totality of Meaning, but for meaning nevertheless; for a reciprocity of *praxis* and representation even when a result of the domination of violence and the violence of domination. The loneliness of violence and domination echoes within every future as its retribution toward the past.

Foucault tells of the lownlyness of history in the wonderful passage summarizing the archive:

In this sense, the diagnosis does not establish the fact of our identity by the play of distinctions. It establishes that we are difference, that our reason is the difference of discourses, our history the difference of times, our selves the difference of masks. That difference, far from being the forgotten and recovered origin, is this dispersion that we are and make.[30]

This characterizes us, fallen into history, our identities local and dispersed. Ownliness echoes one-liness and excess: the fragmentations and dispersions of unisons and their resonances. Identity echoes difference and difference in difference: disharmonies in times, places, and representations, deferrals and their deferrals. Nature echoes locality and its locality. In history, these compose lownlyness, our selves in history polyphonic masks of stillness. Returning to Dewey:

> The contingency of all into which time enters is the source of pathos, comedy, and tragedy. Genuine time, if it exists as anything else except the measure of motions in space, is all one with the existence of individuals as individuals, with the creative, with the occurrence of unpredictable novelties. Everything that can be said contrary to this conclusion is but a reminder that an individual may lose his individuality, for individuals become imprisoned in routine and fall to the level of mechanisms.[31]

That human identity disperses as differences in representation, time, and place gives us the onlyness of history in its representations of other times and places and the loneliness of history in the excesses of its onlyness. That this identity pertains to history as well as human beings gives us the ownliness of history. Ownliness reverberates as the play of disharmony within the onlyness and loneliness of history and *praxis*. It echoes where every locus falls into history's onlyness and exceeds it in virtue of the loneliness of time. Ownliness resounds as the play of harmony and disharmony, the belonging of a locus to itself, thereby departing. Within history, it resounds as multiple deferral, local displacement.

There resounds no totality of beings and no essence of being. There echoes no unity of the world, only the unison of some locale. There resounds only nature dislocated, represented in the stillness of local representations, including their own dislocations and polyphonies. This deferral of locality echoes as its *ergon*. To be is to work somewhere. In history and *praxis*, this *ergon* appears as ownliness. Every locus echoes itself, possesses an identity, but every identity reverberates as only and lonely, yearns for others and exceeds itself. In the yearning for Totality there echoes only locality, including its locality, yet locality exceeds totality as inexhaustibility. The play of onlyness and loneliness as they compose some-thing-local-in-time echoes nature's *ergon* as history's ownliness. The play of onlyness and loneliness as they compose the sacrifices of praxis echoes the ownliness of history. We belong to history and depart from it in the multiple ways that constitute ownliness.

Ownliness reverberates in another silence behind its loneliness. We have heard it in the thought within philosophy of its other, the "its" a gesture within onlyness toward ownliness:

> Philosophy has always insisted upon this: thinking its other. Its other: that which limits it, and from which it derives its essence, its definition, its production.[32]

> *To insist* upon thinking *its other*: its proper other, the proper of its other, an other proper? In thinking it as such, in recognizing it, one misses it. One reappropriates it for oneself, one disposes of it, one misses it, or rather one misses (the) missing (of) it, which, as concerns the other, always amounts to the same. Between the proper of the other and the other of the proper.[33]

The proper themes here within ownliness are otherness and propriety. One appears as one's own in relation to the others that define one, others that also appear as one's own. Ownliness echoes propriety on the side of what belongs and what departs, as propriety falls within the rules of Same and Law.

May we hear in the properness of ownliness gestures against propriety, or do such gestures collapse back into repetition and regulation? Ownliness echoes as a figure that falls from onlyness and loneliness into otherness—as Derrida suggests, into proper otherness. The theme of mastery and control masks the rule of property over otherness: one's own other, what belongs properly to oneself. What may properly be heard within ownliness—therefore within onlyness and loneliness, though we may have missed it until now—gestures repulsively toward exclusion, toward what does not belong. Every propriety, every rule, every regulation, every law, gestures toward repetition and exclusion. This exclusion, toward oneself, within ownliness, repeats history's catastrophes. This repulsion gestures toward stillness without polyphony.

The ownliness of truth sounds the regulation of its untruths and disruption of every regulation. There resounds no Other that imposes a great Departure, but disharmony within every harmony, loneliness within every mastery. Yet the converses are also true: mastery within every disharmony. Our sonorescence questions the way in which the belonging of things to themselves exceeds every belonging. This echoes ownliness, where propriety echoes harmony and disharmony.

Derrida's figure of *le propre* is of the writing machine:

> I am asking in terms of the *manual printing press* the question of the writing machine which is to upset the entire space of the proper body in the unlimited enmeshing of machines-of-machines, hence of machines without hands.[34]

> In terms of the manual printing press, then, there is not one tympan but several.[35]

> It may be about this multiplicity that philosophy, being situated, inscribed, and included within it, has never been able to reason.[36]

The ownliness of history echoes this machine-that-writes its stories upon and by bodies. The figure of ownliness portrays the loneliness of every representation, the excesses it hopes to make its own.

The onlyness and loneliness of history constitute its ownliness, what is proper to it in a gesture that always exceeds its own propriety, whether that of property or rule, even the thought of difference. History gestures toward every every while only toward only. That such a gesture reveals the locality of locality amid its excesses tolls lownlyness.

The triad of onlyness, loneliness, and ownliness rings in Nietzsche in the form of memory, profoundly emphasizing loneliness—a loneliness shared with animals, however romantically, against their repeated sacrifice:

> the animal lives *unhistorically*: for it goes into the present like a number without leaving a curious fraction; it does not know how to dissimulate, hides nothing, appears at every moment fully as what it is and so cannot but be honest. Man on the other hand resists the great and ever greater weight of the past: this oppresses him and bends him sideways, it encumbers his gait like an invisible and sinister burden. And when death finally brings longed-for forgetfulness it also robs him of the present and of existence and impresses its seal on this knowledge that existence is only an uninterrupted having-been, a thing which lives by denying itself, consuming itself, and contradicting itself.[37]

The loneliness forcefully appears in the dissimulation and imperfect tense, the requirements of *praxis* within an already-having-been story. Here loneliness receives its fulfillment in forgetfulness more than remembrance—forgetfulness as the proper other of remembrance. More truly, history's fulfillment tolls of death. "With the smallest as with the greatest happiness, however, there is always one thing which makes it happiness: being able to forget or, to express it in a more learned fashion, the capacity to live *unhistorically* while it endures" (OADHL, p. 9)

Nietzsche equates forgetfulness with living unhistorically where this may be heard not as loss but as oblivion, a requisite of the possibility of life and action, still culling animals for the sacrifice. "All acting requires forgetting, as not only light but also darkness is required for life by all organisms. A man who wanted to feel everything historically would resemble someone forced to refrain from sleeping, or an animal expected to live only from ruminating and ever repeated ruminating" (OADHL, p. 10) He thinks of living historically as living in memory, speaking of the joys and perils of forgetting. We reply that history is lonely, that living in memory echoes different pasts and different futures. Rising above history is collapsing into nothing. That is history's loneliness.

> The stronger the roots of the inmost nature of a man are, the more of the past will he appropriate or master; and were one to conceive the most powerful and colossal nature, it would be known by this, that for it there would be no limit at which the historical sense could overgrow and harm it; such a nature would draw its own as well as every alien past wholly into itself and transform it into blood, as it were. What such a nature cannot master it knows how to forget . . . (OADHL, p. 10)

This capacity of *praxis* to overpower the afflictions of memory does not demand forgetfulness so much as lownlyness. Nietzsche affirms affirmation against the negativities of history. Yet the loneliness of history imposes a kind of armor against which the onlyness of history falls short. "And this is a general law: every living thing can become healthy, strong and fruitful only within a horizon; if it is incapable of drawing a horizon around itself or, on the other hand, too selfish to restrict its vision to the limits of a horizon drawn by another, it will wither away feebly or overhastily to its early demise" (OADHL, p. 10) This limited horizon appears as the place at which *praxis* demands locality for its effectiveness and where history confronts its ownliness with its onlyness and loneliness. The overcoming of memory that *praxis* demands issues in the lownlyness that composes historical being. "As the man of action, according to Goethe's phrase, is always without conscience, so he is also without knowledge; he forgets a great deal to do one thing, he is unjust to what lies behind him and knows only one right, the right of that which is to become" (OADHL, pp. 11–12). Becoming is history's inescapable reality—its ownliness. In the play of memory and forgetting that constitutes history's loneliness, Nietzsche affirms the inescapability of history. This recognition, of history's necessity, therefore its ownliness, passes into superhistory.

> If someone could, in numerous instances, discern and breathe again the unhistorical atmosphere in which every great historical event came to be, then such a one might, as a cognitive being, perhaps elevate himself to a *superhistorical* standpoint. . . . One could call such a standpoint superhistorical, because one who has adopted it could no longer be tempted at all to continue to live and cooperate in making history, since he would have understood that blindness and injustice in the soul of each agent as the condition of all activity; he would even be cured henceforth of taking history excessively seriously . . . (OADHL, p. 12)

Within Nietzsche's dream of the superhistorical we confront past and future together. The vision of improvement unifies history, obscuring its loneliness. Loneliness in Nietzsche is not the absence of history nor of the historical, but affirmation of history itself: its ownliness. Freedom in *praxis* marks escape from the shackles of the past. Yet such a freedom is found only within history. The superhistorical sense echoes loneliness.

> Superhistorical men have never agreed whether the significance of the teaching is happiness or resignation, virtue or penance; but, opposed to all historical ways of viewing the past, they are quite unanimous in accepting the following proposition: the past and the present is one and the same, that is, typically alike in all manifold variety and, as omnipresence of imperishable types, a static structure of unchanged value and eternally the same meaning. (OADHL, p. 13)

The loneliness of history demands a certain strength against the monsters that history holds at bay. We cannot avoid thinking of history as a terrain that includes itself although that thought exceeds itself. *"Only from the standpoint of the highest strength of the present may you interpret the past:* only in the highest exertion of your noblest qualities will you discern what is worthy of being known and preserved, what is great in the past" (OADHL, p. 37). Here history overcomes its loneliness by surpassing its limits, still in the form of privilege and exclusion: "only in the highest." The excesses fall into and outside history. The play of limit and other defines mastery and control. Such control transforms the future. In this play toward a future that repudiates its relationship to the past within the necessity of such a relation, we are brought to insurrection. The ownliness of history unfolds the truth that the only attitude we can take toward the past is that of retribution.

> The historical sense, if it rules *without restraint* and unfolds all its implications, uproots the future because it destroys illusions and robs existing things of their atmosphere in which alone they can live. Historical justice, even when it is practised truly and with pure intentions, is a terrible virtue because it always undermines the living and brings it to ruin; its judging is always annihilating. (OADHL, p. 38)

Benjamin speaks directly to Nietzsche's forgetfulness: "To articulate the past historically does not mean to recognize it 'the way it really was.' It means to seize hold of a memory as it flashes up at a moment of danger."[38] He adds to superhistory's retribution the theme of redemption: "The Messiah comes not only as the redeemer, he comes as the subduer of Antichrist. Only that historian will have the gift of fanning the spark of hope in the past who is firmly convinced that *even the dead* will not be same for the enemy if he wins. And this enemy has not ceased to be victorious."[39] Retribution and redemption materialize as the forms of *praxis* that history imposes. The ownliness of history echoes history's resistance, not by denying its future but by denying its denial.

Nietzsche rejects the representativity of history, imposing upon it the privilege of *praxis*. "Now, is life to rule over knowledge, over science, or is knowledge to rule over life? Which of these two authorities is the higher and decisive one? No one will doubt: life is the higher, the ruling authority, for any knowledge which destroys life would also have destroyed itself" (OADHL, p. 62). He repeats privilege despite his superforgetfulness:

> This is a parable for each one of us; he must organize the chaos within himself by reflecting on his genuine needs. His honest, his sound and truthful character must at some time reel against secondhand thought, secondhand learning and imitation; then he will begin to comprehend that culture can be something other still than *decoration of life*, that is fundamentally always only dissimulation and disguise; for all adornment hides what it adopts. (OADHL, p. 64)

History must pass from truth into simulation to mark the movement of its loneliness. Simulation marks the revenge of history on the untruthfulness of its truth.

The ownliness of history materializes in the giddiness of history's representations. "We can't avoid going a long way with negativity, with nihilism and all. But then don't you think a more exciting world opens up? Not a more reassuring world, but certainly more thrilling, a world where the name of the game remains secret. A world ruled by reversibility and indetermination."[40] This giddiness sounds our retribution upon the past, where redemption echoes simulation. Here ownliness dissolves into loneliness.

The difficulty we may have with Nietzsche's forgetfulness within the memory that composes history is that it is neither oblivion nor memory. History engulfs the traces that defy oblivion, the movements that speak against equating it with memory. History speaks against every privilege, even its own—the echo of its lownlyness.

The difficulty with forgetfulness may be described differently: the play of onlyness, loneliness, and ownliness within their lownlyness. Each dislocates itself against the others, casting itself into its own shadows, coiling itself within and against the others. This play of onlyness, loneliness, and ownliness is lownlyness: an itself that belongs to all the others in their departures.

Here onlyness echoes only onlyness: doubled itself. As such a double, it makes loneliness more lonely, opening it to include and displace itself. Onlyness sounds only onlyness; loneliness sounds lonely; ownliness sounds as this itself, each itself and the others. Each, then, turns back on and away from itself and the others. Here onlyness questions totality and itself. Similarly, the loneliness of loneliness turns away from itself to the others. Finally, what is proper itself within ownliness presents itself as resistance—other to and as itself.

Each of these echoes as and resists itself. This reciprocal movement sounds the ownliness of ownliness. The propriety of one's own divides it into itself and its limits. The play of resistance pertains to history. The resistance of resistance to itself resounds as *praxis*.

Here, then, history meets *praxis* in the resistances of ownliness in the lonely play of onlyness. The truth of local truth divides wherever it sounds its inexhaustibility. One of these divisions echoes history and *praxis*, their onlyness, loneliness, and ownliness. Another division echoes bodily movements. The play of onlyness becomes the dance of earthliness, where bodies fall upon the earth and rise.

The onlyness, loneliness, and ownliness in history lead from lost time to lost bodies, where truth and desire join forces in their displacements. Here the resistances of each to itself as well as the others echo the play of history's others, especially in the forms of sacrifice and loss. The sacrifice of embodiment to its others extrudes as a supreme representation of loneliness. In this sense, we are always, in history and in every representation, lonely in the flesh. The play of incarnation and loneliness emerges as the reaffirmation of lownlyness in the form of the proper body and its inscription in the form of desire.

EIGHT

Embodiment

The frame protrudes from and within a painting as the materiality of its representations, the matter of and in the painting—or any other representation—that marks, that represents, its representativity: the matter extruded within the representation of its representation. "Along with stone, better than stone, wood names matter (*hylē* means wood). These questions of wood, of matter, of the frame, of the limit between inside and outside, must, somewhere in the margins, be constituted together."[1] The painting's frame—its materiality—protrudes as the limit of its representation, in the truth of its truth. To what, we may ask, shall such a truth be restored, and in what act of restitution? Do we find the truth in painting in its matter, or does the truth of its truth weigh upon us as a matter of its excessive materiality?

—Why always say of painting that it renders, that it restitutes?

—to discharge a more or less ghostly debt, . . .; *outside* the picture, inside the *picture*, and, third, as a picture, or to put it very equivocally, *in their painting truth* . . .[2]

Matter extrudes in the frame of the picture, within which irrupts its truth, a truth whose restitution—perhaps among countless other restitutions—conveys us to the matter that composes, frames it. The truth of the truth of truth protrudes in virtue of a frame, its materiality. Yet the work of the frame stands on the invisibility of the matter with which it obtrudes. The truth of truth sings in the silent voice of its materiality. Analogously, our embodiment, already represented, surges forth within its representations as our frame, our materiality, looming within us inseparable from its immateriality as truth echoes its inseparability from untruth: the immateriality of the limit of the truth of our body's frame.

"The–Human–Body"—each word framed and frame—obtrudes as inseparably body and its representations, flesh and excess. At once any body and unique, different from other bodies in how it is inhabited and represented, we dwell within it—it has been said—pervasively and fully. The seat of our humanity, individual and collective, it weighs upon us tempered by the silent truths that animals and plants, even rocks and machines, also have or are bodies and inhabit them fully, that no Seat-of-Humanity touches us, no human essence and no (one) human body with its essence, not even many bodies with their essences. Our body weighs down upon and unfolds within us as the transgressive materiality of the immateriality of our frame.

That human and animal bodies, even trunks and branches of a tree, wires and junctions of a machine, crystals and stones, are inhabited fully gestures toward excess rather than completeness. Whatever pertains to a creature pertains to its body, to its representations and their embodiments, where that body both frames that creature and is framed by it. This insight defines *entelechy*, the excessive plenitude of an inhabited body.

To the excesses of embodiment that define its plenitude, we add the regimentations of embodiment that define its materiality.[3] A truth of power[4] echoes the extrusion of materiality as a site of regulation and excess, power and resistance, among the most transgressive of such sites. Embodiment touches us where power works and where truth is written: by means of and upon The Body.

Kafka's crushing truth represents the representation of truth upon the body in the language of the Law, in words of guilt and blame, expressing the materiality of the *logos*. Guilt and blame weigh upon us as written on the body. The frailty and powers of embodiment extrude the limits of humanity as well as the limits of those limits, materialized for us in disease and pain, race and sexuality, childhood and age. Pain and disease, here, protrude as generic marks of our embodiment. They especially mark the limits of our biology, where our materiality meets its representations.

Among the themes that characterize God's choice of the Jews as his people is that they bear extraordinary responsibility for their suffering. One pole of this theme of persecution manifests blame and guilt; the other echoes the truth of suffering. The truth for the Jews echoes that they are Jews, destined to suffer; the corresponding truth for Kafka echoes that human beings are destined to suffer the merciless injustice of the Law. Embodiment extrudes as the site of humanity and suffering: we suffer because we are human; we are human insofar as we suffer. Our bodies protrude where we are human and where we suffer. Being human, being embodied, here, is harrowing.

> "Whatever commandment the prisoner has disobeyed is written upon his body by the Harrow. This prisoner, for instance,"—the officer indicated the man—"will have written on his body: HONOR THY SUPERIORS!"
>
> . . . "Does he know his sentence?" "No," said the officer, . . . "There would be no point in telling him. He'll learn it on his body."[5]

> ". . . Enlightenment comes to the most dull-witted. It begins around the eyes. From there it radiates. A moment that might tempt one to get under the Harrow oneself. Nothing more happens than that the man begins to understand the inscription, he purses his mouth as if he were listening. You have seen how difficult it is to

decipher the script with one's eyes; but our man deciphers it with his wounds. To be sure, that is a hard task; he needs six hours to accomplish it. By that time the Harrow has pierced him quite through and casts him down into the pit, where he pitches down upon the blood and water and the cotton wool. Then the judgment has been fulfilled, and we, the soldier and I, bury him." (IPC, p. 104)

Many of the darker themes that inhabit the edges of material life crystallize in Kafka's images of embodiment: death, truth, its visibility, understanding, guilt, redemption, the Law, pain, and suffering. Truth inscribes itself upon the body—at least, the truth of domination and oppression, perhaps every truth. These press upon as the essential truths of humanity. In Kafka, the body looms as the site of the Law, even where most passive or resistant. Passivity touches us as resistance; domination touches us as acquiescence. When K. is killed "like a dog," we recognize that there is no noble death, that the body materializes as a transgressive site of the passivity before the Law that marks our relations to pain, disease, and death. Yet pain and death do not force themselves upon us as the essence of our humanity or our embodiments; nor do domination and subjection. All ring around us in divided orbits of limit and transgression, imposed by the limits and transgressions of our embodiment.

Our relationship to our bodies, already a profound question of human identity, touches us intimately and excessively. Merleau-Ponty tells us something of this intimacy in the language of its humanity:

> Whether it is a question of another's body or my own, I have no means of knowing the human body other than that of living it, which means taking up on my own account the drama which is being played out in it, and losing myself in it. I am my body, at least wholly to the extent that I possess experience, and yet at the same time my body is as it were a 'natural' subject, a provisional sketch of my total being. . . . let us look closely at what is implied in the rediscovery of our own body. It is not merely one object among the rest which has the peculiarity of resisting reflection and remaining, so to speak, stuck to the subject. Obscurity spreads to the perceived world in its entirety.[6]

Several themes characterize this understanding: the "withness" of our body, that we belong to it in continuing departure, that our humanity dwells within its polyphonic stillness; the humanity of our body, that we are it as much as we are anything—"wholly"; the obscurity and ambiguity of our relationship to our body, its groundlessness even as it is our ground; the unitariness of our body, inseparable from the unitariness of our humanity. If we supplement these observations with the representativity and reflexivity that mark our sonorescence, we may delineate several principles that characterize how embodiment presses upon us as a site of our time's transgressions:

1. We find ourselves always with our body, inescapably and truly, in the form of deferral. We belong to our embodiment as it belongs to us, through inexhaustible departures.

2. We materialize as human in virtue of our body, inextricably present in every representation, displacing and enforcing the materiality of every human body. Our humanity inhabits this still space between our embodiment and The Body.

3. Embodiment protrudes as both a ground of humanity and its excess, its essence and its supplement, its limit and its transgression.

4. Every representation echoes as a representation of and with the body. Every embodiment of our humanity revolves around us as representation in order to be matter and as embodied to be representation. This is why Foucault can speak of the "materiality of discourse" and Cixous of "writing the body."[7]

5. A consequence is that every human trait unfolds as a site of embodiment and excess, of materiality, history, and truth, of transgression and deferral. The human body extrudes as a site where humanity delimits and exceeds itself, as humanity exceeds itself in thought and desire while they delimit the essence of humanity. It follows that the human body always materializes as many bodies, posing unending questions of the essence of humanity, many essences.

6. Power, desire, and representation press upon us as embodiment's materiality while materiality weighs down as limit and transgression.

7. The excess of the embodiment of embodiment materializes as its immateriality; the representation of representation echoes as misrepresentation and the truth of truth echoes untruth.

8. The excesses of representation obtrude as the immaterialities of its materiality.

9. Many things follow, not least that our embodiment and its representations imprint on us our humanity and its Laws, by necessity and excess, that power and desire materialize as forms of truth as well as humanity. Specifically, this means that sexuality and gender, race and class, irrupt as meeting places of desire, power, and representation, materialize as embodiment, understood among its excesses, and as not only embodiment, understood to include the ways in which excess exceeds itself as well as the ways in which materiality materializes itself in unending deferral.

10. It follows that we, in virtue of our bodies, are men and women, adults and children, colored and white; that our bodies work upon and within us displaced as we find ourselves by the dislocations of truth and power. Within these divisions protrude the presences of the Law and privilege, occupying the sites of embodiment by regimentation and oppression, by transgression and resistance.

The inescapability of our embodiment extrudes as the inescapability of our humanity, in its stillnesses and polyphonies, its limitations and their limitations. Its inescapability echoes its polyphony as disharmony echoes excess.

We pursue embodiment with its presence in all our judgments and the elusiveness of its transgressiveness even within the tradition's understanding of its inescapability. We sound the totality and essentiality of the materiality of our humanity. For embodiment extrudes as the site where humanity materializes, displaced by the transgressions of our materiality and the transformations wrought upon and with our bodies. Embodiment materializes where our biology redefines itself. We are spiritual only in virtue of our embodiment.

If the Greek view of humanity privileges minds and men over bodies and women, a shared privilege, the evidence for the priority of *anthrōpos* is stronger than for that of *nous*. *Eudaimonia* emerges as the fulfillment of a humanity achieved only in a body trained as fully as *nous* can be trained. Even so, to the Greeks, as to most Western philosophers, the fulfillment of the body, even when unique to it, still belongs to *nous*, even to the *logos*. Analogously, the *aretē* of women, traditionally unique to them, belongs to men. The theme of privilege, here, in humanity and gender, reflects the inseparability of humanity from embodiment and of power and law from desire. The privilege of the *logos*, in the form of language or representation, in science or *poiēsis*, continues unabated, even for those who repudiate logocentrism, caught up in the priority of humanity and language.

We need go no further than to Spinoza for a view of humanity and nature, though in part grounded in the *logos* and hostile to imagination, in timeless ideas and infinite reason, that profoundly emphasizes the displaced withness of embodiment. "The object of the idea constituting the human mind is a body, or a certain mode of extension actually existing, and nothing else" (*Ethics*, II, Prop. 11). And this body is the human body: "It follows that man is composed of mind and body, and that the human body exists as we perceive it" (*Ethics*, II, Prop. 13: Corollary). For Spinoza, a human being is thought and extension and, moreover, knows itself as thought and extension—the only two attributes known to humanity of infinite numbers of infinite attributes. In the extreme, there is no human idea that is not an idea of the human body: "The idea of every way in which the human body is affected by external bodies must involve the nature of the human body, and at the same time the nature of the external body (*Ethics*, II, Prop. XVI). Whatever the mind thinks is thought through and of its body. The body is pervasive even within so powerful an emphasis as Spinoza's on ideas. Moreover, it does not merely accompany the body, but belongs to it inextricably. Yet the essence of human being, though on the one hand thought and extension, on the other materializes as desire or *conatus*—endeavor to exercise power: "The effort by which each thing endeavors to persevere in its own being is nothing but the actual essence of the thing itself" (*Ethics*, III, Prop. VII).

Spinoza, no more than Descartes, can avoid the excesses of thought and embodiment over each other. In Descartes, this excess is unbounded except by God, effectively closed. In Spinoza, the distinction that marks such excess resounds not in the presence or absence of embodiment, but in the finite in relation to the infinite, in the modifications of Substance in relation to ideas in God, both present in embodiment, as infinite as finite, as eternal as temporal.

On the one hand, then,

> The human mind perceives no external body as actually existing unless through the ideas of the modifications of its body. (*Ethics*, II, Prop. XXVI)

> About the duration of our body we can have but a very inadequate knowledge. (*Ethics*, II, Prop. XXX)

Finite knowledge is inadequate knowledge; finite being is imperfect. On the other hand,

> Every idea which in us is absolute, that is to say, adequate and perfect, is true. (*Ethics*, II, Prop. XXXIV)

> There will exist in the human mind an adequate idea of that which is common and proper to the human body, and to any external bodies by which the human body is generally affected—of that which equally in the part of each of these external bodies and in the whole is common and proper. (*Ethics*, II, Prop. XXXIX)

What is common to all bodies, part and whole, falls within God's intellect: infinite, universal, and necessary. God, here, is absolutely infinite, in all ways, where the absoluteness is less universality than excess.

The excesses appear in the aporias of necessity and eternity.

> It is not of the nature of reason to consider things as contingent but as necessary. (*Ethics*, II, Prop. XLIV)

> It is of the nature of reason to perceive things under a certain form of eternity. (*Ethics*, II, Prop. XLIV: Corollary)

> Every idea of any body or actually existing individual thing necessarily involves the eternal and infinite essence of God. (*Ethics*, II, Prop. XLV)

Spinoza reaches the extraordinary conclusion that the body mediates between finite and infinite, temporal and eternal: "He who possesses a body fit for many things possesses a mind of which the greater part is eternal" (*Ethics*, V, Prop. XXXIX). We may hear this proposition to suggest that athletes and dancers approach eternity more closely. Such a reading speaks of the eternity of embodiment in the voice of instrumentality. Instead, we have heard the fitness of the body echoing the excessive plenitude of nature. Whatever is true of humanity is true of the body. If nature and humanity are excessive, excess pertains to the body. If we and our ideas always belong to our embodiment, they also depart, here in a plenitude of excesses.

What makes it possible for the body to serve as intermediary is Spinoza's theory of emotion, based on the most famous of his propositions: "The order and connection of ideas is the same as the order and connection of things" (*Ethics*, II, Prop. VII). Ideas and things here are the same: they do not correspond. The attributes of thought and extension independently express a single Substance. The consequence is Spinoza's theory of emotion, still one of the greatest understandings of embodiment in relation to thought: "By emotion I understand the modifications of the body by which the power of acting of the body itself is increased, diminished, helped, or hindered, together with the ideas of these modifications" (*Ethics*, III, Def. III). Emotion is a modification of the body related to its power of acting, together with the ideas of those modifications. The point where mind and body, desire and power, meet is emotion. If we add Spinoza's view that emotions can be active or passive, that we can be adequate causes of our actions or passively moved by external causes, then emotions can be rational or irrational. Reason pertains to embodiment (*Ethics*, III, Def. III).

> An emotion which is a passion ceases to be a passion as soon as we form a clear and distinct idea of it. (*Ethics*, V, Prop. III)

> The emotions which spring from reason or which are excited by it are, if time be taken into account, more powerful than those which are related to individual objects which we contemplate as absent. (*Ethics*, V, Prop. VII)

A consequence is that the rationality of emotions is no more a function of the ideas associated with them than of their embodiment. The body is a seat of reason together with the mind, is rational to the extent that it possesses powers. If we add to this view the body's *conatus*, reason and desire conjoin in Spinoza with the body and its powers.

> The mind, both in so far as it has clear and distinct ideas and in so far as it has confused ideas, endeavors to persevere in its being for an indefinite time, and is conscious of this effort. (*Ethics*, III, Prop. IX)

> This effort, when it is related to the mind alone, is called "will," but when it is related at the same time both to the mind and the body is called "appetite," which is therefore nothing but the very essence of man, from the nature of which necessarily follow those things which promote his preservation, and thus he is determined to do those things. Hence there is no difference between appetite and desire, . . . (*Ethics*, III, Prop. IX: Note)

The essence of human beings materializes as power and desire together in the effort to persevere; success in this endeavor materializes as reason. Power and desire, here, echo the same in their disharmony. The play of power and desire materializes in the body.

We find in Spinoza an extraordinary expression of embodiment and its powers, coordinated with its desires, reason, and truth. The body materializes as rational in virtue of its efforts to persevere and in the exercise of its powers. Yet reason in Spinoza is associated with eternity and with ideas in God. It is a striking aporia that whereas on the one hand we can have no idea that is not associated with the body and its causes, on the other hand there can be no idea of which we cannot form an eternal simulacrum associated with it. The word "simulacrum" here expresses the displacement of these two ideas. For the rationality of the body and its ideas depends on the mediation afforded by the body between the finite and the infinite. This mediation is simulation in both directions. Thought and extension are the same but different. Inadequate ideas, reflected through God, are the same as adequate ideas but different. Spinoza's reality reflects unending deferral and dislocation.

For any mediation between finite and infinite materializes as aporia, one of Spinoza's greatest insights.[8] Where reason triumphs over passion, eternity triumphs over temporality, the infinite triumphs over the finite, and the *conatus*— each finite being's desire and power—vanishes into timelessness. The reason inherent in the materiality of embodiment vanishes into a geometrical paradigm based on necessity and universality. The alternative is that reason be associated with deferral, with embodiment's temporal contingencies along with the eternity of the mind. Here embodiment materializes as rational and reason unfolds as temporal, finite, contingent, and circular. We acknowledge the multiple reflexivities of representation as embodied. The multiple representations that resound as reason and truth repeat the materiality of embodiment. The embodiment of embodiment materializes as transgressive together with the multiple reflexivities of representation. It is known to us univocally as desire.

The multiple reflexivities of representation, thought, and truth—and of the misrepresentation, unthought, and untruth that inhabit and delimit them—must be embodied to be representational and, as embodied, are always representational. Without embodiment, representation is nothing. Representations with their misrepresentations materialize as the multiple disembodiments of embodiment. The circularity of embodiment's materiality repeats the circularity of representation in the form of deferral. If the circularity of embodiment echoes desire, then its primary marks materialize as sexuality, pain, and disease. These transcend their origins to become excessive objects of our desire and marks of the excesses of our desire for power over desire and itself. Without such representations, embodiment cannot materialize. Its materiality is its deferral.

The multiple reflexivities of embodiment protrude in one of Spinoza's most extraordinary insights. The order and connection of ideas is the same as the order and connection of things; that is, bodies. But there are ideas of ideas, and ideas of ideas of ideas, and so forth. There must therefore also be bodies of bodies, and bodies of bodies of bodies. Only one step is lacking: Spinoza minimizes inadequate ideas of inadequate ideas and so on, though he does not entirely neglect them: "The idea of the idea of any modification of the human body does not involve an adequate knowledge of the human mind" (*Ethics*, II, Prop. XXIX). He does not explore the consequences of multiply unending reflexivity for the adequacy of ideas. In our sonorescence, the circularities of representation displace the truthfulness of ideas with untruths and the materialities of bodies with their immaterialities. Inadequate ideas of inadequate ideas of inadequate ideas, ad infinitum, mark finiteness and contingency as well as the representation of representation, ad infinitum. Analogously, the embodiment of embodiment, inexhaustibly, marks the inexhaustible immaterialities of materiality.

The circularity and reflexivity of ideas and bodies echo their inseparability from the untruths whose resonances define truth and the immaterialities whose embodiments define materiality. Embodiment fails to be embodied—or exceeds it—as much as it materializes embodied, exceeds embodiment because embodied. This conjunction of materiality and immateriality extrudes as embodiment's work. The association of embodiment with power, desire, and representation materializes in its departures.

Spinoza may be the only major philosopher in whom one can discern inexhaustible traces of this reciprocity of embodiment with disembodiment. Yet he is not alone in emphasizing the presence of the body and has been in certain respects exceeded in representing the relation of embodiment to representation. In Whitehead, "For we feel *with the body*. There may be some further specialization into a particular organ of sensation; but in any case the '*withness*' of the body is an ever-present, though elusive element in our perceptions."[9] The elusiveness of embodiment results here from the vagueness of causal efficacy: we are more explicitly aware of presentational immediacy—the association of sensory universals with extensive regions—than we are of inheriting such universals from the past. Yet without such inheritance, we could possess no temporal relations, neither historical nor lawful: could not have them and could not know them. Our embodiment is our historicality. We are, then, present in historical and temporal as well as extensive relations, and our bodies are the seat of communication between them.

> Symbolic reference between the two perceptive modes affords the main example of the principles which govern all symbolism. The requisites for symbolism are that there be two species of percepta; and that a perceptum of one species has some "ground" in common with a perceptum of another species, so that a correlation between the pair of percepta is established.[10]

In Whitehead, symbolism falls between two modes of perception: causal and presentational; historical and extensive. He appears less explicitly concerned with embodiment's displacements. Yet actual entities are constituted by their perceptions, or prehensions. It follows that the materiality of an actual entity is dislocated by the prehensions that constitute it even where its being is their unification.

Far more important for our purposes here is the association of embodiment with representation. To be an actual entity is to be multiply representational. Whitehead follows Leibniz's view that monads are fundamentally representational.

> 60. . . . Because God, in regulating all, has had regard to each part, and particularly to each monad, whose nature being representative, nothing can limit it to representing only a part of things; although it may be true that this representation is but confused as regards the detail of the whole universe, and can be distinct only in the case of a small part of things, that is to say, in the case of those which are nearest or greatest in relation to each of the monads; otherwise each monad would be a divinity.[11]

> 62. Thus, although each created monad represents the entire universe, it represents more distinctly the body which is particularly attached to it, and of which it forms the entelechy; and as this body expresses the whole universe through the connection of all matter in a plenum, the soul also represents the whole universe in representing this body, which belongs to it in a particular way.[12]

The living vitality that composes the entelechy of a monad or actual entity echoes embodiment and representation. What follows for us, absent from Leibniz and Whitehead and only obscurely present in Spinoza, materializes in the disembodiment of embodiment as inexhaustible deferral.

The "withness" of embodiment, essential to Whitehead and Merleau-Ponty, echoes its belonging together with representation. The "withness" of embodiment intrudes a "withness" of representation. In Spinoza, Leibniz, and Whitehead, this reciprocity of representation and embodiment pertains to embodiment in its finiteness, temporality, and individuality. The *conatus* of finite things materializes in their striving as bodies to endure as bodies. Yet a body is not only a body, both because bodies are representational and because they are disembodied by their embodiments, by excess and plenitude, disharmony and polyphony.

An important difference between the views of embodiment found in Spinoza, Leibniz, and Whitehead and of Merleau-Ponty—at once repudiation and affirmation of the "metaphysics of the subject"—echoes how embodiment embodies humanity, both in the materiality of nature—the identity of ideas and things—and in how humanity lives. Here our body protrudes as its and our other; we live it in the form of its departures. The belonging together of our relation to our embodiment intrudes as desire.

> There is no explanation of sexuality which reduces it to anything other than itself, for it is already something other than itself, and indeed, if we like, our whole being. Sexuality, it is said, is dramatic *because* we commit our whole personal life to it. But just why do we do this? Why is our body, for us, the mirror of our being, unless because it is a *natural self*, a current of given existence, with the result that we never know whether the forces which bear us on are its or ours—or with the result rather

> that they are never entirely either its or ours. There is no outstripping of sexuality any more than there is any sexuality enclosed within itself.[13]

Our body materializes for itself as its other in a mode of ambiguity represented by Merleau-Ponty as "never its or ours." Embodiment manifests an ambiguity absent from the Cartesian ego that is the foundation of the transcendental Ego in Kant. Yet the same ambiguity cannot be heard in Kant in relation to embodiment, not in this case echoing Leibniz, for whom, like Spinoza, being represents embodiment. Shall we learn from this omission that with embodiment restored to its full ambiguity we recapture an undividedly divided truth or, instead, that embodiment's ambiguities echo only some ambiguities? Here the insistent biological nature of our bodies constricts even its repudiation: the ambiguity of embodiment. For the embodiment of embodiment extrudes as ambiguity of ambiguity.

The body represents, in its ambiguity, an excess of ambiguity in relation to being human—by no means a subject; or rather, and indeed, that being human only ambiguously echoes being a subject—that is, being anything at all: a human essence. Embodiment extrudes as representation of oneself as a body, belonging to it in virtue of that representation and representing, through or in virtue of one's embodiment, one's relations to other things. Embodiment materializes as fundamentally representational—the origin of its reflexivity—though, equally, that reflexivity extrudes as the materiality of embodiment's representations. This representativity is the reason why, though Merleau-Ponty does not say so, sexuality suffuses our embodiment: sexuality and not sex—rather, the two inextricably. Sexuality represents desire as sex, reaches forth as transmutation of a desire that has no site except as represented.[14] Yet desire's representation does not materialize only as sexuality, but includes pain and disease as well as pleasure.

How can we think of a locus—humanity, embodiment, sexuality, gender, subjectivity, representation, historicality—that has no unison except as culturally constituted in determinate and contingent ways while always exceeding itself? How can we represent the historicality of an embodiment that has no materiality except within a cultural milieu, constituted within and as a deployment of powers, that has no universal essence, only particular material embodiments? Like power, desire, and representation, materiality escapes the domination of identity through its univocity.

We return through the excesses of embodiment's immateriality to its human representation. The representation of embodiment is the representation of humanity. Heidegger expresses this embodiment in terms of the hand:

> The hand does not only grasp and catch, or push and pull. The hand reaches and extends, receives and welcomes—and not just things: the hand extends itself, and receives its own welcome in the hands of others. The hand holds. The hand carries. The hand designs and signs, presumably because man is a sign. Two hands fold into one, a gesture, meant to carry man into the great oneness. The hand is all this, and this is the true handicraft. . . . Every motion of the hand in every one of its works

carries itself through the element of thinking, every bearing of the hand bears itself in that element. All the work of the hand is rooted in thinking. Therefore, thinking itself is man's simplest, and for that reason hardest, handiwork, if it would be accomplished at its proper time.[15]

In this context, where we grasp the hand as body and thought—the Essence of Being Human—there obtrudes a theme concerning which Derrida says the following, alluding to a particular sentence more than to the entire thematic of the body-as-hand: "Here in effect occurs a sentence that at bottom seems to me Heidegger's most significant, symptomatic, and seriously dogmatic. . . . 'Apes, *for example* [my emphasis, J.D.], have organs that can grasp, but they have no hand.' "[16] Animals here have no body, or at best only an animal-technical body that can grasp, but that cannot mean—that is, a body (paws, claws, fangs) that can pull and push, but that does not, even cannot, represent; or if it represents, does not autoerotically represent its own representativity. An animal body here is a body whereas a human body represents itself excessively as a represented body. A question we may ask, against this dogmatic privileging of the hand, is Why do we not hear the animality of this represented body as another representation of its excesses? Why do we not hear the materiality of animals as our frame?

Several themes echo in the idea of the represented body, of the hand. Derrida adds to the line, "The hand designs and signs, presumably because man is a sign," that man is a "monstrous" sign, one that shows and exceeds the monstrosity of showing. Yet to introduce this monstrousness is to remonstrate, in this case, against the privilege accorded to The Human in the name of *Geschlecht*.[17] The author of the "Letter on Humanism" privileges the human-German *Geschlecht* "as a blow" (*Schlag*). The human is always spoken of with privilege, and the privilege here is situated in the body, at least (Derrida notes) in "The" hand— never two, never hand*s*, certainly not (dogmatically excluding) four paws. The body permeates our environs as a divided, fragmented, represented body; the hand pervades our humanity as a divided, representational hand; humanity fills our lives as divided humanity—but never (or always?) divided by paws, fangs, or claws. The unity of the divided human hand exercises privilege under a monstrous and essential sign, that of our *Geschlecht*. Its manifest signs are health in relation to disease, men in relation to women, white in relation to yellow or brown skin, skin in relation to feathers or fur, all figures of authorization framing privileged humanity.

Among the presences that define the excesses of human embodiment unfold the privileges that name its *Geschlecht*, even Merleau-Ponty's *Geschlecht*, despite questions of its untranslatability into French or English: the sexual-gendered-ethnic-racial-colonized-medicalized-legalized-classified body that is "our whole being." However divided, or because divided, the body weighs on us as a site of the privileges that define the essence of humanity and despite every repudiation of the autonomous subject. Among these privileges transpire those that circle around humanity in relation to animals and machines as well as to language, *technē*, reason, embodiment, and the gods. The truth of embodiment echoes its *technē*. The *technē* of the body resounds as its and our *Geschlecht*.

The privileges that encircle embodiment range from all those that pertain to The Human, from thinking and language to sexuality, to those that express the immateriality of The Body in contrast with the materialities of bodies, organic and inorganic. The former privileges give us reason and its laws; the latter give us sexual, racial, and class differences. What the German language explicitly gives us is the indissociability (in *Geschlecht*) of humanity, race, sex, gender, and class. The Body, here, in its unitariness, represents the indissociability of humanity from privilege, even the privilege of our relationship to our own body. To say that we are our body, that we belong to it as much as it belongs to us, echoes unending questions of the I (or we) that it is and from which it and we depart. The answer extrudes a body displaced in every way that pertains to embodiment, where the univocity of the every names excess, frees embodiment from the dominion of identity.

These excesses express, in the obscurity of their materiality, the resistances of embodiment to being named, represented, even within our acknowledgment that embodiment exists only as represented. Embodiment is Unthought even as it is the soul. The body is a (monstrous) sign, where the monstrosity is at once showing and excess. The "is" here presses upon us with the excesses of embodiment's materiality. The body extrudes in representation as representation extrudes embodied. In both cases, this extrusion departs from itself as it displaces representation and embodiment. Where the spaces in which multiple representation circles back to itself open difference, embodiment materializes as at once *that* difference, the representation of representation as twice embodied, and *another* difference, the immateriality of embodiment's embodiment. The multiplicity of embodiment obtrudes in the excesses of desire and power, embodied in sexuality, gender, and race. This play of materiality and excess echoes the univocity of the privileged essence of embodied humanity.

This divided truth of embodiment is "fully" expressed, though Derrida never quite says so, in *Geschlecht*—or rather, in the *Geschlecht* of *Geschlecht*— *Geschlechtsgeschlecht*, where the spaces between one *Geschlecht* and the other are filled by a plethora of prepositions: of, in, on, by, from, through, under, over, beside, with, among, near, even far. The dividedness of *Geschlecht* lies at the question of its untranslatability: "We are going to speak of the word '*Geschlecht*.' I am not going to translate it for the moment. Doubtless I shall translate it at no moment. But you know that, according to the contexts that come to determine this word, it can be translated by sex, race, species, genus, gender, stock, family, generation or genealogy, community."[18] This question of translatability—*Geschlecht* is surely repeatable in French and English—marks its Germanness, the monstrous locality within it of a human essence. National socialism here is no less human than is love, no less the essence-of-being-human. *Geschlecht* poses for us questions of its Germanness and its monstrosity.

The dislocations of *Geschlechtsgeschlecht* protrude in its multiple reflexivities as it captures in the play of its different embodiments the displacements that determine humanity: the humanity of the human as the embodiment of the body and representation of representation; but also, the violence of violence and domination of domination that echo repeatedly within humanity. "Humanity does not gradually progress from combat to combat until it arrives at universal reciprocity, where the rule of law finally replaces warfare; humanity installs each of its violences in a system of rules and thus proceeds from domination to domination."[19] The humanity of humanity exercises a point of privilege. *Geschlechtsgeschlecht* poses questions of the humanity of humanity in a way perhaps foreign to any other language, though every language may be twisted into its *Geschlecht* and is twisted in its own ways. Above all, it poses questions of the disembodiment of embodiment, along with its violence and domination, as questions of power and desire. Here we emphasize the suffering of the body as well as its triumphs. Here we find the irresistibility of pain and disease as our *Geschlecht*.

Geschlecht poses three questions for us:

1. Does humanity always materialize at a point of privilege, within and without? Does humanity always extrude The Human?
2. Does the point of privilege appear uniquely German, expressive of a particular historical and cultural site? Or do racial, sexual, and gender differences materialize everywhere, framing humanity's nature?
3. Does humanity extrude its privileges and sufferings at particular sites? Specifically, does the embodiment of privilege materialize in pain, represented as torture and disease?

Such questions do not commit us to the preservation of any embodied points of privilege; patriarchy, for example, or European civilization. They ask us to think of the Essence of Humanity as embodied privilege where embodiment dislocates any privilege. That is why pain and disease define bodily privilege. The gouges that define this privilege carve essence into its departures, so that the privilege of the phallus can be undercut, but only in virtue of either dismembering the Human or by engendering another point of privilege. An appealing prospect, equally a point of privilege, is the domination of difference as difference. Here, in relation to embodiment, the repudiation of its *Geschlecht* passes into infinite tolerance. Every difference becomes Difference—even *Différance*. The danger resounds that difference will lose its identity, its departures from itself, that excess will lack excess.

Human beings materialize as bodies. But so do animals and machines. Human beings exceed their bodies. So do animals and machines. And their bodies exceed them. There can be no body without excess. The question of being human resounds as Metaphysical (in a certain sense) when it hides its locality from itself. Our sonorescence hopes to sound its own locality, even the locality of its sonorescence.

The excesses marked by *Geschlecht* in relation to our humanity fall into embodiment on both sides: human embodiment over or against animals' and machines' bodies; the dominant male over and against the subordinate female body; the Enlightened body over and against the Primitive body; the division of humanity by disease and pain—defective bodies; the ideality of the bodies of the gods. The image of the ideal body shines as image of ideal humanity, a perfectibility grounded in a certain view of *technē*, its *aretē*, implying a technique of the body. It is no wonder, with this sense of perfectibility, that embodiment should inhabit a site whose excesses mark its violences and dominations. The idea of ideality in relation to embodiment marks its excesses excessively, revealed in the excesses of normality that define humanity. Embodiment obtrudes as a site where humanity finds itself in its others, especially in its defects. The idea that embodiment's materiality lies within ideality turns humanity into a *technē*. The art of the body works its escape from its displacements. We respond that embodiment's embodiment echoes repudiation of both its ideality and its defectiveness. Here disease and pain, along with sexuality and old age, press upon us as reminders of our body's insistent materiality.

The embodiments of being's being and truth protrude wherever there is body with its materiality; that is, everywhere in its plenitude. Here, representation, truth, and history, with power and desire, materialize as embodiment as it materializes as they. They extrude through their embodiment, with material influences, but they resound as matter's excesses as it resounds as theirs. They influence the future (or fail to do so) in virtue of their embodiments and can mean or say only in bodily terms. These immaterial materialities constitute humanity's humanity with its inhumanities.[20]

It follows that embodiment and materiality both denote privilege and the law and displace them, situating privilege at the essence of humanity. This essential privilege materializes in *Geschlecht*. It is time to discuss this privilege not as embodiment but on a body. The body, Kafka tells us, oppresses us as both instrument of the Law and its site of pain. We follow the "knowledge" of bodies involved in their discipline, the technology of embodiment.

> But the body is also directly involved in a political field; power relations have an immediate hold upon it; they invest it, mark it, train it, torture it, force it to carry out tasks, to perform ceremonies, to emit signs. . . . there may be a "knowledge" of the body that is not exactly the science of its functioning, and a mastery of its forces that is more than the ability to conquer them: this knowledge and this mastery constitute what might be called the political technology of the body.[21]

This dispersed knowledge of the body, as every dictatorship knows, has two reciprocal poles: silence and torture. Within this silence irrupts the truth of torture, the reason why rape has always been a supreme symbol of domination, not only of men over women: a "carnal knowledge"—incredible phrase—embodied in a silent torture whose violence lies hidden from and under the gaze of social institutions, where the bodiliness of the body, here its sexuality, embodies a painful silence and a silence in pain. Rape inhabits the center of social life, for men and women. It inhabits every space of embodiment's displacement. It materializes, in our culture, as representation of the subordination of women through their bodies, repeated in the everyday mirror of the controls in social life that define women's embodiment as reproduction. The battle over abortion echoes the struggle over women's bodies. The silence of their bodies mirrors the silence of their unborn, whose bodies are the site at which the oppression of women's bodies endlessly and silently mirrors their sexuality.

The silence of the body is a system of control:

> Now, the study of this micro-physics presupposes that the power exercised on the body is conceived not as a property, but as a strategy, that its effects of domination are attributed not to "appropriation," but to dispositions, manoeuvres, tactics, techniques, functionings; that one should decipher in it a network of relations, constantly in tension, in activity, rather than a privilege that one might possess; . . . In short this power is exercised rather than possessed; it is not the "privilege," acquired or preserved, of the dominant class, but the overall effect of its strategic positions.[22]

One corollary of such microstrategies of power is that rape and sexual abuse be regarded not as violence of one person on another, but as an institutional, even cultural strategy of domination in and through sexuality and embodiment.[23] This difference borne by women and children, especially female children, transforms the individual violences in human life into institutional patterns of domination. For this reason, arguments that one cannot distinguish erotic works from pornography, that the testimony of children or even individual women cannot be relied on in criminal prosecutions, that fetuses deserve moral protection—all based on principles of Enlightened Civilization—always echo suspiciously. Institutional practices of pornography, protection of the accused before the law, and protection of life occupy social and political sites where domination and violence are norms that pass for forms of resistance. Here the disharmonies that define the freedoms of desire belong together with and repeat the privileges of our civilization.

The reinterpretation of power against Power reappropriates embodiment in relation to privilege, displacing and perpetuating itself. Both reappropriations resound in the notion of a microphysics of power, though they sound more forcefully in Foucault's propositions concerning power, especially in relation to resistance: "Where there is power, there is resistance, and yet, or rather consequently, this resistance is never in a position of exteriority in relation to power."[24] Yet if resistance always accompanies power as its other, then power always accompanies resistance. Power materializes as "Power" in both directions. The most laudable of institutional norms, the laws of enlightened reason, occupy the social and political spaces of desire for both truth and domination, where enlightenment means oppression. The utopian gesture reemerges not only within our Enlightenment but within our enlightened understanding of its limitations.

May we hear these propositions concerning power and resistance to materialize in embodiment, as we hear the corresponding propositions concerning desire and representation? Discipline echoes among them all: disciplining desire as the exercise of power but most of all in relation to the silence of the body.

> The historical moment of the disciplines was the moment when an art of the human body was born, which was directed not only at the growth of its skills, nor at the intensification of its subjection, but at the formation of a relation that in the mechanism itself makes it more obedient as it becomes more useful, and conversely. . . . The human body was entering a machinery of power that explores it, breaks it down and rearranges it.[25]

The machinery works less by overt torture than by control of space and time. The spaces our bodies occupy envelop our materiality. They nevertheless echo silences of suffering. For we cannot escape the reality of pain. We experience the limits of our bodies in many ways, but overwhelmingly in the midst of pain and poignantly in the throes of disease. What vanishes in moving from the tortures of a microphysics of power to everyday pain and disease materializes as dispersion, of embodiment and law. We return to the locus of the individual body, resisting its recentering.

We reemerge with Kafka and the Harrow, the machine that writes the truth upon the body as an act of torture. But we reemerge as well with the Law.

> 4. With this new economy of power, the carceral system, which is its basic instrument, permitted the emergence of a new form of "law": a mixture of legality and nature, prescription and constitution, the norm. . . .

> 5. . . . Knowable man (soul, individuality, consciousness, conduct, whatever it is called) is the object-effect of this analytical investment, of this domination-observation.[26]

This union of knowability with the *praxis* of embodiment extrudes defined by pain. The first truth of enlightened discipline materializes as a truth of truth and *praxis*, but also *praxis*'s truth and truth's *praxis*, in every case dislocated by the other, an excuse for torture, materializing its untruth. It extrudes a truth that embodies the disembodiment of discipline where pain screams out the story of the triumphs and oppressions of the body. It extrudes where desire collapses into its other, where the will to power forgets itself.

We may contrast within this view of the pervasiveness of the body-politic of power as knowledge the view of Power as the Law it replaces: "it is a power whose model is essentially juridical, centered on nothing more than the statement of the law and the operation of taboos. All the modes of domination, submission, and subjugation are ultimately reduced to an effect of obedience."[27] Whatever materializes as power and desire extrudes embodiment. The body materializes in its relation to the Law, but the rules, prohibitions, and censorship that delimit its materiality extrude in the resistances of power. The transgressiveness lies in embodiment's univocity, everywhere disembodied wherever inscribed.

The essence of embodiment—where it has no essence—lies in pain, where pain and pleasure are each other's excesses. Here the body knows better than the soul and better than Care, which thinks of itself before Death: knows of its mortality through pain and its finiteness through pleasure. We take pleasure in pain as we desire truth and desire, desire even the absence of desire. Yet something obscure intrudes in this silent acquiescence in the pleasures of pain: we accept it only where it extrudes *our* desire and *our* pain. The pains and pleasures of embodiment are again the seat of our humanity, express the specific departures that define the absent presence of a human essence.

These specificities echo ways of being human, embodied in the body, where it extrudes as site of our autonomy and subjection, the site where power, desire, and representation meet. The body is "all" of human being, is "fully" rational, where reason is divided by materiality.

Here a somewhat different theme of materiality emerges in Foucault, that of discourse, returning us to representation.

> In the sense that this slender wedge I intend to slip into the history of ideas consists not in dealing with meanings possibly lying behind this or that discourse, but with discourse as regular series and distinct event, I fear I recognise in this wedge a tiny (odious, too, perhaps) device permitting the introduction, into the very roots of thought, of notions of *chance, discontinuity* and *materiality*.[28]

He calls this wedge "an incorporeal materialism," the "disembodiment of embodiment," and adds the following: "what political status can you give to discourse if you see in it merely a thin transparency that shines for an instant at the limit of things and thoughts?"[29] Discourse speaks in virtue of its materiality, however incorporeal. We add that matter extrudes in virtue of its immateriality, as does embodiment, however material. The entwining of discourse and materiality extrudes an intertwining of embodiment and representation, where each in belonging with the other departs from it as a site of limit and excess.

NINE

Praxis

I n Greek, *praxis*, in English, practice, materializes as judgment in relation to an other through time, or, alternatively, as judgment in relation to time through another, where the other echoes harmony and disharmony and time echoes past and present but especially future. In this harmony of locality and time, *praxis* unfolds as teleological, not possessing an end—*technē*—or striving toward fulfillment, but inescapably though contingently moving toward a future, many futures. *Praxis* makes a difference, to past and present, far and near, and whatever makes that difference materializes as *praxis*.

Practice unfolds as the modality that partakes of the inescapability of judgment's temporality, the displaced truth of which belongs to semasis, but that materializes in practice through failure, in semasis as deferral, in stillness as polyphony. We are historical creatures: we live through time, from past to future, birth to death. Every judgment and every judgmental modality reflects this temporality. In this sense, every judgment materializes as a practical judgment along with its other modalities. The practicality of judgment expresses its temporality. The assertiveness of judgment expresses its representativity. The fabricativeness of judgment expresses its materiality. The syndeticness of judgment expresses its multiple reflexivity. All echo semasis; all materialize as practical judgment. Each modality partakes of and exceeds the others, the displaced truth that composes disciplinariness. The linearity of language, decay of paintings, seriality of music and dance, movement of battle, historicality of metaphysics, all express and defer their semasic temporality. Judgment materializes as both temporal and spatial, and we could not imagine a judgment, as we sometimes think we can imagine forms and laws, that was not with other judgments in space and time. In this sense, we cannot imagine any judgment that does not belong to practice. We can, however, imagine different practices and temporalities.

The inescapability of practical judgment, of semasis and history, nature and *technē*, echoes their univocity, falling between necessity and contingency, transcendentality and empiricity. The inescapability of the temporality of judgment, the historicality of human life and experience, materialize as empirical rather than transcendental conditions—more accurately, transcendental because empirical and conversely. We have noted Dewey's emphasis upon the empirical uncertainty, indeterminacy, and contingency of time. Foucault describes the "quasi-transcendentals" of life, labor, and language,[1] He also describes a certain representation of "Man" as an "empirico-transcendental doublet," at once empirically conditioned and intelligible in virtue of those conditions.[2] The authority of science lies in this doubling of the empirical side of humanity's transcendentals. The contingency of the contingency of experience, the empiricity of the empiricity of nature, the transcendentality of the transcendentals that define judgment, reflexively redefine them. The empiricity of empiricity manifests the temporality of temporality—its dislocatedness as time.

Two considerations speak against understanding the generic conditions of experience empirically: their contingency and the sovereignty of empirical science. The first presents the inescapability and necessity that define transcendentals as neither inescapable nor necessary, but contingent, even as contingency appears unavoidable, necessary. Temporality, one of the empiricals, unfolds in the inescapable field of empiricity, its historicality. Yet no ingredient of historicality sounds inescapably inescapable, not even the future. The necessity of historical contingency and the contingency of historical necessity echo aporias that define the univocity of time.[3] The necessity of empiricity makes the inescapability of temporality contingent.

The transcendental reply to the contingencies of Hume's view of experience is that experience is necessarily synthetic and synthetically necessary. In this joining of necessity with the unity of truth lies reaffirmation of the sovereignty of science, realized supremely in Hegel, because, not in spite, of his historicality. Science's sovereignty unfolds in time, and appears, in part, in virtue of its sovereignty over time. The marks of the sovereignty of science reinscribe necessity, teleology, and eschatology. The marks of the truth of science reinscribe its empiricity. These two sets of inscriptions mark the aporetic truth of the scientific tradition, one side of a tradition whose truth lies in its aporias.[4]

The marks of the practicality of science signify its contingency and imperfectibility, all within the successes of its achievements. Waste and imperfection contribute to its triumphs though incongruous with its necessity, at least with the necessity of that necessity. The necessity science imposes within divided experience belies its temporality, not to mention the temporality of its testimony. The truth science tells echoes its necessity and contingency, sovereignty and displacement, stillness and polyphony. The aporia modern science tells echoes its subjection to the vicissitudes of human experience while imposing dominion over that experience in the form of Law. That science's propositional truth echoes its necessity is affirmed and repudiated by science's history. Science unfolds as an empirical-transcendental truth exercising authority. The truths of truth materialize empirically and transcendentally.

Foucault calls Man, the figure that defines the human sciences, an empirico-transcendental doublet.

> Man, in the analytic of finitude, is a strange empirico-transcendental doublet, since he is a being such that knowledge will be attained in him of what renders all knowledge possible.[5]

> Man's mode of being as constituted in modern thought enables him to play two roles: he is at the same time at the foundation of all positivities and present, in a way that cannot even be termed privileged, in the element of empirical things.[6]

He has in mind the regulation of the unthought in language and humanity by the human sciences' attempt to think it within their forms of reason. "The question is no longer: How can experience of nature give rise to necessary judgements? But rather: How can man think what he does not think, inhabit as though by a mute occupation something that eludes him, animate with a kind of frozen movement that figure of himself that takes the form of a stubborn exteriority?"[7] Scientific judgment, especially the human sciences, attempts to represent the unthought without excess. Yet the necessity of transcendentals manifests excess: of language, humanity, materiality, and practice. Among the far-reaching transcendentals of human experience echoes judgment, where each modality exceeds the others and excess exceeds itself. The temporality and spatiality of judgment resound not as its transcendental conditions but as its excesses.

Among the inescapable excesses of judgment unfold its spatiality and temporality, each exceeding the other's grasp in modalities of truth for which temporality or spatiality appear unessential. Science and art offer themselves as timeless in different ways, the one grounded in the inescapable temporality of evidence leading, however excessively, to timeless laws, the other grounded in the inescapable historicality of representation leading, however excessively, to timeless works. The temporality of science and art appears inescapable while the form of the truths associated with them exceeds their temporality. Timelessness echoes polyphonically within the stillnesses of repetition. Science and art materialize in but not of time; their temporality unfolds in judgment but not in how they represent time. They materialize among the forms in which temporality exceeds itself.

The excesses of practical judgment lie not in escape from temporality but in other modes of query: the excesses that compose the disciplines. Practical judgment moves from a past without which no practice could define itself toward a future marking its fulfillment, all the while resisting. The future emerges as the measure of a practice that exceeds any measure in the materiality of many futures and many truths. Practical judgment, including the work of science and art, speaks against the blindness of a judgment that does not know its own temporality, but practice unfolds blind in its own ways, failing to acknowledge any other truth than its own, the tyranny of practice. Practice in the form of law imposes its own forms of sovereignty and regulation. Judgment inescapably exercises power.

The copresence of different modalities of judgment and truth produces what Foucault calls discontinuity and Lyotard calls *le différend*. Lyotard also speaks of law in ways that seem hostile to its displacement.

> The law prescribes a something, an "I don't know what," and at the same time it prescribes itself: it forbids and prevents us from identifying with it and profiting from it.[8]
>
> Here, without further explanation, I shall call the law the fact that there is a question or that we are questioned about what we ought to become and what we ought to do to become it. That fact Kant calls "factum rationis," the indisputable fact that practical reason is an apriori transcendental condition for any morality whatsoever. It is a pure obligation, a duty, not one, however, to do this or that, but rather the pure "fact" of duty, of being obliged.[9]

In one of these references to the law, he appeals to Levinas: "Emmanuel Levinas, whose books were my companion for twenty years, would say that it is a community of hostages, each of them being in a state of dependency to others or, more precisely, to the capital Other (what I call the law)."[10] This appeal to law echoes the ethical obligation, the necessity within practical being.

Why should we think that politics or ethics—our relation to an other— marks obligation, however pure? Does the law always present the Law? Must practice always be contaminated by law over judgment, by a juridico-logical model based on proof? Might not the movement be reversed, so that our relationship to law would be judicial, where the former rules as practice and the latter appears antagonistic to Law? Can the law of law replace the law of science?

Lyotard says: "In other words, to respond to a case without criteria, which is reflective judgment, is itself a case in its turn, an event to which an answer, a mode of thinking, will eventually have to be found. This condition may be negative, but it is the principle for all probity in politics as it is in art. I am also obliged to say: as it is in thinking."[11] In Kant, reflective judgment moves from individuality to universality without criteria while seeking them within the Law. Only a meager view of Law claims that it always rules. Rather, it rules if and because we seek its refuge. To seek to fall into obligation, to be obliged to seek the Law, is to occupy the castle of our forgetfulness.

Can practice materialize without Law? Can an other materialize without duty? May necessity, however weak, appear as a transcendental condition of any practical judgment? Can we pursue the Good rather than the Law? Foucault has a different view of both transcendentality and the Law. It questions whether power demands the Law as its Power or whether law rules as a transcendental condition of power.

to begin with, this power is poor in resources, sparing of its methods, monotonous in the tactics it utilizes, incapable of invention, and seemingly doomed always to repeat itself. Further, it is a power that only has the force of the negative on its side, a power to say no; in no condition to produce, capable only of posing limits, it is basically anti-energy.[12]

This manifests the Power of the Law, as contrasted with power: "Power is everywhere; not because it embraces everything, but because it comes from everywhere. And 'Power,' insofar as it is permanent, repetitious, inert, and self-reproducing, is simply the over-all effect that emerges from all these mobilities, the concatenation that rests on each of them and seeks in turn to arrest their movement."[13] "Power" here unfolds as the excess that marks one epoch of power, along with its resistances, and Law the excess that marks one epoch of law. It follows that power exceeds Power as (and because) resistance exceeds power. It follows also that law rules through deferral of the Law as the good attracts the deferral of law and law rules by deferral over the Good.

The excesses of power can be heard in the onlyness that defines Power: only negative, only posing limits, centered on the nothing more. The excesses of law can be heard in the prescriptiveness, however empty, that demands pure obligation, an obligation that imposes without domination or dominates without imposition. The Law wars incessantly with law to make its judgments criterial, to rule over past and future.

Our sonorescence poses the practical question of how a politics may be represented without criteria that can inhabit the space of historical experience without oppression or domination—at least, without blindness to its own dogmatisms—where representation materializes as practical judgment. Here the empirical temporality of lived experience must be understood to war with any transcendentals that impose criteria and to be transcendental itself, imposing rules. For that we find ourselves within lived experience entails empirically that we find ourselves within rules. There are always rules, and experience is always temporal. Traditionally, this always echoes either transcendentally or empirically, necessarily or contingently. Yet it unfolds here transcendentally because of its empiricity, not, as Kant says, because experience requires transcendental conditions for its unity but because transcendental conditions require experience for their deferral. This discovery of the empirical transcendental echoes the rule of representation that delimits the representation of rules.

That our pervasive relation to others should be in terms of law, however pure, defines that relation prescriptively and ignores the oppressions of the Law; or, at least, imposes on it another oppression. Its violence remains obscure. Only if we hear these terms as both Prescription and prescription, Law and law, can they speak against themselves, within and without, displacements of violence. Lyotard's model of *le différend* as falling between language games or phrase regimens suffers from this sense of what it excludes: its own *différend* within. The law's purity overthrows the departures that dislocate it, though every locus, including representation, echoes *différends* within and without. Perhaps we may hear the purity of the law as its univocity, including its own displacements.

A utopian dream echoes that the lion may lie down with the lamb, that truth and goodness may find themselves in harmony. A utopian dream also echoes that contingent practice might escape violence. Here the *différends* between law and goodness mark the inexhaustibility of violence's violence. The Law defines our nature as moral, giving privilege to duty over happiness. The good replies that Law does violence to those over whom it rules. Yet no good transpires without regulation, no practice without influence. Practice materializes as displacement of the violence of judgment, retribution against history's waste.

That our pervasive relation to others should be divided between morality and fulfillment, duty and happiness, law and good, right and utility, challenges the sovereignty of the Law in the language of its authority, reaffirming sovereignty under law. Reason demands necessity, either as the sovereignty of the Law or the superiority of the Good. The transcendental movement, here, recapitulates the chains of rational necessity. At the heart of our relation to the good stands an obligation. Reason echoes Law. Being echoes Prescription. Duty and privilege materialize as our *Geschlecht*.

To reject the Law's necessity and sovereignty, to displace its domination, we reject every transcendental that would impose, however covertly, another form of oppression in the name of rule. We reject the necessity of necessity, affirming its contingency. In *Republic*, Plato circumscribes an authoritarian *polis* founded on an oppressive principle of law: each person obligated to do the one thing that fulfills his *areté*. That a complex *areté* might be incompatible with singularity or fulfillment is seemingly overcome in the dialogue by the image of the sovereignty of reason as multiplicity under Law. Many virtues are made one by rule. In *Republic* it is the rule of reason; in *Symposium* it is the rule of desire. Both rules are undermined by the excessive play of reason and desire.

Our relations to ourselves and others echo contingency and empiricity. Stillness and polyphony exceed each other while they echo their togetherness. Empiricity echoes its transcendentality; locality sounds its inexhaustibility. The transcendental movement in which necessity and rule appear contains within itself the deferrals of multiple representation within which sovereignty imposes itself. Empiricity and contingency reverberate in the necessity of necessity—it cannot define its own necessity—as necessity echoes in the empiricity of empiricity, which cannot define its own contingency. Similarly, the sovereignty of sovereignty disperses the sovereignty of Law as violence against violence dislocates itself and as it repeats domination. This circular movement thought as law, however pure, imposes a double obligation. This circular movement thought as the good, however local, imposes a double teleology. These excesses define every relation we bear in experience and time. Experience unfolds as necessarily contingent: the locality of its locality; the stillness of its polyphonies; the polyphonies of its stillnesses. The transcendental univocals here echo aporia.

Heidegger speaks of our relation to Being, in virtue of our finitude, as care.

> Dasein's Being is care. It comprises in itself facticity (thrownness), existence (projection), and falling. As being, Dasein is something that has been thrown; it has been brought into its "there," but *not* of its own accord. As being, it has taken the definite form of a potentiality-for-Being which has heard itself and has devoted itself to itself, but *not* as itself.[14]

Facticity, existence, and falling reveal finitude, define the "not" of *Dasein*'s limits. Heidegger repudiates the ethical and political side of this view of care, although conscience pulls toward its destiny. Care is more a relation toward death than to an other, a relation nevertheless to time. Yet death marks more than a relation of finitude, towards one's limits. It marks a relation towards other creatures' limits: their deaths and beyond. Even these limits do not define the limits of finiteness because what does not live and die is finite. Even if there were unchanging, unyielding things, they would possess limits. Locality echoes the finiteness that engenders care. The care toward locality, together with the locality of care, unfolds charity. It echoes a representation of locality along with its representation and the representation of the locality of locality, and so forth. Charity echoes locality and inexhaustibility, including the locality of representation and the inexhaustibility of materiality. It echoes relation to an other by one that represents itself as an other in a relation of excess. The representation of the inexhaustibility that pertains to individual things materializes as charity. Its materiality echoes historicality and practicality. The form of judgment that embodies charity materializes as practical judgment.

Charity unfolds as care within and toward the inexhaustible plenitude of any locus, any thing. The traditional Greek word describing this plenitude is *entelechy*: a self-moving creature in a world of inexhaustible creatures. In our sonorescence, a locus comes forth as one locale inhabiting many other locales, many and one, expressed in its resonances and unisons, it belongs to and departs from locales to which it is relevant; it materializes polyphonically or stilly. Traditional metaphysical naturalism, from Aristotle through Spinoza to Whitehead, has repeatedly concerned itself with the plenitude of every finite creature, marked by the presence within it of the infinite. In this respect, metaphysical naturalism resounds very differently from scientific naturalism, though as Whitehead and Spinoza suggest, a reverse movement may be taken, to restore science's view of natural things to their plenitude by profoundly rethinking science's nature. Even within its technical limitations, science represents the plenitude of things inexhaustibly.

Charity echoes the sense of plenitude that pertains to every locus, its locality and inexhaustibility. It materializes generically as the foundation of practical judgment, even of a practice without foundation. Charity reverberates as a foundation that speaks against any foundation, rejecting every limit as coercive despite the inexhaustible presence of limits. Charity echoes care in an inexhaustible universe by local creatures who participate in their own inexhaustibility. It unfolds the compassion that grounds practice, the sense of inexhaustibility that inhabits every location.

Charity unfolds as compassion free from interest, except that no freedom can escape interest. Charity unfolds as compassion apart from desire, except that desire cannot fall apart. Charity unfolds as compassion without domination or violence, except that no life can escape violence and domination. These negative movements recapitulate the antinomies of the dialectic of taste in the first part of the *Critique of Judgment*. The suggestion emerges that charity is fundamentally aesthetic, that practical judgment strives toward an aesthetic rather than an ethical goal. Ethics appears under law whereas practice rests on compassion. Charity here unfolds as compassion free from utility. It echoes the inexhaustibility that founds any practice, including the norms of utility. It also ungrounds utility as the basis of practice: the means whose plenitude is forgotten when employed toward another. No creature can act without means and ends: consequently, charity turns back upon itself repeatedly in the form of sacrifice.

Charity sounds the relations of a practical creature to others and itself in their inexhaustibility. That a practical creature also may be theoretical, engaged in propositional and scientific as well as practical judgments, echoes one of its limits, opens itself inexhaustibly while it delimits. That such a practical creature makes as well as does opens another set of limits, to disharmony while it limits. The play of locality and inexhaustibility in time resounds as semasis: its temporal truth unfolds as practice; the play of locality in representation echoes as science; the play of inexhaustibility in materiality resounds as art; the play of materiality in representation extrudes as politics; the play of materiality in practice protrudes as technology.

Sacrifice enacts violence, an inescapable side of practical judgment. Sacrifice also echoes triumph, another side of practical judgment. The relation between time and inexhaustibility echoes charity; the relation between *praxis* and inexhaustibility reverberates in time as sacrifice. Relations among time, locality, and inexhaustibility echo valor, represented by *poiēsis*. *Poiēsis* belongs to practical judgment among its polyphonies.

Creation repeats destruction but still creates. Destruction repeats creation but still destroys. This conjunction echoes a truth of practice: that the belonging together and departing of charity and sacrifice constitute valor as transgression. Power and desire inhabit this transgressive space of sacrifice and charity. On one side, sacrifice appeals to our tragic sense, with the qualification that even that sense must be sacrificed in the name of charity: to comedy, perhaps, or to science. On the other side, charity echoes a care that sounds its limits, along with the limits of whatever echoes inexhaustibility, celebrating its powers. Sacrifice, here, re-peats charity with the supplement that each displaces itself and the other by mul-tiple reflexivity. The limits of charity echo sacrifice; the limits of sacrifice echo charity; the limits of charity and sacrifice together resound as valor. The represen-tation of valor echoes *poiēsis*. Power and desire echo as names of *poiēsis*, fall between charity and sacrifice. Sacrifice fulfills desire as violence over violence and the domination of domination, especially as desire toward desire, expressing the limits of desire and their limits.

Practical judgment enacts relations through time, pervaded by charity and sacrifice. The sacrificial side of charity appears inescapable: that is why we can-not speak of charity without loss. Yet charity remains unspoken within sacrifice, and practice remains inert as we face the monstrous future helpless before its losses. Charity and sacrifice materialize as the relations we bear as practical agents toward a future whose monstrosity requires the past and threatens it with nothingness. Practice rings as teleological, moving toward the future, its histori-cality and practicality; teleology echoes as its defining limit. The recession of the past delimits loss; the advance of the future delimits violence; the space between echoes practice.

Charity echoes aporia. We may hear the aporias not as obstacles to be over-come but as fulfillments to pursue. Yet the obstacles pervade the Western ethical and political tradition, perhaps the most excessive (and obsessive) form of the Law that prescribes duty. What cannot be known determinately cannot be a se-cure ground of *praxis*. Alternatively, while theory can present determinate truths, *praxis* is *phronēsis*. We may go both ways from this Aristotelian distinction, from the certainty of science to *praxis*, seeking a sacrificial science; or from the uncer-tainty of *praxis* to science, disclosing the wastefulness of science.

If we have taken the latter way to this point, it is time to think again about our choice, though not by reopening the question of the legitimation of *praxis*. Even *phronēsis* may be too determinate a notion for practical judgment, as if it pursued necessity while falling into consensus. We find in Habermas and Arendt this almost circular movement, as if granting *praxis* its limitations acknowledges its standards without grounding them scientifically. The norms of community are asserted by both, though with an extraordinary difference. Habermas affirms con-sensus: "Fundamental to the paradigm of mutual understanding is, rather, the performative attitude of participants in interaction, who coordinate their plans for action by coming to an understanding about something in the world."[15] Arendt appears to agree:

> The term "public" signifies two closely interrelated but not altogether identical phe-nomena:
>
> It means, first, that everything that appears in public can be seen and heard by everybody and has the widest possibly publicity. . . .

Second, the term "public" signifies the world itself, in so far as it is common to all of us and distinguished from our privately owned place in it.[16]

Yet she describes this commonality as the space of difference:

the reality of the public realm relies on the simultaneous presence of innumerable perspectives and aspects in which the common world presents itself and from which no common measurement or denominator can ever be devised.[17]

Being seen and being heard by others derive their significance from the fact that everybody sees and hears from a different position.[18]

The public world is common because everyone who shares it occupies a different position.

Arendt comes close to charity, though to approach further would be to give up her sense of the private. She regards a public realm as a sphere of differences. In the extreme, her words are a compelling affirmation of locality: "The end of the common world has come when it is seen only under one aspect and is permitted to present itself in only one perspective."[19] Here, despite the aporia of the common world that must be different, the community that would come to an end if it gained consensus, she asserts the fundamental truth of practice and the public world: its essence rests on difference. It comes forth in virtue of the obstacles that confront it. This insight echoes strongly: practical judgment knows nothing of consensus and agreement. The locality of practical judgment, realized in charity, expresses not a falling short but fulfillment. Charity echoes the only fulfillment possible of a local, historical creature acting in history. Put another way, the truth of practice echoes sacrifice as sacrifice materializes through charity. Charity is fulfilled in practice as sacrifice and violence. Fulfilled! The only fulfillment possible for a local practice in time reverberates as violence, retribution, including violence against violence and domination. We add to this locality, realized in charity and sacrifice, the dislocation of every sacrifice. We add further the celebration of charity as sacrifice.

Practical judgment repeats charity where charity echoes sacrifice. But charity does not echo undivided loss. Temporality sounds loss but makes possible bringing forth—*poiēsis*. Charity expresses the inexhaustibility of loss, the terrible nature of waste, but not only waste. Here, the onlys of practical judgment define it, delimit the relation between locality and inexhaustibility in a way we have not expressed before. On one side echoes the representation of loss as sacrifice; on the other resounds sacrifice as life, both present in practical judgment as valor. The destruction that defines sacrifice, the waste that defines history, on one side echoes *praxis*, on another side echoes *poiēsis*. The plenitude of nature, falling between locality and inexhaustibility, materializes as the site of *praxis*, where we act, in time, in relation to others. Their otherness gives rise to charity; temporality gives rise to sacrifice. *Praxis* lies between charity and sacrifice, occupies them together as they divide each other.

History chants unending stories of sacrifice, of waste and loss, in forms of celebration and grief, traditionally represented in Western literature by comedy and tragedy. That we might have a history without loss rings of utopia, without a sense of its own limits. That loss might be found irrelevant also rings of utopia, loss without waste. That we might sing of sacrifice unambiguously, without deferral, marks utopia again: history's truth untouched by catastrophe. Sacrifices in history echo irreplaceable losses as inexhaustible waste, inescapable deferrals inescapably deferred. What matters in any present shares with its past, lost and recovered, what mattered then, even while unrecoverably displaced. The project of history seeks to recover the unrecoverable, to repeat the unrepeatable. In that sense, history reverberates as practical judgment, the modality that crystallizes between losses of the past and promises of the future, triumphs of the past and sacrifices of the future, between charity and sacrifice. Practice becomes celebration through the sacrifice of sacrifice, where sacrifice remains unforgotten in the chorale of charity.

Simulation and fetishization echo among the recurrent risks of practical judgment. The celebration of sacrifice unfolds in art in a *poiēsis* for which sacrifice emerges only in its representations. The simulation of grief presents as much danger to *praxis* as its refusal. Art presents us repeatedly with the monstrosity of a loss preserved (and canceled) through its representations. In this sense, art overcomes waste through simulation. So does modern technology, in a different way: simulation without memory. *Praxis* struggles constantly with this threat, that it will lose its relevance as *praxis* by becoming—even simulating—simulation. Yet it cannot cease to be *praxis* even as simulation, which unfolds as another *praxis*. If reality without simulation lacks knowledge of the locality of its own locality, simulation without reality forswears the sacrifices of its sacrifices. Aestheticization simulates a *poiēsis* that represents excess in *praxis* without representing its own excesses.

History tells stories of fulfillment, of charity and plenitude. History transpires in the form of movement, and every movement, even repetition, culminates locally. No history can unfold without teleology: without archaeology and teleology,[20] without memory and prolepsis, without past and future, but every such teleology, with its fulfillments and losses, echoes locality. That we might have a history without fulfillment tells not of tragedy but despair, another thought of practice that denies the limits of its limits. A reverse image of utopia echoes the impossibility of fulfillment, another denial of the limits of limits. Practical judgment unfolds as life lived within the representation of locality and inexhaustibility, charity and sacrifice, novelty and plenitude. The monstrosity of the future, confronting every practical judgment, offers promise and terror their own promise and terror. The monstrosity of the past echoes the threat that its future is our present. The monstrosity of the future echoes that its past was our present. The monstrosity of the present resounds as its past and future, present as simulation through representation's deferrals.

This play of terror and promise echoes the monstrosity of the future in the double sense of the horror and illumination of the future and its representations. We may hear, in the sovereignty of the Law, a covert desire to control the monstrosities of the future, sacrificing with them both its promises and its threats. If we cannot know the future, if we cannot know the results of *praxis*, if *praxis* always materializes pregnant with failure, threatened by loss, then our desire reaches toward the future threatened by its imperfections. The relation of desire to perfection virtually defines the Western tradition as *technē*, even within our modernity. We respond by asking why the imperfectibility of desire and power presents an unbroken threat, why it does not echo judgment itself, without rules, if a monstrous threat also is a threat to that threat. Why can judgment not ensue as judgment, in the betweens, the local *différends*, that define it, free from any commitment to ideality?

The West's traditional response to the threat of imperfection has echoed domination, of people and things and of the representations that characterize every living practice. Such domination rules over the darker side of life and experience with its monstrosities, its representations and their promises. It expresses what Nietzsche means by the will to truth—the desire to control representation, where will and desire, truth and practice meet. The promise within practice echoes representation—its simulated truth and truth of simulation. Yet in seeking to withhold itself from its monstrosities, practice seeks to dominate its own representations, sacrificing imagination to domination of the will.

Desire to control the future includes desire to control representation, for, like every judgment, representation materializes as practice. On the one hand, the idea of a knowledge unthreatened by its future unfolds as no knowledge at all. Science echoes refusal of knowledge's monstrosity, embodied in a will to truth that does not know itself as desire, does not even know itself as representation. On the other hand, where representation rules by means of regulation, it exceeds both law and rule, not by another sovereignty that would regulate what regulates it, but by excesses within sovereignty and representation. Foucault suggests that literature befalls us as the form in which language's excesses ring within classical representation.[21] Analogously, certain works of art and literature—*Don Quixote, Las Meninas*—exceed the forms of representation that delimit them. The modernism that began in 1913 may be viewed as a powerful intervention into the representation of representation, where artistic representation displaces the very possibility of representation.

Representation exceeds itself inexhaustibly; practice unfolds among the different ways in which it does so. The future transpires as the monstrous play of materiality together with excess. We may oppose the tradition's view of science by the thought that art and practice, even philosophy, exceed science. Alternatively, we may take science to exceed itself in virtue of its representativity and practicality. Truth exceeds itself. The political question repeats this excess of truth.

The plenitude of nature, its locality and inexhaustibility, gives rise, in time, to sacrifice and loss, threatens the waste of the past and the monstrosity of the future. Yet these do not express countermovements, but belong to valor. The reciprocities here include excess. Practical judgment inhabits these complex and transgressive spaces, fallen into time. Here valor echoes loss, and loss echoes inexhaustibility. Sacrifice and charity, tragedy and comedy, grief and celebration, resound together in their diaphonies.

It is a commonplace that grief may come forth unrepresented, in that sense unknown; celebration, to the contrary, always sounds in representation. We may add two comments, that representation itself appears unrepresented, its deferral; and that celebration and grief together compose the deferral of practice's excesses, charity and sacrifice. Charity echoes representation of inexhaustibility as sacrifice echoes representation of locality and the two together echo valor. Because locality and inexhaustibility echo each other, charity and sacrifice sound the same except for the deferrals of their representations. Valor materializes in judgment as deferral, resounds as semasis.

Representation, knowledge, and truth meet in practice as they meet in judgment. Their meeting here, as practical judgment, echoes representation of our polyphonic relations to time and our surroundings. In time, through practice, we repeatedly depart from a past that we yearn to preserve without loss toward a future that we welcome in its terrible monstrosities, including its violences toward the past. In relation to our surroundings, through practice, we confront terrible losses that we desperately seek to avoid while we materialize as their inescapable causes, agents before a future promising achievements and fulfillments, surrounded by waste.

The play of judgment on judgment ensues as semasis. It inhabits two divided spheres: that of temporality, divided by the losses of the past and monstrosities of the future; and that of representation, the untruths of truth. The monstrous truth of science sounds its representativity and practicality, divided by untruth, waste, and loss. Modern science's reason must ignore the sacrifices its own practices impose, the violences and exclusions that define the practice of science, even while science as practice may depredate life and experience, if only in the form of technology. Yet this depredation divides with practice and representation into its others, and every destruction by technology works productively.

The traditional embodiments of *praxis* materialize as power, desire, and law. Law, here, echoes less the truth of *praxis* than its *technē*, certainly not its fulfillment. We have noted Lyotard's grounding of *praxis* in the form of a law with no content whatever; what happens is the obligation to link.[22] We have questioned the assumption behind such a view of *praxis*, that it rests on rule more than virtue, that duty and the good can be separated, an assumption that marks modernity against the Greeks. Our sonorescence cannot accept law with its obligations, however (or especially) pure. It questions the obligation to be obligated, the law behind the law, questions whether being good can transpire as good, how it must emerge in relation to its other: the badness of the good, the unvalor of valor, echoing the ugliness that rings within the sublime. Our sonorescence seeks to represent its limits and their limits, including knowledge that it will never know itself—or anything else—completely. It profoundly suspects the necessity of the Law, regarding it as another privilege and domination. It accepts necessity as deferral.

The law that grounds practice in the West rules as Law. This conjunction of law and Law resounds dislocated within and by itself. The purity of Law does not speak of its displacement, does not acknowledge transgression. The name of law, here, echoes dislocation, forbidden by the Law. We are reminded again of Foucault, for whom the domination of the Law marks the dislocations of power and desire:

> it seems to me that this analytics [of power] can be constituted only if it frees itself completely from a certain representation of power that I would term—it will be seen later why—"juridico-discursive." It is this conception that governs both the thematics of repression and the theory of law as constitutive of desire. . . . They both rely on a common representation of power which, depending on the use made of it and the position it is accorded with respect to desire, leads to two contrary results: either to the promise of a "liberation," if power is seen as having only an external hold on desire, or, if it is constitutive of desire itself, to the affirmation: you are always-already trapped.[23]

The links Foucault makes here are important for the representation of practice, from the juridico-discursive representation of Power through its authority over desire. The Law and law divide each other repeating the dividedness of Power and power. This sundered truth is not fully acknowledged by Foucault: he contrasts his analytics of power with the juridico-discursive model. Yet although power does not repeat Power, it belongs to power, if only as one of its epochs, within its historicality. "Power" belongs to power as we belong to history. Where Power materializes by exclusion, power includes its other, even Power, as resistance. Resistance repeats power without exclusion. Yet the unlawful falls within law as its other though excluded by the Law. Otherwise there emerges the temptation to think toward a practice founded on a pure law and an analytics of power without loss.

"Power" and Law emerge as juridico-discursive because they relate representation to the law of its own desire, the desire for regulation. It is unclear whether Foucault means to suggest that Power has authority over desire but that desire does not impose itself on power. The excess of power in relation to desire entails Power, realized uncannily in the authority of power over desire, typically in the form of violence and domination. The excess of desire in relation to power entails that desire exceeds authority and itself, first in the form of Law, then in the "immense expanse of shade" that characterizes modernity's desire for desire. "Sade attains the end of Classical discourse and thought. He holds sway precisely upon their frontier. After him, violence, life and death, desire, and sexuality will extend, below the level of representation, an immense expanse of shade which we are now attempting to recover, as far as we can, in our discourse, in our freedom, in our thought."[24] Foucault expresses here the excesses of desire over representation. We add that, although desire, with violence, life and death, and sexuality, exceeds representation, representation also exceeds desire; similarly, power and desire exceed and delimit each other. The bottomless sea drowns us in a plenitude of monstrous excesses.

The Law here, even as the law of desire, exercises power over desire no more than desire over power: each rules as the other's excess; each echoes the other as itself. The Law represents the point at which power, desire, and representation meet, where desire echoes power's resistance and repetition, and power echoes desire's desire insofar as desire defers itself. The distance of power from power echoes desire; the echo resounds as representation. The distance of desire from desire echoes desire again and power, both falling into representation's deferral.

It follows that the way in which power imposes its law on desire, externally or constitutively, enforces its reciprocities and excesses: desire imposes its law on power; law imposes its will on power; power imposes its desire on law. Power echoes everywhere, together with desire. Where these everywheres meet resound deferral, excess, and representation. Foucault calls a certain view of power's relationship to desire juridico-discursive. It manifests a particular historical relation of representation to desire and power.

One theme pertaining to Foucault's discussion of the law of desire is that of repression. Another is the everywhere of power. We have represented the latter as the everywhere of practical judgment. Every judgment unfolds as practical, though practical judgment does not manifest itself as the only mode of judgment. We have represented the former as the untruth of truth, the misrepresentation of representation, as they materialize in practical judgment.

Here practice falls among the limits and excesses that echo power, desire, and law, where repression on the one hand materializes as power over desire and on the other as desire over power, in both cases as their Law, derived from the law of practice, and its Other. Practice falls between law as instrument and domination, where the domination of domination rules as the law of law. We have refused a Law of law. Similarly, no Power materializes over power, only the others of its resistances, but desire reaches toward desire, repeats itself as its other, exceeds itself in its self-representations. Desire and power here manifest excesses that constitute law. Their conjunction ensues as valor.

The major question of our practice may be how these inexhaustible junctures within practice relate to charity and sacrifice. How are locality and inexhaustibility manifested within practical judgment in relation to power, desire, and representation? Charity echoes inexhaustibility; sacrifice mourns locality; valor repeats the togetherness of charity and sacrifice in practice, the interplay of locality and inexhaustibility in judgment.

Power expresses locality as domination and resistance. Acting destroys. It also builds. Power and resistance belong to sacrifice. By contrast, desire reaches forth less as sacrifice than charity. Where desire is thought of exclusively as teleological, it falls within *praxis* as *technē*, lacking excess and deferral. Acknowledging the excesses of desire, not only in relation to power and *praxis*, but in relation to itself, affirms the locality of *technē* and redefines its teleology. Sacrificing *technē* to itself within *praxis* affirms the desire within desire that defines every relation of a living creature to its others, the spaces opened within desire by the play of its multiple representations. Desire inexhaustibly exceeds desire as desire. Realization of this inexhaustibility rings out as charity.

We return with this truth to the law within desire as the power over desire. The law of desire rules as its *technē*. The excesses of desire in relation to desire, over and within itself, echo the excesses of power materialized as resistance. "Power" manifests the *technē* within power, overcoming its displacements through the Law in terms of another displacement. The same Law echoes the law of desire, overcoming its dividedness within itself, controlling its excesses. Desire echoes excess on the side of both its objects and creatures with desires. This sense of the limits of the limits of desire in relation to a practical creature echoes charity. The Law here rules within our tradition as a violent sacrifice of power and desire. We cannot respond by abrogating the Law, for we cannot escape the sacrifices that delimit our historicality.

Law here rules as the play of desire and power, expresses inexhaustibility and locality. These correspond within practical judgment to charity and sacrifice, but within practice, not perhaps within science, philosophy, or art. Locality bears a special relationship to practice, marked by sacrifice, though locality is inescapable within charity, within desire and power. Similarly, inexhaustibility bears a special relationship to practice, marked by charity, though inexhaustibility is inescapable within sacrifice, within power and desire. To say that law rules as Law is to acknowledge this play of locality and inexhaustibility within practical judgment, realized as charity and sacrifice but exceeding them together as they exceed each other. The Law rules as the displaced representation of practical reason. It exercises itself as the unavoidable sacrifice within valor.

That the Law rules as the Law of Practice identifies *praxis* with *technē*, with perfectibility. That the Law rules as an instrument of *praxis* reidentifies *praxis* with *technē*. We may, with Nietzsche and Heidegger, interpret this view of practical judgment as present in the Platonic view of *praxis*, taking sides in the quarrel between philosophy and poetry. Alternatively, we may agree with Adorno and Foucault that it echoes a trait of Enlightenment modernity. In both cases, *praxis* and *technē* mark the poles that delimit the relations of law to power and desire.

Alternatively, we may find in desire, going back to the Greeks and forward through the regimentations of The Body, an excessive relationship to itself, representing charity. Here the sexual violence and domination that characterize Sade's view of desire mark both charity and violence within it. The immaterialities of embodiment and excesses of desire speak against any utopian view of human practice. Even worse, the inexhaustibility that characterizes valor resounds not as sacrifice, even violence, in a finite universe, as if in a more perfect world charity might emerge without sacrifice. Marked as desire's excess in relation to itself, charity echoes sacrifice. Practice works as violence and domination, does so because of inexhaustibility. Violence and domination extrude as the dark sides of valor pervading every living practice.

We have noted Whitehead's similar understanding: "The nature of evil is that the characters of things are mutually obstructive. Thus the depths of life require a process of selection. Selection is at once the measure of evil, and the process of its evasion."[25] Selection is locality, evil and its overcoming, charity and sacrifice, as locality repeats inexhaustibility. Practice obtrudes as that mode of judgment which, in its relationship to time, falls between charity and sacrifice, between power and desire, where these materialize as life and being for a practical creature. To live is to desire, where representation, truth, judgment, and being transpire surrounded by the excesses of desire in relation to itself—charity. To live is to be influenced and influential—power—where locality materializes as power and the locality of practice materializes as sacrifice. The Law, here, both regulates desire as power and rules as the excesses whereby desire exceeds itself. To think that we must follow the Law is as arbitrary as to suppose that we can avoid it. The reason is that law exceeds itself, like desire, as the Law no less than as power and desire. Analogously, practical judgment exceeds itself, in relation to past and future, as the law of practice and as the deferral of desire.

In our tradition, within the *logos*, desire and power, truth and representation, are ruled by Law. Our modernity brings us to a different relation to law, at least within its representation. "Law" exceeds itself as law. This dividedness pertains to natural and human law, to the law of power and the law of desire, to the will to law and the will for Law. The questions posed for us, within *praxis*, are whether its laws belong to it from within its *logos*, its governance by our tradition's Law of Truth, or whether law rules as an instrumentality for practical judgment. And if the latter, if law materializes as something used by *praxis*, is it then only *technē*?

The answers we have sounded are that the only of *technē* echoes aporia, that the perfectibility of *technē* belongs to it within a tradition that imposed a certain relationship upon it, that *technē* may be associated with *poiēsis* as well as with perfectibility and ideality, where the perfection of *poiēsis* is anything but technical perfectibility. Instrumentality suggests the perfectibility of *technē* only where the latter already resounds within perfectibility.

Heidegger associates *technē* with *epistēmē*.

> We must observe two things with respect to the meaning of this word. One is that *technē* is the name not only for the activities and skills of the craftsman, but also for the arts of the of the mind and the fine arts. *Technē* belongs to bringing-forth, to *poiēsis*; it is something poetic.
>
> The other thing that we should with regard to *Technē* is even more important. From earliest times until Plato the word *Technē* is associated with the word *epistēmē*.[26]

More difficult to hear may be the displacement of bringing-forth that defines *technē* as *poiēsis*. The perfectibility that defines *technē* belongs to it within the dividedness of its Law, where *technē* and *poiēsis* come forth as the same. In this space, we find law.

Insofar as *technē* comes forth divided polyphonically, instrumentality emerges, divided by its others, beauty and truth. Instrumentality echoes its polyphonies. Similarly, teleology and desire echo their deferrals. The Law here rules where the *logos* dislocates itself. The teleology of instrumentality suggests perfectibility, stillness, whereas, in lived experience, technology moves disruptively and transgressively, polyphonically. It does so in the form of *praxis*, not in discourse or thought. Moreover, these too echo *praxis*.

Law belongs to practical judgment in at least three ways: as the law of will and desire that governs practice; as the law that delimits the practicality of judgment, ethics in relation to truth; and as the laws that emerge within *praxis*. The first poses a human essence that grounds desire and will, ignoring its own will to truth. The second delimits a multiplicity of judgmental modalities, but grounds practical judgment on law. The third remains within practical judgment in an epoch that thinks of justice as founded on the rule of Law. Here we may seek in practice to understand both the Rule and the Law. The Law, as Kafka knew, governs the site of our monstrous inexhaustibility. Politics cannot escape from law, both as its reason and as its instrument. In both cases, law rules divided. It follows that the movement of reason into law, fundamental in Hegel, is a deferred movement of liberation and oppression. The *logos* imposes chains on a free imagination, defining its measure. The stability of adaptation under law, instrumental and teleological, stands forth as comfort and domination. The law of democracy rules as domination without oppression—at least, without oppressive oppression. The law of politics rules as desire as desire moves as the truth of practice.

No politics, no practice, can transpire without violence and domination. Law rules as the greatest instrument of resistance to such domination and oppression; but resistance repeats power, domination and oppression. Similarly, no practice can unfold without desire. Law governs as the greatest force imposing order on desire, but also the greatest fulfillment of desire for power. Science, here, in relation to nature, acts among the greatest forms of practice, permeated by power and desire.

Law rules as power's and desire's instrument, exceeding their authority and instrumentality, passing into other forms of desire and power. Where law defines the rationality of politics, it imposes itself wherever judgment must proceed without rules. Where law defines the community of politics, it imposes itself wherever judgment must proceed without generality. Where law defines the adjudicative side of practice, it imposes itself within the territories where there are no laws.

The displacement of law challenges several mythologies: that reason demands a law; that representation rules only through law; that law defines truth and judgment; that judgment adjudicates within law. All but the last are outcomes of our prior discussions. The last is very important.

Judgment echoes locality and inexhaustibility, represents without rule, free from and within the law. Where laws exist and are not coercive, they define adjudication within the play of judgment, define rationality as adjudication. Such adjudication presupposes mediation, cannot tolerate unending deferral, echoes measure and universality. In this respect, it differs from judgment, which has no intrinsic relation to law. Thus, adjudication either repeats judgment, without rule and law except as excesses of its *techne*, or it specifies its essence as law.

Where adjudication echoes locality and inexhaustibility, so does law, delimited by its others, power, desire, and representation. Law on one side rules judgment without rules, on another rules within representation, on a third, echoes semasis. Law echoes reason itself, undermined at its limits. Law repeats practical instrumentality, aiming at community and stability, undermined in sacrifice. Law manifests the essence of social practice, transgressed by the sacrifices demanded by charity. Law echoes the realization in social practice of charity, fulfilled and undermined by charity's sacrifices. Law attempts to rationalize charity without sacrifice. In this way, it profoundly echoes the aporias of political practice.

Our sonorescent view of law begins in this space where the utopian image of the Law's perfectibility appears, replacing it by its finiteness: sacrifice without charity. There echoes no charity without sacrifice, but also no sacrifice without charity. The holiness of the Law repeats its oppressiveness, but also represents its dreams of charity. In this aporia, law exercises itself within political practice as its other and itself. Within this aporia practice finds its reason.

Two questions arise within our multiple representation of the pervasiveness of practice. Both are residues of the rule of Law. First, where judgment observes no laws except within a sedimented relation to its time, a customary relation to its culture, and where we think that Truth and Goodness belong to Law, how are we to know justice and liberation when we encounter them, especially if our truths reach us as historically and culturally situated? The question of liberation here echoes the historical and cultural locality of judgment. How are we to know justice and liberation if we are not able to escape locality? We ask in return, why do our historical situations not embody justice as they embody representation, desire, and practice? Why do justice and liberation not belong to history—though not only to history—in the form of multiple deferral? Among the forms of deferral echo the polyphonies of every stillness among modalities of judgment, in particular, between theory and practice. The truth of justice echoes practice along with theory, multiplied by the modalities of judgment and query. We ask instead how we may adjudicate our differences where judgment has no law.

Second, if no law of judgment rules, if judgment has no necessity, what may we reply to those who repudiate it, who do not judge, or who do not judge as we do? The question assumes that the same echoes normatively within judgment, that judgment's differences mark lapses within a striving for universality, at least consensus. This view of normativity in practice repeats the myth of Law. Intelligibility, goodness, and truth all must be lawful twice to be normative: they must be embodied in law and that law must exercise sovereignty.

Our sonorescence views practical judgment as falling into time transgressively, displacing law and its sovereignty. Consensus sounds one norm among others, by no means a supreme Law. Reason and truth echo consensus no more than fragmentation, disturbance no less than equanimity. Disorder and order unfold together in a play of harmony and disharmony, belonging together with truth and goodness, even law, in unending disharmonies.

The question of how to adjudicate our differences where judgment has no law has no law. We judge by judgment, however we do so; we sometimes pursue agreement, sometimes difference. The answer to the question of how we may respond to those who do not judge repeats that they do judge and we judge their judgments in return. Practical creatures cannot avoid judgment. Others may not judge as we do; their judgments may represent insurmountable disharmonies. Our responses endlessly echo tempered by the inescapable demand to ameliorate injustice and the unavoidable deferrals of local practice.

The melancholies that despair at the displacements of practical judgment do not materialize as problems of practice, with or without solutions. They represent one pole of the conditions that define practical judgments: laws belong to and do not rule over practice. Skepticism and nihilism do not fall outside practice, but within: they are not practice's Truth because no truth of practice echoes apart from judgment. They materialize as debilitating and impotent forms of practice. We engage in practice as we live and act, and we cannot avoid practical judgments or the questions that emerge within them. Nor can we resolve practical judgments by law. Endless deferrals of practical query produce nihilism only where it reimposes the absolute it has repudiated. Skepticism, similarly, either echoes deferral of the unending deferral of a displaced truth, which continues into a monstrous future, or separates us from that monstrosity by an absolute barrier. Nihilism, skepticism, and relativism resound as unlimited affirmations of limitation.

The displacement of truth echoes untruth within it—and reciprocally. The displacements of practice echo the polyphonies of law and desire. One consequence repeats the displacements of history: the untruths of history as its truth. Another echoes the dislocations of justice as injustice. Justice transpires as always unjust. It follows that there resounds no *technē* of justice, no ideality to morality or politics, only the concord and discord of justice within injustice. There comes forth no *technē* of justice, no *technē* of *praxis*. Practical query rests on valor rather than perfectibility.

How can we tell justice from injustice? It may be difficult to do so, especially by rule. How can we convince another, bent on injustice, to refrain? It may be difficult to do so, especially when we are unsure ourselves, humble before the play of differences. Why should we expect things to be easier? Why should we expect reason to be able to overcome every resistance? Why should it possess power without being localized by it? Why should we suppose that reason's practice might escape violence? How can we escape from practice's reason, however aporetic?

In the Western tradition, ethics, like *technē*, joins with ideality and perfectibility. Even in Aristotle, where *phronēsis* replaces *technē*, form functions in a sphere of ideality. Excepting Aristotle, the subsequent tradition, largely Christian, found its ideality in God. But the site is of little consequence: the ideality is more germane. Ethics, here, names itself as a *technē* even where it would avoid technique. It presupposes perfection as its ideality. It denies its togetherness with desire and power, which, with representation, possess no perfectibility. In our sonorescence, art represents our paradigm of practice by repudiating technical perfectibility and redefining perfection without ideality, where practical judgment rules without rules except where rules themselves emerge as practical judgments without rules. Here ideals entail neither *technē* nor ideality: ideals without ideality—without perfectibility.[27] One way to represent this contrast is by emphasizing the fundamentally political nature of practice, where ethics represents an ideality founded on *technē*. Another is through a local ethics that rests on locality and disharmony.[28] What defines ideality here is valor.

Practice falls into time as charity and sacrifice. Charity sounds the sense—the inexhaustible representation—of inexhaustibility. Sacrifice sounds the inexhaustible representation of locality. Both echo deferral, where the multiple representation of multiple deferral echoes valor. We find ourselves reapproaching desire on one side, falling into time, but labor and work on the other, already fallen. Of all judgmental forms whose practicality exceeds the Law, labor, work, and desire exceed each other and themselves. Their excesses echo valor.

Arendt distinguishes labor and work, the former caught up in the wastefulness of time, the latter making a difference.

> It is indeed the mark of all laboring that it leaves nothing behind, that the result of its effort is almost as quickly consumed as the effort is spent.[29]

> The work of our hands, as distinguished from the labor of our bodies—*homo faber* who makes and literally "works upon" as distinguished from the *animal laborans* which labors and "mixes with"—fabricates the sheer unending variety of things whose sum total constitutes the human artifice.[30]

Work is practical judgment, including art. Labor is neither science nor art, for it leaves behind no work. This notion of a work is Heidegger's: putting truth into work.[31]

Labor and work respond to sacrifice and loss from within, the one attempting to overpower sacrifice by nullifying loss, the other attempting to overpower it by will. It may appear odd to speak of works of art as overpowering in practice, yet the notion of durability suggests such a power. More important is the life of the mind.

For thinking of the mind as theoretical represents it as free from sacrifice and waste, from *praxis*, thereby from efficacy. Heidegger repeatedly suggests that philosophy is useless, neither labor nor work. It echoes *poiēsis*, bringing forth. And in such bringing, such making and acting, violence and death irrupt. Thinking materializes as violence, destruction and creation. Truth irrupts as violence's result. Here we may return to *technē* as both the supreme violence in our tradition and enduring expression of its excesses.

Technē echoes both extreme violence and perfectibility, echoes its own displacement. In this form, it includes violence and representation. If we with Nietzsche trace back to Socrates the technical view of nature whose violence names our tradition, then this opening into *technē* represents abandonment of technique. If, instead, with Foucault we trace technique and measure to Enlightenment modernity, then the Greek view of *technē* opens an alternative within by tearing it asunder.

Labor works as *praxis*; work labors as *poiēsis*. Combining the two gives *technē*. One of *technē*'s most violent violences imposes measure on every phase of *praxis*—an economic view of *praxis*. Money circulates as the supreme measure of value. Value purchases an economic view of *praxis*: entirely technical.

We may note here capitalism's role as imposing *technē* on itself: instrumentality. Even here, utility under capitalism unfolds as judgment in relation to the future, semasis and deferral, whether or not given over to instrumentality. The dividedness of *technē* materializes as capitalism's abandonment, an impossible task under its rule. Capitalism achieves either *technē* or *poiēsis*; alternatively, it joins the two represented by the break between them. The contradictions of capitalism, ancient within *technē*, echo that it would be *technē* but acts as *poiēsis*. Socialism, here, repeats capitalism, still striving to be *technē* but materializing doubly as *poiēsis*. This setting into work that characterizes capitalism and socialism expresses their practicality. Practical judgment materializes as *poiēsis*, *technē*, and *praxis*, each the other's violence. The break in *technē* reflects its violence as *poiēsis*. It resists the alternatives named as capitalism and socialism, resists representing them as disharmonies. Rather, they express the contemporary forms of political *praxis* inseparably together in the same.

One of the discoveries of our modern *praxis*, one of its forms of regulation, lies in the covert forms of representation of its representations. Capitalism and modern technology meet at the point where technology and representation join forces. Television, cinema, newspapers, and advertising echo as fundamentally the same. The truth of contemporary politics echoes representational media's truth—simulation. The goodness of contemporary politics echoes representational media's goodness—again simulation. Our local form of *alētheia* shines as television.

This last truth echoes the violence present within the most democratic contemporary regimes, violences within unknown to them. And rightly so, because by comparison with repressive governments—Nazi Germany, Soviet Russia, Communist China—their truth is open and disclosed. Missing in this disclosure murmur the secrets of its truth. The truth of our modern democratic *praxis* materializes as capitalism with its technology. Postcolonialism and postcapitalism dwell in the dislocations of our repetitions.

TEN

Humanity

Humanity echoes through representation, power, desire, history, practice, and embodiment—and more. These deferred representations resound in our sonorescence through several univocals: locality, inexhaustibility, judgment; power, desire, representation; onlyness, loneliness, ownliness; unison-resonance, harmony-disharmony, stillness-polyphony. The univocity here echoes aporia: locality, inexhaustibility, and judgment resound against every totality, including their own, echo their necessity in a contingent way. The aporia echoes the belonging together of representation and simulation; these representations harmonize their own disharmonies.

If these representations sound discordantly, and they define humanity, then humanity echoes discordance. Here The Human marks an essence that vanishes into the constitution of humanity through representation. Similarly, nature unfolds as humanity's other while resounding within its representations. At one pole, nature represents Reality against Simulation; at another pole, nature represents the reality of simulation and the unreality of reality.

That humanity echoes representation, in conjunction with the representation of nature, on one side marks the decentering of the Subject—The Human—and on the other marks the reemergence of Humanity within the divided representations of its Others: animal and machine; nature and reality; child and female; representation and misrepresentation. The presence of these different others marks a predominant theme within the multiple representations of humanity—always Human. This representation marks privilege, of man or machine, humanity or nature. Humanity's representation echoes authority.

Decentering the subject presents a variety of different movements, especially two: (1) returning humanity to nature without restitution, therefore at the same time restoring nature to humanity; (2) disallowing a singular point of privilege at which nature and humanity meet, for example, in the autonomy of the will or where genius meets the sublime, even the Clearing of Being and Language. The key word here is "singular," for nature and humanity emerge as points of privilege even where they repudiate precedence. Nature's cacophony, *physis*, echoes neither humanity's lack, for example, in relation to *technē*, nor an undisrupted harmony. Nature and humanity resound within the cacophony of their polyphonies. If we reject the singular point at which genius marks our sense of the sublime, then excess sounds everywhere, where these totalities mark their cancellation in the excesses of excess.

The metaphysical movement, as Heidegger describes it, represents ontotheology, concerned with grounds, totality, and logic. A local metaphysical movement cannot repudiate totality and representation, even within its sonorescence, though it may Repudiate God against any Totalizing Representation. Each of the terms of this local movement belongs with and departs from its predecessors: Being becomes locality, totality passes into inexhaustibility, representation represents itself as judgment. The identities present here are not movements beyond representation to another reality, but movements within representation's excesses where it represents its realities. Each of these withins represents a movement without: the "mis-" of representation, the "meta-" of metaphysics. Truth echoes reality's simulation.

With this recognition, ringing between representation and misrepresentation, truth and untruth, we may return our discussion against metaphysics to metaphysics once more within our sonorescence, first in relation to humanity decentered in relation to representation, then in relation to nature, decentered within itself. These two reciprocal movements compose the concluding chapters of these sonorescences.

Classical American philosophy pursues two principles of continuity: one between theory and practice, the other between humanity and nature. The former, frequently understood to define theory in terms of practice, gives pragmatism its name and represents its historical essence. Yet in almost every way, this representation fails to express the multiply reflexive truth of pragmatism: a theory that represents itself as defined by practice, where practice is always local. In our sonorescent terms, practice materializes as representation and philosophy echoes practice, while representation sounds its locality and inexhaustibility. The metaphysical representation of the locality of representation rings out as aporia. The practical representation of the locality of practice materializes as failure. Charity expresses the representation of practical judgment as failure where failure marks its own excesses.

The second continuity, between humanity and nature, appears iconoclastic toward a modern privileging of the subject and a metaphysical recentering of nature. The recentering of nature here does not present us with the human cast in the form of nature—the Nature of the Human—but with nature and humanity displaced together. The inexhaustible plenitude of nature, consequently of human nature, conflicts with the essences of Humanity and Nature. This theme in American philosophy—its double rejection of essences—may be identified with its naturalism, one that dislocates metaphysics and nature.

Qualities, Dewey says, belong to nature.

If we recognize that all qualities directly had in conscious experience apart from use made of them, testify to nature's characterization by immediacy and finality, there is ground for unsophisticated recognition of use and enjoyment of things as natural, as belonging to the things as well as to us. *Things* are beautiful and ugly, lovely and hateful, dull and illuminated, attractive and repulsive. Stir and thrill in us is as much theirs as is length, breadth, an thickness. Even the utility of things, their capacity to be employed as means and agencies, is first of all not a relation, but a quality possessed, immediately possessed, it is as esthetic as any other quality.[1]

This may be heard to emphasize immediacy and possession, the unity and synthesis of qualitative experience. Here, felt qualities, traditionally belonging to experience only, belong to nature. "Like its congeners, life and history, [experience] includes *what* men do and suffer, *what* they strive for, love, believe and endure, and also *how* men act and are acted upon, the ways in which they do and suffer, desire and enjoy, see, believe, imagine—in short, processes of *experiencing*."[2] Experience and nature mark undivided wholes that reflection divides: unions of what and how, what and who, subject and object.

Such a reading is not the only plausible one, for the dispersions already belong to experience and nature, as well as between them. At least three alternatives for understanding the relation between nature and experience echo here: (1) accepting the terms of reflective experience, accepting representation's representations as nature's undisplaced truths; (2) accepting the global field of experience, the lived world, that grounds the terms of reflection, accepting another representation of representation as undivided; (3) accepting the inescapable reciprocities and excesses of experience, nature, and representation as expressing stillness and polyphony. With respect to the last alternative, philosophy has no unitary truth to tell either of things and human beings or of its own global representations: being, experience, and nature. Its truths echo as dispersed truths, untrue as well as true, misrepresentative as well as representative. The plenitude of experience, nature, and being manifests itself in deferral and transgression. The pervasiveness of qualities and the unity of experience represent aporias in nature and humanity.

The striking movement in Dewey's account of experience is from humanity to nature.

experience is *of* as well as *in* nature. . . . Things interacting in certain ways *are* experience; they are what is experienced. Linked in certain other ways with another natural object—the human organism—they are *how* things are experienced as well. Experience thus reaches down into nature; it has depth. It also has breadth and to an indefinitely elastic extent. It stretches.[3]

A totalizing movement echoes here, resisted in two remarkable ways. One is that, although qualities belong to nature, they echo there in a plenitude that resists every attempt to capture it. This is a nature with everything in it, where the totality includes the inexhaustible reality of human experience: inchoate, abyssal, and incommensurate. It is a local and inexhaustible nature: reality indistinguishable from simulation, truth inseparable from untruth. "[Pragmatism] finds that 'reality' is a *denotative* term, a word used to designate indifferently everything that happens. Lies, dreams, insanities, deceptions, myths, theories are all of them just the events which they specifically are."[4] The everything that happens expresses inexhaustibility. It cannot be a Totality and there is no way to represent it, for it is everything without being anything.

James denies the totality of the universe by asserting its plurality: "Something always escapes. 'Ever not quite' has to be said of the best attempts made anywhere in the universe at attaining all-inclusiveness."[5] Dewey univocally asserts all-inclusiveness. Each represents aporia. In both, there is something that escapes, the one that falls without, the other that falls irresistibly within, shattering the complacency of its limits.

The second way in which the totality of nature resists totalization is that nature includes its multiple representations. The theories and meanings of reflective experience occupy many local historical spaces: they resound as theories for a human purpose, and human purposes belong to local nature. Pragmatism tells a pragmatistic, culturally and historically situated truth of nature, experience, and itself.

When Dewey says that experience is of as well as in nature, that experience stretches into nature, he does not discuss how the prepositions clash, how the ways in which experience is of—representationally—relate to the ways in which it is in. It is tempting to interpret him as resolving without conflict the locality of experience and nature.

The alternative is that the relation between of and in falls aporetically into nature and experience. Experience is of nature through representation, but representation belongs to nature in departure, echoes nature polyphonically. The transgressions of representation lie at the point where of and in belong together. The conflicts between experience and nature are either resolved without remainder or remain within nature in the form of aporia. Dewey speaks directly to this aporia in response to criticism that he does not keep nature and experience apart:

> There is a circularity in the position taken regarding the connection of experience and nature. . . . Upon one side, analysis and interpretation is made dependent upon the conclusions of the natural sciences, . . .
>
> The other aspect of the circle is found in the fact that it is held that experience itself . . . contains the materials and the processes and operations which, when they are rightly laid hold of and used, lead to the methods and conclusions of the natural sciences; namely, to the very conclusions that provide the means for forming a theory of experience. That this circle exists is not so much admitted as claimed. It is also claimed that the circle is not vicious; for instead of being logical it is existential and historic.[6]

The circle exists but is not vicious, not because it is free from aporia, but because it is existential and historical. It is experienced and belongs to history. The circle is local. Experience is an inexhaustible mélange of qualities and processes, situations and their locality, where the locality of locality echoes inexhaustibility, the humanity of humanity sounds its locality, and the empiricity of empiricity echoes excess. Science exists within this mélange on both sides: within representation it transpires divided by the multiplicities of judgment and its modalities; within nature it unfolds divided by the excesses of experience in nature. The *of* in relation to the *in* echoes transgression. This transgression echoes locality; its deferral expresses inexhaustibility.

Totalities of Nature and Experience are Metaphysical, except that they ring for us not as Totalities, but as excesses, univocals, divided superaltern unisons that express incomprehensiveness in their comprehensiveness. Although Dewey writes as if these univocals were somehow synthetic, they are displaced by two great reciprocal excesses: experience and nature, and theory and practice. The continuities between experience and nature and between theory and practice emerge as disharmonious unisons.

Dewey is not alone in presenting a nature whose unity echoes transgression and aporia. Spinoza is widely known but Aristotle may be included, especially in Heidegger's reading of *physis* and Randall's reading of *ousia*.[7] The plenitude of *physis* includes what has been forgotten within the metaphysical tradition in the reverberations of *technē*.[8]

Spinoza is a remarkable example. For the attributes of thought and extension in an undivided God whose absolutely infinite nature entails an infinite number of attributes, each infinite, and the finite and infinite meet in a double causation in which each mode follows from God but also from other modes ad infinitum. Nature is at once many and one: *natura naturans* and *natura naturata*. The aporia is the mark of the transgressiveness of Spinoza's metaphysics. Metaphysics has always been transgressive, if not only transgressive.

> An individual thing, or a thing which is finite and which has a determinate existence, cannot exist nor be determined to action unless it be determined to existence and action by another cause which is also finite and has a determinate existence; and again, this cause cannot exist nor be determined to action unless by another cause which is also finite and determined to existence and action, and so on *ad infinitum*.[9]

> In Nature there is nothing contingent, but all things are determined from the necessity of the divine nature to exist and act in a certain manner.[10]

The togetherness of thought and extension in God is Spinoza's naturalism, analogous to the naturalism found in James and Dewey. The belonging together of *natura naturans* and *natura naturata* as nature marks nature's excesses in relation to God and God's in relation to nature. Nature is excess within, divided by infinite differences. But it is still one, excessive. Metaphysics here is not a *technē* but inexhaustible representation of inexhaustible excesses.

A metaphysical excess rings in Dewey, belonging to his pragmatism, that is difficult to hear in Spinoza: the representation of metaphysics as representation. Although he writes of the interpretation of the Bible, Spinoza does not write of his own writings. Although they appear to fall within knowledge from sense and signs, appear therefore to be inadequate knowledge, he presents them as the truth of truth, as ideas in God. This aporia is no less powerful for its recessiveness. What Spinoza leaves unthought is the question of the unthought of his own thought.

Something, not a thing at all, always remains unthought, not because we cannot think everything in a finite time or place but because thought and everything echo as transgressive notions, ringing in the betweens where we encounter nature and humanity. The reason why the essence of humanity remains unthought, in Dewey, Aristotle, and Spinoza, is that it is transgressive at every limit, every boundary within. Humanity echoes our contingent individuality and its excesses, marked on one side by The Human and on the other by Our *Geschlecht*.

It is as if the entire universe were at stake in our Humanity, all of it, every note or quantum of it. This is, of course, supremely ontotheological, except that here ontotheology echoes its own multiple displacement. Our sonorescent representation of excess falls between representation and misrepresentation, shattering the complacency of any thought that would think itself without deferral. Here Derrida's remark about Hegel, representing his tradition, rings its truth: "Philosophy has always insisted upon this: thinking its other. Its other, that which limits it, and from which it derives its essence, its definition, its production."[11] The other to be thought echoes philosophy's limits and may be thought there in an act of appropriation or transgression. Metaphysics in the tradition has frequently occupied the space Derrida describes: thinking its other without transgression. Yet it has never succeeded in doing so, has always been displaced by its own transgressions. The sites where metaphysics acknowledges the transgressiveness of its representations include the plenitude of humanity. Here humanity falls outside itself into its others, disrupted by them, as they fall into it, disrupting themselves. The Human echoes Our *Geschlecht*.

When Sartre sought to reinstate humanism within existentialism, Heidegger replied that such a movement forgets the question of Being. The forgetting here echoes oblivion and obstruction. "Every humanism is either grounded in a metaphysics or is itself made to be the ground of one. . . . In defining the humanity of man humanism not only does not ask about the relation of Being to the essence of man; because of its origin humanism even impedes the question by neither recognizing nor understanding it."[12] Sartre is concerned with practice, and his remarks on humanism may betray more than anything else an unresolved conflict between action and the insecurities of its future. Indeed, Heidegger opens his discussion with reference to action. "We are still far from pondering the essence of action decisively enough. We view action only as causing an effect. The actuality of the effect is valued according to its utility. But the essence of action is accomplishment."[13] Sartre assumes that he cannot avoid a universalization that speaks against the absurdity of existence. Our soniferous reply is that being, for- and in-itself, does indeed echo absurdity, that correspondingly practice materializes as its own absurdity; practice's absurdity, however, remains local, in intimate relation to divided reason. Sartre remains within the authority of the subject and totality.

> Man is nothing else but what he makes of himself. Such is the first principle of existentialism. . . . existentialism's first move is to make every man aware of what he is and to make the full responsibility of his existence rest on him. And when we say that a man is responsible for himself, we do not only mean that he is responsible for his own individuality, but that he is responsible for all men.[14]

Three themes here are striking. First, Man makes *something* of *himself*. The making here materializes as *praxis* while the something stands forth grounded in *technē*. Both may be heard instead as *poiēsis*. The Himself that Man Makes both exceeds every humanity and making and marks the excesses within humanity and *poiēsis*. Existence does not precede essence: it belongs to it as transgression. The essence of a work of art is . . . no thing. Both the making and the essence of Man are more discordant than Sartre acknowledges, even within the absurdity of existence. For both Man and *poiēsis* are absurd; no way can be found to represent their nature, of maker or of what is made, without transgression. Absurdity, here, echoes its inseparability from reason. The essentializing movement in Sartre's humanism sounds particularly striking in the appearance of the phrase, nothing else, an only that betrays the limits circumscribing a totalizing movement. Humanity is never a nothing else but always something else, on the way to elsewhere while fallen into somewhere.

Second, the full responsibility that each Man must take for his own existence is itself absurd, divided within itself so nothing is full, especially responsibility but also *praxis* and *poiēsis*. The fullness of responsibility rings of *technē*. It poses for us the emptiness of *technē* and *praxis*.

Third, this responsibility posits another universalizing movement, in that to be responsible is for All, not just for One. This All denotes both a multiplicity of autonomous subjects within the absurdity of their existence and a totality of The Human. It reaffirms the break in Sartre's existentialism between the in-itself and for-itself, inscribing the limits of humanity in relation to nature. Totality echoes either a fully present metaphysical movement or a univocal totality that repudiates every totality. Among these rejected totalities echoes humanity's essence.

Sartre explicitly denies a human essence, yet covertly reinstates it: "If existence really does precede essence, there is no explaining things away by reference to a fixed and given human nature. In other words, there is no determinism, man is free, man is freedom."[15] Man *is* freedom, and existence *really does* precede essence. Also, there *really is* no determinism. Sartre does not appear to hear that each of these movements repudiates locality, for the human nature that is denied reappears as freedom, and existence really does come first. Sartre explicitly affirms the universality of the denial of universality: "if it is impossible to find in every man some universal essence which would be human nature, yet there does exist a human condition."[16] In vain, we listen for locality.

Existentialism as a Humanism is a popular work. Why should we, why should Heidegger, take it seriously enough to substitute it for Sartre's more technical works where absurdity appears as aporia? Even within this popular work, he emphasizes excess. There is a meaning of humanism "which takes man as an end and as a higher value."[17]

> But there is another meaning of humanism. Fundamentally it is this: man is constantly outside of himself; in projecting himself, in losing himself outside of himself, he makes for man's existing; and, on the other hand, it is by pursuing transcendent goals that he is able to exist; man, being this state of passing-beyond, and seizing upon things only as they bear upon this passing-beyond, is at the heart, at the center of this passing-beyond.[18]

This outside is excess and transgression, though we may wonder at the self of which Man is outside—wonder at Sartre's understanding of *eksistence*. The transcendence sounds another story, for universality reappears without its locality, even though the subject's presence appears to displace it. There is still a human center, inscribed by the Absolute. Sartre's beyond still looks for God. It may instead accept God's death, leaving behind inexhaustible transcendences and beyonds, each local and inexhaustible. Humanity is so far outside itself and transcendence that the freedom that is human is inseparable from confinement, and the responsibility humanity bears is arbitrary, indistinguishable from no responsibility at all.

It is striking to compare Sartre with Beauvoir, whose representation of existentialism has another side while representing itself entirely as Sartrean, even while repeating our *Geschlecht*:

> From the very beginning, existentialism defined itself as a philosophy of ambiguity.[19]

> Man knows and thinks this tragic ambivalence which the animal and the plant merely undergo. . . . He is still a part of this world of which he is a consciousness. He asserts himself as a pure internality against which no external power can take hold, and he also experiences himself as a thing crushed by the dark weight of other

things. At every moment he can grasp the non-temporal truth of his existence. But between the past which no longer is and the future which is not yet, this moment when he exists is nothing.[20]

This view of ambiguity expresses an extreme contrast between mediateness and mediation. Human life is always betwixt and between, defined in terms of temporality and nontemporality, absolute freedom and externality, consciousness and inertness. It is a weakness of Beauvoir's discussion to follow Sartre's extreme formulations of the pure negativities of consciousness, of being for itself. The ambiguity is that there is no such being, that being in itself cannot be determinate without negativity. Being for itself is always situated mediately, influencing and being influenced by other things.

Sartre's existentialism does not turn its interrogative gaze upon itself to ask what kind of ambiguity pertains to freedom itself and what mediateness entails for human practices. Beauvoir sets herself the task of rectifying these omissions. Yet she accepts Sartre's definition of freedom.[21] "Man, Sartre tells us, is 'a being who *makes himself* a lack of being *in order that there might be* being.' That means, first of all, that his passion is not inflicted upon him from without. He chooses it."[22] Her achievement is to know that mediateness is ambiguity—a gesture toward aporia. "An ethics of ambiguity will be one which will refuse to deny *a priori* that separate existents can, at the same time, be bound to each other, that their individual freedoms can forge laws valid for all."[23] Ambiguity is mediateness, neither inexhaustibility nor excess. It is centered on an individual located within social and collective milieux. But these milieux are defined in terms of absolute freedom without ambiguity.

Heidegger's response to Sartre's reinscription of the essence of humanity in humanism is that every form of humanism is metaphysical, oblivious to the question of Being.

> Metaphysics does indeed represent beings in their Being, and so it thinks the Being of beings. But it does not think the difference of both. Metaphysics does not ask about the truth of Being itself.[24]

> Are we really on the right track toward the essence of man as long as we set him off as one living creature among others in contrast to plants, beasts, and God?[25]

Two themes recurrently echo here, one nostalgia toward Being, forgotten by any humanism, repeating the privilege of our *Geschlecht*, the other denial that the essence of humanity must be defined by exclusion, men from animals and plants, God, machines, but also women. The movement of exclusion in the preceding passage is marked by "really," a sign that representation is far from transgression. The two themes circle around each other in the authority of Our Humanity. They meet in the movement toward Being that Heidegger regards as impossible for metaphysics, in the "lighting of Being,"[26] the place where Man's Essence resides. "Metaphysics closes itself to the simple essential fact that man essentially occurs only in his essence, where he is claimed by Being. Only from that claim 'has' he found that wherein his essence dwells."[27] The place where humanity finds itself, outside itself—its *eksistence*—is Being: *eksistence* marks the relation between Being and beings as one of difference and inclusion, still Man's essential Place.

> Ek-sistence, thought in terms of *ecstasis*, does not coincide with *existentia* in either form or content. In terms of content ek-sistence means standing out into the truth of Being.[28]
>
> in the determination of the humanity of man as ek-sistence what is essential is not man but Being—as the dimension of the *ecstasis* of ek-sistence.[29]

Shall we hear the outside of every human relation to itself as nostalgia or transgression? Should we repudiate the or along with the only? Heidegger makes it difficult for us to answer, for what is involved is man's essence,[30] but also when he preserves the moment of contrast against the nearness of Being.

> Yet Being—what is Being? It is It itself. The thinking that is to come must learn to experience that and to say it. "Being"—that is not God and not a cosmic ground. Being is farther than all beings and is yet nearer to man than every being, be it a rock, a beast, a work of art, a machine, be it an angel or God. Being is the nearest. Yet the near remains farthest from man.[31]

The nostalgia for Being that sounds the primary theme in the rejection of humanism keeps circling back to the space in which Man divides Himself from other beings, represented earlier as plants, beasts, and God, now as rocks, beasts, works, machines, angels, and God. This nostalgia marks a tension within the Human as desire for Being.

May we rehabilitate humanism from the vantage point of our recollection of Being? Heidegger asks and answers Sartre's question twice:

> Should we still keep the name "humanism" for a "humanism" that contradicts all previous humanism—although it in no way advocates the inhuman? And keep it just so that by sharing in the use of the name we might perhaps swim in the predominant currents, stifled in metaphysical subjectivism and submerged in the oblivion of Being? Or should thinking, by means of open resistance to "humanism," risk a shock that could for the first time cause perplexity concerning the *humanitas* of *homo humanus* and its basis?[32]
>
> But—as you no doubt have been wanting to rejoin for quite a while now—does not such thinking think precisely the *humanitas* of *homo humanus*? Does it not think *humanitas* in a decisive sense, as no metaphysics has thought it or can think it? Is

> this not "humanism" in the extreme sense? Certainly. It is a humanism that thinks the humanity of man from nearness to Being.[33]
>
> The essence of man lies in ek-sistence.[34]

The essence of humanity unfolds as *eksistence*; humanity is always outside itself and its being, where beings are always outside themselves, in Being. *Eksistence* is the Being of human beings in their being, always other. The other, however, reinscribes the privilege of exclusion within the essence of humanity. The essence of humanity either turns back to Being in transgression, where every exclusion that defines its truth is set aside, or the essence of humanity reinscribes itself as privilege, here in virtue of its nearness to Being. It is the human against the unhuman, even within, for we are forbidden to advocate the unhuman, even within the human. Heidegger is still concerned with the threat to Man and Being of rocks, beasts, works, machines, angels, and God. Within this "in-" or "un-" of humanity we hear the drone of Being's *Geschlecht*.

Even in Heidegger, though resisted at many points, the human seeks definition as a form of exclusion. We ask whether the human can be thought, even as *eksistence*, except in opposition. Humanism seeks the essence of the human as male, white, and rational against females, children, people of color, mad people, animals, and machines. This against marks a movement that posits a certain view of representation. Because locality and inexhaustibility define representation and reality, there is no against, even in opposition to locality and inexhaustibility. These and their others have their locales.

Humanity is not represented by humanism but Represented as Human. Shall we call this Representation Humanism, or shall we relinquish humanism, with representation and its metaphysics, to metaphysics? Shall we give up the history of Humanistic Metaphysics as a Mistake—and from what Nonmetaphysical standpoint—or shall we rehabilitate it as a mistake within representation as our metaphysical sonorescence?

Derrida calls "dogmatic" the side of Heidegger that preserves the opposition of humanity and inhumanity within the repudiation of every such opposition. Man still exercises privilege over animals and machines under the name of *Geschlecht*. "This sentence in sum comes down to distinguishing the human *Geschlecht*, our *Geschlecht*, and the animal *Geschlecht*, called 'animal.'"[35] The key word here is "our": Our *Geschlecht*. This is a humanism if "certainly" not metaphysical: "In its very content, this proposition marks the text's essential scene, marks it with a humanism that wanted certainly to be nonmetaphysical—Heidegger underscores this in the following paragraph—but with a humanism . . . that inscribes not *some* differences but an absolute oppositional limit."[36] What makes it humanistic is its inscription in the hand, marking an infinite difference, the gift:

the name of man, his *Geschlecht*, becomes problematic itself. For it names what has the hand, and so thinking, speech or language, and openness to the gift.

> Man's hand then will be a thing apart not as separable organ but because it is different, dissimilar from all prehensive organs (paws, claws, talons); man's hand is far from these in an infinite way through the abyss of its being. This abyss is speech and thought.[37]

The gift—of language, speech, or thinking—is not given to animals or machines, but only to "us." Similarly, *Geschlecht* is always "ours." Language, the gift, representation, in a movement that opposes dogmatism, reinscribes it dogmatically both within *Geschlecht* and against those who do not think like Us. The difference between humans who do not think and other creatures is infinite, marking the absolute limit of Man. "Apes, too, have organs that can grasp, but they do not have hands. The hand is infinitely different from all the grasping organs—paws, claws, or fangs—different by an abyss of essence. Only a being who can speak, that is, think, can have hands and can handily achieve works of handicraft."[38] This infinite difference represents the gift absolutely, though no representation can represent without transgression. The hand reinscribes both dogma and the limits of representation within itself—within Heidegger's writing—so that it no longer exceeds itself. The edges between humanity and animality, humanity and mechanicality, *poiēsis* and *technē*, representation and humanity, vanish as the gap widens into infinity. The between falls into oblivion both where difference disappears and where it expands into an absolute.

By and within the gift of the hand Heidegger explicitly reinscribes *Geschlecht*.[39] He explicitly refers back to the High German, emphasizing sexual difference within the field of its differences: humanity's nature as sexual duality.[40] The human within our *Geschlecht*, Derrida notes, is struck two blows, both explicit in Heidegger: one its sexuality, the second the violence that characterizes sexual difference.[41] *Unser Geschlecht* marks Us (if we are German) as essentially given by our sexual difference—here dual—and its movement to violence.

Our *Geschlecht* marks a dogmatic space in which The Body extrudes in its transgressions but which, at its own absolute limits, repudiates the dislocations within itself that truth requires. The truth that resounds as untruth can acknowledge no difference as Absolute or Infinite. The movement to truth from within language, recognized by us but not by Heidegger as a movement *within* representation, marks the hand as transgressive, entirely inseparable from paws, fangs, and claws.

Humanity unfolds divided. It transpires as aporia, where aporia marks an unthought that cannot but must be thought despite and in virtue of its monstrous transgressions. The positivity of transgression in Nietzsche and Foucault is no less monstrous for being affirmed: "Transgression contains nothing negative, but affirms limited being—affirms the limitlessness into which it leaps as it opens this zone for the first time. But correspondingly, this affirmation contains nothing positive: no content can bind it, since, by definition, no limit can possibly restrict it."[42] To hear God as the Good once more within the flashing line of transgression is utopian. This affirmation is a good but not The Good—not God. The absence of content keeps us at the abyss; reciprocally, the presence of content echoes aporia; aporia, however enthusiastically affirmed, rings in the abyss. Here humanity is abyssal even as Human, echoing in transgression, transgressing even that transgression. The transgressive movement within transgression echoes transgression of itself, violence against violence, the humanity that displaces humanity. Here nothing can be human, except that everything is. Everything is human, except that nothing *is* human.

Our Geschlecht presents us with the monstrous question whether humanity can be represented in any way without reinstating an unthought point of privilege, without recentering an opposition against which the movement opposing humanism moves. Humanity and inhumanity, representation and reality, move and remove their representations of their representativity.

Here we may return to Foucault's peculiar gesture toward the constitution of a subject that exists only when constituted, those gestures toward the "pure itself" that disappears as soon as it appears. The deferrals in representation and humanity mark an absent content that terrifies as well as pleases, our *jouissance*. The play of desire terrifies because it utilizes power; power terrifies because it overwhelms desire. Humanity echoes in all these spaces, which, as nonspaces, cannot be filled. No thing can fill the space of the representation of human being, neither on the side of representation nor on the sides of humanity and being.

"Man" appears in *The Order of Things* within the space opened up within modernity between knower and known, the figure that defines the human sciences. "Man's mode of being as constituted in modern thought enables him to play two roles: he is at the same time at the foundation of all positivities and present, in a way that cannot even be termed privileged, in the element of empirical things."[43] This figure of Man echoes profoundly doubled within the Same, at the same time and with the form of privilege, but in particular as "the difficult object and sovereign subject of all possible knowledge";[44] in a "communication between nature and human nature, on the basis of two opposite but complementary functions";[45] an "empirico-transcendental doublet": "Man, in the analytic of finitude, is a strange empirico-transcendental doublet, since he is a being such that knowledge will be attained in him of what renders all knowledge possible."[46] This doubled figure constitutes the basis of the human sciences, which unfold in virtue of the possibility they define for understanding themselves and finitude in a single double. This self-constitution and self-knowledge define the humanity of the human sciences, doubling the figure of Man as they constitute it and themselves. No nature or human nature echoes apart from this constitution; Man emerges at a moment in the history of representation. These notions present us with some questions.

Man emerges:

> Before the end of the eighteenth century, *man* did not exist—any more than the potency of life, the fecundity of labour, or the historical density of language. He is a quite recent creature, which the demiurge of knowledge fabricated with its own hands less than two hundred years ago; but he has grown old so quickly that it has been only too easy to imagine that he had been waiting for thousands of years in the darkness for that moment of illumination in which he would finally be known.[47]

This positivity of Man materializes as his emergence at a time and place, in a configuration of representations.[48] The positivity doubles, at once empirical object of a science and figure of the dividedness of representation within its emergence, definitive of the human subject and its history.[49] Foucault speaks of this historical irruption as the constitution of the subject. This Subject who is constituted—here Man—echoes as an aporetic moment in a history of constitutions: a *that* whose name always displaces it. "The author is undoubtedly only one of the possible specifications of the subject."[50] How may we represent this realm of possibility? "We can easily imagine a culture where discourse would circulate without any need for an author."[51] Can we imagine a discourse without a subject? Without language or representation?

Representation: "man for the human sciences . . . is that living being who, from within the life to which he entirely belongs and by which he is traversed in his whole being, constitutes representations by means of which he lives, and on the basis of which he possesses that strange capacity of being able to represent to himself precisely that life."[52] Classical representation collapses into modern representation where finitude is at stake; and Man is constituted as the figure of finitude that can be fully understood *as finite*, as representer and represented. "The object of the human sciences is not language (though it is spoken by men alone); it is that being which, from the interior of the language by which he is surrounded, represents to himself, by speaking, the sense of the words or propositions he utters, and finally provides himself with a representation of language itself."[53] The "men alone" reiterates *Geschlecht*. "Man" is defined, for the human sciences, as the figure that establishes their authority by establishing Man's authority. Representation doubles along with Man as that which expresses his doubled truth.

History: The emergence of Man transpires at a moment in the history of representation. The history here echoes truth. The truth of human being echoes a historical truth. The truth of truth resounds as a truth of history and representation. Foucault says, however, that his histories tell no such truth, have no restoration of another totality as their goal:[54]

—my aim is most decidedly not to use the categories of cultural totalities (whether world-views, ideal types, the particular spirit of an age) in order to impose on history, despite itself, the forms of structural analysis. The series described, the limits fixed, the comparisons and correlations made are based not on the old philosophies of history, but are intended to question teleologies and totalizations.[55]

Foucault's restriction of his work to "history," rejecting its continuity as memory, echoes a striking refusal to diminish the monstrosity of the future.

By comparison, then, and in contrast to the various projects which aim to inscribe knowledges in the hierarchical order of power associated with science, a genealogy should be seen as a kind of attempt to emancipate historical knowledges from that subjection, to render them, that is, capable of opposition and of struggle against the coercion of a theoretical, unitary, formal and scientific discourse.[56]

These genealogies echo disorder and fragmentation; correspondingly, so do Man, History, and Representation: genealogies of the Subject. The question emerges how we are to represent this subject and its humanity in relation to its emergence within history. How are we to echo human being within the figures that define its fragmentation? How are We to think at all?

Foucault recurrently offers figures of the pure itself in gestures toward an origin.

We must try to return, in history, to that zero point in the course of madness at which madness is an undifferentiated experience, a not yet divided experience of division itself.[57]

between the already "encoded" eye and reflexive knowledge there is a middle region which liberates order itself: . . . in every culture, between the use of what one might call the ordering codes and reflections upon order itself, there is the pure experience of order and of its modes of being.[58]

[In *Las Meninas*] representation, freed finally from the relation that was impeding it, can offer itself as representation in its pure form.[59]

In the zero point of madness itself Derrida hears a return of the origin.[60] We might hear a similar nostalgia in his own *archē-trace*. It is time to hear nostalgia as another transgression. The pure, the itself, the vanishing origin may be heard as fragmenting rather than reaffirming gestures. The essence emerges slashed to pieces. Yet nostalgia may be finally irresistible, even in Heidegger, where the Rift between world and earth is marked by the *Geschlecht* of the Hand.

Foucault gestures toward this displaced purity in another figure, perhaps not without nostalgia but more clearly without the presence of an origin, that of the archive:

It is obvious that the archive of a society, a culture, or a civilization cannot be described exhaustively; or even, no doubt, the archive of a whole period. On the

> other hand, it is not possible for us to describe our own archive, since it is from within these rules that we speak, . . . The archive cannot be described in its totality; and in its presence it is unavoidable. It emerges in fragments, regions, and levels, more fully, no doubt, and with greater sharpness, the greater the time that separates us from it . . .[61]

Paraphrasing Derrida on Heidegger, this is Foucault at his most dogmatic, not on the presence or nature of the archive, but on what is not possible for us: another figure of *Geschlecht*, both in the for us and in what is possible. Necessity and possibility, stillness and polyphony echo always with us, where we echo our displacement.

Another dogma echoes here: the past emerges more fully the greater our separation from it. No doubt we are blinded in our present to its conditions; we are surely not privileged absolutely by what is "closer" to us. Yet the future is not another point of privilege. These notions of fully and closer are always to and for us, another *Geschlecht*. The present—temporal and phenomenological—is always human, always our *Geschlecht*. The archive is a point of privilege: "The analysis of the archive, then, involves a privileged region: at once close to us, and different from our present existence, it is the border of time that surrounds our presence, which overhangs it, and which indicates it in its otherness; it is that which, outside ourselves, delimits us."[62] Foucault repeats the themes of nostalgia for a humanity that can be named even within this gesture to limit and transgression: privilege, close to us, our present existence, even, astonishingly, that which delimits *us*. The result, we have heard, rings for us among the most sublime accounts of human being: "we are difference, [that] our reason is the difference of discourses, our history the differences of times, our selves the difference of masks. That difference, far from being the forgotten and recovered origin, is this dispersion that we are and make."[63] To understand this displaced gesture toward an origin that is but dispersion we must add that the We here still appears as Our *Geschlecht*. "We" must represent our nature so as to avoid nostalgia for the origin and to escape the arbitrariness of privilege, although every thought rings as both nostalgic and privileged. Humanity is Our *Geschlecht* even as the archive and the supplement. This thought marks the locality and inexhaustibility of humanity.

The question of humanity always appears before us in the guise of *Geschlecht*, where *Geschlecht* is always our *Geschlecht* and where our *Geschlecht* is always *unser Geschlecht*, always German. Each of these representations—our, *unser*, *Geschlecht*, German—represents a particular, situated humanity, and there transpires no other; yet locality and situatedness echo as always other, to themselves and as themselves. Humanity is to *Geschlecht* as Power is to power: deferrals and their deferrals.

Without translating *Geschlecht*, for it may be unspeakable, Derrida tells us that: "it can be translated by sex, race, species, genus, gender, stock, family, generation or genealogy, community."[64] Within this list, or any other, we find humanity's essence *as Geschlecht*—our very own. Our sonorescent marking of humanity echoes representation, power, and desire, embodiment, sexuality, gender, and history, where power includes privilege, domination, and violence and where history includes life and death. This list, far from exhaustive, marks our representation of our humanity.

Humanity materializes as *Geschlecht*: sex, race, species, genus, gender, stock, family, generation or genealogy, and community among others. Among the others appear representation, power, and desire; also history and embodiment, including sexuality, closing the circle defined by *Geschlecht*. Each of these exercises privilege, a site of oppression and violence, of the oppression of oppression and violence against violence. The locality of humanity lies in its *Geschlecht*. Its inexhaustibility lies in the limits of *Geschlecht*, where the latter delimits the limits of our humanity. The reciprocal movement of stillness and polyphony, harmony and disharmony, echoes nature's inexhaustible cacophonies.

Among the movements that define humanity, not unique to it among living creatures, unfolds the circle of life and death. Within this circle, we may say, death stands forth as privileged, never succeeded by its life, whereas life always leads to death. The privilege here echoes another *Geschlecht* within humanity: the finitude of care, which belongs to us. Locality does not repeat finitude, and charity does not echo care, belongs to other loci, not only to us. Rather, locality echoes *Geschlecht* and inexhaustibility marks the displacement of *Geschlecht*. Here *Geschlecht* marks sacrifice and charity.

Life and death belong to other human beings as well as to me, to other animals and plants as well as to us. What, then, does death represent? Within the Western tradition, with some important exceptions, awareness of death represents our Humanity: *Our Geschlecht*. The forms of our awareness vary, from the Infinite Beyond Death to human finitude, but always the form in which human beings stand apart. Our *Geschlecht* echoes *our* thought of our mortality, found in language and thought, represented within metaphysics as the thought that exceeds its locality.

In the forms in which death expresses our humanity, set apart from animals and machines, even in which death echoes my humanity, apart from other human beings, death echoes finitude and contingency. Yet its finiteness sounds absolute, stillness without polyphony. This absoluteness represents what our *Geschlecht* represents, a point of privilege that exceeds every representation of humanity. Humanity here echoes a stillness absolutely marked within metaphysics, without excess. Death, however, always appears disharmonious, finite and inexhaustible. The abyss that marks the future presents deferral everywhere, the deferral of and in death, that even its close does not appear absolute. We never die in vain, if that means that we die without a deferred trace whose meaning remains to be determined. The truth of death exemplifies the truth of locality, always inexhaustibility.

To have lived is to die, though the necessity refuses inexhaustibility. Inexhaustibility remains within death in two ways, in the polyphonies of the closure and the contingencies of death. It marks a utopian gesture to think that we might not die, but even death is local. We may remain influential in memory; we may remain relevant for a time. Locality entails the limits of every being—but also the limits of every limit.

Geschlecht appears within death as a figure of its closure, an absolute mark of our finite humanity. The representation of finiteness somehow transcends it; the locality of representation becomes the figure of our absoluteness. We may think to evade this absolute by emphasizing the finiteness of our humanity, although to speak of it reinstates the Geschlecht that we echo in a figure that exceeds finiteness. The locality of Geschlecht, then, sounds the Geschlecht of our Geschlecht, the humanity of our humanity. It is marked by the realization that we can represent our humanity at some organic or inorganic site only in a gesture that exceeds its representation. Death whispers among the supreme embodiments of this excessive gesture, whose excess appears in the comic figures within the tragic expression of our finiteness and in the desperation within memory to reinstate a history marked by loss. Memory and comedy portray excessive gestures against the closure of human finitude. They represent our humanity.

Humanity echoes Geschlecht but not only Geschlecht. Geschlecht itself does not only repeat Geschlecht, as representation, power, and desire, but also history, embodiment, sexuality, domination, and oppression do not only repeat what they are. The only marks a closure that is neither local nor inexhaustible. We may add that the closure of the only may not only repeat closure. All these denials of onlyness are local. They echo nature. The Geschlecht of humanity, understood as its excesses, belongs to nature. Nature too is our Geschlecht.

ELEVEN

Nature

We conclude our representation of representation as we began it, with nature's sonance, closing the circle. We began our representation of representation as we now end it, with nature's music, opening the circle. Closing and opening here reverberate as soniferous themes of query, local representations of locality. Opening and closing the circle reverberate as multiply reflexive figures of judgment, semasis and query, and there echoes no outside, no place from which we can judge judgment or represent representation, that does not belong within them, inseparable from disharmonies within and without. Similarly, no representation can be heard of the nature of nature or the reality of reality, that does not echo within our locality—again inseparable from without. Within and without belong together in their departures. This togetherness sounds our sonorescence: the ring of nature's truth.

Our pathway to nature rings through representation and its representation. To question nature is to represent nature's reality as simulation: the reality of nature's artifice. This path defines the locality of our sonorescence. On it we have sounded everything we could within nature and representation—not "every thing in its complete being," but sonorescent univocals echoing nature, representation, power, desire, time, and embodiment. These do not drone the categories of being, being's being, but represent a particular historical epoch's representation of nature through unending disharmonies. The particularity of this representation echoes its locality. The discord of locality in relation to nature and representation, to power, desire, history, and embodiment, rings displacements within our local sonorescence: simulation again. Locality occupies the spaces between nature and its simulations. The work of nature's artifice materializes as simulation, where artifice both belongs to nature and inexhaustibly dislocates it. Query echoes nature judging itself and its judgments, where we as judges embody nature's work, echoing for us as our sonorescence.

Nature and judgment echo locality, along with power, desire, space and time, and materiality. This locality echoes inexhaustibility, excess, as inexhaustibility echoes locality, its excess. The singular name of each of these representations presents and obscures multiple locality. The singular word representation,

like power and desire but especially reality and nature, resounds as a local sonor-
ific figure that obscures nature and presents it in its obscurity from within the
aporias that define it. This doubled obscurity within the judgments of nature
names our local sonorescence. It echoes within the recurrent ring of aporia. To
represent aporia as nature's truth is to judge metaphysically. The judgment of the
nature of nature represents the relation of as aporia. Nature echoes aporia as its
work.

Heidegger claims, still "dogmatically," that the form of representation we
represent as the history of Western metaphysics is characterized by the forgetting
of Being, by oblivion to the difference between Being and beings, obscuring the
self-originating plenitude of nature as *physis* behind a notion of its perfectibility
as *technē*. The "ontological difference" appears here in two forms: between Being
and beings, and between *physis* and *technē*. The difference between *physis* and
technē, nature and artifice, echoes representation three times: artifice echoes representation even where nature exceeds its representations, while the difference
calls for representation. In our sonorescence, it calls for multiply local representation. Nature's music resounds in multiple representation, polyphonic artifices.
Nature echoes artifice where artifice echoes nature's judgments, no more art than
science or philosophy, where each displaces the other. Artifice echoes the ring of
representation in nature as nature echoes artifice in judgment's judgments and
query's queries. Nature's *ergon* materializes for us as judgment and query. These
sound the cacophonies of nature as themselves, where they echo nature's music.
The differences between representation and judgment, judgment and artifice, artifice and representation, sound the discordant locality that rings the cacophonies
of nature.

The drone of Being sounds metaphysical, a gesture in which the relation
between Being and beings remains unthought. Yet this phrase, "remains unthought," remains ambiguous, like the ambiguity—itself ambiguous—of nature
and judgment. The oblivion in which the difference between nature and its nature
remains unthought whispers the appearance of that difference and its disappearance, both belonging to nature. The difference that remains unthought must be
thought to remain unthought, must be present as a trace. The drone of the unthought within nature defines and defiles it.

The necessities of this transcendental formulation echo aporias, but must
not therefore be refused. Aporia tolls the locality within metaphysics, the form in
which it exceeds and refuses itself. It echoes one form of nature's cacophony, a
local form whose music exceeds itself. Still, the aporia of necessity violently
explodes within a refusal of metaphysics, even within its transformation by locality, and obscures its own obscurities. Attempting to disengage the violence from
the point at which it manifests itself, we may represent the locality of the unthought somewhat differently. The ambiguity of the thought that the excessive
plenitude of nature remains unthought echoes that that unthought whispers caco-

phonically within representation and nature. Its ambiguity falls on it only within its representations. The ambiguity of the unthought appears as an only within representation. To represent nature is to represent this unthought as transgression and the unthought within representation as another transgression. The nature of what resounds as unthought transgresses nature as its work.

The nature of nature remains unthought. Because it remains, however obscurely, it belongs to nature even where nature has no totality. Because it remains unthought, it departs from representation, so that we cannot represent the nature of nature. Shall we think of this thought away from representation as a thought outside its representation? Representation's representation has no outside or inside to be thought or represented. Similarly, nature has no outside or inside. As a consequence, it sounds the cacophonies of its excesses.

The Unthought, like Nature, names itself within a gesture—a representation—of Refusal; conversely, it refuses itself a name even while it represents itself. To question the nature of nature is to question both judgment and nature, but most of all the of. Of belongs to judgment—always of; of belongs to nature—always the nature of and the of of nature. Nature's of echoes artifice, its truth semasis. The of rings the truth of nature, its semasis. The of of semasis and query echoes the ring of nature's artifice. The of within metaphysics sounds what our sonorescence is of: nature's work. This of, the *technē* of ergonality, nature's work, echoes valor.[1] Nature's *technē* possesses no measure, comes forth as *poiēsis*. The of in nature echoes *poiēsis* as semasis.

Heidegger distinguishes *physis* from *poiēsis* in that *poiēsis* belongs to *technē*, moved from without; nature is the self-originating movement of that which moves out of and toward itself.[2] The bringing forth of *poiēsis* is making but not origination, certainly not self-movement. Yet the other that originates production in *technē* and the self that originates movement in *physis* reverberate as centered, originary notions, whereas *physis* has no center or origin. Where we sharply distinguish nature and art, each represents the other's excesses so that the excess has no excess. Nature always moves from without because ingredience presupposes excess. Artifice echoes production from within because causes exceed themselves. These excesses appear in Aristotle where *physis* always acts as if by art and in Kant where art always presents itself as if by nature. The as if of nature echoes its artifices. The artifices of nature echo judgment.

In our sonorescence, nature and artifice compose each other's excesses and their excesses. *Physis*, *poiēsis*, and *technē* compose each other's nature and that nature's excesses as work. The plenitude of nature resounds as the origination of a cacophony that rings in virtue of its artifices. *Technē* echoes nature's nature and its transgressions, both resounding in *poiēsis* as semasis.

Our sonorescent univocals, locality, inexhaustibility, and ergonality, with their sonoriferous pairs, unison-resonance, harmony-disharmony, and stillness-polyphony, represent the locality of nature and representation excessively and inexhaustibly, fall between them, where nature meets representation as its work. This work, echoing judgment, echoes judgment's judgment, semasis and its truths. These truths cacophonically sound the sonances and dissonances of nature's work, where nature and representation relate to each other unisonally but not identically, echoing unending resonances, belong to each other in inexhaustible departures, sound their stillness together polyphonically. The ring of representation echoes the sonorescence of nature in the ways in which nature and representation echo each other.

Nature's self-originating movement of that which moves belongs to time but especially to *place*, of which Heidegger says two things:

> we should note that in a certain sense what Aristotle means by "change of place" is something different from the modern conception of the change of location of some mass in space.[3]
>
> We of today have to do two things: first, free ourselves from the view that movement is *first and above all* change of place, and second, learn to see how, for the Greeks movement as a mode of *Being* has the character of emerging into presence.[4]

The second passage redefines the first: we rethink movement and place, relinquish the view that movement is change of place or that place belongs to space. Rest and movement are of place where place displaces itself. The self-origination of nature echoes inexhaustibility.

Nature's cacophonies echo multiple locality. Time and space echo nature's locality. Multiple locality finds expression in the times and spaces of nature, where these represent the locality of nature and where the expression represents nature's artifice. Space and time generically express what belongs to nature and its departures. They delimit the displacements of nature's locality.

Space materializes as repetition with its dislocations: there as well as here. Time repeats the repetitions of repetition: here and there again and again, displacements in the repetitions of repetition. In both cases, location in a place echoes location in other places, not here, not then. Locality's locality echoes multiple places and their multiple displacements, polyphonies of nature, where space and time represent univocal location and where the of represents representation. Locality has its place in virtue of representation. Nature, then, sounds locality and inexhaustibility, echoing in place as representation.

Nature drones being's being in time and space, where time and space are not being's being in general. Heidegger appears to say this twice in relation to being-moved, though within its refusal.

> Rest is a kind of movement; only what can move can rest. It is absurd to speak of the number 3 as "resting."

it was Aristotle who first attained—thus, first created—that level of questioning where (movement is not considered as something merely given along with other things, but rather where) *Being-moved* is explicitly questioned and understood as the basic mode of Being.[5]

The number 3 neither moves nor rests, though we may question the absurdity of thinking otherwise. *"Being-moved* . . . is the basic mode of Being"—more explicitly, "Being is the self-concealing revealing, *physis* in the original sense."[6] If Being is *physis* and *physis* is being-moved, then the number 3 either moves or is not, either has its time or does not belong to nature. Although it may be absurd to think that the number 3 rests, it is not absurd to question how it may be if it does not emerge.

Remarkably, time disappears in Heidegger into the already.

> The *mathēmata*, the mathematical, is that "about" things which we really already know. Therefore we do not first get it out of things, but, in a certain way, we bring it already with us. From this we can now understand why, for instance, number is something mathematical. We see three chairs and say that there are three. What "three" is the three chairs do not tell us, nor three apples, three cats, nor any other three things. Rather, we can count three things only if we already know "three." In thus grasping the number three as such, we only expressly recognize something which, in some way, we already have.[7]

The mathematical represents the already; numbers are what we already have, apparently, therefore, always have had. This already and always define Platonism historically (but not Plato's writings, which exceed any doctrine), becoming transcendental with Kant and continuing into Heidegger. In every being there is already that which gives its Being. The already is traditionally timeless, seen in Aristotle's Unmoved Mover, in Spinoza's ideas of God, and in Whitehead's primordial nature of God. Whitehead, for whom time is fundamental to nature, still cannot think of it without its opposite. "The things which are temporal arise by their participation in the things which are eternal."[8] Nature is temporal and eternal, despite complex inversion. "It is as true to say that God is permanent and the World fluent, as that the World is permanent and God is fluent."[9]

Nature is temporal and eternal, fluent and permanent. God is likewise temporal and eternal: the former on his consequent side, the latter on his primordial side. On his consequent side, God asks us to rethink the meaning of temporality. On his primordial side, God is undividedly eternal: "One side of God's nature is constituted by his conceptual experience. This experience is the primordial fact in the world; limited by no actuality which it presupposes. . . . This side of his nature is free, complete, primordial, eternal, actually deficient, and unconscious."[10] The already here is an unbroken always, unsounding stillness. Temporality appears only in the succession of creative occasions emerging into actuality. Whitehead rejects the possibility that the primordial nature of God might be an already subsequent to his consequent nature,[11] that every already might be after, that the a priori might be constituted historically.[12]

Why does Whitehead make the primordial nature of God complete and eternal? Why must the already appear unbroken, obscuring its aporias? Why must God's stillness be unaffected by his polyphonies while the latter always repeat the same stillness? Whitehead explicitly acknowledges the aporias of God in relation to the unity of Nature:

> No reason can be given for the nature of God, because that nature is the ground of rationality.
>
> . . . There is a metaphysical need for a principle of determination, but there can be no metaphysical reason for what is determined.[13]

The already appears as absence of an ultimate reason for everything. In this form, the already rings of excess, and the nature of nature, with the temporality of time, echoes excesses of excesses. We are questioning why this excessive already belongs together with eternity. Rather, the already echoes the of in the stillness of the repetition of repetition.

For Heidegger, the already reappears in modern science as *axiomata*: "As axiomatic, the mathematical project is the anticipation of the essence of things, of bodies; thus the basic blueprint of the structure of every thing and its relation to every other thing is sketched in advance."[14] It reemerges in Kant as transcendental. Even the already, then, unfolds into time, not timelessly but historically a priori, already present in the representativity of nature's multiple repetitions. The spaces between locality and nature unfold, occupied by an already given as the of in the representation of nature, nature's artifices, but especially the of in repetition's disharmonies. The already present in the movement of being-moved echoes the excesses of time's temporality. The of belongs to judgment. Only in virtue of judgment does mathematical truth unfold. Mathematical truth sounds a historical truth whose aporia echoes that it appears in the form of eternity.

The regions between nature and judgment are occupied by space and time, nature's excesses as its artifice. The locality of space and time opens a locale in which nature exceeds itself as time and space, exceeded by many times and spaces and by locales other than time and space, exceeded in time and space. The locality of space and time belongs to nature in virtue of judgment. The already of mathematical truth emerges in virtue of judgment's excesses. Judgment echoes in virtue of the work of locality, its inexhaustibility.

Time resounds polyphonically as the stillness in the repetition of repetition. Nature's work echoes repetition's repetitions. In our tradition, repetition materializes as space, form, and law. Yet the repetition of repetition does not repeat space, form, and law. For there unfolds no law of law, no form of form, not to mention law of law of law or form of form of form. Locality echoes the dislocations of its multiple locations; similarly, time echoes the temporalities of its historicality. Law and form echo displacement and deferral. Nature's cacophony sounds the locality of its locality, appearing in our time as the temporality of temporality, its differences from itself, excess exceeding its own excessiveness.

One form of such excess, marking our epoch, echoes judgment. Law echoes one form of the repetition of judgment. Representation expresses one form of the repetition of repetition—its temporality—essential for the truth of law but dismantling the Law of law. Multiple representation—semasis—expresses one form of the repetition of multiple repetition, echoing the truth of the truth of repetition: nature's artifice. Nature knows nothing of representation's representations except as particular historical representations of its artifices.

Nature appears in Aristotle as self-originating movement, by nature, contrasted with movement from without:

> Of things that exist, some exist by nature, some from other causes.
>
> . . .
>
> All the things mentioned . . . has *within itself* a principle of motion and of stationariness (in respect of place, or of growth and decrease, or by way of alteration). On the other hand, a bed and a coat and anything else of that sort, *qua* receiving these designations—i.e. in so far as they are products of *art* [*technē*]—have no innate impulse to change. . . . *nature is a source or cause of being moved and of being at rest in that to which it belongs primarily*, in virtue of itself and not in virtue of a concomitant attribute. (Aristotle, *Physics*, II, 1, 7–23)

Because the self-originating movement includes rest, nature is not movement but origination. To be by nature is to belong to time, whether in motion or at rest. To be by artifice, by *technē* or *poiēsis*, is not in the same way to belong to time. Works come into being and pass away, but insofar as their ends express their perfectibility—however incompletely realized—they fall outside time.

In one reading of Aristotle, *physis* is displaced by its temporality, but artifice is not similarly displaced, is only *technē*. In another reading, the self-originating movement of nature belongs to every form of origination including *technē*, in part because nature includes *technē* and *poiēsis* while they include nature in their representations, but also because the self of nature's self-origination univocally echoes stillness. The separation of nature from artifice, if it appears in Aristotle and Kant, reappears in both repeatedly in the form of cancellation. Aristotle can speak of nature only as art; Kant can speak of art only as if by nature. These reciprocal movements repeat the aporetic space of temporality between nature and its work.

The distinction between nature and artifice, *physis* and *technē*, echoes in Aristotle to be negated. Yet it appears inescapable even within the gestures of its refusal. Judgment echoes not only *technē* but *poiēsis*. To represent this difference we may refuse to rethink *technē* into *poiēsis*. Yet our refusal echoes but another refusal and can be reechoed as the reemergence of *technē* as *poiēsis* against its perfectibility. Works by artifice come forth in mysterious and excessive splendor.

Generation from without, in *technē*, centers the maker among materials and products dispersed through nature's generation. Artifice, here, belongs to Edison and Cézanne. Nature, art, and *technē* all unfold in virtue of their excesses. Each exceeds itself.

The presence of artifice within nature echoes nature's cacophonies as its *poiēsis*. Judgment exceeds nature in its perfectibility—or rather, each exceeds the other's perfections, for nature and query are perfect in their own ways. *Technē* questions whether the distinction between nature and query, *physis* and *technē*, becomes something different in our sonorescence: not the timeless perfectibility of art against nature, but the polyphonies of nature's artifices. Here, we echo the repetitions of judgment as a manifestation of the polyphonies of nature: *technē* as nature rather than its other; the music of representation as nature's cacophonies.

In Aristotle, in Heidegger's reading, nature's aporias ring in the hollows between *physis* and *technē*. Other openings echo in Aristotle's view of nature, between *physis* and *ousia* or nature and being. These can be represented in terms of time and movement: the plenitude of a nature that exceeds itself in the forms of being, *technē*, and *ousia*, each of which has its local places of movement.

By way of contrast, Spinoza's and Leibniz's representations of repetition's repetitions, inexhaustibility, exceed nature's temporality, still within its polyphonies. The representativity of nature appears in Spinoza's attributes: always the attribute of thought along with the attribute of extension among infinite attributes. The inexhaustibility of nature appears in the absolutely infinite nature of Substance. Nature is not God, is both *natura naturata* and *natura naturans*. God is the latter; finite, temporal beings are the former. Nature is both cause and effect; God is only the cause (but not the only cause) (*Ethics,* I, Prop. XXIX, Note; Prop. XVII, Note).[15]

The representativity of nature appears explicitly in Spinoza in God's ideas and implicitly in Spinoza's writings. The representativity of nature appears in Leibniz in the relation of monads to one another. In both cases, nature unfolds as repetition, in Spinoza the repetition ad infinitum of causal succession that coexists with the causation of God;[16] in Leibniz, the representation of each monad by each monad, mirroring all others even as self-determined.[17] In Spinoza and Leibniz there echoes the aporia of the self-determination of what exists only in causal determination. There also echoes the aporia of the repetition of repetition, where each thing endlessly repeats the repetitions of others. The infinite mirrors of representation express the self-determination of each entelechy and the infinite repetitions that inscribe it. Infinite representations of representation in Leibniz replace the divisibility of space and time.

We may hear Leibniz and Spinoza as presenting the individuality of each finite thing in conflict with its exteriority: inner as against outer causation. We may hear them instead as presenting the individuality of each finite thing as a repetition of the repetitions of others: repetition's repetitions as individuality. Here self-origination echoes relations with others, discordances and displacements. The disharmonies within the individuality of a finite thing that ring in virtue of its repetitions express causal succession in Spinoza and change in Leibniz, both expressions of history. The disharmonies of repetition's repetitions echo time. Time transpires as a local representation of judgment.

In Whitehead, an actual entity is a singular act of creation: many become one. Its becoming repeats the becomings, now objectified, of all past events; its future repeats the becomings of others as a repetition of its becoming. Becoming, here, is repetition and repetition of repetition. Yet each creative act is a disharmony; each becoming expresses an individual's decisions to be itself. Many become one only to become many others. The self-determination of each actual entity is a circle of repetition.

Nature materializes where space and time repeat repetition and repetition exceeds itself. The future transpires as the place at which the repetition of repetition becomes different. This multiple reflexivity in repetition distinguishes natural plenitude in time as history from Natural Law and *Technē*, where nature repeats repetition but not its multiple reflexivity. Because repetition always repeats repetition, the repetition that falls under law, within the *logos*, is always different. But Law does not represent its repetitions as disharmonies; *Technē* does not represent its norms as departures. It represents perfectibility as stillness without polyphony.

Nature transpires in time and space as repetition and its repetition, where neither repetition nor its repetition materializes metrically. *Technē* imposes measure on nature. The self-originative power of *physis* has no measure, external or internal, but originates and becomes itself as repetition without norms. The difference between the repetition of repetition in a discontinuous temporality or catastrophic history and metrical repeatability is that the latter imposes normativity on its exemplars. The former has no examples, only events and repetitions. A catastrophic history unfolds through terrible events exemplifying nothing. The cacophony of nature rings without a measure, without a norm or standard, in which locality rules by refusing rules, by repetitions that displace themselves. Nature's displacements fall into every space they open up, especially the sites of repetition's repetitions that compose representation.

The univocals of our sonorescence represent nature's locality, inexhaustibility, and work in reciprocal excess. This representation of the limits of representation rings in a univocity for which every every echoes aporia. Nature's univocity echoes a refusal of metaphysics that reaffirms it locally and historically. Refusal here echoes denial and affirmation, refusal as belonging within. Locality and inexhaustibility belong within the discordant drone of metaphysics even as they dislocate it.

The univocals of our sonorescence refuse the traditional nature of metaphysics while still metaphysical. This refusal echoes another refusal, echoes representation of the limits of representation, within and without, limits of its totalities and specificities. The necessity of refusal, here, like universality, sounds another figure of the limits of representation's representations. For the necessity in metaphysics and its representations falls within metaphysics as the questioning of necessity exceeds it as metaphysics. The questioning here does not proclaim skepticism toward necessity; for example, assertion of its contingency. Skepticism obliquely reaffirms the undivided truth of being. Our sonorescence sounds the refusal of skepticism from within its own refusal.

The relation of nature to itself materializes as *poiēsis*. The displacements marked by the of that characterizes nature's work marks *poiēsis*, bringing into work as nature. The displacement of nature in relation to itself, by representation, echoes its locality. This displacement rings in our sonorescent univocals voicing nature's work. They belong to nature as its excesses. *Poiēsis* and *technē* belong to nature while each departs from the other as *poiēsis* and *technē*.

The multiplicities, excesses, and aporias of our sonorescent univocals represent transgression and its transgression as their unities and solidarities echo aporia. We may name this transgression the refusal of metaphysics, as if metaphysics were a category of representation, giving way to its other, or we may name this transgression metaphysics where it sounds its own refusal from within the univocity of that refusal. All the forms of our sonorescence ring in this judgmental space of excess and deferral.

Western metaphysics traditionally seeks to represent nature's nature from within oblivion toward the representativity of the of. It acknowledges the irresistibility of neither the ring of representation in relation to nature nor the representativity at its heart. Metaphysics forgets both its work as query and the transgressions present within judgment. It represents nature without representing representation as nature or nature as representation, both figures of excess.

The univocity of representation, the all-inclusive names that label it, defines our sonorescence. It knows that the more generic the name, the more displaced, including the name of metaphysics. Among these displacements echo the aporias within the tradition, the disruptions and violences within metaphysics, moments of oblivion within the appearance of our sonorescence.

When Derrida calls our attention to the universal insistence in philosophy "to think its other," he calls our attention to two movements in philosophy: *our Geschlecht* and its insistence. Metaphysics represents the being of being to delimit and control it. Metaphysics cannot escape this movement; no judgment can. Otherwise we would be captive to a representation of difference that escaped from power and desire, from materiality, relevance, and excess, from history.

Every judgment manifests a will to truth whose will, desire, power, and truth exceed themselves and each other. Metaphysics traditionally imagines that these excesses can be controlled somehow, if only by a gesture toward God and Reason. Our sonorescence disdains such a gesture. The excesses in nature and judgment displace desire, power, truth, and history, but also god and reason. The judgment echoes nature's locality; its locality echoes nature's inexhaustibility; the inexhaustibility of locality repeats nature's work. This work repeats artifice in nature: judgment, semasis, and query.

Our sonorescence still echoes metaphysics. It represents nature locally as excess: truth, power, desire, materiality, and history. This list can be extended; the univocals in it define it only locally. Excess has always sounded within metaphysics, wherever representational gestures toward nature's generality exceeded every generality—every every—turning representation back onto itself in the form of aporia. The locality of nature echoes in the excesses of the aporias of its generality.

Nature rings its local work, its excesses and inexhaustibility, through semasis, the locality of judgment's judgment. Such a judgment sounds the limits of representation and nature: artifice and simulation. Yet such a judgment sounds metaphysical even as it echoes excesses. It sounds its limits, including its power and authority. Such a representation of nature's limits expresses the project of metaphysics. A representation of the limits of the representation of nature unfolds as the artifice of metaphysics, which does not give up the representation of nature in representing its limits, though it may find such representations present in other modalities of judgment and query. And there must be other modalities; without them reason could not interrogate itself. Metaphysics cannot materialize as a supreme or final form of truth, able finally to represent itself.

Our sonorescence sings but one of manifold songs of nature as transgression. The danger is that another form of representation—even a sonorescent one—will attempt to control nature's limits in the name of refusing control. The refusal of control exercises another control. More important, refusal of the coercion of representation through multiple representation entails that our sonorescence accept the challenge of representing both the limits of nature and its own limits. The language of our sonorescence speaks against itself. Yet this against does not destroy its metaphysicality; nor does it reinstate it. Rather, it calls our attention to nature's unending excesses, including the excesses of our sonorescence. The project of our sonorescence unfolds in the hope of carrying metaphysical query to such an extreme that even metaphysics and query may be violently torn apart by the cacophonies of nature's work. By such displacement we return to the excesses of *poiēsis*, where *poiēsis* brings forth every representation. Nature's work sings its artifices, realized as semasis, in the locality and inexhaustibility of a multiplicity of modalities of query, one of which may be metaphysics.

Judgment sings as *poiēsis*; *poiēsis* brings stillness forth from polyphony, unison from ingredience, belonging from departing, and reciprocally. Nature also brings forth stillness from polyphony and polyphony from stillness, with the others: its *poiēsis*. *Poiēsis* echoes nature's *ergon*. In our sonorescence, the line dividing nature from representation, nature's artifice, echoes transgression. Here, our sonorescent query echoes judgment of the judgment of the nature of nature where both metaphysics and nature echo *poiēsis*. Nature's *ergon* sings the music of its semasis. *Poiēsis* echoes that we, with our artifices and *Geschlecht*, belong to nature, where belonging echoes transgression.

Nature's nature, its *ergon* and *technē*, rings as *poiēsis*, composed in human life as judgment, semasis and query. We do not know if nature must reverberate only in that form, even in human life, or whether other forms of sonorescence may echo forth. The representation of nature and judgment, also of power, desire, time, and materiality, all ring of limits and their limits, in that way metaphysical. Here the nature of nature rings at a time and place through judgments that exceed themselves. This excess sings the excesses of metaphysics, nature, and artifice over themselves: none at all. A nothing that makes all the difference in the world. Our sonorescence sounds each of these words inexhaustibly. Nature rings as a no thing that makes all the difference in the world. The cacophony of the world. The ring of nature's representations.

NOTES

ANACRUSIS

1. The sonorescent voice echoing here hopes to represent its own representativity. How can such a philosophy speak in a traditional disciplinary voice? Can this or any voice hope for perfection?
2. Jacques Derrida, "Tympan," Introduction to *Margins of Philosophy*, trans, A. Bass (Chicago: University of Chicago Press, 1982), pp. x–xi.
3. Michel Foucault, "Theatrum Philosophicum," *Language, Countermemory, Practice* (Ithaca, N.Y.: Cornell University Press, 1977), p. 192.

I. SONANCE

1. Heraclitus, fragments 5.22 and 5.45, from John Mansley Robinson, *An Introduction to Early Greek Philosophy* (Boston: Houghton Mifflin, 1968), pp. 93, 96 (DK 22 B 80; DK 22 B 8)
2. See Anacrusis. "The univocity of Being. . . ."
3. Luce Irigaray, *The Speculum of the Other Woman*, ed. G. C. Gill (Ithaca, N.Y.: Cornell University Press, 1985), p. 134.
4. Hans-Georg Gadamer, *Truth and Method* (New York: Seabury, 1975), pp. 438–39.
5. Derrida, "Tympan," p. xi.
6. Ibid.
7. Ibid., p. xii.
8. Ibid., p. xiii.
9. Ibid., p. xv.
10. Irigaray, *Speculum of the Other Woman*, p. 136.
11. Ibid., p. 142.
12. Michel Foucault, "The Discourse on Language" (translation of *L'ordre du discours*), trans. R. Swyer, Appendix to *The Archaeology of Knowledge* (New York: Pantheon, 1972), p. 216.
13. Trinh T. Minh-ha, *Woman, Native, Other: Writing Postcoloniality and Feminism* (Bloomington: Indiana University Press, 1989), pp. 98–99.
14. Martin Heidegger, "The End of Philosophy and the Task of Thinking," *Basic Writings*, ed. D. Krell (New York: Harper & Row, 1977), p. 374.

15. Quotations from E. Hamilton and H. Cairns eds., *The Collected Dialogues of Plato* (Princeton, N.J.: Princeton University Press, 1969).
16. Immanuel Kant, *Critique of Judgment*, trans. J. H. Bernard (New York: Hafner, 1951), p. 89.
17. Ibid., p. 108.
18. Michel Foucault, "A Preface to Transgression," *Language, Countermemory, Practice* (Ithaca, N.Y.: Cornell University Press, 1977), p. 35.
19. The notion of "deferral" is Derrida's. See especially "Differance," from *Speech and Phenomena*, trans. D. B. Allison (Evanston, Ill.: Northwestern University Press, 1973), p. 129: "The verb 'to differ' (*différer*) seems to differ from itself. On the one hand, it indicates difference as distinction, inequality, or discernibility; on the other, it expresses the interposition of delay, the interval of a *spacing* and *temporalizing* that puts off until 'later' what is presently denied, the possible that is presently impossible. Sometimes the *different* and sometimes the *deferred* correspond [in French] to the verb 'to differ.' " It has been taken over by others in ways relevant to the discussion here.

    Deferral echoes in our sonorescence as locality, inexhaustibility, and work, each the same as and deferral of the others. Although commonly understood as temporal, deferral is no more temporal than spatial, no more futural than mathematical. Nor is it a difference that presupposes identity. It is a multiply reflexive figure of otherness within the same, including the otherness of otherness within the sameness of the same. The infinity of which Trinh Minh-ha speaks in the following is neither future nor past, neither near nor far.
20. Trinh T. Minh-ha, *Woman, Native, Other*, p. 101.
21. Alfred Jarry's notion of "pataphysics" should be noted. See Ruy Latour, *Clefs pour La 'Pataphysique'* (Paris: Éditions Seghers, 1969). Any metaphysical representation of itself places itself at risk.
22. Heidegger, "The End of Philosophy and the Task of Thinking," p. 374.
23. Derrida, "Tympan," p. xxvii.
24. The ideas through which we may attempt to represent the limits of limitation here are locality, inexhaustibility, and ergonality (or functionality), nature's work. I have discussed these notions in several other works in different contexts. See *Inexhaustibility and Human Being: An Essay on Locality, The Limits of Language*, and *Locality and Practical Judgment: Charity and Sacrifice* (all New York: Fordham University Press, the first 1989, the latter two forthcoming). See also *Metaphysical Aporia and Philosophical Heresy* (Albany: State University of New York Press, 1989).

    Locality, inexhaustibility, and ergonality express multiple reflexivity as a cultural embodiment of *our or any* modernity. They appear in the Western metaphysical tradition as aporia, at its limits and in the betweens that fragment that or any tradition and the identity of The West against its Non-Western Others.

25. Martin Heidegger, "The Origin of the Work of Art," *Poetry, Language, Thought*, trans. A. Hofstadter (New York, Harper & Row, 1971), p. 62.

26. See Jürgen Habermas, *The Philosophical Discourse of Modernity* trans. F. Lawrence (Massachusetts: MIT Press, 1987), p. 295.

27. These principles are as follows:

"—Power . . . is exercised from innumerable points, in the interplay of non-egalitarian and mobile relations.
—Relations of power are not in a position of exteriority with respect to other types of relationships . . .; they have a directly productive role, wherever they come into play.
—Power comes from below; that is, there is no binary and all-encompassing opposition between rulers and ruled at the root of power relations, . . .
—Power relations are both intentional and nonsubjective. . . .
—Where there is power, there is resistance, and yet, or rather consequently, this resistance is never in a position of exteriority in relation to power" (Michel Foucault, *The History of Sexuality, Volume I*, trans. R. Hurley [New York, Vintage, 1980], pp. 94–95).

28. Ibid., p. 93.

29. Ibid., p. 96.

30. Foucault, "The Discourse on Language," p. 219: "True discourse, liberated by the nature of its form from desire and power, is incapable of recognising the will to truth which pervades it, and the will to truth, having imposed itself upon us for so long, is such that the truth it seeks to reveal cannot fail to mask it."

31. John Dewey, "The Need for a Recovery of Philosophy," *On Experience, Nature, and Freedom*, ed. R. Bernstein (Indianapolis, Bobbs-Merrill, 1960), p. 59.

32. Such univocity in reality bears affinities with Baudrillard's hyperreality (see Jean Baudrillard, *Forget Foucault* [New York: Semiotext(e), 1987], pp. 51–52). Nevertheless, there are important differences. One is that reality is local, turned reflexively back onto itself, not a closing of reality onto itself. The other is that simulation is not unreality but displacement within the circularity of reality. At stake are locality and deferral.

33. See Hans-Georg Gadamer, "Hermeneutics and Historicism," Supplement I to the English edition of *Truth and Method* (New York, Seabury, 1975), p. 483.

34. Ibid.

35. Aristotle, *Physics*, IV, 208a. All quotations from Aristotle are from *The Basic Works of Aristotle*, ed. R. McKeon (New York: Random House, 1941).

36. Aristotle, *Physics*, II, 192b.
37. Gross unison and resonances, belonging and departing, can be given a formal description as follows. If we have superaltern locales L_i, each composed of loci l_{ij}, then each of the latter is composed of ingredients, some of which compose its unison in L_i, others of which compose its resonances. Let us call the unisons of l_{ij} in L_i, u_{ij}, and call the associated resonances r_{ij}, where u_{ij} and r_{ij} together compose the ingredients of l_{ij} in L_i. The locus l_{ij} can be the "same" over a range of locations only if there is a supersuperaltern locale, *SSL*, in which the L_i are located relative to which each l_{ij} possesses a unison over some subset of its unisons u_{ijk}. Among the range of the locus's unisons in L_i, only some may compose a functional unison in *SSL*. The relationship among *SSL* and the subaltern set of unisons that composes a gross unison, including their ingredients, is fourfold. The other unisons, relative to *SSL*, that are not functionally included in the gross unison are ways in which L_i *departs* from *SSL* and from its "identity" in *SSL*.
38. See my *Metaphysical Aporia and Philosophical Heresy* for a detailed discussion of these univocals.
39. This is Baudrillard's criticism of Foucault's generic view of power.
40. Charles Sanders Peirce, *Collected Papers of Charles Sanders Peirce*, ed. C. Hartshorne and P. Weiss (Cambridge, Mass.: Harvard University Press, 1931–35), 2.228.
41. Foucault, *The History of Sexuality, Volume I*, pp. 82–92.
42. Foucault, "The Discourse on Language," p. 224.
43. See my *Metaphysical Aporia and Philosophical Heresy*.

II. JUDGMENT

1. Immanuel Kant, *Critique of Judgment*, trans. J. H. Bernard (New York: Hafner, 1951), p. 11.
2. Ibid., p. 12.
3. Ibid., p. 13.
4. Ibid., p. 89.
5. Ibid., p. 186.
6. That is why Lyotard can so conclusively take sides with Kant against Hegel—reading Hegel without aporia, even the aporia of the Absolute. "126. You qualify presentation, entailed by a phrase, as *absolute*. By qualifying it in this way, you are presenting it. Its quality as absolute is situated in the universe presented by your phrase, and is relative to it. This is why the absolute is not presentable. With the notion of the sublime (and on the condition that *Darstellung* be understood as we have here), Kant will always get the better of Hegel. The *Erhabene* persists, not over and beyond, but right in the

heart of the *Aufgehobenen*" (Jean-François Lyotard, *The Differend*, G. Van Den Abbeele trans., [Minneapolis, University of Minnesota Press, 1988], p. 77).

7. Kant, *Critique of Judgment*, p. 86.
8. Ibid., p. 88.
9. Ibid., p. 93.
10. Ibid., p. 99.
11. Ibid., p. 101.
12. Ibid., p. 91.
13. Jacques Derrida, "Parergon," *The Truth in Painting*, trans. G. Bennington and I. McLeod (Chicago: University of Chicago Press, 1987), p. 125.
14. Ibid.
15. Ibid., p. 129.
16. Ibid., p. 136.
17. Kant, *Critique of Judgment*, p. 83.
18. Ibid., p. 99.
19. Ibid., p. 108.
20. Immanuel Kant, *Critique of Pure Reason* trans. N. Kemp Smith (London: Macmillan, 1956), p. 105: "Judgment is therefore the mediate knowledge of an object, that is, the representation of a representation of it."
21. Foucault, *The Archaeology of Knowledge* (New York: Pantheon, 1972), pp. 130–31.
22. Hannah Arendt, *Between Past and Future* (New York, Meridian, 1954), p. 220.
23. Hannah Arendt, *The Human Condition* (Chicago, University of Chicago Press, 1958), p. 52.
24. Ibid., p. 53.
25. Habermas, *The Philosophical Discourse of Modernity*, p. 295.
26. Ibid.
27. Kant, *Critique of Judgment*, par. 50: "Taste, like the judgment in general, is the discipline (or training) of genius; it clips its wings, it makes it cultured and polished; but, at the same time, it gives guidance as to where and how far it may extend itself if it is to remain purposive. . . . If, then, in the conflict of these two properties in a product something must be sacrificed, it should be rather on the side of genius; and the judgment, which in the things of beautiful art gives its decision from its own proper principles, will rather sacrifice the freedom and wealth of the imagination than permit anything prejudicial to the understanding."
28. Hannah Arendt, *Lectures on Kant's Political Philosophy*, ed. R. Beiner (Chicago: University of Chicago Press, 1982), p. 40. The quotation from Kant is from the *Critique of Judgment*, par. 40.
29. Heidegger, "The Origin of the Work of Art," *Poetry, Language, Thought*, trans. A. Hofstadter (New York, Harper & Row, 1971), pp. 61–62. The

complete passage is as follows: "One essential way in which truth establishes itself in the beings it has opened up is truth setting itself into work. Another way in which truth occurs is the act that founds a political state. Still another way in which truth comes to shine forth is the nearness of that which is not simply a being, but the being that is most of all. Still another way in which truth grounds itself is the essential sacrifice. Still another way in which truth becomes is the thinker's questioning, which, as the thinking of Being, names Being in its question-worthiness. By contrast, science is not an original happening of truth, but always the cultivation of a domain of truth already opened, specifically by apprehending and confirming that which shows itself to be possible and necessarily correct within that field. When and insofar as science passes beyond correctness and goes on to a truth, which means that it arrives at the essential disclosure of what is as such, it is philosophy."

30. Martin Heidegger, "The End of Philosophy and the Task of Thinking," *Basic Writings*, ed. D. Krell (New York: Harper & Row, 1977), p. 374.
31. "We have yet to write the history of that other form of madness, by which men, in an act of sovereign reason, confine their neighbors, and communicate and recognize each other through the merciless language of non-madness" (Michel Foucault, *Madness and Civilization* [New York: Random House, 1965], p. v).
32. Things of experience "are things *had* before they are things cognized" (John Dewey, *Experience and Nature* 2nd ed. [New York: Dover, 1958], p. 21.)
33. This, I believe, is what Dewey had in mind when he wrote that primary experience occurs "as it does chiefly in modes of action and undergoing." (ibid., p. 22).
34. Habermas, *The Philosophical Discourse of Modernity*, p. 339.
35. Foucault, "The Discourse on Language," Appendix to *The Archaeology of Knowledge*, p. 219.
36. Ibid., p. 225.
37. Michel Foucault, *Discipline and Punish: The Birth of the Prison*, trans. A. Sheridan (New York, Vintage, 1979), p. 215.
38. Martin Heidegger, "Letter on Humanism," *Basic Writings*, p. 202.
39. Michel Foucault, *The Order of Things* (New York: Vintage, 1973), p. 315.
40. See note 31.
41. Charles Sanders Peirce, "Logic as Semiotic: The Theory of Signs," *Philosophical Writings of Peirce*, ed. J. Buchler (New York: Dover, 1955), p. 99, from *Collected Papers*, 2.229: "The Third must indeed stand in such a relation, and thus must be capable of determining a Third of its own; but besides that, it must have a second triadic relation in which the Representamen, or rather the relation thereof to its Object, shall be its own (the Third's) Object, and must be capable of determining a Third to this relation. All this must equally be true of the Third's Thirds and so on endlessly."

42. See my *The Limits of Language* (New York: Fordham University Press, forthcoming), Chapter IVB. Semasis is closely related to what Derrida calls "iterability" though without emphasizing its judgmental nature.
43. See my *Locality and Practical Judgment: Charity and Sacrifice* (New York: Fordham University Press, forthcoming).
44. Arendt, *The Human Condition*, p. 183.
45. Heidegger, "The Origin of the Work of Art," p. 62.
46. Ibid., pp. 61–62.
47. See the discussion of the intensification of contrasts in Alfred North Whitehead, *Process and Reality*, corrected ed., ed. D. R. Griffin and D. W. Sherburne (New York: Free Press, 1978); and my *A Theory of Art: Inexhaustibility by Contrast* (Albany: State University of New York Press, 1982).
48. Baudrillard, "Forget Baudrillard," in *Forget Foucault* (New York: Semiotext(e), 1987), p. 71.
49. See Theodor Adorno, *Aesthetic Theory*, trans. C. Lenhardt (London and New York: Routledge & Kegan Paul, 1984), pp. 19–21, for a discussion of the fetish character of art.
50. Whitehead, *Process and Reality*, pp. 15–16.

III. REPRESENTATION

1. Baudrillard calls this "simulation." See *Forget Foucault* (New York: Semiotext(e), 1987).
2. Thomas Hobbes, *Leviathan* (Indianapolis: Liberal Arts Press, 1958), p. 132).
3. Ibid.
4. Ibid.
5. Ibid., p. 29.
6. Ibid., p. 38.
7. Niccolò Machiavelli, *The Prince*, trans. L. Ricci, rev. by E. R. P. Vincent (New York: Random House, 1950), p. 82.
8. Arendt, *The Human Condition*, p. 45.
9. Ibid., p. 48.
10. Ibid., p. 53.
11. Ibid., pp. 53–54.
12. Hobbes, *Leviathan*, pp. 143–44.
13. Ibid., p. 135.
14. Hilaire Belloc and G. K. Chesterton, *The Party System* (London, S. Swift, 1911), p. 12; quoted in Hanna Fenichel Pitkin, "Commentary: the Paradox of Representation," in J. Roland Pennock and John W. Chapman, eds., *Representation* (New York: Atherton Press, 1968), p. 40.

15. Lord Brougham, *Works*, XI, pp. 35–36; quoted in Pitkin, "Commentary," p. 40.

16. "I think that this paradoxical requirement, that a thing be both present and not present at the same time, is precisely what appears in the mandate and independence theorists' conflicting views on the meaning of representation. The mandate theorist says: If the situation is such that we can no longer see the constituents as present, there is no representation, and if the man habitually votes the opposite of their wishes they do not seem present in his voting (except, at most, formally, in the sense that he has the authority to commit them). The independence theorist says: If the situation is such that the constituents seem to be acting for themselves directly, if there is no intermediary or if the intermediary is a mere puppet in their hands, there is no representation; '*he* is to act, not *they*.' Both theorists are right" (Pitkin, "Commentary," pp. 41–42).

17. Ibid., p. 42.

18. See my "Translation as Transgression," *Translation Perspectives*, V, ed. D. J. Schmidt, (State University of New York at Binghamton, 1990).

19. Hanna Fenichel Pitkin, *The Concept of Representation* (Berkeley: University of California, 1967), p. 10.

20. Ibid., pp. 10–11.

21. Ibid., pp. 209–10.

22. Ibid., p. 240.

23. A quite different idea appears in Rousseau: "Sovereignty cannot be represented, for the same reason that it cannot be alienated. It consists essentially of the general will, and will cannot be represented. Either it is itself or it is different. There is no middle term" (Jean-Jacques Rousseau, *The Social Contract*, trans. G. D. H. Cole [New York: Dutton & Co., 1950], p. 94). Also, "the moment a People allows itself to be represented, it is no longer free: it no longer exists" (ibid., p. 96). A general will not divided by many wills, into unresolvable conflicts, disrupted by aporia and transgression, dissipates itself into another form of slavery.

24. "[I]t is, as we know, theoretically possible to deduce in advance of experience all the possible arrangements into which members of the group can enter with one another" (Marie Collins Swabey, *The Theory of the Democratic State* [Cambridge, Mass.: Harvard University Press, 1937]; reprinted in Hanna Fenichel Pitkin, *Representation* (New York: Atherton, 1969), p. 87.

25. Strawson's view of the reidentification of particulars is closely allied with substitution and exchange, as is most of classical empiricism, since the "re" accommodates no fundamental sense of alterity. The "purely auditory experience" Strawson posits (P. F. Strawson, *Individuals* [Garden City, N.Y.: Doubleday, 1963], p. 56) allows for no unambiguous reidentification. Yet is

not our experience frequently rather like the one Strawson rejects? Is not its refrain more auditory than visible, indeed both? Are not the difficulties of reidentification more of plenitude than ambiguity, of inexhaustibility rather than vagueness?

26. See especially Whitehead, *Process and Reality*, Part IV, where Whitehead develops a geometry without a metric to make sense of his notion of extensive order.

27. Foucault, *The Order of Things*, p. 169.

28. "All wealth is *coinable*; and it is by this means that it enters into *circulation*—in the same way that any natural being was *characterizable*, and could thereby find its place in a *taxonomy*; that any individual was *nameable* and could find its place in an *articulated language*; that any representation was *signifiable* and could find its place, in order to be known, in a *system of identities and differences*" (ibid., p. 175).

29. "The bond between the signifier and the signified is arbitrary. Since I mean by the sign the whole that results from the associating of the signifier with the signified, I can simply say: 'the linguistic sign is arbitrary'" (Ferdinand de Saussure, *Course in General Linguistics*, trans. W. Baskin [New York: McGraw-Hill, 1966], p. 67). Also, "in language there are only differences. Even more important, a difference generally implies positive terms between which the difference is set up; but in language there are only differences *without positive terms*" (ibid., p. 120).

30. Foucault, *The Order of Things*, p. 177.

31. Ibid., pp. 189–90.

32. Ibid., p. 192.

33. An interesting parallel may be drawn with synonymy in language, that metrical notion of equivalence without which meaning has no systematic relevance. See W. V. O. Quine, "Two Dogmas of Empiricism," *Philosophical Review*, 60 (1950): 20–43; and *Ontological Relativity and Other Essays* (New York: Columbia University Press, 1969).

34. Foucault, *The Order of Things*, p. 211.

35. Ibid.

36. Michel Foucault, "Two Lectures," *Power/Knowledge*, ed. C. Gordon, trans. A. Fontana and P. Pasquino (New York: Pantheon, 1980), p. 78. See also, "What, do you imagine that I would take so much trouble and so much pleasure in writing, do you think that I would keep so persistently to my task, if I were not preparing—with a rather shaky hand—a labyrinth into which I can venture, in which I can move my discourse, opening up underground passages, forcing it to go far from itself, finding overhangs that reduce and deform its itinerary, in which I can lose myself and appear at last to eyes that I will never have to meet again. I am no doubt not the only one who writes in

order to have no face. Do not ask who I am and do not ask me to remain the same" (Michel Foucault, *The Archaeology of Knowledge* [New York: Pantheon, 1972], p. 17).

37. Foucault, *The Order of Things*, p. xx. All further references to *The Order of Things* are indicated in the text as OT.

38. "What historical *a priori* provided the starting-point from which it was possible to define the great checkerboard of distinct identities established against the confused, undefined, faceless, and, as it were, indifferent background of differences?" (OT, p. xxiv).

39. "Between the *language* (*langue*) that defines the system of constructing possible sentences, and the *corpus* that passively collects the words that are spoken, the *archive* defines a particular level: that of a practice that causes a multiplicity of statements to emerge as so many regular events, as so many things to be dealt with and manipulated. . . . *It is the general system of the formation and transformation of statements*" (Foucault, *The Archaeology of Knowledge*, p. 130).

40. Ibid., pp. 130–131.

41. Among the strengths of *The Order of Things* is to make intelligible other orders than those we find familiar, to open up possibilities and alternatives. Foucault calls the most striking of these alternative orders "the prose of the world." (Foucault, *The Order of Things*, Chapter I.) The title of the chapter is from Merleau-Ponty.

42. "It is here [in the middle region] that a culture, imperceptibly deviating from the empirical orders prescribed for it by its primary codes . . . frees itself sufficiently to discover that these orders are perhaps not the only possible ones or the best ones" (OT, p. xx).

43. "It is comforting, however, and a source of profound relief to think that man is only a recent invention, a figure not yet two centuries old, a new wrinkle in our knowledge, and that he will disappear again as soon as that knowledge has discovered a new form" (OT, p. xxiii).

44. "[The human sciences] also permit the dissociation, which is characteristic of all contemporary knowledge about man, of consciousness and representation. They define the manner in which the empiricities can be given to representation but in a form that is not present to the consciousness . . . It must not be forgotten, therefore, that the increasingly marked importance of the unconscious in no way compromises the primacy of representation" (OT, p. 363)

45. "So the human sciences speak only within the element of the representable, but in accordance with a conscious/unconscious dimension, a dimension that becomes more and more marked as one attempts to bring the order of systems, rules, and norms to light" (OT, p. 363).

46. "This passage quotes a 'certain Chinese encyclopaedia' in which it is written that 'animals are divided into: (a) belonging to the Emperor, (b) embalmed, (c) tame, (d) suckling pigs, (e) sirens, (f) fabulous, (g) stray dogs, (h) included in the present classification, (i) frenzied, (j) innumerable, (k) drawn with a very fine camelhair brush, (l) *et cetera*, (m) having just broken the water pitcher, (n) that from a long way off look like flies.' In the wonderment of this taxonomy, the thing we apprehend in one great leap, the thing that, by means of the fable, is demonstrated as the exotic charm of another system of thought, is the limitation of our own, the stark impossibility of thinking *that*" (OT, p. xv).

47. "Man is a mode of being which accommodates that dimension—always open, never finally delimited, yet constantly traversed—which extends from a part of himself not reflected in a *cogito* to the act of thought by which he apprehends that part; and which, in the inverse direction, extends from that pure apprehension to the empirical clutter, the chaotic accumulation of contents, the weight of experiences constantly eluding themselves, the whole silent horizon of what is posited in the sandy stretches of non-thought" (OT, pp. 322–23).

48. "In the Classical age, nothing is given that is not given to representation; but, by that very fact, no sign ever appears, no word is spoken, no proposition is ever directed at any content except by the action of a representation that stands back from itself, that duplicates and reflects itself in another representation that is its equivalent" (OT, p. 78).

49. "Those things are 'convenient' which come sufficiently close to one another to be in juxtaposition" (OT, p. 18). "There is something in emulation of the reflection and the mirror: it is the means whereby things scattered through the universe can answer one another" (OT, p. 19). "Through [analogy], all the figures in the whole universe can be drawn together" (OT, p. 20). "Sympathy is an instance of the *Same* so strong and so insistent that it will not rest content to be merely one of the forms of likeness; . . . This is why sympathy is compensated for by its twin, antipathy" (OT, pp. 23–24).

50. Foucault continues: "The system of signatures reverses the relation of the visible to the invisible. Resemblance was the invisible form of that which, from the depths of the world, made things visible; but in order that this form may be brought out into the light in its turn there must be a visible figure that will draw it out from its profound invisibility" (OT, p. 26).

51. "Every resemblance receives a signature; but this signature is no more than an intermediate form of the same resemblance. As a result, the totality of these marks, sliding over the great circle of similitudes, forms a second circle which would be an exact duplication of the first, point by point, were it not for that tiny degree of displacement which causes the sign of sympathy to

reside in an analogy, that of analogy in emulation, that of emulation in convenience, which in turn requires the mark of sympathy for its recognition" (OT, p. 29).

52. "Resemblance never remains stable within itself; it can be fixed only if it refers back to another similitude, which then, in turn, refers to others; each resemblance, therefore, has value only from the accumulation of all the others, and the whole world must be explored if even the slightest of analogies is to be justified and finally take on the appearance of certainty. . . . And for this reason, from its very foundations, this knowledge will be a thing of sand" (OT, p. 30).

53. "[I]n the sixteenth century, one asked oneself how it was possible to know that a sign did in fact designate what it signified; from the seventeenth century, one began to ask how a sign could be linked to what it signified. A question to which the Classical period was to reply by the analysis of representation; and to which modern thought was to reply by the analysis of meaning and signification. But given the fact itself, language was never to be anything more than a particular case of representation (for the Classics) or of signification (for us). The profound kinship of language with the world was thus dissolved" (OT, pp. 42–43).

54. "[I]n Classical terms, a knowledge of empirical individual can be acquired only from the continuous, ordered, and universal tabulation of all possible differences" (OT, p. 144).

55. "The first thing we observe is that *analysis of wealth* obeys the same configuration as *natural history* and *general grammar*" (OT, p. 201).

56. "From this event onward, what gives value to the objects of desire is not solely the other objects that desire can represent to itself, but an element that cannot be reduced to that representation: *labour*; what makes it possible to characterize a natural being is no longer the elements that we can analyse in the representations we make for ourselves of it and other beings, it is a certain relation within this being, which we call its *organic structure*; what makes it possible to define a language is not the way in which it represents representations, but a certain internal architecture, . . . its *inflectional system*. In all these cases, the relation of representation to itself, and the relations of order it becomes possible to determine apart from all quantitative forms of measurement, now pass through conditions exterior to the actuality of the representation itself" (OT, p. 237).

57. "It is probably impossible to give empirical contents transcendental value, or to displace them in the direction of a constituent subjectivity, without giving rise, at least silently, to an anthropology—that is, to a mode of thought in which the rightful limitations of acquired knowledge (and consequently of all empirical knowledge) are at the same time the concrete forms of existence, precisely as they are given in that same empirical knowledge, (OT, p. 248).

58. "Confronting Ideology, the Kantian critique, on the other hand, marks the threshold of our modernity; it questions representation, . . . on the basis of its rightful limits. Thus it sanctions for the first time that event in European culture which coincides with the end of the eighteenth century: the withdrawal of knowledge and thought outside the space of representation" (OT, pp. 242–43).

59. Marx maintains the distinction between *vertreten* and *darstellen* in *The Eighteenth Brumaire of Louis Bonaparte*. Spivak quotes the following: "The small peasant proprietors . . . cannot represent [*vertreten*] themselves; they must be represented. Their representative must appear simultaneously as their master, as an authority over them, as unrestricted governmental power that protects them from the other classes and sends them rain and sunshine from above" (Gayatri Spivak, "Can the Subaltern Speak?" *Marxism and the Interpretation of Culture*, ed. Cary Nelson [Urbana: University of Illinois, 1988], pp. 276–77).

60. Spivak, ibid., p. 275.

61. Ibid., p. 277.

62. Among Spivak's arguments are the following, mostly in her own words:

1. The critique of the sovereign subject for which poststructuralism is famous, especially in Deleuze and Foucault, reinaugurates a European Subject.

2. The two systematically ignore the question of ideology and their own implication in intellectual and economic history.

3. They ignore the international division of labor, a gesture that often marks poststructuralist political theory.

4. They ignore the international division of labor, render "Asia" (and on occasion "Africa") transparent, reestablish the legal subject of socialized capital . . .

5. Deleuze and Foucault failed to consider the relation between desire, power, and subjectivity, rendering them incapable of articulating a theory of interests.

6. These philosophers seem obliged to reject all arguments naming the concept of ideology as schematic rather than textual and seem equally obliged to produce a mechanistically reductive opposition between interest and desire.

7. These philosophers would not entertain the thought of constitutive contradiction, that is where they admittedly part company from the Left.

8. Neither Deleuze nor Foucault seems aware that the intellectual within socialized capital, brandishing concrete experience, can help consolidate the international division of labor.

9. Two senses of representation are run together: representation as "speaking for," as in politics, and representation as "re-presentation," as in art or philosophy. Radical practice should attend to this double session of representation rather than reintroducing the individual subject through totalizing concepts of power and desire.

10. Said's critique of power in Foucault was as a captivating and mystifying category that allowed him "to obliterate the role of classes, the role of economics, the role of insurgency and rebellion."

11. It is impossible for contemporary French intellectuals to imagine the kind of Power and Desire that would inhabit the unnamed subject of the Other of Europe.

12. The clearest example of such epistemic violence is the . . . project to constitute the colonial subject as Other.

13. According to Foucault and Deleuze . . . the oppressed, if given the chance . . . *can speak and know their conditions*.

14. The seduction for them, and fearfulness for us, is that they might allow the complicity of the investigating subject (male or female professional) to disguise itself in transparency.

63. Spivak, "Can the Subaltern Speak?" p. 276.

64. Trinh T. Minh-ha, *Woman, Native, Other* (Bloomington: Indiana University Press, 1989), pp. 98–99, 101.

IV. POWER

1. Foucault, *The History of Sexuality, Volume I*, trans. R. Hurley (New York: Vintage, 1980), pp. 92–93.

2. Ibid., p. 93.

3. The writer who portrays the transgressions within and of the Law within "Power" is, of course, Kafka. "Many aver that the story confers no right on anyone to pass judgment on the doorkeeper. Whatever he may seem to us, he is yet a servant of the Law; that is, he belongs to the Law and as such is beyond human judgment. In that case one must not believe that the doorkeeper is subordinate to the man. Bound as he is by his service, even only at the door of the Law, he is incomparably greater than anyone at large in the world. The man is only seeking the Law, the doorkeeper is already attached to it. It is the Law that has placed him at his post; to doubt his dignity is to doubt the Law itself" (Franz Kafka, *The Trial*, trans. W. and E. Muir [New York: Modern Library, 1956], p. 276).

4. Foucault, *The History of Sexuality, Volume I*, p. 93.

5. Ibid., pp. 83–84.

6. Foucault, "Nietzsche, Genealogy, History," *Language, Countermemory, Practice* (Ithaca, N.Y.: Cornell University Press, 1977), pp. 150–51.

7. Foucault, *The History of Sexuality, Volume I*, p. 85

8. Ibid., p. 94.

9. Ibid.

10. Ibid.

11. Ibid., pp. 94–95.

12. Ibid., p. 95.

13. Ibid., pp. 95–96.

14. Ibid., p. 96.

15. Foucault, "Nietzsche, Genealogy, History," p. 151.

16. Foucault, *The History of Sexuality, Vol. I*, p. 96.

17. Ibid.

18. Aristotle, *Metaphysics*, V, 12.

19. John Locke, *An Essay Concerning Human Understanding* (New York: Dover, 1959), II, XXI, 1–3 (quoted by Whitehead in *Process and Reality* [New York: Free Press, 1978], pp. 57–58).

20. Whitehead, *Process and Reality*, p. 56.

21. Ibid., p. 340.

22. Benedict de Spinoza, *Ethics* (New York: Hafner, 1949), I, Prop. XXXIV.

23. Ibid., III, Prop. VII.

24. Ibid., IV, Def. VIII.

25. Ibid., IV, Def. of the Emotions I.

26. Jacques Derrida, "Plato's Pharmacy," *Disseminations*, trans. B. Johnson (Chicago: University of Chicago Press, 1981). See also my *Metaphysical Aporia and Philosophical Heresy*, Chapter 1.

27. Gadamer, *Truth and Method* (New York: Seabury, 1975), p. 180.

28. Ibid., pp. 180–81.

29. Ibid., p. 181.

30. Ibid.

31. Ibid.

32. A related but alternative view of power is found in Deleuze. In the words of his translators: "*Puissance* refers to a range of potential. It has been defined by Deleuze as a 'capacity for existence,' 'a capacity to affect or be affected,' a capacity to multiply connections that may be realized in a given 'body' to varying degrees in different situations. It may be thought of as a scale of intensity or fullness of existence (or of a degree on such a scale), analogous to the capacity of a number to be raised to a higher 'power.' . . . Here, *puissance* pertains to the virtual (the plane of consistency), *pouvoir* to the actual (the plane of organisation)" (Gilles Deleuze and Félix Guattari, *A Thousand Plateaus: Capitalism and Schizophrenia*, trans. and ed. B. Massumi [Minneapolis: University of Minnesota Press, 1987], p. xvii). The potential within

puissance is Spinozistic: inseparable from its actuality, especially in relation to a "body" on which it is imposed. If we distinguish *puissance* from *pouvoir* as potency from actuality, then power is divided within by its actualizations in a way quite different from the divisions within power or within stillness and polyphony.

33. Foucault, "Nietzsche, Genealogy, History," p. 151.

34. The passage continues: "How were these power relations linked to one another according to the logic of a great strategy, which in retrospect takes on the aspect of a unitary and voluntarist politics of sex? In general terms: rather than referring all the infinitesimal violences that are exerted on sex, all the anxious gazes that are directed at it, and all the hiding places whose discovery is made into an impossible task, to the unique form of a great Power, we must immerse the expanding production of discourses on sex in the field of multiple and mobile power relations" (Foucault, *The History of Sexuality, Volume I*, pp. 97–98).

35. Foucault, "The Discourse on Language," p. 229.

36. Foucault, *The History of Sexuality, Volume I*, pp. 100–1.

37. Arendt, *The Human Condition*, p. 179.

38. Ibid., p. 181.

39. Ibid., p. 182.

40. Ibid., p. 179.

41. Ibid., p. 183.

42. Ibid., pp. 52–53.

43. The passage continues: "The facts of nature are the actualities; and the facts into which the actualities are divisible are their prehensions, with their public origins, their private forms, and their private aims. But the actualities are moments of passage into a novel stage of publicity; and the coordination of prehensions expresses the publicity of the world, so far as it can be considered in abstraction from private genesis. Prehensions have public careers, but they are born privately" (Whitehead, *Process and Reality*, p. 290).

44. Michel Foucault, "Truth and Power," *Power/Knowledge*, ed. and trans. C. Gordon (New York: Pantheon, 1980), p. 131.

45. Ibid., p. 133.

V. DESIRE

1. In German, this schism is called *Geschlecht*. See notes 16–18 in Chapter VIII.

2. Sigmund Freud, "Femininity," *New Lectures on Psycho-Analysis*, quoted from *The Standard Edition of the Complete Psychological Works of Sigmund*

Freud, ed. J. Strachey (London: Hogarth Press, 1953–74), p. 113; quoted in Irigaray, *The Speculum of the Other Woman* (Ithaca, N.Y.: Cornell University Press, 1985), pp. 13–14.

3. Ibid.: Freud, p. 113; in Irigaray, p. 14.
4. Irigaray, *The Speculum of the Other Woman*, p. 14.
5. Ibid., p. 25.
6. Ibid., p. 133.
7. Irigaray has Lacan in mind. "The phallus is the privileged signifier of that mark in which the role of the logos is joined with the advent of desire. It can be said that this signifier is chosen because it is the most tangible element in the real of sexual copulation, and also the most symbolic in the literal (typographical) sense of the term, since it is equivalent there to the (logical) copula. It might also be said that, by virtue of its turgidity, it is the image of the vital flow as it is transmitted in generation" (Jacques Lacan, *Écrits*, trans. A. Sheridan [New York: Norton, 1977], p. 287).
8. Irigaray, *The Speculum of the Other Woman*, p. 135.
9. Derrida, "Plato's Pharmacy," *Disseminations* (Chicago: University of Chicago Press, 1981).
10. Ibid., p. 169.
11. Ibid., p. 105.
12. Spinoza, *Ethics*, III, Prop. IX. All further page references are given in the text.
13. See Chapter VIII, note 8.
14. G. W. F. Hegel, *Phenomenology of Mind*, trans. J. Baillie (London: George Allen & Unwin, 1931), p. 220
15. G. W. F. Hegel, *The Logic of Hegel* (the *Encyclopaedia Logic*), trans. W. Wallace (Oxford: Oxford University Press, 1892), pp. 24–25.
16. G. W. F. Hegel, *Hegel's Science of Logic*, trans. A. V. Miller (London: George Allen & Unwin, 1969), p. 149.
17. Hegel, *Phenomenology of Mind*, p. 225.
18. Foucault, *The Archaeology of Knowledge* (New York: Pantheon, 1972), p. 186.
19. Sigmund Freud, *Civilization and Its Discontents*, trans. J. Riviere, International Psycho-analytical Library (London: Hogarth Press, 1953), p. 7.
20. Ibid.
21. Foucault, *The Order of Things*, p. 211.

VI. TRUTH

1. Aristotle, *De Anima*, III, 4.
2. "Actual knowledge is identical with its object" (ibid., III, 7).

3. Spinoza, *Ethics*, II, Prop. 7.
4. Ibid., I, Ax. VI.
5. Ibid., II, Prop. XLIII
6. Ludwig Wittgenstein, *Tractatus Logico–Philosophicus,* trans. D. F. Pears and B. F. McGuiness (London: Routledge & Kegan Paul, 1961), 1
7. Ibid., 1.1
8. Ibid., 2.21
9. Hegel, *Phenomenology of Mind* (London: George Allen & Unwin, 1931), Preface, pp. 81–82.
10. Hegel, *Encyclopaedia Logic* (Oxford: Oxford University Press, 1892), Preliminary Notion, pp. 51–52.
11. Aristotle, *Metaphysics*, IV, 8.
12. Aristotle, *De Interpretatione*, 16a.
13. Perhaps we should call it the misogyny of brotherhood: "But perhaps, someone will ask, whether women are under men's authority by nature or institution? . . . But if we consult experience itself, we shall find that the origin of it is in their weakness. . . . one may assert with perfect propriety, that women have not by nature equal right with men: but that they necessarily give way to men, and that thus it cannot happen, that both sexes should rule alike, much less that men should be ruled by women" (Benedict de Spinoza, *A Theologico-Political Treatise and A Political Treatise*, trans. R. H. M. Elwes [New York: Dover, 1951], pp. 386–87).
14. Spinoza, *Ethics*, II, Prop. XXXV.
15. Hegel, *Phenomenology of Mind*, p. 99.
16. Charles Sanders Peirce, "How to Make Our Ideas Clear," CP 5.388–410; reprinted in J. Buchler ed., *Philosophical Writings of Peirce* (New York: Dover, 1955), p. 38.
17. Martin Heidegger, "On the Essence of Truth," *Basic Writings,* ed. D. Krull (New York: Harper & Row, 1977), p. 117.
18. Ibid., p. 130.
19. Foucault, *The Archaeology of Knowledge* (New York: Pantheon, 1972), p. 224.
20. Heidegger, "On the Essence of Truth," p. 133.
21. Heidegger, "The Origin of the Work of Art," *Basic Writings*, p. 53.
22. Heidegger, "On the Essence of Truth," p. 133.
23. Ibid., pp. 135–36.
24. Ibid., p. 136.
25. Hegel, *Phenomenology of Mind*, pp. 81–82.
26. Hegel, *Encyclopaedia Logic*, p. 225.
27. Ibid., p. 363.
28. Ibid., p. 352.

29. Ibid., pp. 355–56.
30. Hegel, *Phenomenology of Mind*, p. 68.
31. Ibid., p. 69.
32. Ibid., p. 70.
33. Ibid., p. 134.
34. Ibid., p. 115.
35. Hegel, *Encyclopaedia Logic*, p. 30.
36. Hegel, *Phenomenology of Mind*, pp. 70–71.
37. Hegel, *Encyclopaedia Logic*, p. 267.
38. Ibid., p. 232.
39. "Consciousness furnishes its own criterion in itself, and the inquiry will thereby be a comparison of itself with its own self; for the distinction, just made, falls inside itself. . . . Thus in what consciousness inside itself declares to be the essence or truth we have the standard which itself sets up, and by which we are to measure its knowledge" (Hegel, *Phenomenology of Mind*, p. 140).
40. Heidegger, "On the Essence of Truth," p. 125.
41. Ibid., p. 128.
42. "Freedom now reveals itself as letting things be" (ibid., p. 127).
43. Hegel, *Phenomenology of Mind*, p. 802.
44. Heidegger, "On the Essence of Truth," p. 132.
45. Martin Heidegger, *Identity and Difference*, trans. J. Stambaugh (New York: Harper & Row, 1969), p. 31.
46. "Considered with respect to truth as disclosedness, concealment is then undisclosedness and accordingly the untruth that is most proper to the essence of truth" (Heidegger, "On The Essence of Truth," p. 132).
47. Ibid., pp. 132–33.
48. *"[K]ata to chreōn didonai gar auta dikēnkai tisin allēlois tēs adikias"* (Anaximander fragment, quoted from Martin Heidegger, "The Anaximander Fragment," *Early Greek Thinking* [San Francisco: Harper & Row, 1984], p. 29); *"according to what must be; for they make reparation to one another for their injustice according to the ordinance of time"* (Anaximander Fragment 2.34, from John Mansley Robinson, *An Introduction to Early Greek Thinking* [Boston: Houghton Mifflin, 1968], p. 34). The age of injustice speaks against any privilege, echoing the unending risk of domination, even by the one mystery.
49. Heidegger, *On The Essence of Truth,"* p. 133.
50. "The errancy in which any given segment of historical humanity must proceed for its course to be errant is essentially connected with the openness of Dasein. By leading him astray, errancy dominates man through and through. But, as leading astray, errancy at the same time contributes to a possibility

that man is capable of drawing up from his ek-sistence—the possibility that, by experiencing errancy itself and by not mistaking the mystery of Da-sein, he does *not* let himself be led astray" (ibid., p. 136).

51. Ibid., p. 137.
52. Heidegger, "The Origin of the Work of Art," p. 61.
53. Ibid., p. 62. See Chapter II p. 25, pp. 32–37.
54. Heidegger, "On the Essence of Truth," p. 130
55. Foucault, "The Discourse on Language," *The Archaeology of Knowledge*, pp. 223–24.
56. Ibid., p. 219.
57. Baudrillard, *Forget Foucault* (New York: Semiotext(e), 1987), p. 50.
58. "[P]ower starts off from something (otherwise there would not even be those resistances noted on p. 96), something like an exclusion, a division, or a denial, and on that basis power can 'produce something real' or produce *the* real. It is only from this point on that we can conceive of a new peripateia of power—a catastrophic one this time—where power no longer succeeds in producing the real, in reproducing itself as real, or in opening new spaces to the reality principle, and where it falls into the hyperreal and vanishes: *this is the end of power*, the end of the strategy of the real" (ibid., p. 33)
59. Ibid., p. 124.
60. "The real—all things considered, perhaps it exists—no, it doesn't exist—is the insurmountable limit of theory. The real is not an objective status of things, it is the point at which theory can do nothing. In any case, power lures us on and truth lures us on. Everything is in the lightning-quick contraction in which an entire cycle of accumulation, of power, or of truth comes to a close. There is never any inversion or any subversion: the cycle must be accomplished. But it can happen instantaneously. It is death that is a stake in this contraction" (ibid., p. 125).
61. Ibid., pp. 127–28.

VII. HISTORY

1. Hegel, *Phenomenology of Mind*, trans. J. Baillie (London, George Allen & Unwin, 1931), p. 220.
2. Ibid., p. 806.
3. Ibid., p. 802.
4. Hegel, *Encyclopaedia Logic* (Oxford: Oxford University Press, 1892), p. 363.
5. Ibid., p. 355.
6. Ibid., p. 357.
7. Ibid., p. 225.

8. Hegel, *Phenomenology of Mind*, pp. 806–7.
9. Hegel, *Encyclopaedia Logic*, p. 10.
10. Hegel, *Phenomenology of Mind*, pp. 791–92.
11. Ibid., p. 802.
12. Trinh T. Minh-ha, *Woman, Native, Other* (Bloomington: Indiana University Press, 1989), p. 101.
13. Gadamer, *Truth and Method* (New York: Seabury, 1975), p. xxv.
14. Ibid., p. 271.
15. Ibid., p. 324.
16. Dewey, "Time and Individuality," *Experience, Nature, and Freedom* (Indianapolis: Bobbs-Merrill, 1960), p. 239.
17. Ibid., p. 240.
18. Ibid.
19. Foucault, *The Archaeology of Knowledge* (New York: Pantheon, 1972), p. 31.
20. "The Discourse on Language," in ibid., p. 229.
21. Ibid.
22. Foucault, *The Archaeology of Knowledge*, p. 55.
23. Ibid., p. 135.
24. Ibid., p. 136.
25. Foucault, "Two Lectures," *Power/Knowledge* (New York: Pantheon, 1980), p. 78.
26. Ibid., p. 81.
27. Ibid.
28. Foucault, "Nietzsche, Genealogy, History," *Language, Countermemory, Practice* (Ithaca, N.Y.: Cornell University Press, 1977), pp. 150–51.
29. Ibid., p. 151.
30. Foucault, *The Archaeology of Knowledge*, p. 131.
31. Dewey, "Time and Individuality," p. 241.
32. Derrida, "Tympan," *Margins of Philosophy* (Chicago: University of Chicago Press, 1982), p. x.
33. Ibid., pp. x–xi.
34. Ibid., p. xxv.
35. Ibid., p. xxvi.
36. Ibid., p. xxvii.
37. Friedrich Nietzsche, *On the Advantage and Disadvantage of History for Life*, trans. P. Preuss (Indianapolis: Hackett, 1980), pp. 8–9. All further page references are given in the text as OADHL.
38. Walter Benjamin, "Theses on the Philosophy of History," *Illuminations*, trans. H. Zohn (New York: Schocken, 1969) p. 255.
39. Ibid.
40. Baudrillard, *Forget Foucault*, p. 71.

VIII. EMBODIMENT

1. Jacques Derrida, "Parergon," *The Truth in Painting* (Chicago: University of Chicago Press, 1987), pp. 54–55.
2. Derrida, "Restitutions," in ibid., pp. 258–59.
3. I have in mind here Foucault's archaeologies, especially *Discipline and Punish*, *Birth of the Clinic*, and *The History of Sexuality, Volume I*. But similar themes turn on the biological side of the taxonomies that define the human sciences in *The Order of Things*.
4. I am extending here Foucault's distinction between Power under Law and power: "Power is everywhere; not because it embraces everything, but because it comes from everywhere. And 'Power,' insofar as it is permanent, repetitious, inert, and self-reproducing, is simply the over-all effect that emerges from all these mobilities, the concatenation that rests on each of them and seeks in turn to arrest their movement" (Foucault, *The History of Sexuality, Volume I*, p. 93).
5. "In the Penal Colony," *Selected Short Stories of Franz Kafka*, trans. W. Muir and E. Muir (New York: Modern Library, 1952), p. 96. Further references to this story are indicated in the text as IPC.
6. Maurice Merleau-Ponty, *The Phenomenology of Perception* trans. C. Smith (London: Routledge & Kegan Paul, 1962), pp. 199–200.
7. Hélène Cixous, "The Laugh of the Medusa," *Signs* (Summer 1976); reprinted in E. Marks and I. de Courtivron, eds., *New French Feminisms* (New York: Schocken, 1981).
8. See my *Metaphysical Aporia and Philosophical Heresy* (Albany: State University of New York Press, 1989), Chapter 5, for a detailed discussion of the aporias that pertain to Spinoza's view of the relationship between Substance and its modes.
9. Whitehead, *Process and Reality* (New York: Free Press, 1978), pp. 311–12.
10. Ibid., pp. 180–81.
11. G. W. F. Leibniz, *Monadology*, in *Leibniz Selections*, ed. P. P. Wiener (New York: Scribner's, 1951), p. 545.
12. Ibid.
13. Merleau-Ponty, *Phenomenology of Perception*, p. 171.
14. See my "The Limits of Sexuality," *Philosophy and Social Criticism* 9, nos. 3–4 (Spring 1984); and *Inexhaustibility and Human Being* (New York: Fordham University Press, 1989), Chapter 4, for a detailed discussion of sexuality as representation.
15. Martin Heidegger, "What Calls for Thinking;" *Basic Writings* (New York: Harper & Row, 1977), p. 357.
16. Jacques Derrida, "Geschlecht II: Heidegger's Hand," *Deconstruction and Philosophy*, ed. J. Sallis (Chicago: University of Chicago Press, 1987), p. 173.
17. Derrida quotes David Krell on *Geschlecht* as follows: "Paul lists three prin-

cipal meanings for *Geschlecht* (Old High German *gislahti*). First, it translates the Latin word *genus*, being equivalent to *Gattung: das Geschlecht* is a group of people who share a common ancestry, especially if they constitute a part of the hereditary nobility. Of course, if the ancestry is traced back far enough we may speak of *des menschliche Geschlecht*, 'humankind.' Second, *das Geschlecht* may mean one generation of men and women who die to make way for a succeeding generation. Third, there are male and female *Geschlechter*, and *Geschlecht* becomes the root of many words for the things males and females have and do for the sake of the first two meanings: *Geschlechts-glied* or *-teil*, the genitals; *-trieb*, the sex drive; *-verkehr*, sexual intercourse; and so on" (Derrida, "*Geschlecht* II"; quoted from David Krell, *Intimations of Mortality* [University Park: Pennsylvania State University Press, 1986], Chapter 11).

18. Ibid., p. 162.
19. Foucault, "Nietzsche, Genealogy, History," *Language, Countermemory, Practice* (Ithaca, N.Y.: Cornell University Press, 1982), p. 151.
20. Foucault speaks of an "incorporeal materialism"; I speak of immaterial materiality and disembodied embodiment. See Foucault, "The Discourse on Language," *The Archaeology of Knowledge* (New York: Pantheon, 1972), p. 231.
21. Foucault, *Discipline and Punish: The Birth of the Prison* (New York: Vintage, 1979), pp. 25–26.
22. Ibid., p. 26.
23. Foucault has proposed the opposite, that rape not be treated as a sexual crime. This proposal reflects a desire to undermine the constitution of sexuality by public institutions but fails to acknowledge its cultural relations.
24. Foucault, *The History of Sexuality, Volume I*, p. 95.
25. Foucault, *Discipline and Punish*, pp. 137–38.
26. Ibid., pp. 304–5.
27. Foucault, *The History of Sexuality, Volume I*, p. 85.

"These are some of its principal features.
—*The negative relation*. It never establishes any connection between power and sex that is not negative: . . .
—*The insistence of the rule*. Power is essentially what dictates its law to sex. . . .
—*The cycle of prohibition*. . . .
—*The logic of censorship*. . . .
—*The uniformity of the apparatus*. Power over sex is exercised in the same way at all levels" (ibid., pp. 83–84.)

28. Foucault, "The Discourse on Language," p. 231.
29. Foucault, *The Archaeology of Knowledge*, p. 209.

IX. PRAXIS

1. Foucault, *The Order of Things*, p. 250.
2. Ibid., p. 319.
3. Foucault also speaks of the archive as the "historical a priori" (*The Archaeology of Knowledge* [New York: Pantheon, 1972], p. 127)
4. See my *Metaphysical Aporia and Philosophical Heresy* (Albany: State University of New York Press, 1989).
5. Foucault, *The Order of Things*, p. 318.
6. Ibid., p. 344.
7. Ibid., p. 323
8. Jean-François Lyotard, *Peregrinations* (New York: Columbia University Press, 1988), p. 10.
9. Ibid., p. 35.
10. Ibid., pp. 38–39.
11. Ibid., p. 27.
12. Foucault, *The History of Sexuality, Volume I* (New York: Vintage, 1980), p. 85
13. Ibid., p. 93
14. Martin Heidegger, *Being and Time*, trans. J. Macquarrie and E. Robinson (New York: Harper & Row, 1962). pp. 531–32.
15. "Fundamental to the paradigm of mutual understanding is, rather, the performative attitude of participants in interaction, who coordinate their plans for action by coming to an understanding about something in the world" (Habermas, *The Philosophical Discourse of Modernity*, p. 296).
16. Arendt, *The Human Condition* (Chicago: University of Chicago Press, 1958), pp. 45, 48
17. Ibid., p. 52.
18. Ibid.
19. Ibid., p. 53.
20. Paul Ricoeur, *Freud and Philosophy: an Essay on Interpretation*, trans. D. Savage (New Haven, Conn.: Yale University Press, 1970), pp. 459–551.
21. Foucault, *The Order of Things*, p. 44.
22. Lyotard, *The Differend*, p. xii.
23. Foucault, *The History of Sexuality, Volume I*, pp. 82–83.
24. Foucault, *The Order of Things*, p. 211.
25. Whitehead, *Process and Reality* (New York: Free Press, 1978), p. 340.
26. Martin Heidegger, "The Question Concerning Technology," *Basic Writings*, p. 294.
27. See John Dewey, *A Common Faith*, in *Intelligence in the Modern World*, ed. J. Ratner (New York: Modern Library, 1939), for an ideality without God or perfectibility, without *technē*.

28. See Emmanuel Levinas, *Otherwise than Being or Beyond Essence*, trans. A. Lingis (The Hague: Martinus Nijhoff, 1981); see also my *Locality and Practical Judgment: Charity and Sacrifice*, forthcoming.
29. Arendt, *The Human Condition*, p. 76.
30. Ibid., p. 119.
31. Heidegger, "The Origin of the Work of Art," *Poetry, Language, Thought* (New York: Harper & Row, 1971), p. 77. In both Arendt and Heidegger, the notion of work repeats the *Geschlecht* of our humanity against animality.

X. HUMANITY

1. Dewey, *Experience and Nature* 2nd ed. (New York: Dover, 1958), p. 108.
2. Ibid., p. 8.
3. Ibid., pp. 4a–1.
4. John Dewey, "On the Need for a Recovery of Philosophy," *On Experience, Nature, and Freedom*, ed. R. Bernstein (Indianapolis: Bobbs-Merrill, 1960), p. 59.
5. William James, *A Pluralistic Universe* (New York: Longmans Green, 1909), p. 321.
6. John Dewey, "Nature in Experience," *On Experience, Nature, and Freedom*, p. 246–47.
7. Martin Heidegger, "On the Being and Conception of *Physis* in Aristotle's *Physics* B. 1," trans. T. J. Sheehan *Man and World* 9, no. 3 (August 1976). John Herman Randall, Jr., *Nature and Historical Experience* (New York: Columbia University Press, 1958), pp. 143–94.
8. Martin Heidegger, "Modern Science, Metaphysics, and Mathematics, *Basic Writings* (New York: Harper & Row, 1977), pp. 259–61.
9. Spinoza, *Ethics*, I, Prop. XXVIII.
10. Ibid., I, Prop. XXIX.
11. Derrida, *Margins of Philosophy* (Chicago: University of Chicago Press, 1982), p. x.
12. Heidegger, "Letter on Humanism," *Basic Writings*, p. 202.
13. Ibid., p. 193.
14. Jean-Paul Sartre, *Existentialism as a Humanism*, trans. B. Frechtman (New York: Philosophical Library, 1947), p. 20.
15. Ibid., p. 27.
16. Ibid., p. 45.
17. Ibid., p. 58
18. Ibid., pp. 59–60.
19. Simone de Beauvoir, *The Ethics of Ambiguity*, trans. B. Frechtman (New York: Philosophical Library, 1948), p. 9
20. Ibid., p. 7.

21. "[I]t is still necessary for the failure to be surmounted, and existentialist ontology does not allow this hope. Man's passion is useless; he has no means
for becoming the being he is not. That too is true. And it is also true that in
Being and Nothingness Sartre has insisted above all on the abortive aspect of
the human adventure. It is only in the last pages that he opens up the perspective for an ethics. However, if we reflect upon his descriptions of existence,
we perceive that they are far from condemning man without recourse" (ibid.,
p. 11).
22. Ibid., p. 11.
23. Ibid., p. 18.
24. Heidegger, "Letter on Humanism," pp. 202–3.
25. Ibid., p. 203.
26. Ibid., p. 205.
27. Ibid., p. 204.
28. Ibid., p. 206.
29. Ibid, p. 213.
30. Ibid., p. 206.
31. Ibid., pp. 210–11.
32. Ibid., p. 225.
33. Ibid., p. 222.
34. Ibid., p. 223.
35. Derrida, "*Geschlecht* II," *Deconstruction and Philosophy* (Chicago: University of Chicago Press, 1987), p. 173.
36. Ibid., pp. 173–74.
37. Ibid., p. 174.
38. Martin Heidegger, "What Calls for Thinking?" *Basic Writings*, p. 357.
39. "*Geschlecht* becomes the root of many words for the things males and females have and do for the sake of the first two meanings: *Geschlechts-glied*
or *-teil*, the genitals; *-trieb*, the sex drive; *-verkehr*, sexual intercourse; and so
on" (Derrida, "*Geschlecht* II," pp. 191–92).
40. "The word [*Geschlecht*, then] signifies the human species (*Menschenge-
schlecht*) in the sense of humanity (*Menschheit*) as well as the species in the
sense of tribes, stocks, and families, all that struck again [*dies alles widerum
geprägt:* struck in the sense of what receives the imprint, the *typos*, the typi-
cal mark] with the generic duality of the sexes (*in das Zwiefache der
Geschlechter*)" (ibid., p. 185).
41. "What comes to *Geschlecht* as its decomposition (*Verwesung*), its corrup-
tion, is a *second* blow that comes to strike the sexual difference and to trans-
form it into dissension, war, savage opposition" (ibid., p. 193).
42. Foucault, "Preface to Transgression," *Language, Countermemory, Practice*
(Ithaca, N.Y.: Cornell University Press, 1977), pp. 35–36.
43. Foucault, *The Order of Things*, p. 344
44. Ibid., p. 310

45. Ibid.
46. Ibid., p. 318.
47. Ibid., p. 308.
48. "The human sciences are not, then, an analysis of what man is by nature; but rather an analysis that extends from what man is in his positivity (living, speaking, labouring being) to what enables this same being to know (or seek to know) what life is, in what the essence of labour and its laws consist, and in what way he is able to speak" (ibid., p. 353)
49. "To describe a group of statements not as the closed, plethoric totality of a meaning, but as an incomplete, fragmented figure; to describe a group of statements not with reference to the interiority of an intention, a thought, or a subject, but in accordance with the dispersion of an exteriority; to describe a group of statements, in order to rediscover not the moment or the trace of their origin, but the specific forms of an accumulation, is certainly not to uncover an interpretation, to discover a foundation, or to free constituent acts; nor is it to decide on a rationality, or embrace a teleology. It is to establish what I am quite willing to call a *positivity*" (Foucault, *The Archaeology of Knowledge* [New York: Pantheon, 1972], p. 125).
50. Foucault, "What Is an Author?," *Language, Countermemory, Practice*, p. 138.
51. Ibid.
52. Foucault, *The Order of Things*, p. 352
53. Ibid., p. 353.
54.. "None of it does more than mark time. Repetitive and disconnected, it advances nowhere" (Foucault, "Two Lectures," *Power/Knowledge* [New York: Pantheon, 1980], p. 78).
55. Foucault, *The Archaeology of Knowledge*, p. 16.
56. Foucault, "Two Lectures," p. 85.
57. Foucault, *Madness and Civilization* [New York: Random House, 1965], p. ix.
58. Foucault, *The Order of Things*, p. xxi.
59. Ibid., p. 16.
60. Jacques Derrida, "Cogito and the History of Madness," *Writing and Difference*, trans. A. Bass (Chicago: University of Chicago Press, 1978), pp. 34–35.
61. Foucault, *The Archaeology of Knowledge*, p. 130.
62. Ibid.
63. Ibid., p. 131.
64. Derrida, "*Geschlecht II*," p. 162.

XI. NATURE

1. See my *Locality and Practical Judgment* (New York: Fordham University Press, forthcoming), Chapter 4.

2. Heidegger, "On the Being and Conception of *Physis* in Aristotle's *Physics* B. 1," trans. T. J. Sheehan, *Man and World* 9, no 3 (August 1976): 260: "Then we see that making, *poiēsis*, is *one* kind of production, whereas 'growing' (the going back into itself and emerging out of itself), *physis*, is *another*."

3. Ibid., p. 232.

4. Ibid., p. 231.

5. Ibid., pp. 228, 225.

6. Ibid., p. 269.

7. Heidegger, "Modern Science, Metaphysics, and Mathematics," *Basic Writings* (New York: Harper & Row, 1977), p. 252.

8. Whitehead, *Process and Reality* (New York: Free Press, 1978), p. 40.

9. Ibid., p. 348.

10. Ibid, p. 345.

11. I develop this alternative in detail in my *Perspective in Whitehead's Metaphysics* (Albany: State University of New York Press, 1983), pp. 244–49.

12. Foucault, *The Archaeology of Knowledge* (New York: Pantheon, 1972), pp. 126–31.

13. Alfred North Whitehead, *Science and the Modern World* (New York: Macmillan, 1925), p. 250.

14. Heidegger, "Modern Science, Metaphysics, and Mathematics," p. 268.

15. "Therefore a thing which is the cause both of the essence and of the existence of any effect must differ from that effect both with regard to its essence and with regard to its existence."

16. "An individual thing, or a thing which is finite and which has a determinate existence, cannot exist nor be determined to action unless it be determined to existence and action by another cause which is also finite and has a determinate existence; and again, this cause cannot exist nor be determined to action unless by another cause which is also finite and determined to existence and action, and so on *ad infinitum*" (Spinoza, *Ethics*, I, Prop. XXVIII). "In Nature there is nothing contingent, but all things are determined from the necessity of the divine nature to exist and act in a certain manner" (Prop. XXIX).

17. "Because God, in regulating all, has had regard to each part, and particularly to each monad, whose nature being representative, nothing can limit it to representing only a part of things; although it may be true that this representation is but confused as regards the detail of the whole universe, . . . souls in general are the living mirrors or images of the universe of creatures, but minds or spirits are in addition of the Divinity itself, or of the author of nature, able to know the system of the universe and to imitate something of it by architectonic samples, each mind being like a little divinity in its own department" (Leibniz, *Monadology*, Pars. 60, 83.)

INDEX

A Priori, 60, 164, 193, 208, 224, 238

Abandonment, 131, 133, 182

Abgrund, 21; *see also* Abyss

Abnormality, 25–26

Abortion, 158

Absence, 44, 46, 51, 55–56, 63, 89, 91, 96, 98–99, 107, 113, 120–21, 131–32, 140, 148–49, 152–53, 160, 197, 208; *see also* Silence

Absolute, 10, 12, 20, 44, 76, 102, 104, 112, 116–17, 119–20, 124, 128–29, 131, 148, 180, 192–93, 195–96, 201–202, 218

Absoluteness, 10, 124, 130–31, 148, 201–202

Abstraction, 29, 35, 112, 116–17, 121, 128, 230

Absurdity, 76, 191–92, 207

Abyss, 21, 23, 123, 187, 196–97, 201

Achievement, 54, 57, 73, 96, 98–99, 112, 119, 147, 182, 193

Action, 24, 28, 40, 50–52, 54–56, 82–83, 87, 104, 129, 139–40, 149, 169, 179, 182, 189, 191, 205, 220, 225, 238, 241–42

Activity, 54, 69, 76, 82, 84–85, 105, 135, 140, 149, 158

Actuality, 14, 81, 83–85, 88, 117, 120, 191, 207, 226, 230

Actualization, 81, 230

Adikias, 233; *see also* Injustice, Justice

Adjudication, 179–80; *see also* Judgment

Adorno, T., 43, 176, 221

Aesthetic, 20–22, 168, 187, 221; *see also* Art

Aestheticization, 43, 171; *see also* Fetishization

Affirmation, 107, 116, 140, 152, 169–70, 174, 176, 180, 192, 197, 211

Agathon, 98

Age, 114, 144, 157, 199, 225, 233

Agency, 69, 76

Agon, 25, 42, 79–80, 84, 129

Agreement, 24–25, 54, 112, 114, 140, 169–70, 176, 180; *see also* Consensus

Alcibiades, 95, 99

Alētheia, 121–22, 183; *see also* Truth, Untruth

Alienation, 89, 120, 222

All-inclusiveness, 76, 188, 212; *see also* Totality

Alsoness, 117

Alterity, 9, 31, 65, 97, 124, 222

Ambiguity, 96, 116, 145, 153, 192–93, 204–205, 223, 239

Analogy, 52, 63, 73, 143, 147, 151, 172, 177, 189, 225–26, 229

Analysis, 52, 57, 60, 65, 188, 199–200, 226, 241

Anarchy, 71

Anaximander, 121, 233

De Anima, 231; *see also* Aristotle

Animal, 30, 139, 143–44, 154–57, 182, 185, 192–93, 195–96, 201, 225, 239

Anthropology, 64–65

Aporia, 10, 16–17, 19–20, 35, 37, 44–46, 49, 54–55, 59, 62, 69, 71, 73, 76, 80–82, 87, 93, 113–14, 117–20, 122, 129–30, 148, 150, 162, 167, 169–70, 177, 179, 181, 185–90, 192–93, 196–98, 204,

Aporia (*cont.*)
    208–13, 216, 218, 222, 229, 236, 238
Apparatus, 28, 70–71, 73–74, 237
Appetite, 92–95, 101, 103; 149; *see also* Desire
Appropriation, 121, 134, 158, 190
Arbitrariness, 30–31, 58, 112, 177, 192, 200, 223
Archaeology, 60–61, 89, 171, 215, 219, 224, 231–32, 235–38, 241–42
Architectonic, 21, 242
Archive, 22, 60–61, 136, 199–200, 224, 238
Arendt, H., 24–25, 36, 40, 52–53, 86, 87–88, 169–70, 181, 219–21, 230, 238–39
Aretē, 147, 157, 166; *see also* Virtue
Argument, 26, 66, 102, 158, 227
Aristophanes, 97–98
Aristotle, 12, 14, 22, 27–28, 31, 33, 57, 81, 84–85, 111–13, 167, 169, 181, 189–90, 205–207, 209–10, 217–18, 229, 231–32, 239, 242
Art, 5, 10, 25–30, 32–33, 36–38, 41–43, 49–50, 63, 66, 100, 157, 159, 163–64, 168, 171–72, 176, 178, 181–82, 191, 194, 204–205, 209–10, 217, 219, 221, 228, 232, 234, 239
Artifact, 40, 52–53; *see also* Art, *Technē*
Artifice, 6, 10, 16, 30, 49–52, 54, 56, 87, 114, 182, 203–206, 208–10, 213–14; *see also* Art, Simulation, *Technē*
Assertion, 11, 33, 212
Attributes, 104–105, 113, 147, 149, 189, 210
Aufgehobenen, 219; *see also* Dialectic, Hegel, Spirit
Augustine, St., 92
Author, 50, 98, 100, 135, 154, 198, 241–42; *see also* Writing
Authority, 2–6, 8–10, 12, 15, 27–28, 33–37, 42–45, 51–54, 67–68, 71, 75–78, 108, 111, 122–23, 132, 141, 162, 166, 174, 179, 185, 191, 193, 198, 213, 222, 227, 232
Authorization, 2–3, 154
Autonomy, 26–27, 29, 31, 47, 55, 61, 70, 76, 107, 154, 160, 185, 191

Baudrillard, J., 124, 217–18, 221, 234–35
Beast, 193–95; *see also* Animal
Beautiful, 2, 22, 84, 92, 98–100, 178, 187, 219
Beauty, 84, 92, 94, 98, 99, 100, 178
Beauvoir, S. de, 192–93, 239
Becoming, 42, 78, 80, 119, 131, 140, 207, 211, 240
Being, 2–7, 9–10, 12, 15, 17, 19, 21, 23–24, 29–30, 32, 34, 40, 42, 45–46, 50–53, 55–56, 60–64, 66, 69, 71, 76, 80–84, 87–88, 93, 96–98, 101, 103, 107, 111, 114–16, 118, 120–23, 128, 130, 133–34, 137–41, 144–45, 147–49, 151–55, 157, 160, 163–64, 166–67, 170, 173, 177, 181, 185–88, 190–200, 203–204, 206–207, 209–10, 212, 215–16, 220, 223, 225–26, 236–42
Beings, 4, 6, 16, 25, 30–32, 41, 50, 56, 69, 83, 88, 93, 95–97, 104–105, 115, 120–22, 137, 144, 149, 156, 187, 193–95, 201, 204, 210, 220, 226
Belonging, 13–14, 26, 30–31, 34, 38, 42, 50, 52, 54, 63, 65, 67, 78–79, 89, 100, 107, 111–13, 115–17, 122, 127, 130, 133–34, 137–38, 152–53, 160, 168, 180, 185, 187, 189–90, 204, 211, 213–14, 218, 225; *see also* Departing
Benjamin, W., 141, 235
Berkeley, G., 222
Bernstein, R., 217, 239
Betweens, 23, 47, 55, 62, 190, 216
Bible, 190

Binary, 73–74, 76, 80, 217
Biology, 97, 106, 144, 147, 153, 236
Bodies, 6, 17, 30, 41, 80, 86, 91–92,
    96–97, 102–107, 138, 142–60,
    177, 182, 196, 208
Bonaparte, N., 66, 227
Borges, J., 61
Buchler, J., 220, 232

Cacophony, 6, 8, 11, 22, 27, 34, 37, 69,
    134, 185–86, 204–206, 209–11,
    213–14
Calculation, 58–59, 77
Canon, 27–28, 43, 91, 112–13,
    119–21, 123
Canonicity, 27, 32, 34, 43, 59, 84,
    104, 120–21, 123
Capitalism, 25, 182–83, 229
Care, 56, 98–99, 122, 160, 167–68, 201
Catastrophe, 131–32, 134–35, 138,
    171, 211, 234
Categories, 14, 21, 61, 81, 84, 96,
    199, 203, 212, 228
Causation, 81–83, 103–106, 151, 189,
    210–11
Celebration, 170, 171, 173
Censorship, 73, 160, 237
Certitude, 117, 128
Cézanne, P., 210
Change, 81–82, 116, 206, 209, 211
Charity, 40, 46, 132, 167–71, 173,
    175–77, 179, 181, 186, 201,
    216, 220; see also Care, Ethics,
    Sacrifice, Valor
Children, 86, 95, 97, 99, 101, 144,
    146, 158, 185, 195
Christ, 44
Christianity, 92, 99, 181
Circularity, 50, 61–62, 69, 74, 90,
    106–107, 120, 130, 155, 188–89,
    193, 201, 203, 211, 225
Cixous, H., 146, 236
Classical, 58–65, 68, 108, 172, 174,
    186, 198, 222, 225–26
Codes, 60, 62, 199, 224

Coercion, 87, 168, 179, 199, 213; see
    also Law, Violence
Cogito, 225, 241; see also Descartes
Cognition, 19, 140; see also Knowledge
Collectivity, 29, 51, 77, 88, 143, 193
Colonization, 66, 228, 236
Colossal, 21, 139
Combat, 74, 136, 156; see also
    Violence, War
Comedy, 98–99, 137, 168, 171, 173,
    202
Commentary, 221–22
Commitment, 152, 156, 172, 222
Commodities, 57
Commonality, 24–25, 51–53, 57–58,
    72, 88, 112, 148, 151, 170, 174,
    237–38; see also Agreement,
    Consensus
Commonwealth, 50–51, 54
Communication, 24–25, 55, 151, 197,
    220
Communism, 183
Community, 24, 107, 134, 155, 164,
    169–70, 179, 200–201
Completeness, 98, 101, 112–13, 116,
    130, 144; see also Totality
Conatus, 81, 83, 103, 105, 147,
    149–50, 152; see also Spinoza
Concealment, 73, 96, 100, 115,
    121–22, 124, 233; see also
    Truth, Untruth
Concept, 19–21, 55, 57, 85, 222,
    227–28
Conditions, 17, 24, 29, 39, 41, 45, 53,
    64, 76, 78, 82, 87, 114, 162–63,
    165, 180, 200, 226, 228
Conflict, 9, 16, 19, 25, 28, 41–42, 56,
    88, 93, 122, 133, 186, 188, 190,
    210, 219, 222
Conscience, 140, 167
Consciousness, 60, 89, 106, 120, 134,
    149, 159, 187, 192–93, 224,
    233
Consensus, 24–25, 169–70, 180
Consequences, 11, 38–39, 46, 54, 95,
    103, 146, 149, 151, 181, 205

Contemporary, 58, 69, 183, 224, 228

Context, 154–55, 216

Contingency, 30, 35–37, 104, 135, 137, 148, 150–51, 153, 161–62, 165–66, 185, 189–90, 201–202, 212, 242; *see also* Necessity

Continuity, 66, 129, 186, 199, 226

Contract, 222

Contradiction, 70, 113, 117–18, 119, 139, 182, 194

Contrasts, 20, 24, 133, 174, 221

Countermemory, 216, 229, 241

Creation, 54, 59, 137, 168, 182, 207, 211

Creativity, 22

Creatures, 53, 61, 102, 122, 144, 161, 167–168, 170, 176–77, 180, 193, 196, 198, 201, 242

Critique, 1–6, 15, 19–20, 22, 24–25, 44–45, 66, 168, 216, 218–19, 227–28

Culture, 4, 10, 15, 25–26, 29, 41, 61–62, 67, 76, 91, 127, 141, 153, 156, 158, 179, 188, 198–99, 216, 224, 227

Dance, 17, 41, 43, 45, 53, 92, 142, 161

Danger, 2–5, 8, 12, 15, 43, 67, 108, 115, 141, 156, 171, 213; *see also* Violence

Darstellen, 21, 65, 67, 218, 227

Dasein, 115, 121, 167, 234; *see also* Being

Death, 95, 118, 141, 167, 201, 202, 237, 240

Deferral, 5–6, 9, 11–12, 14–18, 20, 22–23, 25, 27, 30, 32–34, 37–41, 43–44, 46–47, 49–50, 54–56, 59, 67, 71–76, 78–80, 82, 84, 91, 99, 101–102, 106–107, 112–14, 116–17, 123, 127, 130–33, 137, 145–46, 150, 152, 161, 165, 171, 173–77, 179–82, 187, 189–90, 201, 209, 212, 216–17

Defilement, 9, 50, 204

Definition, 3, 8, 55, 57, 74, 77, 103, 114, 138, 190, 193, 195, 197

Deleuze, G., 65, 227–29

Demiurge, 198

Democracy, 56, 178, 183, 222

Demonstration, 103

Departing, 13–14, 18, 25–27, 36, 42, 49–50, 52, 64, 66, 74, 77–80, 89, 91–92, 106, 108, 111–13, 115, 120–22, 129–30, 134, 137–38, 148, 155, 160, 167–68, 173, 186, 205, 212–13, 218; *see also* Belonging

Derrida, J, 2–3, 21, 39, 130, 138, 154–55, 190, 195–96, 199–200, 212, 215–16, 219–20, 229, 231, 235–37, 239–41

Descartes, R., 57, 147, 153

Desire, 2, 6–9, 12, 15–18, 23, 25–26, 28–30, 32–33, 36, 39–41, 49, 51, 56, 58–59, 66–67, 69–73, 75–79, 81, 83–85, 88–109, 111, 118, 123–25, 127, 129–30, 133, 142, 146–47, 149–53, 155–60, 166, 168–69, 172–81, 185, 187, 194, 197, 201–204, 212–14, 217, 226–28, 231, 237

Despair, 80, 171, 180, 202

Destiny, 81, 114, 124, 167

Determinateness, 8, 14, 20, 26, 29–30, 34, 38–39, 54, 58, 71, 74, 81–83, 85, 97–98, 103–104, 107, 135, 149, 153, 169, 189, 193–94, 201, 208, 210, 242

Determinism, 83, 192

Dewey, J., 6, 10, 135, 137, 162, 186–87, 188–90, 217, 220, 235, 238–39

Dialectic, 8, 27, 36, 85, 106, 168

Dialogue, 84, 95, 99–100, 102, 166

Difference, 5, 7, 9, 14, 16, 22–23, 25, 29–32, 40, 53, 55, 58, 60–61, 67, 69, 75–77, 79–81, 83, 88, 90, 94, 97, 112–14, 116, 118, 121, 130–32, 134–35, 137, 139,

149, 152, 155–56, 158, 161,
169–70, 180–81, 193–96, 200,
204, 209, 211–12, 214, 216,
223, 233, 240–41
Différance, 101, 156, 216; *see also*
Deferral, Derrida
Différend, 164–66, 172; *see also*
Lyotard
Diotima, 98; *see also* Symposium
Discipline, 16–17, 27–28, 31, 35,
43–44, 72, 114, 123, 157,
159, 161, 163, 215, 219–20,
236–37
Discontinuity, 87, 135, 160, 164
Discourse, 2–4, 14, 22–23, 28, 39, 59,
60–61, 63, 65, 86–87, 89,
101–102, 108, 123, 135, 137,
160, 174–75, 178, 198–200, 215,
217–20, 223, 230, 234–35,
237–38; *see also* Language,
Representation
Disembodiment, 150–52, 156, 159–60;
see also Bodies, Embodiment
Disharmony, 13–16, 23, 26, 28, 33–36,
38, 41, 43, 45–46, 66–67, 76,
78–81, 85, 91–92, 94, 102, 106,
111, 113–14, 117, 119–20,
122–24, 128–30, 132–33,
137–38, 146, 149, 152, 158,
161, 168, 180–81, 183, 185,
189, 201, 203, 208, 211
Dislocation, 10–11, 14–16, 18, 26–27,
26, 31, 33, 35, 37–40, 45–46,
49–50, 56, 62, 68–69, 78–79,
84–85, 90–92, 102, 114, 118,
124, 127, 132, 134, 137, 146,
150, 156, 166, 170, 174, 181,
183, 196, 206, 208, 211
Disorder, 12–13, 23, 26, 61–62, 71,
74, 78–79, 97, 180, 199
Dispersion, 23, 27, 29–30, 52–53,
60–62, 66, 69–70, 77, 79–80,
86–87, 90, 135, 137, 159, 187,
200, 241
Displacement, 12–13, 26–27, 55, 58,
63, 65, 67, 69, 71, 84, 88, 92,

112, 115, 137, 150, 158, 162,
164, 166, 174, 176, 178–79,
181–82, 190, 200–201, 209,
212–13, 217, 225
Disruption, 9, 26, 29, 37, 41, 43–46,
67–68, 71, 75–76, 81, 84, 91,
101–102, 108, 133, 138, 178,
190, 212, 222
Diversity, 58, 113, 116–17
Divinity, 92, 98, 152, 189, 242; *see
also* God, Religion
Dogmatism, 45, 64, 154, 195–96, 200,
204, 223
Domination, 73–75, 80, 82, 86, 90,
136, 157, 159, 165, 234
Don Quixote, 172
Doubt, 104, 111, 141, 194, 199, 200,
223, 228; *see also* Knowledge,
Truth
Duty, 164, 166, 169, 173; *see also*
Ethics, Obligation

Eksistence, 114–15, 192, 194–95; *see
also* Heidegger
Embodiment, 2, 15, 17, 29–30, 33, 41,
54, 57, 67, 70–71, 78, 92,
94–95, 98–100, 106, 111, 123,
127, 130, 142–60, 172–73, 177,
180, 201–203, 216, 237; *see also*
Bodies, Materiality
Emergence, 32, 43–44, 46, 73, 159,
198–99, 206–207, 242
Emotion, 45–46, 93, 105, 148–49, 229
Empirical, 2, 29–30, 35, 37, 60–61,
64, 82, 161–63, 165–66, 189,
197–98, 224–26; *see also*
Experience
Empiricism, 222–23
Empirico-transcendental, 62, 64, 163,
197
Enlightenment, 57, 144, 159, 176, 182
Entelechy 144, 152, 167, 210
Entity, 82–83, 87–88, 151–52, 211
Epistemic, 5, 28, 35–36, 37, 67, 228;
see also Knowledge
Epistēmē, 64, 178

Ergon, 6, 14, 23, 41, 46, 49, 129, 137, 204, 213–14; *see also* Work

Ergonality, 10, 12–17, 23, 27, 34, 40, 133, 205, 216

Erhabene, 218; *see also* Sublime

Eros, 84, 92, 158; *see also* Care, Charity, Desire, Love

Errancy, 115, 121–122, 233–34

Error, 89, 96, 104, 108, 115, 117, 123; *see also* Truth

Essence, 3, 28–30, 55, 65, 83, 103–106, 114–15, 120–22, 137–38, 144–49, 153–57, 160, 170, 178–79, 185–86, 190–96, 199–200, 208, 232–34, 241–42; *see also* Being

Eternal, 3, 45–46, 105–106, 113, 140, 148–50, 207–108

Ethics, 24, 33, 40, 46, 103–106, 147–50, 164, 167–69, 178, 181, 193, 210, 229, 231–32, 239–40, 242

Eudaimonia, 147

Europe, 65–66, 156, 227–28

Event, 86, 140, 160, 164, 226–27

Everything, 3–4, 9–15, 17, 20–22, 26, 30, 32–33, 52, 54, 70–79, 82, 84–85, 87–89, 91, 104, 112–13, 122, 124, 137, 139, 156–57, 160, 165, 169, 175, 186–88, 190, 197, 201, 203, 208, 217, 234, 236; *see also* Totality

Everywhere, *See* Everything

Evil, 52, 83–84, 101–102, 113, 177

Excess, 1, 4–6, 8, 11–16, 19–26, 26–29, 30–32, 35–36, 38–41, 45, 47, 49–50, 55–59, 61–65, 70, 73–76, 78–80, 82–85, 87, 89, 90–99, 102–109, 111, 114, 121–22, 124, 137–39, 141, 143–44, 146–48, 150–57, 160–61, 163, 165–67, 171–77, 179, 181–82, 186–87, 189–93, 196, 207–214

Exchange, 57–60, 102, 222

Exclusion, 2, 16–17, 25, 28, 33–34, 36, 41–42, 44, 70, 73, 75, 85, 97, 113, 138, 141, 173–74, 193, 195, 234

Existence, 4, 30, 60, 86, 100, 104–105, 117, 131, 135, 137, 139, 152, 167, 189, 191–93, 200, 226, 229, 240, 242; *see also* Being

Existentialism, 190–93, 239–40

Experience, 24, 26–27, 29–31, 34–36, 44, 58, 61–62, 65, 72–73, 76, 84, 118, 121, 124, 132, 159, 161–63, 165–66, 172–73, 178, 187–89, 194, 199, 207, 217, 220, 222–23, 227, 232, 235, 239

Explanation, 56, 98, 119, 152, 164

Expression, 3, 10, 26, 41, 84, 85, 92, 128, 133, 149, 182, 202, 206; *see also* Language, Representation

Extension, 104, 105, 147, 149, 150, 189, 210; *see also* Space

Exteriority, 9, 25, 27, 29, 35, 61, 76–77, 85, 120, 135, 158, 163, 210, 217, 226

Externality, 37, 104, 120, 147–49, 192–93, 211

Fabricative judgment, 28, 32–33, 38–39, 41–44, 52–53, 161, 182, 198; *see also* Art, Artifice, Judgment

Failure, 37–40, 42–43, 46, 49, 56, 161, 172, 186, 240; *see also* Judgment, Practical Judgment, *Praxis*

Faith, 33, 117, 128, 238; *see also* God, Religion

Falsity, 28, 34, 63, 89, 101–102, 108, 112–114, 116, 118–20, 123–24, 128; *see also* Truth, Untruth

Familiarity, 1–4, 15, 224

Family, 19, 155, 200–201, 240

Female, 66, 95–97, 121, 157–58, 185, 195, 228, 237, 240; *see also* Feminism, Gender, Woman

Feminism, 215, 230, 236; *see also* Female, Gender

Fetishization, 43, 90, 97, 171, 221
Fiction, 24, 50–52, 54
Finiteness, 6, 21, 29–30, 37, 103–106,
    117, 121–22, 128, 133, 148,
    150–52, 160, 163, 167, 177,
    179, 189–90, 197–98, 201–202,
    210–11, 242
Force, 70, 72, 75, 87–89, 92–93, 104,
    108, 124, 136, 142, 145, 152,
    157, 165, 178, 183
Forgetting, 8, 29, 108, 139–40, 159,
    164, 190, 204, 212, 217, 221,
    234–35
Forgotten, 7, 11, 23, 34, 60, 137, 168,
    189, 193, 200, 224
Foucault, M., 3, 8–9, 11, 16–17, 22,
    28, 39, 57–66, 69–70, 72, 75,
    81, 85–90, 108, 114–15, 130,
    135–36, 146, 158, 160, 162–64,
    172, 174–76, 182, 196–200,
    215–21, 223–25, 227–32,
    234–38, 240–42
Foundation, 30, 153, 163, 167–68,
    197, 226, 241
Freedom, 6, 19, 22, 24, 50, 59, 76,
    94, 101, 106–108, 114–15,
    119–24, 134, 140, 158, 168,
    175, 192–93, 217, 219, 233,
    235, 239; see also Liberation
French, 108, 154, 155, 216, 228, 236
Freud, S., 58, 96–97, 108, 230–31,
    238
Functionality, 216, 218; see also
    Ergonality, Instrumentality
Future, 9, 11, 15, 26, 29, 34, 37–40,
    42–44, 47, 54, 76, 81, 83–84,
    95, 127–29, 132–34, 136,
    139–41, 157, 161–63, 165, 169,
    171–73, 177, 180, 182, 191,
    193, 199–201, 211, 216, 219;
    see also History, Temporality,
    Time

Gadamer, H-G., 2, 11, 84–85, 133–34,
    215, 217, 229, 235
Galileo, G., 57

Gender, 7, 67, 73, 146–47, 153,
    155–56, 200–201
Genealogy, 60, 89, 136, 155, 199–201,
    229–30, 235, 237; see also
    Archaeology, Foucault, Nietzsche
Generality, 28–29, 44–46, 72–73, 82,
    144, 162, 179, 212–13, 218,
    240; see also Totality,
    Universality
Generation, 155, 200–201, 210, 231, 237
Genitals, 237, 240; see also Gender,
    Sexuality
Genius, 24–25, 185–86, 219
German, 65, 155–56, 183, 196, 200,
    230, 237
Geschlecht, 154–57, 166, 190, 192–93,
    195–202, 212, 214, 230, 236–37,
    239–41
Gift, 87, 141, 195–96
God, 44, 83, 91–92, 99, 103–107, 113,
    144, 147–50, 152, 181, 186,
    189–90, 192–95, 197, 207–208,
    210, 212, 238, 242; see also
    Divine, Religion
Goddesses, 97
Gods, 95–96, 155, 157
Goethe, J., 140
Good, 52, 56, 58–59, 82, 84, 92–95,
    98–101, 107, 130, 164–66,
    173–74, 179–80, 183, 197
Governance, 50, 80, 107, 174, 177–78
Government, 50, 55, 227
Great, 19, 20, 21, 22, 52, 59, 65, 87,
    92, 94, 105, 139, 148, 200, 228
Greek, 65, 99, 147, 161, 167, 173,
    177, 182, 206, 215, 233
Ground, 6, 19–20, 25–26, 29–30, 35,
    36–37, 42, 58, 77, 96–97, 116,
    130, 145–47, 151, 157, 163,
    168–69, 173–74, 178, 186–87,
    190–91, 194, 208, 220
Guilt, 71, 82, 144–45
Gulliver's Travels, 50

Habermas, J., 24–27, 169, 217, 219–20,
    238

Hand, 52, 89, 97, 101–102, 104, 106,
    112, 120, 138–40, 147–48, 150,
    153–54, 172, 175, 192, 182,
    195–96, 198–200, 209, 216, 222,
    227, 236
Handicraft, 153–54, 196
Harmony, 1, 7, 13–14, 16, 23, 26, 33,
    38, 43, 45–46, 52, 71, 78, 81,
    85, 106, 111, 117, 128–30, 133,
    137–38, 161, 166, 180, 186, 201
Harmony-disharmony, 15–16, 27, 185,
    205
Hartshorne, C., 218
Hegel, G., 17, 24, 27, 36, 84–85,
    106–107, 112–13, 116–21, 124,
    128, 130–31, 162, 178, 190,
    218, 231–35
Hegemony, 4, 9, 27–28, 33, 39, 71,
    76, 78–79, 90, 123–24
Heidegger, M., 4–6, 22, 25, 29, 41,
    81, 84, 93, 114–15, 120–22,
    130, 134, 153–54, 167, 176,
    178, 182, 186, 189–96, 199–200,
    204–208, 210, 216–17, 219–21,
    232–34, 236, 238–40, 242
Heraclitus, 1, 112–13, 215
Hermeneutics, 217
Heterogeneity, 4, 15, 34, 37–38,
    46–47, 66–67, 80, 124
Highest, 5, 99, 107, 141
Historicism, 11, 217
History, 2, 5–11, 15–18, 22–23, 25,
    28–34, 36–41, 43, 45, 53, 60,
    64, 67, 69–72, 75–76, 78,
    80–81, 83–86, 90–92, 106, 108,
    117, 119, 123, 127–42, 146,
    151, 153, 156–57, 159–63,
    165–66, 170–71, 174–75,
    179–81, 185–89, 195, 198–204,
    208–209, 211–13, 217–18, 220,
    224, 226–30, 233, 235–39, 241
Hobbes, T., 50–54, 68, 221
Holiness, 45, 179
Homo faber, 182
Hope, 1, 6, 16, 26, 90, 111, 118–19,
    134, 141, 213, 215, 240

Human, 2, 9, 15–17, 23, 29–32,
    35–36, 40–41, 43–44, 46, 50–53,
    56, 61–64, 69–70, 74, 76–77,
    80, 84, 87–88, 93, 95–97, 101,
    103–106, 108, 122–24, 132, 134,
    136–37, 143–50, 152–63,
    177–78, 182, 185–202, 214, 216,
    219–21, 224, 228–30, 233,
    236–41
Humanism, 29, 154, 190–95, 197, 220,
    239–40
Hume, D., 93, 162
Hyperreality, 124, 217, 234; see also
    Baudrillard

Ideal, 57, 99, 121, 123, 128, 157, 172,
    177, 181, 199, 238
Identity, 1, 3–5, 7, 14–15, 23, 28, 31,
    49, 56–57, 62, 64, 81, 90, 93,
    101–102, 105, 116–17, 128, 130,
    137, 152–53, 155–56, 186,
    216–18, 223–24, 233
Ideology, 9, 24, 89, 108, 123–24, 227
Illicit, 73–74, 95–96; see also Law,
    Licit
Imagination, 21, 41–42, 51–52, 97,
    147, 172, 178, 219
Immanence, 9, 42, 70, 76, 105
Immateriality, 143–44, 146, 151, 153,
    155, 160, 177; see also Bodies,
    Materiality
Imperfection, 162, 172
Impossibility, 61, 97, 134, 171, 225
Incommensurate, 19, 188
Incompleteness, 113, 115, 130; see also
    Totality
Indeterminate, 20, 26, 34, 37, 39, 81,
    96, 107, 142
Individuality, 57, 81, 87–88, 135, 137,
    152, 159, 164, 190, 210–11,
    222, 235
Inescapability, 43, 83, 89–90, 129,
    134, 140, 146–47, 161–62
Inexhaustibility, 2, 5, 12–19, 23, 25,
    27, 31–32, 34, 36, 39–40, 49,
    59, 70, 72–73, 91, 93–94, 97,

107–108, 114, 128–30, 133,
135–37, 142, 166–71, 173,
175–79, 181, 185–86, 188–89,
193, 195, 200–201, 203,
205–206, 208, 210–11, 213, 216,
221, 223, 236; *see also* Locality
Infinite, 5, 10–11, 14, 19–23, 25,
40, 58, 67, 91–92, 103–105,
107, 113, 117, 123, 128,
131–33, 147–48, 150, 156,
167, 189, 195–96, 201, 210,
216
Ingredient, 12–14, 16, 31, 35, 39,
72–73, 82, 162, 205, 213, 218
Inhumanity, 195, 197; *see also* Human,
Justice
Injustice, 131–32, 140, 144, 180–81,
233; *see also* Ethics, Justice,
Politics
Inquiry, 34, 233; *see also* Knowledge,
Science
Institutions, 57, 70, 71, 158, 237
Instrumentality, 14, 41, 148, 177–79,
182; *see also* *Technē*
Insurrection, 89, 97, 136, 141; *see also*
Freedom, Genealogy
Intelligibility, 25, 32, 34–36, 61, 73,
123, 135, 180
Intensification, 159, 221; 229; *see also*
Art, Contrasts
Intentionality, 77, 241
Intermodality, 29, 42, 38, 46–47; *see*
also Judgment, Mode of
Judgment, Mulltimodality
Interpretant, 16, 34
Interpretation, 25, 29, 57, 63, 188,
190, 227, 238, 241
Intransitivity, 14–15, 69
Invisibility, 143, 225
Irrelevance, 15, 17, 67, 72, 171
Iterability, 220

Jouissance, 197
Judgment, 2, 18–20, 22–47, 49–50, 52,
55–56, 61, 70, 78, 80, 89, 129,
134, 145, 147, 161–73, 175–82,

185–86, 189, 203–206, 208–14,
216, 218–20, 228, 241; *see also*
Knowledge, Representation,
Semasis, Truth
Juridical, 73, 160, 174–75; *see also*
Law
Justice, 1, 55, 81, 101, 113, 131, 141,
178–81; *see also* Ethics, Politics

Kafka, F., 102, 144–45, 157, 159, 178,
228, 236
Kant, I., 4–5, 19–20, 22–28, 31, 53,
84, 153, 164–65, 205, 207–209,
216, 218–19, 227
Knowledge, 2, 8, 11, 18, 22, 24–28,
30–32, 60–64, 67, 76, 84–85,
101, 104–105, 108, 111, 113,
118–19, 123, 128, 131, 134–36,
139–41, 147–48, 150, 157–59,
163, 169, 171–74, 189–90,
197–99, 215, 219, 223–24,
226–27, 230–33, 235, 237–38,
241–42; *see also* Judgment,
Representation, Truth
Krell, D., 216, 237

Labor, 64, 162, 181–82, 227
Lacan, J., 231
Lack, 58, 93, 98, 102, 113, 156, 185,
193
Language, 12, 26, 30, 49–50, 58,
60–65, 74, 108, 113, 144–45,
147, 155–56, 161–63, 165–66,
172, 185, 196, 198, 201, 213,
215–20, 223–24, 226, 229, 237,
241; *see also* Discourse,
Representation
Las Meninas, 62, 172, 199; *see also*
Foucault
Latin, 51, 237
Laughter, 124–25; *see also* Comedy
Law, 3, 7, 16, 19, 35–37, 40, 70–77,
80–81, 83, 90, 103, 106–108,
119, 132, 136, 138, 140,
144–47, 151, 155–66, 168–69,

Law (*cont.*)
    172–81, 193, 208–209, 211, 228,
    236–37, 241; *see also* Justice,
    Technē
Legitimacy, 5, 27–28, 33, 67, 101,
    132, 169
Leibniz, G., 22, 57, 152–53, 210–11,
    236, 242
Letting-be, 115, 121
Leviathan, 50, 221; *see also* Hobbes
Levinas, E., 164, 238
Liberation, 24, 57, 78–80, 87, 174,
    178–80; *see also* Freedom
Licit, 73–74, 95–96; *see also* Illicit
Life, 4, 29, 31, 36, 42, 44, 51–53, 59,
    61, 64–65, 70, 83, 87–88, 90,
    92–93, 98–102, 106–109, 112,
    124–25, 127, 132, 134, 139,
    141, 145, 152, 158, 161–62,
    168, 170–73, 175, 177, 182,
    187, 193, 198, 201, 214, 235,
    241
Limit, 2–15, 20, 22–23, 26–28, 30–34,
    36–37, 39–40, 42–47, 50, 52,
    54–57, 61–65, 68, 72, 75,
    79–80, 83, 90–91, 94, 100,
    104–107, 111, 114, 119, 121,
    123–24, 128–29, 131, 133–35,
    138–46, 152, 159–60, 165,
    167–69, 171, 174–76, 179–80,
    188, 190–91, 195–97, 199–202,
    207, 211–214, 216, 220, 225–27,
    234, 236, 242; *see also* Locality
Literature, 171–72
Living, 40, 58, 61, 82, 95, 98–99,
    101–103, 118, 121, 128, 130–31,
    139–41, 145, 152, 172, 176–77,
    193, 198, 201, 241–42; *see also*
    Life
Local, 6, 9, 11–18, 22–23, 25, 28–31,
    36–37, 40, 43, 45–46, 68–69,
    71–74, 76, 80–81, 86, 89, 115,
    122, 133, 136–37, 142, 166,
    168, 170, 172, 180–81, 183,
    186, 188–89, 191–92, 202–204,
    210–11, 213, 217

Locale, 9, 12–14, 16, 26, 30–32, 49,
    68, 72, 76, 81, 133, 137, 167,
    195, 208, 218
Locale-ingredient, 13, 15–16, 27
Locality, 6, 10–18, 23, 26–27, 29,
    31–34, 36–37, 39–41, 44–45, 49,
    56, 65, 69–73, 75, 78–79, 81,
    84, 87, 97, 111, 114–15, 123,
    125, 127–33, 136–37, 139–40,
    155, 157, 161, 166–68, 170–71,
    173, 175–77, 179–81, 185–86,
    188–89, 192, 195, 200–206,
    208–209, 211–13, 216–17, 220,
    241
Location, 12–14, 19, 77, 87, 97, 108,
    168, 206, 208, 218
Locke, J., 81–82, 229
Locus, 12–14, 32, 40, 49, 72–73,
    77–78, 89, 114, 137, 159,
    166–67, 201, 218
Logic, 11, 29, 36, 73, 103, 108, 117,
    128, 186, 220, 230–35, 237
Logocentrism, 147
Logos, 1, 9, 101, 144, 147, 177–78,
    211, 231
Loneliness, 116, 122, 128–42, 185; *see
    also* Lownlyness, Onlyness,
    Ownliness
Lorde, A., 5, 67, 132
Loss, 11, 99, 133–34, 139, 142,
    169–74, 182, 202
Love, 84, 92, 94–95, 97–99, 101, 107,
    156, 187; *see also* Charity, *Eros*
Lownlyness, 129–32, 135–37, 139–40,
    142; *see also* History,
    Loneliness, Lownlyness,
    Ownliness
Lyotard, J-F., 164–65, 173, 218–19,
    238

Machiavelli, N., 52–53, 221
Machine, 138, 143–44, 155–57, 159,
    185, 193–96, 201
Madness, 26–27, 33–34, 66, 72, 199,
    220, 241
Magic, 84, 100–101

Magnitude, 20–22
Making, 27, 53, 81, 90, 96, 101, 108,
    140, 181–82, 191, 205, 242; see
    also Fabricative Judgment
Male, 6, 10, 65, 68, 95–97, 121, 129,
    157, 195, 228, 237, 240; see
    also Gender
Marx, K., 24, 66, 227
Masculine, 66, 92, 96–97; see also
    Gender, Male
Masks, 22, 29, 35, 51, 60, 69, 73, 77,
    89, 101, 118, 123–24, 138,
    200, 217; see also Foucault,
    Nietzsche
Mastery, 4, 15, 37, 39, 67, 69, 73–74,
    87, 90, 107–108, 114, 121,
    138–39, 141, 157, 227
Materialism, 160, 237
Materiality, 3, 7, 14, 16–17, 31,
    38–39, 42–44, 46, 57, 71–72,
    74, 82, 85, 87, 90, 102, 106,
    111, 123, 143–45, 146–47,
    150–57, 159–61, 163, 167–68,
    172, 203, 212–14, 237; see also
    Body, Embodiment, Matter
Mathematics, 20–22, 35, 41, 57,
    207–208, 216, 239, 242
Matter, 1, 24, 39, 81, 117–18, 143,
    146, 152, 160; see also
    Embodiment, Materiality
Meaning, 37–38, 54–55, 66, 86, 88,
    99, 103–104, 113, 136, 140,
    160, 178, 188, 192, 201, 207,
    222–23, 226, 237, 240–41
Measure, 1, 4–6, 11, 14, 21–22, 24,
    27, 36, 40, 57–58, 64, 83,
    87–88, 100, 108, 112–13,
    137, 163, 170, 177–79, 182,
    205, 211, 226, 233; see also
    Technē
Mechansim, 57, 86, 89, 137, 159
Mediation, 16, 22–23, 27, 55, 105,
    150, 179, 193
Memory, 10, 34, 100, 129, 139–42,
    171, 199, 202, 215; see also
    History, Time

Merleau-Ponty, M., 145, 152–54, 224,
    236
Merleau-Ponty-at, 152
Message, 74
Messiah, 124, 141
Metaphysics, 1–6, 9–10, 12, 15, 17,
    22, 25–26, 29, 44–46, 57, 65,
    69–70, 130, 152, 157, 161, 167,
    186, 189–91, 193–95, 201,
    204–205, 208, 211–14, 216, 218,
    229, 232, 236, 238–39; see also
    Being, Philosophy
Method, 34–35, 75, 119, 123, 134,
    165, 188, 215, 217, 229, 235
Metric, 57–59, 211, 223; see also
    Measure
Midworldliness, 15, 18, 22–23,
    26–27, 29, 31–32, 41–44, 46–47,
    55–56
Mimesis, 4, 49, 92, 98, 101
Minorities, 121, 125
Mirrors, 57, 64, 79, 91–92, 101,
    105–106, 152, 158, 210, 225,
    242
Misrepresentation, 18, 42–43, 45,
    49–52, 54, 60–62, 67–68, 91,
    115, 124, 146, 150, 175,
    185–86, 190; see also Falsity,
    Representation, Truth
Mode of judgment, 26–39, 36, 38,
    42–47, 49, 85, 104, 147, 153,
    161, 163–64, 171, 175, 177–78,
    180, 189, 197, 206–207, 213,
    225–26; see also Intermodality,
    Judgment, Query, Semasis
Modern, 8, 10, 17, 25–26, 35–37,
    41–42, 44, 57, 60–61, 63–64,
    106, 129, 162–63, 171, 173,
    183, 186, 197–98, 206, 208,
    226, 228, 236, 239, 242; see
    also Modernism, Modernity,
    Postmodern
Modernism, 172
Modernity, 6, 8–11, 16, 22, 26, 31,
    35–37, 41, 43–45, 61–64, 71–72,
    75, 90–91, 109, 118, 172–74,

Modernity (*cont.*)
    176–77, 182, 197, 216–17,
    219–20, 227, 238; *see also*
    Modern, Postmodern
Monadology, 236, 242
Monads, 22, 152, 210, 242
Money, 57–59, 64, 182
Monstrosity, 21, 54, 59, 61, 123, 129,
    132, 140, 154–56, 169, 171–73,
    175, 178, 180, 196–97, 199
Morality, 40, 60, 95, 158, 164, 166,
    181; *see also* Charity, Ethics,
    Valor
Mortality, 160, 201, 237; *see also*
    Death
Multimodality, 29, 35, 37–38, 42,
    46–47; *see also* Intermodality,
    Judgment, Mode of judgment
Multiplicity, 5–16, 18, 22–23, 26–34,
    36–37, 39–40, 42–46, 58–59,
    61–62, 65–72, 75–77, 81, 84,
    89, 95, 101, 109, 124, 128–30,
    137–38, 150, 155–56, 161, 166,
    169, 176, 178–81, 185, 188–91,
    203–204, 206, 208–209, 211–13,
    216, 227, 230
Music, 1–2, 5, 9, 14, 16, 22, 43, 45,
    52–53, 111, 161, 203–204, 210,
    213
Mystery, 115, 121–22, 135, 233–34
Myth, 100, 180, 188
Mythology, 32, 179

Nameable, 223
Naming, 68, 115, 223, 227; *see also*
    Language, Representation
Narrative, 36, 64–67, 91, 102; *see also*
    Writing
Natura naturans, 104, 189, 210; *see*
    also Nature, Spinoza
Natura naturata, 104, 189, 210; *see*
    also Nature, Spinoza
Naturalism, 167, 186, 189
Nature, 1–12, 14–23, 25–27, 30–32,
    35–39, 41, 46, 49–55, 57–58,
    61, 63–64, 69, 77, 80, 83, 85,
    87–88, 95–97, 100, 103–104,
    106, 111–12, 114–19, 123, 125,
    128–31, 133–34, 136–37, 139,
    145, 147–49, 152–53, 156, 159,
    161–63, 166–67, 170, 173, 177,
    179, 181–82, 185–92, 196–98,
    200–14, 216–17, 220, 223, 226,
    230, 232, 235, 239, 241–42; *see*
    also Physis, World
Nearness, 152, 194–95, 220
Necessity, 1, 14, 19, 27, 30, 33, 35,
    50, 61–62, 76–77, 80, 103–104,
    106–108, 114, 117, 119–20,
    122–24, 140–41, 148–50,
    161–66, 169, 174 180, 185, 189,
    200–201, 204, 211–12, 220, 232,
    240, 242
Need, 41–42, 55, 59, 77, 84, 95, 101,
    119, 141, 145, 147, 198, 208,
    217, 239
Negativity, 54, 59, 71, 73–75, 107,
    116, 120, 140, 142, 164–65,
    168, 193, 196, 237
Nietzsche, F., 5–6, 39, 44, 69, 81–82,
    84–85, 89, 92–93, 139–42, 172,
    176, 182, 196, 229–30, 235, 237
Nihilism, 180
Nonbeing, 9, 31; *see also* Being,
    Nothingness
NonWestern, 8, 32, 37, 217
Norm, 14, 24–25, 35–36, 39–40, 46,
    120, 158–59, 169–69, 180, 211,
    224
Normality, 24–26, 39, 56, 75, 96, 157
Normativity, 24–25, 57, 180, 211
Nostalgia, 74, 121, 133–34, 193–94,
    199–200
Nothingness, 107, 169, 240; *see also*
    Negation, Nonbeing

Objectivity, 53, 107, 117, 128, 234
Obligation, 74, 164–66, 173
Oblivion, 95, 123, 134, 139, 142, 190,
    193–94, 196, 204, 212; *see also*
    Death, Forgetting, Nonbeing
Obscurity, 69, 140, 204, 208

Obsession, 91–93, 96, 98–99, 101, 107–108, 169
Obstruction, 83, 132, 177, 190
Onlyness, 6, 74, 115, 117–18, 121, 124, 128–40, 142, 165, 185, 202; *see also* Hegel, History, Loneliness, Lownlyness, Ownliness
Ontology, 16, 69, 79, 81, 134, 204, 223, 240; *see also* Metaphysics
Ontotheology, 130, 186, 190
Openness, 124, 134, 196, 234
Opposition, 52, 74, 80–81, 86, 93, 97, 116–18, 120, 123, 128, 195, 197; *see also* Negativity
Oppression, 4, 7, 24–25, 51, 66, 68, 71, 75–80, 90, 125, 139, 145–46, 157–59, 165–66, 178–79, 201–202, 228; *see also* Domination, Injustice, Liberation
Order, 3, 12–13, 19, 21, 23, 25, 30, 32, 34, 40, 56–66, 71, 74, 78–79, 82–83, 89, 97, 103, 106, 111, 123, 146, 148–50, 179–80, 193, 197, 199, 220, 223–26, 231, 234–36, 238, 241
Orifices, 92, 96; *see also* Bodies, Embodiment
Origin, 23, 27, 60–62, 64–65, 79, 91–92, 130, 136–37, 150, 153, 190, 199–200, 205, 217, 219, 221, 230, 232, 234, 239, 241
Others, 4, 6–9, 13–15, 17–18, 24–27, 29, 31–35, 37–44, 46–47, 49–53, 55–56, 58–60, 64, 66–70, 72, 75–82, 85, 87–91, 96, 98, 102, 108, 111–12, 114, 123–25, 127–29, 131–34, 137–38, 142, 153, 157, 161, 163–66, 168, 170, 173, 175–76, 178–80, 185, 190, 193, 195, 201, 210–11, 213, 216–18, 226
Ousia, 189, 210
Ownliness, 116, 128–29, 132–34, 135, 137–42, 185; *see also* History, Loneliness, Lownlyness, Onlyness

Pain, 92, 144, 145, 150, 153, 156, 157, 158, 159, 160
Painting, 143, 161, 219, 236
Paradox, 54–56, 75, 80, 221
"Parergon," 219, 236
Passivity, 82, 85, 145
Past, 129, 139; *see also* History, Time
Pataphysics, 216; *see also* Jarry, Metaphysics
Pausanias, 95, 97; *see also Symposium*
Paws, 154, 196; *see also* Animal
Peirce, C., 16, 28, 34, 114, 218, 220, 232
Penis, 96–97; *see also* Gender, Sexuality
Perception, 60, 151, 236
Perfection, 98–99, 157, 172, 176–79, 181–82, 204, 209–11, 215, 238; *see also Technē*
Performance, 51, 53, 100, 106
Performative, 169, 238
Peril, 2–3, 38–39, 43, 139; *see also* Danger, Violence
Person, 32, 34, 50–55, 62, 87, 93, 95–96, 99, 102, 152, 158, 166
Perspective, 2, 24–25, 30–32, 34, 36–37, 39–40, 53, 68, 88–89, 170, 222, 240, 242
Persuasion, 66
Phaedrus, 4, 84, 92–95, 98, 100–102; *see also* Plato
Phallus, 156, 231; *see also* Male, Gender, Penis
Pharmakeus, 101
Pharmakon, 101–102; *see also Phaedrus*
Philebus, 93, 95, 100; *see also* Plato
Philosophy, 1–4, 6, 8–9, 17, 22–23, 25, 29, 32, 36–37, 41–42, 44–46, 49–50, 57, 64, 66, 68–69, 82, 84, 92–94, 103, 106, 119, 137–38, 172, 176, 182, 186–87, 190, 192, 204, 212, 215–17, 219–20, 228, 235–36, 238–39
Phronēsis, 169, 181; *see also* Practical Judgment, *Praxis*

Physics, 12, 28, 209, 217–18, 239, 242
Physis, 22, 185, 189, 204–205, 207,
    209–11, 239, 242; *see also* Nature
Pitkin, H., 54–57, 221–22
Place, 1, 3–5, 8, 12–13, 15, 17, 20,
    24, 52, 55–57, 63, 68, 73, 78,
    81–82, 84–86, 94–95, 101, 106,
    115, 123, 129, 133, 137, 140,
    170, 190, 194, 198, 203, 206,
    209–11, 214, 216, 223; *see also*
    Locality
Plato, 4–5, 35, 69, 81, 84, 92–95,
    99–100, 102–103, 166, 176, 178,
    207, 216, 229, 231
Pleasure, 58, 73, 92, 97, 100, 108,
    153, 160, 223; *see also* Desire
Plenitude, 22, 144, 148, 152, 157,
    167–68, 170–71, 173, 175,
    186–87, 189–90, 204–205,
    210–11, 223; *see also*
    Inexhaustibility
Plenum, 152
Plethora, 63, 155, 241
Plurality, 8–9, 27–29, 32, 37, 46, 77,
    127–28, 188, 239
Poetry, 4, 6, 176, 217, 219; *see also*
    Poiēsis
Poiēsis, 6–7, 23, 26, 41–42, 147,
    168–71, 177–78, 182, 191, 196,
    205, 209–20, 212–14, 242
Polis, 101, 166
Political, 3, 6, 17, 25–26, 32–33,
    36–38, 40–43, 46, 50–51, 55–57,
    65–66, 68, 77, 89, 91, 101, 111,
    157–60, 164–65, 167–69, 172,
    178–79, 181, 183, 219–20,
    227–28, 230, 232; *see also*
    Practical Judgment, *Praxis*
Polyphony, 13–14, 16, 23, 33–38, 42,
    45–47, 69, 71–72, 79–81, 85,
    92, 94, 98, 106, 109, 114–15,
    122–23, 127–29, 130, 132–34,
    136–38, 146, 152, 161–62,
    166–68, 178, 180–81, 186–87,
    200–201, 206, 208, 210–11, 213,
    230; *see also* Stillness

Pornography, 158
Positivities, 30, 75, 85, 135, 163,
    196–97, 241
Possibility, 5–6, 9–11, 13–15, 20, 23,
    25, 32–35, 38–40, 52–53, 62,
    65–66, 81, 85, 99, 122, 124,
    136, 139, 172, 197–98, 200,
    207, 224, 234
Postcoloniality, 183, 215
Poststructuralism, 26, 46, 67, 227
Post-capitalism, 183
Potency, 81, 84–85, 87, 198, 230; *see*
    also Possibility, Potentiality,
    Power
Potentiality, 81, 84–85
Pouvoir, 229–30; *see also* Power
Power, 2, 6–9, 11–12, 14–18, 23–26,
    28–30, 32–33, 36, 39–41, 44,
    46, 49–59, 66–95, 97, 99–109,
    111, 122–25, 127, 129–30, 133,
    136, 139, 144, 146–47, 149–51,
    153, 155–60, 164–65, 168–69,
    172–79, 181–82, 185, 192, 197,
    199–204, 211–14, 217–18, 223,
    227–30, 234–37, 241; *see also*
    Powers, Relevance
Powers, 3, 44, 51, 56, 69, 77, 79,
    81–83, 88–89, 92–93, 96,
    105–106, 144, 149, 153, 169
Practical judgment, 19, 28–29, 31–32,
    38–40, 42–44, 46, 55–56, 67,
    129–30, 161–65, 167–71,
    172–73, 175–82, 186, 216, 220,
    241
Practice, 8–9, 15, 17, 23, 28–30, 33,
    37–44, 49–51, 57, 66–67, 74,
    79, 86, 90, 130, 161, 163–64,
    166, 168–82, 185–86, 189–91,
    215–16, 224, 228–29, 241; *see*
    also Practical Judgment, *Praxis*
Pragmatism, 186, 188, 190
Praxis, 2, 6–7, 23, 26–27, 41, 127–32,
    136–37, 139–42, 159, 161,
    168–73, 176–78, 181–83, 191;
    see also Practical judgment,
    Practice

Prehension, 88–89, 151, 230; *see also* Whitehead

Prejudice, 19, 134

Principles, 8, 14, 36–37, 43–44, 58, 81, 86, 145, 158, 164, 166, 186, 191, 208, 219, 234

Private, 31, 52–54, 68, 88–90, 170, 230; *see also* Public

Privilege, 5, 11–12, 15, 21, 30, 33–34, 60–61, 68, 70, 113–15, 120–24, 141–42, 146–47, 154–58, 163, 166, 174, 185, 193, 195, 197, 200–201, 231, 233

Process, 70, 82–83, 86, 117–19, 128, 131, 177, 221, 229–30, 236, 238; 242; *see also* Time

Producing, 32, 37, 46, 70–71, 80, 89, 96, 219, 234

Productivity, 72, 74–75

Products, 33, 209–10

Profane, 98

Progress, 74, 107, 136, 156

Prohibition, 6, 16, 17, 73, 74, 92, 96–97, 160, 237

Proper, 115, 121, 138, 139, 142, 148, 154, 219, 233

Property, 121, 128, 131, 138–39, 158

Propositional judgment, 25, 28, 32, 33, 34, 35, 36, 37, 38, 39, 41, 42, 43, 44, 45, 103, 105, 114, 122–23, 128, 140, 148, 158, 159, 162, 168, 195, 198, 225

Propre, 138

Psychoanalysis, 46, 230–31

Psychohistory, 46

Public, 16, 24–25, 30–31, 34, 36, 40, 51–54, 57, 68, 70, 77, 79, 86–90, 101, 169–70, 230, 237; *see also* Private

Puissance, 229–30; *see also* Potency, *Pouvoir*

Purity, 41, 66, 91, 100, 102, 166, 174, 199

Purpose, 21, 60, 65, 77, 86, 117, 134, 188

Pythagoras, 57

Quality, 87, 113, 187, 218

Query, 34–37, 39–42, 44–46, 163, 180–81, 203–205, 210, 212–14

Questioning, 5–12, 15, 17–19, 21, 23, 26, 28–29, 33–34, 42, 51, 59, 61, 65, 76, 86, 89, 94, 96–98, 111, 114, 117–18, 120, 122, 125, 133, 138, 145, 154–55, 157, 163–65, 169, 172, 175, 179–80, 190, 193–94, 197, 199–200, 203, 205, 207, 226–27, 238

Quine, W., 223

Race, 67, 155–56

Radiance, 1–2, 52

Radical, 3, 24, 30, 80, 130, 228

Randall, J., 189, 239

Rape, 158, 237

Rationality, 6, 8, 27, 33–35, 41–43, 57, 93, 114, 118, 149–50, 160, 179, 195, 208, 241; *see also* Query, Reason

Reality, 5–6, 8–10, 15–18, 20, 24, 39, 50, 52–53, 57, 71, 81–82, 85, 88, 106, 111–14, 117, 124, 133, 135, 150, 159, 170–71, 185–88, 195, 197, 203–204, 217, 221, 229–31, 234, 236, 238, 242; *see also* Nature

Reason, 6, 8–9, 19, 22–38, 40–47, 56, 60, 63, 66, 73–74, 80, 88, 91–95, 100, 102, 107–108, 117–20, 123, 128, 132, 137–38, 147–50, 153–55, 158–60, 163–64, 166, 173, 176–81, 190–91, 200, 208, 212–13, 219–20, 222, 226; *see also* Query, Rationality

Reflexivity, 8, 10–12, 15–16, 18, 22, 27–28, 30, 36, 39, 42–43, 58–59, 89, 109, 120, 124, 129–30, 145, 151, 153, 161, 169, 211, 216

Regulation, 22, 40, 63–64, 89, 92, 95–98, 101, 106, 112, 124, 138, 144, 163–64, 166, 172, 174, 183

Relation, 2, 6–7, 9–11, 13–16, 20,
    24–25, 27–28, 35, 37–40, 44–47,
    52–53, 58, 62–63, 70–77, 79–80,
    82–83, 85–86, 89–90, 92–96,
    98–101, 103–106, 108, 111–12,
    114, 116–17, 120–21, 130–32,
    138, 141, 145, 148–49, 151–61,
    164–70, 172–79, 182, 185–91,
    194, 199, 203–204, 206, 208,
    210, 212, 217, 220, 225–27,
    230, 237; see also Power,
    Relevance
Relativism, 180
Relativity, 223
Relevance, 12–15, 17, 27, 30–31,
    37–38, 60, 69–74, 76–77, 81,
    83–84, 90, 117, 171, 212, 223;
    see also Power, Relation
Religion, 8, 32–33, 37, 42, 44–46
Repetition, 6–7, 15, 27, 31–37, 40–43,
    46, 49, 55–56, 58, 63, 77,
    79–80, 85, 89–92, 98–101, 106,
    111–12, 116, 121, 124, 127,
    129–30, 133–34, 138, 163, 171,
    175, 183, 206, 208–11
Representation, 1–10, 12–32, 34–36,
    39–47, 49–73, 77–82, 86–92, 95,
    97, 99–103, 106–109, 111–15,
    119, 122–24, 127–33, 136–38,
    142–44, 146–47, 150–60,
    162–63, 165–77, 179–83,
    185–93, 195–206, 208–16, 219,
    221–22, 224–28, 236
Republic, 4, 84, 92–93, 95, 99, 166;
    see also Plato
Resemblance, 62–63, 225–26
Resistance, 8–9, 11–12, 14–15, 17, 40,
    46, 49–50, 67, 69, 72–75,
    77–81, 85–86, 89–91, 102, 111,
    141–42, 144–46, 155, 158–60,
    165, 174–76, 178, 181, 194,
    217, 234; see also Power
Responsibility, 144, 191–92; see also
    Charity, Ethics, Practical
    judgment
Restitution, 132, 143, 185, 236

Retribution, 131–32, 136, 141–42, 166,
    170
Ricoeur, P., 238
Rule, 3, 6–7, 14–15, 50, 55, 71–76,
    79–80, 84, 90, 94, 96, 120, 136,
    138–39, 141, 156, 165–66,
    172–73, 178–82, 232, 237
Rules, 20, 22, 28, 55, 74, 80, 85–86,
    90, 96, 114, 136, 138, 141, 156,
    160, 164–66, 172, 174–81, 200,
    211, 224

Sacrifice, 11, 40, 42–43, 46–47, 49, 59,
    62, 78, 83, 85, 94, 116, 124, 128,
    131–34, 136–37, 139, 142,
    168–71, 173, 175–77, 179,
    181–82, 201, 216, 219–20
Sade, M. de, 59, 64, 96, 108, 177, 174
Sallis, J., 236
Sartre, J-P., 190–94, 239–40
Schlag, 154
Schmidt, D., 222
Science, 5, 8, 10, 12, 22–26, 29,
    32–38, 41–45, 49, 57, 61,
    63–64, 66, 92, 96, 117–20,
    122–24, 141, 147, 157, 162–64,
    167–69, 172–73, 176, 179, 182,
    189, 198–99, 204, 208, 220,
    231, 239, 242
Self, 22–23, 39, 60–61, 63, 98, 107,
    118, 128, 131, 137, 152, 192,
    200, 205, 209, 233
Semasis, 34, 38–39, 41, 45–47, 49–50,
    129, 133, 161, 168, 173, 179,
    182, 203, 205–206, 213–14, 220;
    see also Judgment, Meaning,
    Query
Sex, 73–75, 86, 91, 96, 152–53, 155,
    200–201, 230, 237, 240
Sexes, 96–97, 232, 240; see also
    Gender
Sexuality, 7, 59, 69–70, 72–74, 76, 86,
    91–92, 95–97, 108, 124, 144,
    146, 150, 152–58, 175, 177,
    196, 201–202, 217–18, 228–31,
    236–38, 240

Signified, 56, 68, 223, 226
Signifier, 56, 68, 86, 223, 231
Similitude, 63–64, 225–26
Simulation, 49, 56, 114, 124–25,
    141–42, 150, 171–72, 183,
    185–86, 188, 203, 213, 217,
    221
Skepticism, 180, 212
Social, 36–37, 41, 70, 79, 87–88, 106,
    158–59, 179, 193, 222, 236
Socialism, 155, 182
Society, 3, 25, 45, 80, 89, 199
Socrates, 44, 92–95, 98–102, 182; see
    also Plato
Sonorescence, 1, 6, 10–18, 22–23, 25,
    27, 31–32, 35–36, 38, 40, 44,
    49, 52, 57, 67, 69, 71–73,
    79–81, 89, 114, 127, 130, 133,
    138, 145, 151, 157, 165, 167,
    173–74, 179–81, 185–86, 190,
    195, 200, 203–206, 210–16
Sophists, 100
Soul, 4, 77, 84, 98, 100–102, 111,
    140, 152, 155, 159–60, 242
Sovereignty, 9, 20, 44, 50–51, 53–54,
    63, 86, 90, 94, 108, 114, 118,
    123, 132, 162, 164, 166, 172,
    180, 197, 220, 222, 227
Space, 6, 9, 16–17, 25, 31, 37, 40–44,
    46–47, 51–54, 61–62, 64, 67,
    73, 86–91, 131, 135, 137–38,
    146, 155, 158–59, 161, 165,
    168–70, 173, 176, 178–79, 188,
    190, 194, 196–97, 203, 206,
    208–12, 227, 234
Spinoza, B. de, 22, 81, 84, 103–106,
    111–13, 147–53, 167, 189–90,
    207, 210–11, 229, 231–32, 236,
    239
Spirit, 36, 45, 106, 116–17, 121, 131,
    199
Spivak, G., 65–67, 227
Stillness, 13–14, 16, 23, 33–34, 36–38,
    45–47, 69, 71–72, 81, 85, 92,
    98, 114–15, 122, 127–28, 130,
    133, 137–38, 145–46, 161–63,

    166–67, 178, 180, 187, 200–201,
    206–209, 211, 213, 230; see also
    Polyphony
Stillness-polyphony, 15, 27, 185, 205
Strawson, P., 222–23
Structuralism, 46
Structure, 55, 64, 103, 140, 208, 226
Subaltern, 13, 66–67, 72, 75, 218, 227
Subject, 2–3, 9, 24, 30–31, 41, 57, 62,
    65–66, 69, 76–77, 93, 96, 100,
    103, 106–108, 112, 116, 118,
    128, 135, 145, 152–54, 185–87,
    191, 197–99, 227–28, 241
Subjection, 145, 159–60, 162, 199
Subjectivity, 23, 26, 53, 67, 69, 77,
    106, 117, 128, 153, 194, 226–27
Sublation, 27, 36, 107; see also
    Deferral, Hegel
Sublimation, 58; see also Freud
Sublime, 4, 19–22, 174, 185–86, 200,
    218
Substance, 14, 22, 82, 104, 120,
    148–49, 210, 236
Suffering, 3, 81, 104, 122, 131, 144–45,
    156, 159, 165, 187; see also Pain
Superaltern, 13, 16, 75, 189, 218
Superforgetfulness, 141
Supplement, 101, 145–46, 169, 200,
    217
Surplus, 26, 80; see also Excess
Symposium, 84, 93–95, 97–100, 166;
    see also Plato
Syndetic judgment, 32, 38, 42–46, 161

Taxonomy, 61, 96, 223, 236, 225
Technē, 6–7, 9, 11, 14, 16, 23, 26, 41,
    46, 49, 57, 76, 111, 129–30,
    155, 157, 161, 172–73, 176–79,
    181–82, 185, 189–91, 196,
    204–205, 209–12, 214, 238;
    see also Art, Instrumentality,
    Poiēsis
Technical, 97, 122, 167, 177, 181–82,
    192
Technology, 28, 157, 168, 171, 173,
    178, 183, 238

Teleology, 3, 17, 77, 161–62, 166, 169, 171, 176, 178, 199, 241

Temporality, 34, 38–39, 43, 45–46, 53, 83–85, 106, 113, 134–35, 148, 150–52, 161–63, 165, 168, 170, 173, 193, 200, 207–11, 216; *see also* History, Time

Thinking, 2–4, 6, 25, 82, 86, 111, 118, 134–35, 138, 140, 154–55, 164, 182, 190, 194, 196, 207, 216, 220, 225, 233, 236, 240

Third-world, 66

Time, 5–7, 9–10, 24, 30, 34, 37–39, 42–43, 53, 57, 60–61, 64–65, 68–69, 81, 83, 91, 99, 103–104, 107, 111, 114–15, 117, 119, 121, 124, 127–29, 131–37, 141–42, 145, 147, 149, 154, 157, 159, 161–64, 166–70, 173, 177, 179–81, 185, 190, 193–94, 197–200, 202–203, 206–11, 214, 219, 222, 226–27, 233–35, 238, 241; *see also* History, Temporality

Timelessness, 30, 84, 150, 163

Torture, 156–59; *see also* Pain, Suffering

Totality, 2, 9–14, 22–24, 57–59, 66–67, 70–71, 75, 78, 106, 112–13, 115–17, 119–22, 127–30, 132–33, 135–37, 142, 147, 185–88, 191, 198, 200, 205, 225, 241

Totalization, 1, 17, 45, 67, 70, 116, 130, 186–88, 191, 199, 228

Trace, 182, 201, 204, 241

Tractatus Logico-Philosophicus, 232; *see also* Wittgenstein

Tradition, 6, 10, 15–18, 22, 25, 28, 31, 33, 36–37, 39–40, 42, 57, 65, 71, 81, 83, 91–93, 95, 112–14, 120, 133–34, 162, 167, 169, 172–73, 176–77, 181–82, 189–90, 201, 208, 211–12, 215–17

Tragedy, 99, 125, 137, 168, 171, 173, 192, 202

Transcendence, 192

Transcendental, 15, 24, 64–65, 114, 153, 161–67, 197, 204, 207–208

Transgression, 1, 5–6, 9–12, 20, 24, 26, 32, 43, 45, 49–50, 55, 57–58, 60–62, 65, 69, 71, 73–77, 79–82, 107, 111, 121, 132, 144–47, 150, 168, 173–74, 187–97, 199–200, 205, 212–14, 216, 222, 228, 240

Transitivity, 14

Translation, 45, 55, 155, 200, 215, 222, 229

Trinh, M-H., 3, 215–16, 228, 235

Truth, 2–4, 6–9, 12, 15, 17–18, 23–30, 32–47, 49–52, 54, 59–60, 62–64, 66–69, 71, 74, 76, 78, 80–82, 84, 86, 89, 91–104, 106–109, 111–25, 127–36, 138, 141–46, 149–51, 153, 155, 157–64, 166, 168, 170–83, 186–88, 190, 193–96, 198, 201, 203–205, 208–209, 212–13, 215, 217, 219–20, 229–30, 232–36

"Tympan," 138, 215–16, 235

Tyranny, 164

Ultimate, 30, 40, 42, 46, 83, 87, 208

Unconcealment, 24, 115, 121–22, 124

Unconditioned, 11

Unconscious, 60–61, 207, 224

Understanding, 7–8, 19–20, 22, 24–25, 27, 29, 35–36, 39, 44, 53, 64, 69, 87–88, 97, 104, 116, 118, 127, 145, 147, 159, 162, 169, 177, 187, 190, 192, 197, 219, 229, 238; *see also* Knowledge, Truth

Undisclosedness, 115, 233

Unforgotten, 171

Uniformity, 73–74, 237

Uniqueness, 58–59

Unison, 13–14, 16, 23, 33–34, 38, 47, 52, 54, 68, 71–72, 102, 111–12, 117, 127, 133, 135, 137, 153, 167, 189, 213, 218

Unison-resonances, 15–16, 27, 185, 205

Unity, 19–20, 29, 54, 70–71, 77,
    84–85, 105–107, 113, 116–19,
    121, 127–28, 130, 137, 154,
    162, 165, 187, 189, 208
Universality, 1, 7, 11, 25, 30, 37, 58,
    64, 69–74, 90, 97, 133–34,
    136, 148, 150–51, 153, 156,
    164, 179–80, 191–92, 211–12,
    226
Universe, 79, 103, 105, 152, 168, 177,
    188, 190, 218, 225, 239, 242;
    see also Nature
University, 1, 215–16, 218–19,
    222–23, 227, 229, 231, 236–39,
    241
Univocity, 1–3, 7, 9–16, 18, 23, 27,
    35–36, 38, 44, 67, 69–72, 78,
    81, 117, 150, 153, 155, 160–62,
    166–67, 185, 188–89, 191, 203,
    205, 206, 209, 211–13, 215,
    217–18
Unlimit, 20, 50, 91–92, 94, 105, 138,
    180; see also Excess, Limit,
    Locality, Inexhaustibility
Unreality, 9, 18, 50, 114, 124, 185,
    217
Unreason, 9, 24, 27, 33, 36, 49, 72,
    117; see also Madness, Reason
Unrepresentable, 40
Unthought, 20, 61–62, 64, 85, 150,
    155, 163, 190, 196–97, 204–205
Untruth, 6, 9, 25, 27, 33, 39, 41, 44–47,
    49–52, 66–69, 91, 111–16,
    119–24, 127–28, 131, 138, 143,
    146, 150–51, 159, 173, 175, 181,
    186, 188, 196, 233; see also
    Truth, Unconcealment
Utilitarianism, 58–59, 97
Utility, 59, 166, 168, 182, 187
Utopia, 66, 80, 91, 159, 166, 171,
    177, 179, 197, 202

Vagueness, 151, 223
Valid-on, 112
Valor, 40, 45–46, 58–59, 168–70,
    173–77, 181, 205

Value, 24, 33, 56, 59–60, 108
Vertreten, 65–67, 227
Violence, 74, 80, 82, 85–86, 107, 136,
    156–58, 166, 173, 182–83, 212,
    230
Virtue, 98, 101, 166; see also Aretē
Visible, 62–63, 223, 225
Vision, 98, 140
Volume, 69, 217–18, 228–30, 236–38

War, 1, 74, 119, 136, 156, 165, 240
Waste, 79, 131–36, 162, 166, 169–71,
    173, 181–82
Wealth, 57–59, 64, 91, 94, 219, 223,
    226
West, 3–6, 8, 10, 15, 18, 22, 25, 27,
    29, 32–34, 37, 39, 42, 44,
    57–58, 66, 70–71, 81, 103, 107,
    113, 120, 127, 129, 132, 147,
    169, 171–72, 181, 201, 204,
    212, 216
Whitehead, A., 22, 45, 57, 81–84, 88,
    151–52, 167, 177, 207–208, 211,
    221, 223, 229–30, 236, 238, 242
Wisdom, 54, 84, 92–94, 102
Wittgenstein, L., 6, 232
Woman, 59, 86, 96–97, 99, 113,
    120–21, 129, 146–47, 154, 158,
    193, 215–16, 228, 231–32, 235,
    237; see also Feminism, Gender
Work, 6, 10, 12–15, 23, 25, 27, 31,
    33–34, 37, 39–44, 49, 53, 69,
    74, 86, 89, 99–100, 102–104,
    111, 114–16, 123, 133, 137,
    143–44, 146, 151, 153–54,
    157–59, 163, 172–73, 177,
    181–82, 191–92, 194–96, 199,
    203–206, 208–209, 211–13,
    216–17, 219–22, 230, 232, 234,
    239; see also Art, Ergon,
    Ergonality, Fabricative Judgment,
    Technē
World, 4, 6, 19, 24, 26, 30, 32, 37,
    40–41, 52–54, 56, 63–64, 82–85,
    87–89, 96, 99, 101, 112, 115,
    117–18, 121, 124, 128–29, 131,

World (*cont.*)
    135, 137, 142, 145, 167, 169–70,
    177, 187, 192, 199, 207, 214,
    224–26, 228, 230, 238–39, 242;
    see also Nature, Universe

Writing, 3–5, 32, 72, 81, 99–102,
    130–31, 138, 146, 159, 189–90,
    196, 207, 210, 215–16, 220,
    223, 228, 232, 236, 239–242